NEW PERSPECTIVES SERIES

Microsoft® Windows® 95

COMPREHENSIVE

The New Perspectives Series

The New Perspectives Series consists of texts and technology that teach computer concepts and the programs listed below. Both Windows 3.1 and Windows 95 versions of these programs are available. You can order these New Perspectives texts in many different lengths, software releases, bound combinations, CourseKits™ and Custom Editions. Contact your CTI sales representative or customer service representative for the most up-to-date details.

The New Perspectives Series

Computer Concepts®

dBASE®

Internet/World Wide Web/Netscape Navigator®

Lotus 1-2-3®

Microsoft Access®

Microsoft Excel®

Microsoft Office Professional®

Microsoft PowerPoint®

Microsoft Windows 3.1®

Microsoft Windows 95®

Microsoft Word®

Microsoft Works®

Novell Perfect Office®

Paradox®

Presentations®

Quattro Pro®

WordPerfect®

Microsoft®
Windows® 95

COMPREHENSIVE

June Jamrich Parsons
University of the Virgin Islands

Dan Oja
GuildWare, Inc.

Joan Carey
Carey Associates, Inc.

A
Susan
Solomon
Book

CTI

A DIVISION OF COURSE TECHNOLOGY
ONE MAIN STREET, CAMBRIDGE, MA 02142

an International Thomson Publishing company I(T)P®

Cambridge • Albany • Bonn • Boston • Cincinnati • London • Madrid • Melbourne • Mexico City
New York • Paris • San Francisco • Singapore • Tokyo • Toronto • Washington

New Perspectives on Microsoft Windows 95—Comprehensive is published by CTI.

Managing Editor	Mac Mendelsohn
Series Consulting Editor	Susan Solomon
Product Manager	Susan Solomon
Production Editor	Debbie Masi
Text and Cover Designer	Ella Hanna
Cover Illustrator	Nancy Nash

© 1997 by CTI.
A Division of Course Technology—I⊤P®

For more information contact:

Course Technology
One Main Street
Cambridge, MA 02142

International Thomson Publishing Europe
Berkshire House 168-173
High Holborn
London WCIV 7AA
England

Thomas Nelson Australia
102 Dodds Street
South Melbourne, 3205
Victoria, Australia

Nelson Canada
1120 Birchmount Road
Scarborough, Ontario
Canada M1K 5G4

International Thomson Editores
Campos Eliseos 385, Piso 7
Col. Polanco
11560 Mexico D.F. Mexico

International Thomson Publishing GmbH
Königswinterer Strasse 418
53227 Bonn
Germany

International Thomson Publishing Asia
211 Henderson Road
#05-10 Henderson Building
Singapore 0315

International Thomson Publishing Japan
Hirakawacho Kyowa Building, 3F
2-2-1 Hirakawacho
Chiyoda-ku, Tokyo 102
Japan

Trademarks
Course Technology and the open book logo are registered trademarks of Course Technology.
I⊤P® The ITP logo is a registered trademark of International Thomson Publishing.
Microsoft and Windows 95 are registered trademarks of Microsoft Corporation.

Some of the product names and company names used in this book have been used for identification purposes only and may be trademarks or registered trademarks of their respective manufacturers and sellers.

Disclaimer
CTI reserves the right to revise this publication and make changes from time to time in its content without notice.

ISBN 1-56527-998-0

Printed in the United States of America

10 9 8 7 6

At CTI, we have one foot in education and the other in technology. We believe that technology is transforming the way people teach and learn, and we are excited about providing instructors and students with materials that use technology to teach about technology.

Our development process is unparalleled in the higher education publishing industry. Every product we create goes through an exacting process of design, development, review, and testing.

Reviewers give us direction and insight that shape our manuscripts and bring them up to the latest standards. Every manuscript is quality tested. Students whose backgrounds match the intended audience work through every keystroke, carefully checking for clarity and pointing out errors in logic and sequence. Together with our own technical reviewers, these testers help us ensure that everything that carries our name is error-free and easy to use.

We show both *how* and *why* technology is critical to solving problems in college and in whatever field you choose to teach or pursue. Our time-tested, step-by-step instructions provide unparalleled clarity. Examples and applications are chosen and crafted to motivate students.

As the New Perspectives Series team at CTI, our goal is to produce the most timely, accurate, creative, and technologically sound product in the entire college publishing industry. We strive for consistent high quality. This takes a lot of communication, coordination, and hard work. But we love what we do. We are determined to be the best. Write us and let us know what you think. You can also e-mail us at **newperspectives@course.com**.

The New Perspectives Series Team

Joseph Adamski	Jessica Evans	Dan Oja
Judy Adamski	Kathy Finnegan	June Parsons
Roy Ageloff	Robin Geller	Sandra Poindexter
David Auer	Roger Hayen	Ann Shaffer
Rachel Bunin	Charles Hommel	Susan Solomon
Joan Carey	Chris Kelly	Christine Spillett
Patrick Carey	Terry Ann Kremer	Susanne Walker
Barbara Clemens	Melissa Lima	John Zeanchock
Kim Crowley	Nancy Ludlow	Beverly Zimmerman
Kristen Duerr	Mac Mendelsohn	Scott Zimmerman

Preface The New Perspectives Series

What is the New Perspectives Series?

CTI's **New Perspectives Series** is an integrated system of instruction that combines text and technology products to teach computer concepts and microcomputer applications. Users consistently praise this series for innovative pedagogy, creativity, supportive and engaging style, accuracy, and use of interactive technology. The first New Perspectives text was published in January of 1993. Since then, the series has grown to more than 40 titles and has become the best-selling series on computer concepts and microcomputer applications. Others have imitated the New Perspectives features, design, and technologies, but none have replicated its quality and its ability to consistently anticipate and meet the needs of instructors and students.

What is the Integrated System of Instruction?

You hold in your hands a textbook that is one component of an integrated system of instruction—text, graphics, video, sound animation, and simulations that are linked and that provide a flexible, unified, and interactive system to help you teach and help your students learn. Specifically, the *New Perspectives Integrated System of Instruction* consists of five components: a Course Technology textbook, Course Labs, Course Online, Course Presenter, and Course Test Manager. These components—shown in the graphic on the back cover of this book—have been developed to work together to provide a complete, integrative teaching and learning experience.

How is the New Perspectives Series different from other microcomputer applications series?

The **New Perspectives Series** distinguishes itself from other series in at least four substantial ways: sound instructional design, consistent quality, innovative technology, and proven pedagogy. The texts in this series consist of two or more tutorials, which are based on sound instructional design. Each tutorial is motivated by a realistic case that is meaningful to students. Rather than learn a laundry list of features, students learn the features in the context of solving a problem. This process motivates all concepts and skills by demonstrating to students why they would want to know them.

Instructors and students have come to rely on the high quality of the **New Perspectives Series** and to consistently praise its accuracy. This accuracy is a result of CTI's unique multi-step quality assurance process that incorporates student testing at three stages of development, using hardware and software configurations appropriate to the product. All solutions, test questions, and other Course Tools (see below) are tested using similar procedures. Instructors who adopt this series report that students can work through the tutorials independently, with a minimum of intervention or "damage control" by instructors or staff. This consistent quality has meant that if instructors are pleased with one product from the series, they can rely on the same quality with any other New Perspectives product.

The **New Perspectives Series** also distinguishes itself by its innovative technology. This series innovated Course Labs, truly *interactive* learning applications. These have set the standard for interactive learning.

How do I know that the New Perspectives Series will work?

Some instructors who use this series report a significant difference between how much their students learn and retain with this series as compared to other series. With other series, instructors often find that students can work through the book and do well on homework and tests, but still not demonstrate competency when asked to perform particular tasks outside the context of the text's sample case or project. With the **New Perspectives Series**, however, instructors report that students have a complete, integrative learning experience that stays with them. They credit this high retention and competency to the fact that this series incorporates critical thinking and problem solving with computer skills mastery.

How does this book I'm holding fit into the New Perspectives Series?

New Perspectives microcomputer applications books are available in the following categories:

Brief books are about 100 pages long and are intended to teach only the essentials of the particular microcomputer application.

Introductory books are about 300 pages long and consist of 6 or 7 tutorials. An Introductory book is designed for a short course on a particular application or for a one-term course to be used in combination with other introductory books. The book you are holding is an Introductory book.

Comprehensive books consist of all of the tutorials in the Introductory book, plus 3 or 4 more tutorials on more advanced topics, which are called **Intermediate** modules.

Advanced books begin by covering topics similar to those in the Comprehensive books, but cover them in more depth. Advanced books then go on to present the most high-level coverage in the series.

Concepts *New Perspectives on Computer Concepts* is available in Brief, Introductory, Comprehensive, and chapter-by-chapter versions.

Custom Books offer you two ways to customize the New Perspectives Series to fit your course exactly: *CourseKits*, 2 or more texts packaged together in a box, and *Custom Editions*, your choice of books bound together. Both options offer significant price discounts.

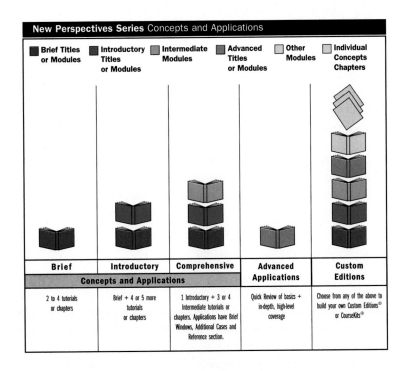

New Perspectives Series Concepts and Applications

- ■ Brief Titles or Modules
- ■ Introductory Titles or Modules
- ■ Intermediate Modules
- ■ Advanced Titles or Modules
- □ Other Modules
- ■ Individual Concepts Chapters

Brief	Introductory	Comprehensive	Advanced Applications	Custom Editions
Concepts and Applications				
2 to 4 tutorials or chapters	Brief + 4 or 5 more tutorials or chapters	1 Introductory + 3 or 4 Intermediate tutorials or chapters. Applications have Brief Windows, Additional Cases and Reference section.	Quick Review of basics + in-depth, high-level coverage	Choose from any of the above to build your own Custom Editions® or CourseKits®

In what kind of course could I use this book?

You can use this book in any course in which you want students to learn the most important Microsoft Windows 95 topics, including basic navigation and file management skills. It is particularly recommended for a short course on Windows 95. This book assumes students have no previous experience with Windows 95.

How do the Windows 95 editions differ from the Windows 3.1 editions?

Larger Page Size   If you've used a New Perspectives text before, you'll immediately notice that the book you're holding is larger than the Windows 3.1 series books. We've responded to user requests for a larger page, which allows for larger screen shots and associated callouts. Look on page WIN95 24 for an example of how we've made the screen shots easier to read.

Sessions   We've divided the tutorials into sessions. Each session is designed to be completed in about 45 minutes to an hour (depending, of course, upon student needs and the speed of your lab equipment). With sessions, learning is broken up into more easily-assimilated chunks. You can more accurately allocate time in your syllabus. Students can better manage the available lab time. Each session begins with a "session box," which quickly describes the skills students will learn in the session. Furthermore, each session is numbered, which makes it easier for you and your students to navigate and communicate about the tutorial. Look on page WIN95 30 for the session box that opens Session 2.1.

Quick Checks   Each session concludes with meaningful, conceptual questions—called Quick Checks—that test students' understanding of what they learned in the session. Answers to all of the Quick Checks are at the back of the book preceding the Index. You can find examples of Quick Checks on pages WIN95 13 and 25.

New Design   We have retained the best of the old design to help students differentiate between what they are to *do* and what they are to *read*. The steps are clearly identified by their shaded background and numbered steps. Furthermore, this new design presents steps and screen shots in a larger, easier to read format. Some good examples of our new design are pages WIN95 64 and 65.

What features are retained in the Windows 95 editions of the New Perspectives Series?

"Read This Before You Begin" Page   This page is consistent with CTI's unequaled commitment to helping instructors introduce technology into the classroom. Technical considerations and assumptions about hardware and software are listed to help instructors save time and head off problems. The "Read This Before You Begin" pages for this book are on pages WIN95 2 and WIN95 I 2.

Tutorial Case   Each tutorial begins with a problem presented in a case that is meaningful to students. The problem turns the task of learning how to use an application into a problem-solving process. The problems increase in complexity with each tutorial. These cases touch on multicultural, international, and ethical issues—so important to today's business curriculum. See page WIN95 57 for the case that begins Tutorial 3.

Step-by-Step Methodology This unique CTI methodology keeps students on track. They enter data, click buttons, or press keys always within the context of solving the problem posed in the tutorial case. The text constantly guides students, letting them know where they are in the course of solving the problem. In addition, the numerous screen shots include callouts that direct students' attention to what they should look at on the screen. On almost every page in this book, you can find an example of how steps, screen shots, and callouts work together.

TROUBLE?

TROUBLE? *Paragraphs* These paragraphs anticipate the mistakes or problems that students are likely to have and help them recover and continue with the tutorial. By putting these paragraphs in the book, rather than in the Instructor's Manual, we facilitate independent learning and free the instructor to focus on substantive conceptual issues rather than on common procedural errors. Two representative examples of Trouble?s are on pages WIN95 32 and 33.

Reference Windows Reference Windows appear throughout the text. They are succinct summaries of the most important tasks covered in the tutorials. Reference Windows are specially designed and written so students can use them for their reference value when doing the Tutorial Assignments and Case Problems, and after completing the course. Page WIN95 67 contains the Reference Window for Renaming a Folder.

Task Reference The Task Reference is a summary of how to perform common tasks using the most efficient method, as well as helpful shortcuts. It appears as a table at the end of the book. In this book the Task Reference is on pages WIN95 257 to 264.

Tutorial Assignments Each tutorial concludes with Tutorial Assignments, which provides students additional hands-on practice of the skills they learned in the tutorial. If a Lab (see below) accompanies the tutorial, Lab Assignments are included. Look on pages WIN95 141 through 144 for the Tutorial Assignments for Tutorial 4. The Lab Assignments for Tutorial 3 are on page WIN95 93.

Exploration Exercises The Windows environment allows students to learn by exploring and discovering what they can do. Exploration Exercises can be Tutorial Assignments or Case Problems that might challenge students, encourage them to explore the capabilities of the program they are using, and extend their knowledge using the Windows Help facility and other reference materials. Page WIN95 92 contains Exploration Exercises for Tutorial 3.

The New Perspectives Series is known for using technology to help instructors teach and administer, and to help students learn. What CourseTools are available with this textbook?

All of the teaching and learning materials available with the **New Perspectives Series** are known as CourseTools. Most of them are available in the Instructor's Resource Kit.

Course Labs: Now, Concepts Come to Life   Computer skills and concepts come to life with the New Perspectives Course Labs—highly interactive tutorials that combine illustrations, animations, digital images, and simulations. The Labs guide students step-by-step, present them Quick Checks, allow them to explore on their own, test their comprehension, and provide printed feedback. Lab Assignments are included at the end of each relevant tutorial. The Labs available with this book and the tutorials in which they appear are:

Using a Keyboard		Introductory Tutorial 1
Using a Mouse		Introductory Tutorial 1
Using Files		Introductory Tutorial 2
Windows Directories, Folders, and Files		Introductory Tutorial 3
Deframentation and Disk Operations		Intermediate Tutorial 6
Data Backup		Intermediate Tutorial 6

Course Online: A Site Dedicated to Keeping You and Your Students Up-To-Date   When you use a New Perspectives product, you can access CTI's faculty and student sites on the World Wide Web. You may browse the password-protected Faculty Online Companion to obtain all the materials you need to prepare for class. Please see your Instructor's Manual or call your Course Technology customer service representative for more information. Students may access their Online Companion in the Student Center using the URL **http://www.coursetools.com/cti/concepts2**.

Course Presenter: Ready-Made or Customized Dynamic Presentations
Course Presenter is a CD-ROM-based presentation tool that provides instructors with a wealth of resources for use in the classroom, replacing traditional overhead transparencies with computer-generated screenshows. Course Presenter includes a structured presentation for each tutorial of the book, and also gives instructors the flexibility to create custom presentations, complete with matching student notes and lecture notes pages. Instructors can also use Course Presenter to create traditional transparencies.

Course Test Manager: Testing and Practice Online or On Paper   Course Test Manager is cutting-edge Windows-based testing software that helps instructors design and administer pretests, practice tests, and actual examinations. This full-featured program allows students to randomly generate practice tests that provide immediate online feedback and detailed study guides for questions incorrectly answered. Online pretests help instructors assess student skills and plan instruction. Instructors can also use Course Test Manager to produce printed tests. Also, students can take tests at the computer that can be automatically graded and generate statistical information on students' individual and group performance.

Instructor's Manual   Instructor's Manuals are written by the authors. They are available in printed form and through the Course Technology Faculty Online Companion on the World Wide Web. Call your customer service representative for the URL and your password. Each Instructor's Manual contains the following items:

- Instructor's Notes for each tutorial prepared by the authors and based on their teaching experience. Instructor's Notes contain a tutorial overview, tutorial outline, troubleshooting tips, and lecture notes.
- Printed solutions to all of the Tutorial Assignments and Lab Assignments.
- Solutions disk(s) containing every file students are asked to create or modify in the Tutorials and Tutorial Assignments.

Student Files Disks   Student Files Disks contain all of the data files that students will use for the Tutorials and Tutorial Assignments. A README file includes technical tips for lab management. These files are also available online. See the inside covers of this book and the "Read This Before You Begin" page before Tutorial 1 and for more information on student files.

Instructor's Resource Kit   You will receive the following Course Tools in the Instructor's Resource Kit:

- Course Labs Setup Disks
- Course Test Manager Test Bank Disks
- Course Presenter CD-ROM
- Instructor's Manual and Solutions Disks
- Student Files Disks

Acknowledgments

We want to thank all of the New Perspectives Team members for giving us input on essential Windows 95 skills. Their insights and team spirit were invaluable. Many thanks to Patrick Carey, Harry Phillips, and Tevya Rachelson for their contributions. Thanks to the technology support we received from Jeff Goding, Jim Valente, Larry Goldstein, and Lyle Korytkowski. Our appreciation goes to Catherine Griffin, Debbie Masi, Patty Stephan, and the staff at Gex for their excellent production work. Finally we appreciate the editorial support of Mark Reimold, Mac Mendelsohn, Kristen Duerr, Barbara Clemens, and Susan Solomon.

June Parsons
Dan Oja

A special acknowledgement to my four little sons, Michael, Peter, Thomas, and John Paul, for their unfailing love, cheer, and faith in me, and an extra thanks to Susan—you can add me to your ever-growing list of grateful authors. You are mentor, guide, and friend.

Joan Carey

Brief Contents

Table of **Contents**

TUTORIAL 1

Exploring the Basics

Session 1.1   **5**

Session 1.2   **14**

TUTORIAL 2

Working with Files

Your First Day in the Lab—Continued 29

Session 2.1 30

Session 2.2 41

TUTORIAL 3

Organizing Files with Windows Explorer

Kolbe Climbing School 57

Session 3.1 58

TUTORIAL 4

Customizing Windows 95 for Increased Productivity

Companions, Inc.   **95**

Microsoft Windows 95 Intermediate Tutorials   I 1

TUTORIAL 1

Finding Files and Data

Speechwriter's Aide   I 3

TUTORIAL 2

Working with Graphics

Kiana Ski Shop   I 45

CONTENTS NEW PERSPECTIVES SERIES

TUTORIAL 6

Disk Maintenance

U.S. Patent and Trademark Office   I 191

NEW PERSPECTIVES SERIES

Microsoft®
Windows® 95

INTRODUCTORY

TUTORIALS

Read This **Before You Begin**

STUDENT DISKS

To complete the Introductory tutorials and Tutorial Assignments you need two Student Disks. Your instructor will either provide you with Student Disks or ask you to make your own.

If you are supposed to make your own Student Disks, you will need two blank, formatted high-density disks. Follow the instructions in the section called "Creating Your Student Disk" in Tutorial 2 to create your Student Disk for Tutorials 1 and 2. Follow the instructions in the section called "Preparing Your Student disk with Quick Format" in Tutorial 3 to create your Student Disk for Tutorials 3 and 4.

The following table shows you which disk you should use with each tutorial:

Student Disk	Write this on the label
1	Student Disk 1: Introductory Tutorials 1-2
2	Student Disk 2: Introductory Tutorials 3-4

When you begin each tutorial, be sure you are using the correct Student Disk. See the inside front or inside back cover of this book for more information on Student Disk files, or ask your instructor or technical support person for assistance.

COURSE LABS

The Introductory tutorials feature four interactive Course Labs to help you understand Windows concepts. There are Lab Assignments at the end of the tutorials that relate to these Labs. To start a Lab, click the **Start** button on the Windows 95 Taskbar, point to **Programs**, point to **CTI Windows 95 Applications**, point to **Windows 95 New Perspective Brief** or **Windows 95 New Perspectives Introductory**, and click the name of the Lab you want to use.

USING YOUR OWN COMPUTER

If you are going to work through this book using your own computer, you need:

■ **Computer System** Windows 95 must be installed on your computer. This book assumes a complete installation of Windows 95.

■ **Student Disks** Ask your instructor or lab manager for details on how to get the two Student Disks. You will not be able to complete the tutorials or exercises in this book using your own computer until you have the Student Disks. The student files may also be obtained electronically over the Internet. See the inside front or inside back cover of this book for more details.

■ **Course Labs** See your instructor or technical support person to obtain the Course Lab software for use on your own computer.

VISIT OUR WORLD WIDE WEB SITE

Additional materials designed especially for you are available on the World Wide Web. Go to **http://coursetools.com**.

To complete the Introductory tutorials and Tutorial Assignments, your students must use a set of files on two Student Disks. The Instructor's Resource Kit CD-ROM for this text contains two setup programs that generate the Student Disks—one in a folder named "Brief" (containing the setup program for Tutorials 1 and 2) and one in a folder named "Introductory" (containing the setup program for Tutorials 3 and 4). To install this software on your server or on standalone computers, follow the instructions in the Readme file.

If you prefer to provide Student Disks rather than letting students generate them, you can run the program that will create Student Disks yourself by following the instructions in Tutorial 2 (for Student Disk 1) and Tutorial 3 (for Student Disk 2).

COURSE LAB SOFTWARE

The Introductory tutorials feature four online, interactive Course Labs that introduce basic Windows concepts. The Instructor's Resource Kit CD-ROM for this text contains two separate Lab installations—one in a folder named "Brief" (which installs the Using a Keyboard, Using a Mouse, and Using Files Labs) and one in a folder named "Introductory" (which installs the Windows Directories, Folders, and Files Lab). To install the Course Lab software, follow the setup instructions in the Readme file on the CD-ROM. Refer also to the Readme file for essential technical notes related to running the labs in a multiuser environment.

Once you have installed the Course Lab software, your students can start the Labs from the Windows 95 desktop by clicking the **Start** button on the Windows 95 taskbar, pointing to **Programs**, pointing to **CTI Windows 95 Applications**, pointing to **Windows 95 New Perspectives Brief** or **Windows 95 New Perspectives Introductory**, and then clicking the name of the Lab they want to use.

CTI COURSE LAB SOFTWARE AND STUDENT FILES

You are granted a license to copy the Student Files and Course Labs to any computer or computer network used by students who have purchased this book.

Exploring the Basics

OBJECTIVES

In this tutorial you will learn to:

- Identify the controls on the Windows 95 desktop

- Use the Windows 95 Start button to run software programs

- Identify and use the controls in a window

- Switch between programs using the taskbar

- Use Windows 95 controls such as menus, toolbars, list boxes, scroll bars, radio buttons, tabs, and check boxes

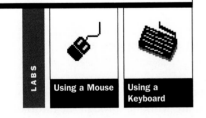

LABS

Using a Mouse   **Using a Keyboard**

CASE

Your First Day in the Lab

You walk into the computer lab and sit down at a desk. There's a computer in front of you, and you find yourself staring dubiously at the stack of software manuals. Where to start? As if in answer to your question, your friend Steve Laslow appears.

Gesturing to the stack of manuals, you tell Steve that you were just wondering where to start.

"You start with the operating system," says Steve. Noticing your slightly puzzled look, Steve explains that the **operating system** is software that helps the computer carry out basic operating tasks such as displaying information on the computer screen and saving data on your disks. Your computer uses the **Microsoft Windows 95** operating system—Windows 95, for short.

Steve tells you that Windows 95 has a "gooey" or **graphical user interface (GUI)**, which uses pictures of familiar objects, such as file folders and documents, to represent a desktop on your screen. Microsoft Windows 95 gets its name from the rectangular-shaped work areas, called "windows," that appear on your screen.

Steve continues to talk as he sorts through the stack of manuals on your desk. He says there are two things he really likes about Windows 95. First, lots of software is available for computers that have the Windows 95 operating system and all this software has a standard graphical user interface. That means once you have learned how to use one Windows software package, such as word-processing software, you are well on your way to understanding how to use other Windows software. Second, Windows 95 lets you use more than one software package at a time, so you can easily switch between your word-processing software and your appointment book software, for example. All in all, Windows 95 makes your computer an effective and easy-to-use productivity tool.

Steve recommends that you get started right away by using some tutorials that will teach you the skills essential for using Microsoft Windows 95. He hands you a book and assures you that everything on your computer system is set up and ready to go.

You mention that last summer you worked in an advertising agency where the employees used something called Windows 3.1. Steve explains that Windows 3.1 is an earlier version of the Windows operating system. Windows 95 and Windows 3.1 are similar, but Windows 95 is more powerful and easier to use. Steve says that as you work through the tutorials you will see notes that point out the important differences between Windows 95 and Windows 3.1.

Steve has a class, but he says he'll check back later to see how you are doing.

Using the Tutorials Effectively

These tutorials will help you learn about Windows 95. The tutorials are designed to be used at a computer. Each tutorial is divided into sessions. Watch for the session headings, such as Session 1.1 and Session 1.2. Each session is designed to be completed in about 45 minutes, but take as much time as you need. It's also a good idea to take a break between sessions.

Before you begin, read the following questions and answers. They are designed to help you use the tutorials effectively.

Where do I start?

Each tutorial begins with a case, which sets the scene for the tutorial and gives you background information to help you understand what you will be doing in the tutorial. Read the case before you go to the lab. In the lab, begin with the first session of the tutorial.

How do I know what to do on the computer?

Each session contains steps that you will perform on the computer to learn how to use Windows 95. Read the text that introduces each series of steps. The steps you need to do at a computer are numbered and are set against a color background. Read each step carefully and completely before you try it.

How do I know if I did the step correctly?

As you work, compare your computer screen with the corresponding figure in the tutorial. Don't worry if your screen display is somewhat different from the figure. The important parts of the screen display are labeled in each figure. Check to make sure these parts are on your screen.

What if I make a mistake?

Don't worry about making mistakes—they are part of the learning process. Paragraphs labeled "TROUBLE?" identify common problems and explain how to get back on track. Follow the steps in a TROUBLE? paragraph *only* if you are having the problem described. If you run into other problems:

- Carefully consider the current state of your system, the position of the pointer, and any messages on the screen.

- Complete the sentence, "Now I want to...." Be specific, because you are identifying your goal.

- Develop a plan for accomplishing your goal, and put your plan into action.

How do I use the Reference Windows?

Reference Windows summarize the procedures you learn in the tutorial steps. Do not complete the actions in the Reference Windows when you are working through the tutorial. Instead, refer to the Reference Windows while you are working on the assignments at the end of the tutorial.

How can I test my understanding of the material I learned in the tutorial?

At the end of each session, you can answer the Quick Check questions. The answers for the Quick Checks are at the end of the book.

After you have completed the entire tutorial, you should complete the Tutorial Assignments. The Tutorial Assignments are carefully structured so you will review what you have learned and then apply your knowledge to new situations.

What if I can't remember how to do something?

You should refer to the Task Reference at the end of the book; it summarizes how to accomplish commonly performed tasks.

What are the 3.1 Notes?

The 3.1 Notes are helpful if you have used Windows 3.1. The notes point out the key similarities and differences between Windows 3.1 and Windows 95.

What are the Interactive Labs, and how should I use them?

Interactive Labs help you review concepts and practice skills that you learn in the tutorial. Lab icons at the beginning of each tutorial and in the margins of the tutorials indicate topics that have corresponding Labs. The Lab Assignments section includes instructions for how to use each Lab.

Now that you understand how to use the tutorials effectively, you are ready to begin.

SESSION
1.1

In this session, in addition to learning basic Windows terminology, you will learn how to use a mouse, to start and stop a program, and to use more than one program at a time. With the skills you learn in this session, you will be able to use Windows 95 to start software programs.

Using a Keyboard

Starting Windows 95

Windows 95 automatically starts when you turn on the computer. Depending on the way your computer is set up, you might be asked to enter your user name and password. If prompted to do so, type your assigned user name and press the Enter key. Then type your password and press the Enter key to continue.

To start Windows 95:

1. Turn on your computer.

The Windows 95 Desktop

In Windows terminology, the screen represents a **desktop**—a workspace for projects and the tools needed to manipulate those projects. Look at your screen display and locate the objects labeled in Figure 1-1 on the following page.

Because it is easy to customize the Windows environment, your screen might not look exactly the same as Figure 1-1. You should, however, be able to locate objects on your screen similar to those in Figure 1-1.

TROUBLE? If the Welcome to Windows 95 box appears on your screen, press the Enter key to close it.

Icons are small pictures that represent objects such as your computer, your computer network, a specific computer program, or a document. Your desktop probably contains several icons, such as My Computer, Network Neighborhood, and the Recycle Bin. You'll use these icons in later tutorials to work with files stored on your computer or on other computers on the network.

Figure 1-1 ◀
The Windows 95 desktop

The **desktop** is your workspace on the screen.

The **Start** button is one of the most important controls in Windows 95. You use the Start button to access essential Windows 95 functions, programs, and documents.

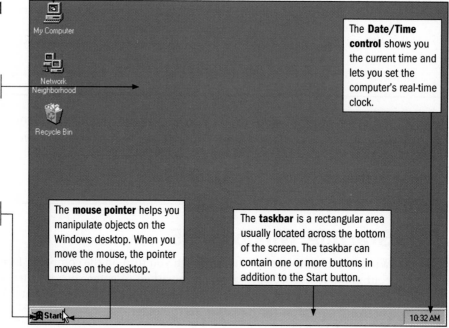

The **Date/Time control** shows you the current time and lets you set the computer's real-time clock.

The **mouse pointer** helps you manipulate objects on the Windows desktop. When you move the mouse, the pointer moves on the desktop.

The **taskbar** is a rectangular area usually located across the bottom of the screen. The taskbar can contain one or more buttons in addition to the Start button.

TROUBLE? If the screen goes blank or starts to display a moving design, press any key to restore the image.

Using the Mouse

Using a Mouse

A **mouse,** like those shown in Figure 1-2, is a pointing device that helps you interact with objects on the screen. In Windows 95 you need to know how to use the mouse to point, click, and drag. In this session you will learn about pointing and clicking. In Session 1.2 you will learn how to use the mouse to drag objects.

You can also interact with objects by using the keyboard; however, the mouse is much more convenient for most tasks, so the tutorials in this book assume you are using one.

Pointing

The **pointer,** or **mouse pointer,** is a small object that moves on the screen when you move the mouse. The pointer is usually shaped like an arrow. As you move the mouse on a flat surface, the pointer on the screen moves in the direction corresponding to the movement of the mouse. The pointer sometimes changes shape depending on where it is on the screen or the action the computer is completing.

Find the arrow-shaped pointer on your screen. If you do not see the pointer, move your mouse until the pointer comes into view.

Figure 1-2 ◀
The mouse

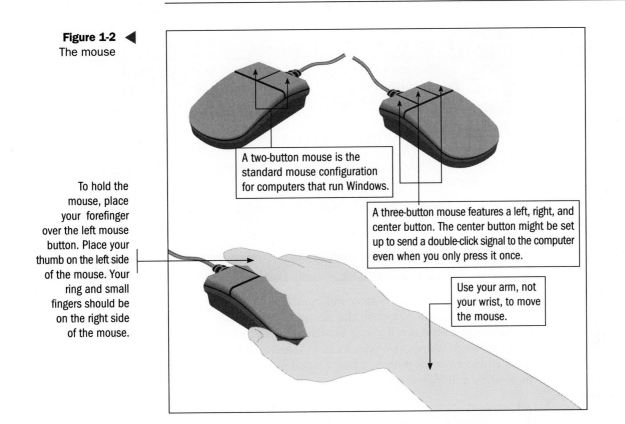

A two-button mouse is the standard mouse configuration for computers that run Windows.

A three-button mouse features a left, right, and center button. The center button might be set up to send a double-click signal to the computer even when you only press it once.

To hold the mouse, place your forefinger over the left mouse button. Place your thumb on the left side of the mouse. Your ring and small fingers should be on the right side of the mouse.

Use your arm, not your wrist, to move the mouse.

Basic "mousing" skills depend on your ability to position the pointer. You begin most Windows operations by positioning the pointer over a specific part of the screen. This is called **pointing**.

To move the pointer:

1. Position your right index finger over the left mouse button, as shown in Figure 1-2. Lightly grasp the sides of the mouse with your thumb and little finger.

   TROUBLE? If you want to use the mouse with your left hand, ask your instructor or technical support person to help you use the Control Panel to change the mouse settings to swap the left and right mouse buttons. Be sure you find out how to change back to the right-handed mouse setting, so you can reset the mouse each time you are finished in the lab.

2. Locate the arrow-shaped pointer on the screen.

3. Move the mouse and watch the movement of the pointer.

If you run out of room to move your mouse, lift the mouse and move it to a clear area on your desk, then place the mouse back on the desk. Notice that the pointer does not move when the mouse is not in contact with the desk.

When you position the mouse pointer over certain objects, such as the objects on the taskbar, a "tip" appears. These "tips" are called **ToolTips**, and they tell you the purpose or function of an object.

To view ToolTips:

1. Use the mouse to point to the **Start** button ![Start]. After a few seconds, you see the tip "Click here to begin" as shown in Figure 1-3 on the following page.

Figure 1-3 ◀
Viewing ToolTips

Start button ──────→

> **TROUBLE?** If you accidentally pressed a mouse button, press it again to get the Start menu off your screen.

2. What tip appears when you point to the date on the right end of the taskbar?

Clicking

When you press a mouse button and immediately release it, it is called **clicking**. Clicking the mouse selects an object on the desktop. *You usually click the left mouse button, so* unless the instructions tell you otherwise, always click the left mouse button.

Windows 95 shows you which object is selected by highlighting it, usually by changing the object's color, putting a box around it, or making the object appear to be pushed in, as shown in Figure 1-4.

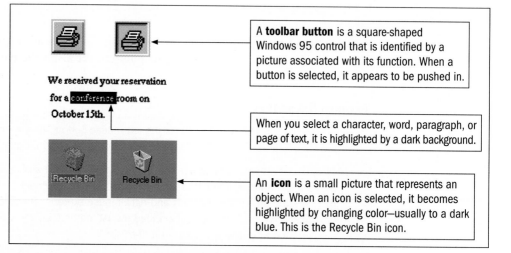

Figure 1-4 ◀
Selected objects

A **toolbar button** is a square-shaped Windows 95 control that is identified by a picture associated with its function. When a button is selected, it appears to be pushed in.

When you select a character, word, paragraph, or page of text, it is highlighted by a dark background.

An **icon** is a small picture that represents an object. When an icon is selected, it becomes highlighted by changing color—usually to a dark blue. This is the Recycle Bin icon.

To select the Recycle Bin icon:

1. Position the pointer over the **Recycle Bin** icon.

2. Click the mouse button and notice how the color of the icon changes to show that it is selected.

Starting and Closing a Program

The software you use is sometimes referred to as a program or an application. To use a program, such as a word-processing program, you must first start it. With Windows 95 you start a program by clicking the Start button. The Start button displays a menu.

A **menu** is a list of options. Windows 95 has a **Start menu** that provides you with access to programs, data, and configuration options. One of the Start menu's most important functions is to let you start a program.

The Reference Window below explains how to start a program. Don't do the steps in the Reference Window now; they are for your later reference.

REFERENCE window	**STARTING A PROGRAM**
	■ Click the Start button.
	■ Point to Programs.
	■ Point to the group that contains your program.
	■ Click the name of the program you want to run.

3.1 NOTE

WordPad is similar to Write in Windows 3.1.

Windows 95 includes an easy-to-use word-processing program called WordPad. Suppose you want to start the WordPad program and use it to write a letter or report.

To start the WordPad program from the Start menu:

1. Click the **Start** button 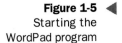 as shown in Figure 1-5. A menu appears.

Figure 1-5 ◄
Starting the
WordPad program

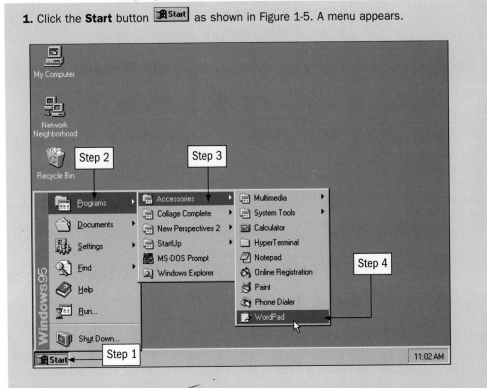

2. Point to **Programs**. After a short pause, the next menu appears.

   TROUBLE? If you don't get the correct menu, go back and point to the correct menu option.

3. Point to **Accessories**. Another menu appears.

4. Click **WordPad**. Make sure you can see the WordPad program as shown in Figure 1-6 on the following page.

Figure 1-6 ◀
The WordPad
program

WordPad program
window

Figure 1-6 The WordPad program
WordPad program window
The Close button

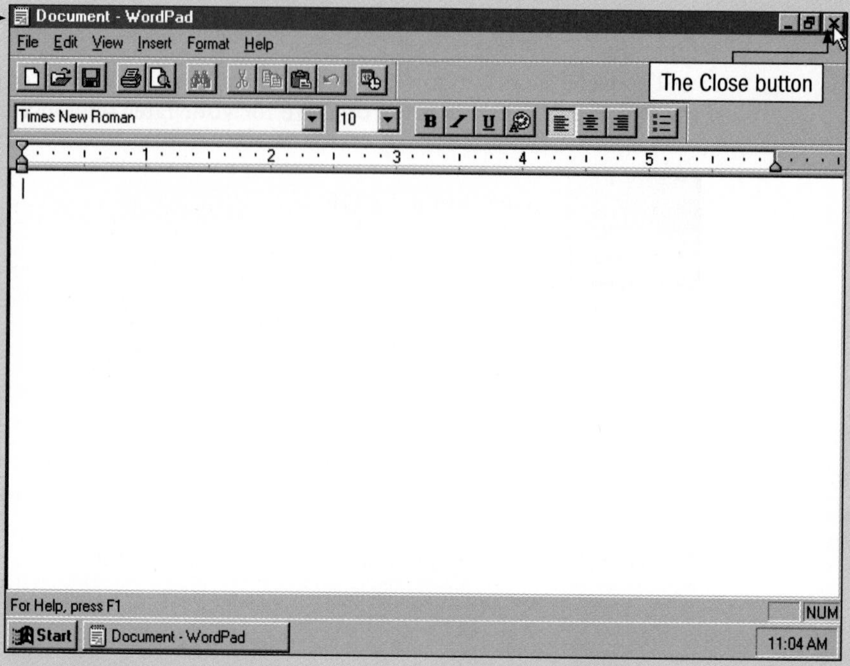

TROUBLE? If the WordPad program does not fill the entire screen, click the ⬜ button in the upper right corner.

3.I NOTE

*As with Windows 3.1,
in Windows 95 you
can also exit a
program using the
Exit option from the
File menu.*

When you are finished using a program, the easiest way to return to the Windows 95 desktop is to click the Close button ✖.

To exit the WordPad program:

> **1.** Click the **Close** button ✖. See Figure 1-6. You will be returned to the Windows 95 desktop.

Running More than One Program at the Same Time

3.I NOTE

*Paint in Windows 95
is similar to
Paintbrush in
WIndows 3.1.*

One of the most useful features of Windows 95 is its ability to run multiple programs at the same time. This feature, known as **multi-tasking**, allows you to work on more than one task at a time and to quickly switch between tasks. For example, you can start WordPad and leave it running while you then start the Paint program.

To run WordPad and Paint at the same time:

> **1.** Start WordPad.
>
> TROUBLE? You learned how to start WordPad earlier in the tutorial: Click the Start button, point to Programs, point to Accessories, and then click WordPad.
>
> **2.** Now you can start the Paint program. Click the **Start** button 🏁Start again.
>
> **3.** Point to **Programs**.
>
> **4.** Point to **Accessories**.
>
> **5.** Click **Paint**. The Paint program appears as shown in Figure 1-7. Now two programs are running at the same time.

TROUBLE? If the Paint program does not fill the entire screen, click the button in the upper right corner.

Figure 1-7
The Paint
Program

Paint program
window

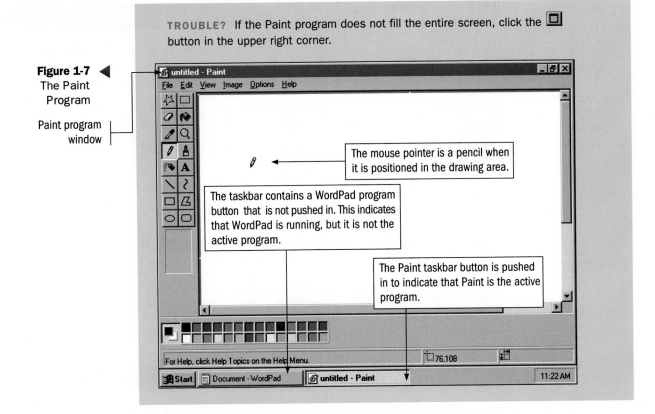

What happened to WordPad? The WordPad button is still on the taskbar, so even if you can't see it, WordPad is still running. You can imagine that it is stacked behind the Paint program, as shown in Figure 1-8.

3.1 NOTE

With Windows 3.1, some users had difficulty finding program windows on the desktop. The buttons on the Windows 95 taskbar make it much easier to keep track of which programs are running.

Other projects might be hidden under the project you are working on. For example, you might have worked on a letter earlier, but it is now under the picture you are currently drawing.

You might keep other projects handy on your desk. Anytime you want to work with one of them, you bring it to the center of your desk.

Figure 1-8
Programs
stacked on top
of a desk

Think of your screen
as the main work
area of your desk.

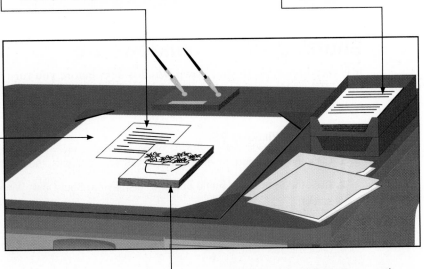

The project with which you are currently working is in your main work area. This project might be a multi-page document.

Switching Between Programs

3.1 NOTE

In Windows 95, you can still use Alt-Tab to switch between programs. You can also click on any open window to switch to it.

Although Windows 95 allows you to run more than one program, only one program at a time is active. The **active** program is the program with which you are currently working. The easiest way to switch between programs is to use the buttons on the taskbar.

REFERENCE
window

SWITCHING BETWEEN PROGRAMS

- Click the taskbar button that contains the name of the program to which you want to switch.

To switch between WordPad and Paint:

1. Click the button labeled **Document - WordPad** on the taskbar. The Document - WordPad button now looks like it has been pushed in to indicate it is the active program.

2. Next, click the button labeled **untitled - Paint** on the taskbar to switch to the Paint program.

Closing WordPad and Paint

It is good practice to close each program when you are finished using it. Each program uses computer resources such as memory, so Windows 95 works more efficiently when only the programs you need are open.

To close WordPad and Paint:

1. Click the **Close** button ☒ for the Paint program. The button labeled "untitled - Paint" disappears from the taskbar.

2. Click the **Close** button ☒ for the WordPad program. The WordPad button disappears from the taskbar, and you return to the Windows 95 desktop.

Shutting Down Windows 95

It is very important to shut down Windows 95 before you turn off the computer. If you turn off your computer without correctly shutting down, you might lose data and damage your files.

To shut down Windows 95:

1. Click the **Start** button 🏁Start on the taskbar to display the Start menu.

2. Click the **Shut Down** menu option to display the Shut Down Windows options screen.

3. Make sure the **Shut down the computer?** option is selected.

4. Click the **Yes** button.

5. Wait until you see a message indicating it is safe to turn off your computer, then switch off your computer.

You should typically use the option "Shut down the computer?" when you want to turn off your computer. However, other shut-down options are available. For example, your school might prefer that you select the option to "Close all programs and log on as a different user." This option logs you out of Windows 95, leaves the computer turned on, and allows another user to log on without restarting the computer. Check with your instructor or technical support person for the preferred method for your school's computer lab.

Quick Check

1 Label the components of the Windows 95 desktop in the figure below:

Figure 1-9 ◄

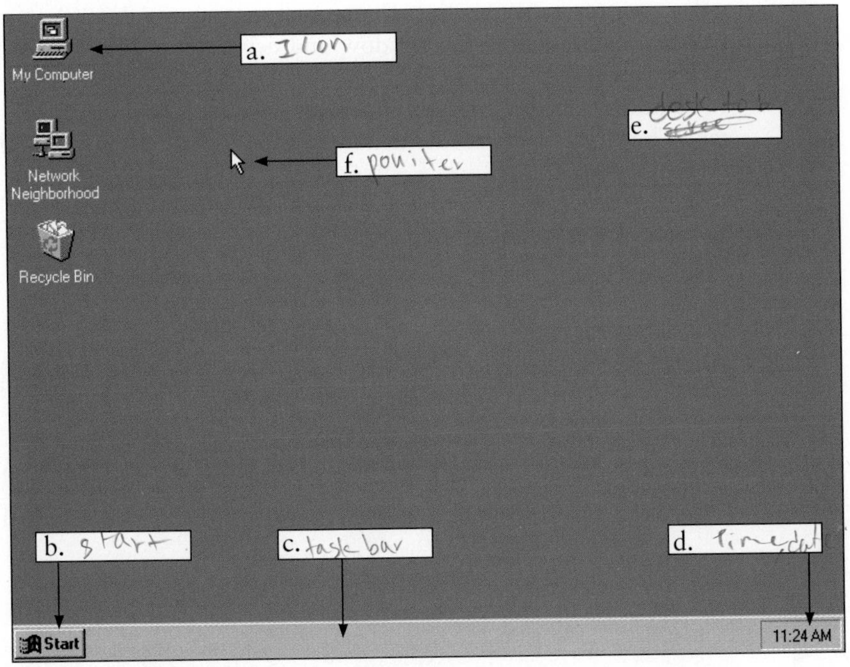

a. *Icon*

e. *desk top* ~~screen~~

f. *pointer*

b. *start*   c. *task bar*   d. *time-date*

My Computer

Network Neighborhood

Recycle Bin

Start   11:24 AM

2 The *multitasking* feature of Windows 95 allows you to run more than one program at a time.

3 The *start button* is a list of options that provides you with access to programs, data, and configuration options.

4 What should you do if you are trying to move the pointer to the left edge of your screen, but your mouse runs into the keyboard?

5 Windows 95 shows you that an icon is selected by *hilighthing* it.

6 Even if you can't see a program, it might be running. How can you tell if a program is running?

7 Why is it good practice to close each program when you are finished using it?

8 Why do you need to shut down Windows 95 before you turn off your computer?

SESSION

1.2

In this session you will learn how to use many of the Windows 95 controls to manipulate windows and programs. You will learn how to change the size and shape of a window and to move a window so that you can customize your screen-based workspace. You will also learn how to use menus, dialog boxes, tabs, buttons, and lists to specify how you want a program to carry out a task.

Anatomy of a Window

When you run a program in Windows 95, it appears in a window. A **window** is a rectangular area of the screen that contains a program or data. A window also contains controls for manipulating the window and using the program. WordPad is a good example of how a window works.

Windows, spelled with an uppercase "W," is the name of the Microsoft operating system. The word "window" with a lowercase "w" refers to one of the rectangular windows on the screen.

To look at window controls:

1. Make sure Windows 95 is running and you are at the Windows 95 desktop screen.

2. Start WordPad.

> **TROUBLE?** To start WordPad, click the **Start** button, point to Programs, point to Accessories, and then click **WordPad**.

3. Make sure WordPad takes up the entire screen.

> **TROUBLE?** If WordPad does not take up the entire screen, click the 🔲 button in the upper right corner.

4. On your screen, identify the controls labeled in Figure 1-10.

Figure 1-10 ◀
Window
controls

The **menu bar** contains the titles of menus, such as File, Edit, and Help.

The **toolbar** contains buttons that provide you with a shortcut to the commands listed on the menus.

The **status bar** provides you with abbreviated help relevant to the task you are doing.

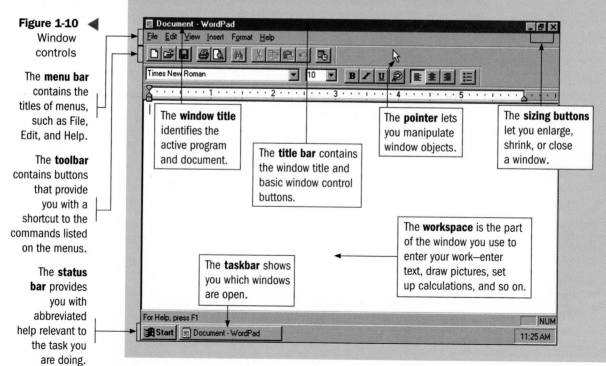

The **window title** identifies the active program and document.

The **title bar** contains the window title and basic window control buttons.

The **pointer** lets you manipulate window objects.

The **sizing buttons** let you enlarge, shrink, or close a window.

The **workspace** is the part of the window you use to enter your work—enter text, draw pictures, set up calculations, and so on.

The **taskbar** shows you which windows are open.

Manipulating a Window

There are three buttons located on the right side of the title bar. You are already familiar with the Close button. The Minimize button hides the window. The other button either maximizes the window or restores it to a predefined size. Figure 1-11 shows how these buttons work.

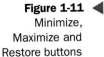

Figure 1-11
Minimize, Maximize and Restore buttons

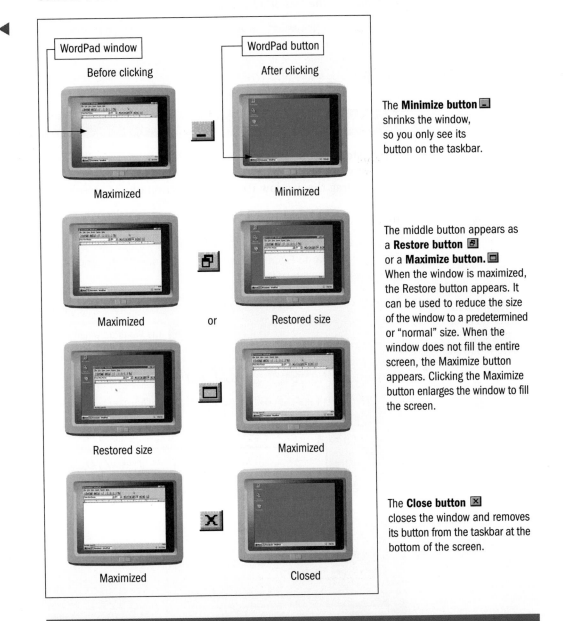

The **Minimize button** 🗕 shrinks the window, so you only see its button on the taskbar.

The middle button appears as a **Restore button** 🗗 or a **Maximize button.** 🗖 When the window is maximized, the Restore button appears. It can be used to reduce the size of the window to a predetermined or "normal" size. When the window does not fill the entire screen, the Maximize button appears. Clicking the Maximize button enlarges the window to fill the screen.

The **Close button** ⊠ closes the window and removes its button from the taskbar at the bottom of the screen.

Minimizing a Window

The **Minimize button** 🗕 shrinks the current window so that only the button on the taskbar remains visible. You can use the Minimize button when you want to temporarily hide a window but keep the program running.

To minimize the WordPad window:

1. Click the **Minimize** button 🗕. The WordPad window shrinks so only the Document - WordPad button on the taskbar is visible.

   TROUBLE?   If you accidentally clicked the Close button and closed the window, use the Start button to start WordPad again.

Redisplaying a Window

You can redisplay a minimized window by clicking the program's button on the taskbar. When you redisplay a window, it becomes the active window.

To redisplay the WordPad window:

1. Click the **Document - WordPad** button on the taskbar. The WordPad window is restored to its previous size. The Document - WordPad button looks pushed in as a visual clue that it is now the active window.

Restoring a Window

The **Restore** button 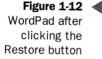 reduces the window so it is smaller than the entire screen. This is useful if you want to see more than one window at a time. Also, because of its small size, you can drag the window to another location on the screen or change its dimensions.

To restore a window:

1. Click the **Restore** button on the WordPad title bar. The WordPad window will look similar to Figure 1-12, but the exact size of the window on your screen might be slightly different.

Figure 1-12 ◀
WordPad after
clicking the
Restore button

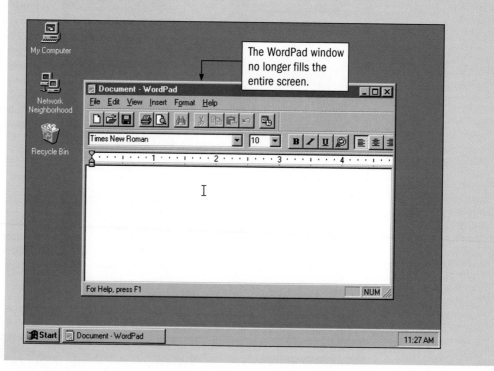

The WordPad window no longer fills the entire screen.

Moving a Window

You can use the mouse to **move** a window to a new position on the screen. When you hold down the mouse button while moving the mouse, it is called **dragging**. You can move objects on the screen by dragging them to a new location. If you want to move a window, you drag its title bar.

To drag the WordPad window to a new location:

1. Position the mouse pointer on the WordPad window title bar.

2. While you hold down the left mouse button, move the mouse to drag the window. A rectangle representing the window moves as you move the mouse.

3. Position the rectangle anywhere on the screen, then release the left mouse button. The WordPad window appears in the new location.

4. Now drag the WordPad window to the upper-left corner of the screen.

Changing the Size of a Window

3.1 NOTE

You can also change the size of a window by dragging the top, bottom, sides, and corners of the window, as you did in Windows 3.1.

You can also use the mouse to change the size of a window. Notice the sizing handle at the lower right corner of the window. The **sizing handle** provides a visible control for changing the size of a current window.

To change the size of the WordPad window:

1. Position the pointer over the sizing handle. The pointer changes to a diagonal arrow.

2. While holding down the mouse button, drag the sizing handle down and to the right.

3. Release the mouse button. Now the window is larger.

4. Practice using the sizing handle to make the WordPad window larger or smaller.

Maximizing a Window

The **Maximize button** enlarges a window so that it fills the entire screen. You will probably do most of your work using maximized windows because you can see more of your program and data.

To maximize the WordPad window:

1. Click the **Maximize** button on the WordPad title bar.

Using Program Menus

Most Windows programs use menus to provide an easy way for you to select program commands. The **menu bar** is typically located at the top of the program window and shows the titles of menus such as File, Edit, and Help.

Windows menus are relatively standardized—most Windows programs include similar menu options. It's easy to learn new programs, because you can make a pretty good guess about which menu contains the command you want.

Selecting Commands from a Menu

When you click any menu title, choices for that menu appear below the menu bar. These choices are referred to as **menu options**. To select a menu option, you click it. For example, the File menu is a standard feature in most Windows programs and contains the options related to working with a file: creating, opening, saving, and printing a file or document.

To select Print Preview from the File menu:

1. Click **File** in the WordPad menu bar to display the File menu.

   TROUBLE? If you open a menu but decide not to select any of the menu options, you can close the menu by clicking its title again.

2. Click **Print Preview** to open the preview screen and view your document as it will appear when printed. This document is blank because you didn't enter any text.

3. After examining the screen, click the button labeled "Close" to return to your document.

Not all menu options immediately carry out an action—some show submenus or ask you for more information about what you want to do. The menu gives you hints about what to expect when you select an option. These hints are sometimes referred to as **menu conventions**. Study Figures 1-13a and 1-13b so you will recognize the Windows 95 menu conventions.

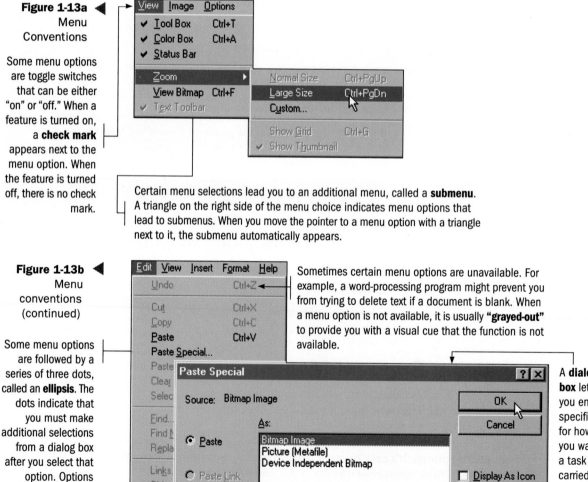

Figure 1-13a ◄
Menu
Conventions

Some menu options are toggle switches that can be either "on" or "off." When a feature is turned on, a **check mark** appears next to the menu option. When the feature is turned off, there is no check mark.

Certain menu selections lead you to an additional menu, called a **submenu**. A triangle on the right side of the menu choice indicates menu options that lead to submenus. When you move the pointer to a menu option with a triangle next to it, the submenu automatically appears.

Figure 1-13b ◄
Menu conventions (continued)

Some menu options are followed by a series of three dots, called an **ellipsis**. The dots indicate that you must make additional selections from a dialog box after you select that option. Options without dots do not require additional choices—they take effect as soon a you click them.

Sometimes certain menu options are unavailable. For example, a word-processing program might prevent you from trying to delete text if a document is blank. When a menu option is not available, it is usually **"grayed-out"** to provide you with a visual cue that the function is not available.

A **dialog box** lets you enter specification for how you want a task carried out.

Using Toolbars

A **toolbar** contains buttons that provide quick access to important program commands. Although you can usually perform all program commands using the menus, the toolbar provides convenient one-click access to frequently-used commands. For most Windows 95 functions, there is usually more than one way to accomplish a task. To simplify your introduction to Windows 95 in this tutorial, you will learn only one method for performing a task. As you become more accomplished using Windows 95, you can explore alternative methods.

In Session 1.1 you learned that Windows 95 programs include ToolTips that indicate the purpose and function of a tool. Now is a good time to explore the WordPad toolbar buttons by looking at their ToolTips.

To find out a toolbar button's function:

1. Position the pointer over any button on the toolbar, such as the Print Preview icon 🔍. After a short pause, the name of the button appears in a box and a description of the button appears in the status bar just above the Start button.

2. Move the pointer to each button on the toolbar to see its name and purpose.

You select a toolbar button by clicking it.

To select the Print Preview toolbar button:

1. Click the **Print Preview** button 🔍.

2. The Print Preview dialog box appears. This is the same dialog box that appeared when you selected File, Print Preview from the menu bar.

3. Click ⬜Close⬜ to close the Print Preview dialog box.

Using List Boxes and Scroll Bars

As you might guess from the name, a **list box** displays a list of choices. In WordPad, date and time formats are shown in the Date/Time list box. List box controls include arrow buttons, a scroll bar, and a scroll box, as shown in Figure 1-14.

Figure 1-14 ◀
List Box

Date and Time dialog box.

You can click the **up arrow button** to move toward the top of the list.

The list box shows the available date formats.

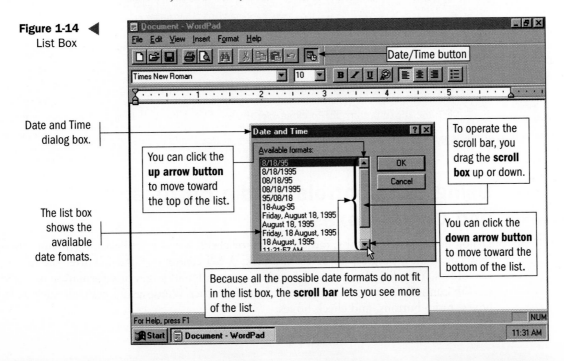

To operate the scroll bar, you drag the **scroll box** up or down.

You can click the **down arrow button** to move toward the bottom of the list.

Because all the possible date formats do not fit in the list box, the **scroll bar** lets you see more of the list.

To use the Date/Time list box:

1. Click the **Date/Time** button 🖼 to display the Date and Time dialog box. See Figure 1-14.

2. To scroll down the list, click the **down arrow** button 🔽. See Figure 1-14.

3. Find the scroll box on your screen. See Figure 1-14.

4. Drag the **scroll box** to the top of the scroll bar. Notice how the list scrolls back to the beginning.

5. Find a date format similar to "October 2, 1997." Click that date format to select it.

6. Click the **OK** button to close the Date and Time list box. This inserts the current date in your document.

A variation of the list box, called a **drop-down list box**, usually shows only one choice, but can expand down to display additional choices on the list.

To use the Type Size drop-down list:

1. Click the **down arrow** button 🔽 shown in Figure 1-15.

Figure 1-15 ◀
Type-size drop-down list box

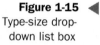

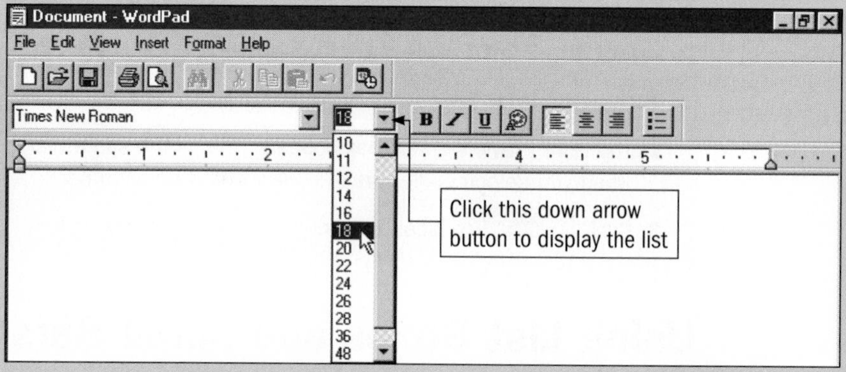

2. Click **18**. The drop-down list disappears and the type size you selected appears at the top of the pull-down list.

3. Type a few characters to test the new type size.

4. Click the **down arrow** button 🔽 in the Type size drop-down list box again.

5. Click **12**.

6. Type a few characters to test this type size.

7. Click the **Close** button ☒ to close WordPad.

8. When you see the message "Save changes to Document?" click the **No** button.

Using Tab Controls, Radio Buttons, and Check Boxes

Dialog boxes often use tabs, radio buttons, or check boxes to collect information about how you want a program to perform a task. A **tab control** is patterned after the tabs on file folders. You click the appropriate tab to view different pages of information or choices. Tab controls are often used as containers for other Windows 95 controls such as list boxes, radio buttons, and check boxes.

Radio buttons, also called **option buttons**, allow you to select a single option from among one or more options. **Check boxes** allow you to select many options at the same time. Figure 1-16 explains how to use these controls.

Figure 1-16 ◀
Tabs, radio buttons, and check boxes

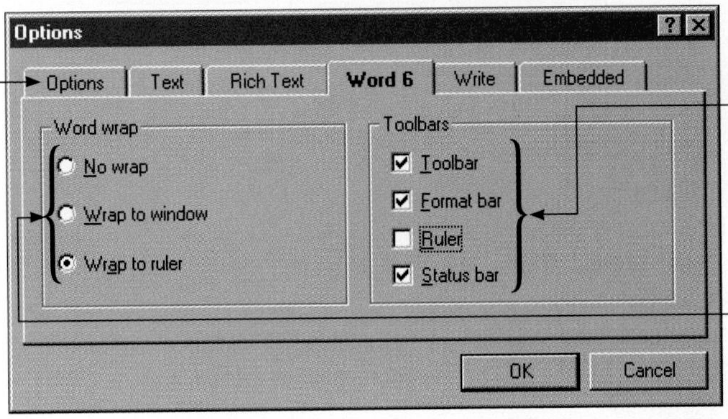

A **tab** indicates an "index card" that contains information or a group of controls, usually with related functions. To look at the functions on an index card, click the tab.

Check boxes allow you to select one or more options from a group. When you click a check box, a check mark appears in it. To remove a check mark from a box, click it again.

Radio buttons are round and usually come in groups of two or more. You can select only one radio button from a group. Your selection is indicated by a black dot.

Using Help

Windows 95 **Help** provides on-screen information about the program you are using. Help for the Windows 95 operating system is available by clicking the Start button on the taskbar, then selecting Help from the Start menu. If you want Help for a program, such as WordPad, you must first start the program, then use the Help menu at the top of the screen.

REFERENCE window	**STARTING WINDOWS 95 HELP**
	▪ Click the Start button.
	▪ Click Help.

To start Windows 95 Help:

1. Click the **Start** button.

2. Click **Help**.

Help uses tabs for each section of Help. Windows 95 Help tabs include Contents, Index, and Find as shown in Figure 1-17 on the following page.

Figure 1-17 ◀
Windows 95
Help

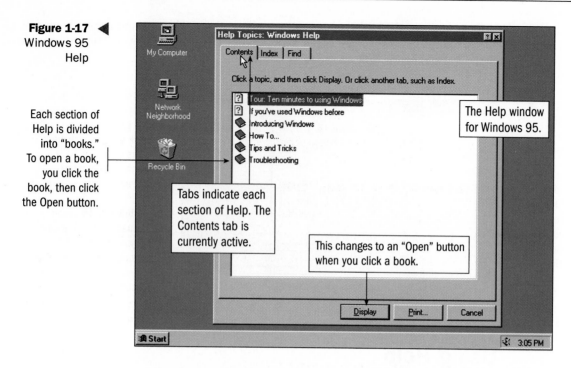

Each section of
Help is divided
into "books."
To open a book,
you click the
book, then click
the Open button.

The **Contents tab** groups Help topics into a series of books. You select a book, which then provides you with a list of related topics from which you can choose. The **Index tab** displays an alphabetical list of all the Help topics from which you can choose. The **Find tab** lets you search for any word or phrase in Help.

Suppose you're wondering if there is an alternative way to start programs. You can use the Contents tab to find the answer to your question.

3.1 NOTE

You can also double-click to select and open a topic in a single step.

To use the Contents tab:

1. Click the **Contents** tab to display the Contents window.

2. Click the **How To...** book title, then click the **Open** button. A list of related books appears below the book title. See. Figure 1-18.

Figure 1-18 ◀
Help Window

Click this book,
then click the
Open button to
display a list of
related books.

Books related to
the "How To" topic.

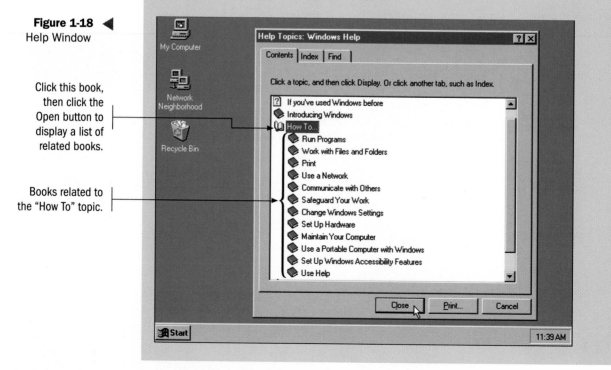

3. Click the **Run Programs** book, then click the **Open** button. The table of contents for this Help book is displayed.

4. Click the topic **Starting a Program**, then click the **Display** button. A Help window appears and explains how to start a program.

Help also provides you with definitions of technical terms. You can click any underlined term to see its definition.

To see a definition of the term "taskbar":

1. Point to the underlined term, **taskbar** until the pointer changes to a hand. Then click.

2. After you have read the definition, click the definition to deselect it.

3. Click the **Close** button ☒ on the Help window.

The **Index tab** allows you to jump to a Help topic by selecting a topic from an indexed list. For example, you can use the Index tab to learn how to arrange the open windows on your desktop.

To find a Help topic using the Index tab:

1. Click the **Start** button.

2. Click **Help**.

3. Click the **Index** tab.

4. A long list of indexed Help topics appears. Drag the scroll box down to view additional topics.

5. You can quickly jump to any part of the list by typing the first few characters of a word or phrase in the line above the Index list. Type **desktop** to display topics related to the Windows 95 desktop.

6. Click the topic **arranging open windows on** in the bottom window.

7. Click the **Display** button as shown in Figure 1-19.

Figure 1-19 ◀
Displaying a
Help Topic

Click here to type
words or phrases.

Index topics are
displayed here.
Click the topic to
select it.

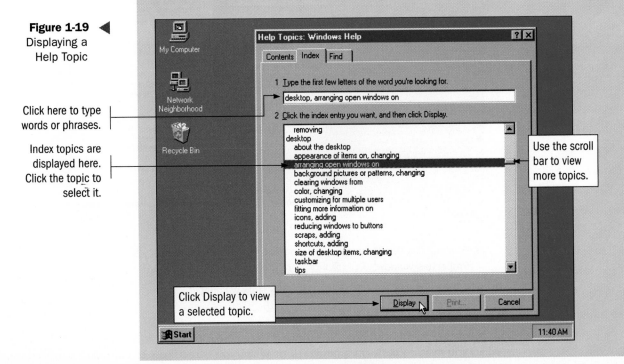

8. Click the **Close** button ☒ to close the Windows Help window.

The **Find tab** contains an index of all words in Windows 95 Help. You can use it to search for Help pages that contain a particular word or phrase. For example, suppose you heard that a screen saver blanks out your screen when you are not using it. You could use the Find tab to find out more about screen savers.

To find a Help topic using the Find tab:

1. Click the **Start** button 🎆 Start.

2. Click **Help**.

3. Click the **Find** tab.

   TROUBLE? If the Find index has not yet been created on your computer, the computer will prompt you through several steps to create the index. Continue with Step 4 below after the Find index is created.

4. Type **screen** to display a list of all topics that start with the letters "screen."

5. Click **screen-saver** in the middle window to display the topics that contain the word "screen-saver."

6. Click **Having your monitor automatically turn off**, then click the **Display** button.

7. Click the **Help window** button shown in Figure 1-20. The screen saver is shown on a simulated monitor.

   TROUBLE? If you see an error message, your lab does not allow students to modify screen savers. Click the OK button and go to Step 9.

Figure 1-20 ◄
Clicking a
Button in Help

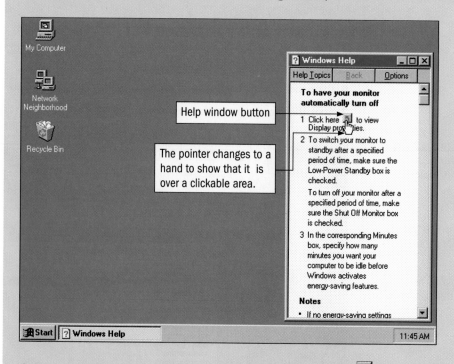

8. To close the Display properties window, click the **Close** button ☒ in the Display Properties window.

9. Click the **Close** button ☒ to close the Help window.

Now that you know how Windows 95 Help works, don't forget to use it! Use Help when you need to perform a new task or when you forget how to complete a procedure.

Quick Check

1. Label the parts of the window shown in Figure 1-21.

Figure 1-21 ◀

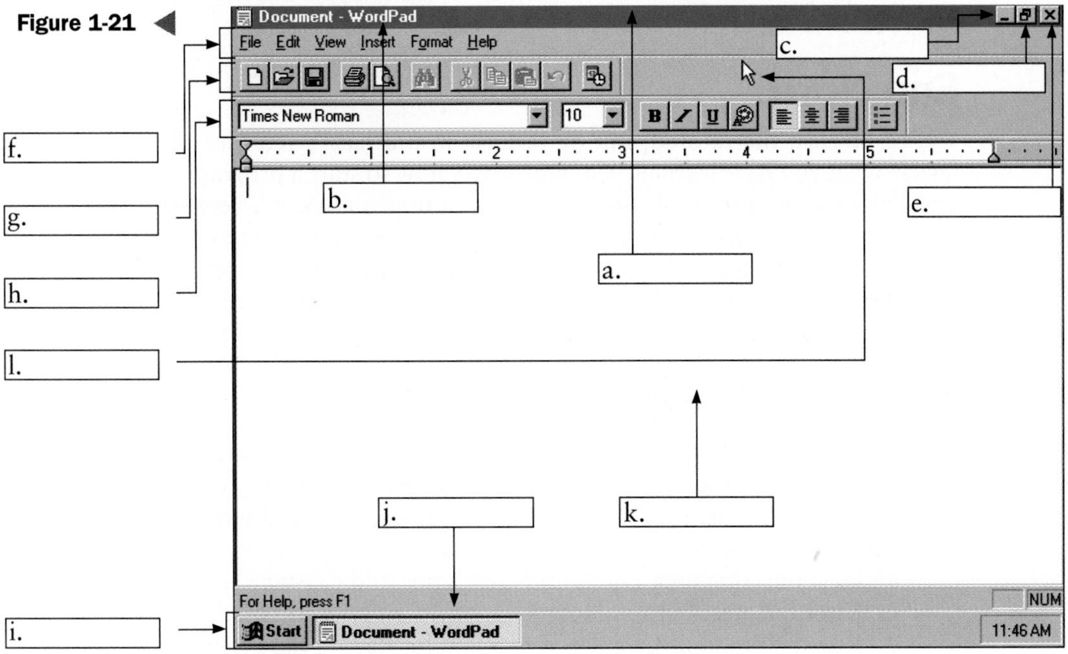

Document - WordPad

File   Edit   View   Insert   Format   Help

Times New Roman   10   B I U   · · · 1 · · · 2 · · · 3 · · · 4 · · · 5 · · ·

f.

g.

h.

l.

b.

a.

c.

d.

e.

j.

k.

For Help, press F1   NUM

i.

Start   Document - WordPad   11:46 AM

2. Provide the name and purpose of each button:
   a. ▬
   b. ▢
   c. ▣
   d. ✖

3. Explain each of the following menu conventions:
   a. Ellipsis...
   b. Grayed out
   c. ▶
   d. ✔

4. A(n) _____ consists of a group of buttons, each of which provides one-click access to important program functions.

5. Label each part of the dialog box below:

Figure 1-22 ◀

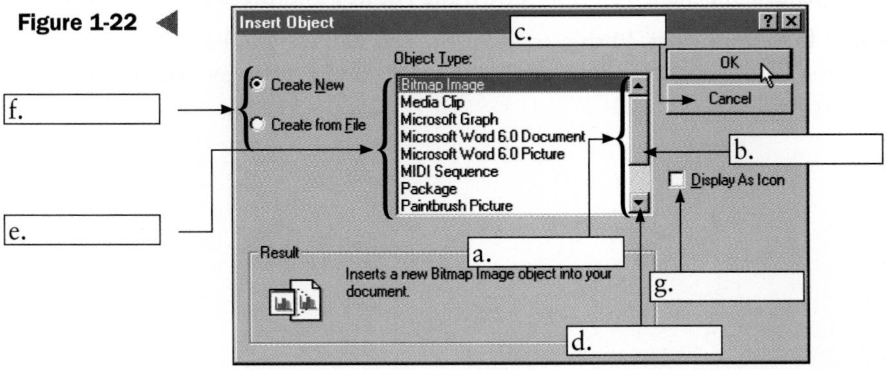

Insert Object   ? ✖

Object Type: c.

f.   ◉ Create New   Bitmap Image   OK
             ○ Create from File Media Clip
                                Microsoft Graph   Cancel
                                Microsoft Word 6.0 Document
                                Microsoft Word 6.0 Picture
                                MIDI Sequence   b.
                                Package
                                Paintbrush Picture   □ Display As Icon

e.

Result   a.

                Inserts a new Bitmap Image object into your
                document.   g.

                                    d.

6 Radio buttons allow you to select _____ option(s) at a time, but _____ allow you to select one or more options.

7 It is a good idea to use _____ when you need to learn how to perform new tasks, simplify tedious procedures, and correct actions that did not turn out as you expected.

End Note

You've finished the tutorial, but Steve Laslow still hasn't returned. Take a moment to review what you have learned. You now know how to start a program using the Start button. You can run more than one program at a time and switch between programs using the buttons on the taskbar. You have learned the names and functions of window controls and Windows 95 menu conventions. You can now use toolbar buttons, list boxes, drop-down lists, radio buttons, check boxes, and scroll bars. Finally, you can use the Contents, Index, and Find tabs in Help to extend your knowledge of how to use Windows 95.

Tutorial Assignments

1. Running Two Programs and Switching Between Them In this tutorial you learned how to run more than one program at a time using WordPad and Paint. You can run other programs at the same time, too. Complete the following steps and write out your answers to questions b through f:

    a. Start the computer. Enter your user name and password if prompted to do so.
    b. Click the Start button. How many menu options are on the Start menu?
    c. Run the program Calculator program located on the Programs, Accessories menu. How many buttons are now on the taskbar?
    d. Run the Paint program and maximize the Paint window. How many application programs are running now?
    e. Switch to Calculator. What are the two visual clues that tell you that Calculator is the active program?
    f. Multiply 576 by 1457. What is the result?
    g. Close Calculator, then close Paint.

2. WordPad Help In Tutorial 1 you learned how to use Windows 95 Help. Just about every Windows 95 program has a help feature. Many computer users can learn to use a program just by using Help. To use Help, you would start the program, then click the Help menu at the top of the screen. Try using WordPad Help and complete steps a, b, and c:

    a. Start WordPad.
    b. Click Help on the WordPad menu bar, then click Help Topics.
    c. Using WordPad help, write out your answers to questions 1 through 3.
        1. How do you create a bulleted list?
        2. How do you set the margins in a document?
        3. What happens if you hold down the Alt key and press the Print Screen key?

3. Using Help to Explore Paint In this assignment, you will use the Paint Help to learn how to use the Paint program. Your goal is to create and print a picture that looks like the one in Figure 1-23.

Figure 1-23 ◀

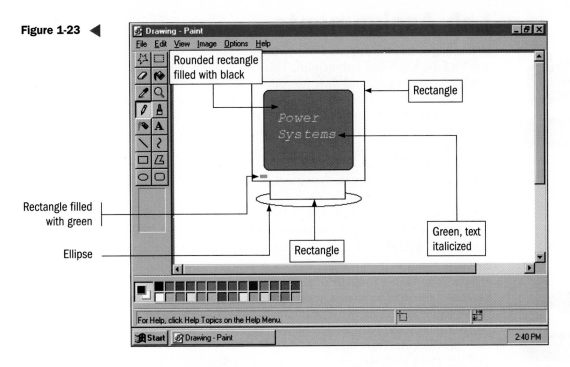

a. Start Paint.
b. Click Help, then click Help Topics.
c. Use Paint Help to learn how to put text in a picture and how to draw rectangles and circles.
d. Draw a picture of a monitor using rectangles, circles, and text as shown in Figure 1-23.
e. Print your picture.

4. The Windows 95 Tutorial Windows 95 includes a five part on-line tutorial. In Tutorial 1 you learned about starting programs, switching windows, and using Help. You can use the on-line Windows 95 Tutorial to review what you learned and pick up some new tips for using Windows 95. Complete the following steps and write out your answers to questions f, g, and h:

a. Click the Start button to display the Start menu.
b. Click Help to display Windows help.
c. Click the Contents tab.
d. From the Contents screen, click Tour: Ten minutes to using Windows.
e. Click the Display button. If an error message appears, the Tour is probably not loaded on your computer. You will not be able to complete this assignment. Click Cancel, then click OK to cancel and check with your instructor or technical support person.
f. Click Starting a Program and complete the tutorial. What are the names of the seven programs on the Accessories menu in the tutorial?
g. Click Switching Windows and complete the on-line tutorial. What does the Minimize button do?
h. Click Using Help and complete the tutorial. What is the purpose of the ? button?
i. Click the Exit button to close the Tour window.
j. Click the Exit Tour button to exit the Tour and return to the Windows 95 desktop.

Lab Assignments

Using a Keyboard

1. Learning to Use the Keyboard If you are not familiar with computer keyboards, you will find the Keyboard Lab helpful. This Lab will give you a structured introduction to special computer keys and their function in Windows 95. As you work through the Lab, you will be asked to answer Quick Check questions about what you have learned. At the end of the lab, you will see a summary report of your answers. If your instructor wants you to print out your answers to these questions, click the Print button on the summary report screen.

    a. Click the Start button.
    b. Point to Programs, then point to CTI Windows 95 Applications.
    c. Click Windows 95 New Perspectives Brief.
    d. Click Using a Keyboard. If you cannot find Windows 95 New Perspectives Brief or Using a Keyboard, ask for help from your instructor or technical support person.

Using a Mouse

2. Mouse Practice If you would like more practice using a mouse, you can complete the Mouse Lab. As you work through the Lab, you will be asked to answer Quick Check questions about what you have learned. At the end of the lab, the Quick Check Report shows you how you did. If your instructor wants you to print out your answers to these questions, click the Print button on the summary report screen.

    a. Click the Start button.
    b. Point to Programs, then point to CTI Windows 95.
    c. Point to Windows 95 New Perspectives Brief.
    d. Click Using a Mouse. If you cannot find Windows 95 New Perspectives Brief or Using a Mouse, ask for help from your instructor or technical support person.

TUTORIAL 2

Working with Files

OBJECTIVES

In this tutorial you will learn to:

- Format a disk

- Enter, select, insert, and delete text

- Create and save a file

- Open and edit a file

- Print a file

- Create a Student Disk

- View the list of files on your disk

- Move, copy, delete, and rename a file

LABS

Using Files

CASE

Your First Day in the Lab—Continued

Steve Laslow is back from class, grinning. "I see you're making progress!"

"That's right," you reply. "I know how to run programs, control windows, and use Help. I guess I'm ready to work with my word-processing and spreadsheet software now."

Steve hesitates before he continues, "You could, but there are a few more things about Windows 95 that you should learn first."

Steve explains that most of the software you have on your computer—your word-processing, spreadsheet, scheduling, and graphing software—was created especially for the Windows 95 operating system. This software is referred to as **Windows 95 applications** or **Windows 95 programs**. You can also use software designed for Windows 3.1, but Windows 95 applications give you more flexibility. For example, when you name a document in a Windows 95 application, you can use descriptive filenames with up to 255 characters, whereas in Windows 3.1 you are limited to eight-character names.

You typically use Windows 95 applications to create files. A **file** is a collection of data that has a name and is stored in a computer. You typically create files that contain documents, pictures, and graphs when you use software packages. For example, you might use word-processing software to create a file containing a document. Once you create a file, you can open it, edit its contents, print it, and save it again—usually using the same application program you used to create it.

Another advantage of Windows 95 is that once you know how to save, open, and print files with one Windows 95 application, you can perform those same functions in *any* Windows 95 application. This is because Windows 95 applications have similar controls. For example, your word-processing and spreadsheet software will have identical menu commands to save, open, and print documents. Steve suggests that it would be worth a few minutes of your time to become familiar with these menus in Windows 95 applications.

You agree, but before you can get to work, Steve gives you one final suggestion: you should also learn how to keep track of the files on your disk. For instance, you might need to find a file you have not used for a while or you might want to delete a file if your disk is getting full. You will definitely want to make a backup copy of your disk in case something happens to the original. Steve's advice seems practical, and you're eager to explore these functions so you can get to work!

Tutorial 2 will help you learn how to work with Windows 95 applications and keep track of the files on your disk. When you've completed this tutorial, you'll be ready to tackle all kinds of Windows 95 software!

In Session 2.1 you will learn how to format a disk so it can store files. You will create, save, open, and print a file. You will find out how the insertion point is different from the mouse pointer, and you will learn the basic skills for Windows 95 text entry, such as inserting, deleting, and selecting.
For this session you will need two blank 3 ½-inch disks.

Formatting a Disk

Before you can save files on a disk, the disk must be formatted. When the computer **formats** a disk, the magnetic particles on the disk surface are arranged so data can be stored on the disk. Today, many disks are sold preformatted and can be used right out of the box. However, if you purchase an unformatted disk, or if you have an old disk that you want to completely erase and reuse, you can format the disk using the Windows 95 Format command.

The following steps tell you how to format a 3 ½-inch high-density disk using drive A. Your instructor will tell you how to revise the instructions given in these steps if the procedure is different for your lab equipment.

All data on the disk you format will be erased, so don't perform these steps using a disk that contains important files.

To format a disk:

1. Start Windows 95, if necessary.

2. Write your name on the label of a 3 ½-inch disk.

3. Insert your disk in drive A. See Figure 2-1.

Figure 2-1 ◄
Inserting a
disk into the
disk drive

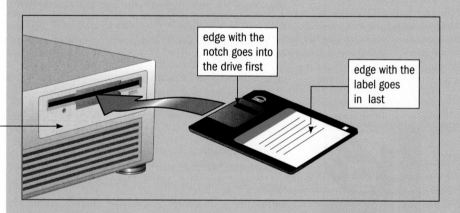

floppy disk drive

edge with the notch goes into the drive first

edge with the label goes in last

TROUBLE? If your disk does not fit in drive A, put it in drive B and substitute drive B for drive A in all of the steps for the rest of the tutorial.

4. Click the **My Computer** icon to select it, then press the **Enter** key. Make sure you can see the My Computer window. See Figure 2-2.

TROUBLE? If you see a list instead of icons like those in Figure 2-2, click View. Then click Large Icon.

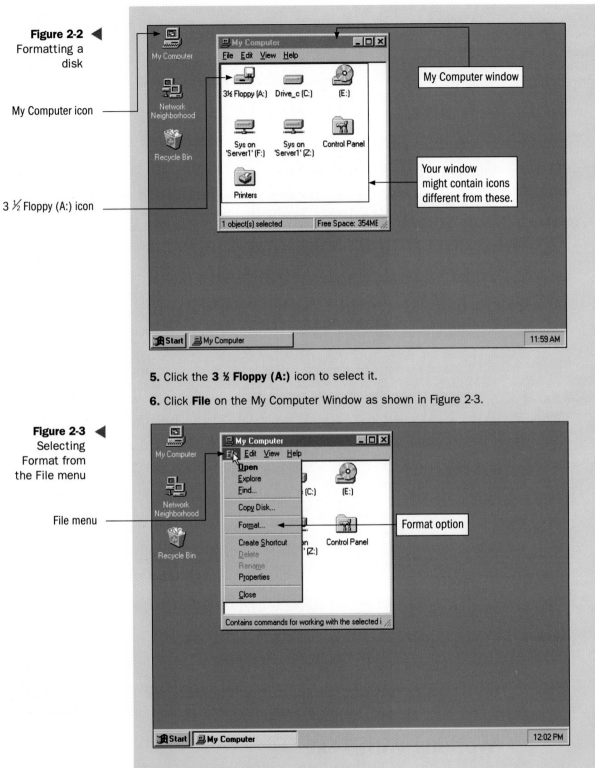

Figure 2-2 ◀
Formatting a
disk

My Computer icon

3 ½ Floppy (A:) icon

5. Click the **3 ½ Floppy (A:)** icon to select it.

6. Click **File** on the My Computer Window as shown in Figure 2-3.

Figure 2-3 ◀
Selecting
Format from
the File menu

File menu

7. Click **Format** to open the Format dialog box.

8. Make sure the dialog box settings on your screen match those in Figure 2-4.

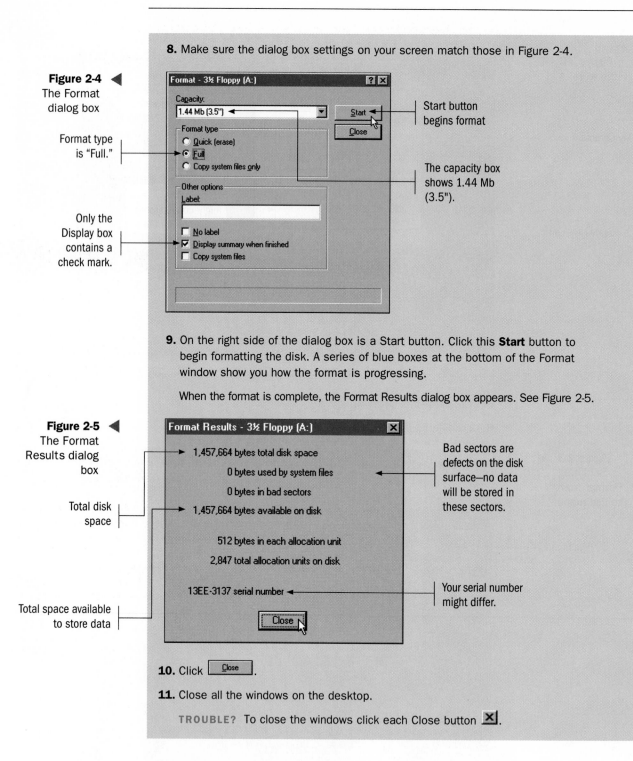

Figure 2-4 ◀
The Format
dialog box

Format type
is "Full."

Only the
Display box
contains a
check mark.

Start button
begins format

The capacity box
shows 1.44 Mb
(3.5").

9. On the right side of the dialog box is a Start button. Click this **Start** button to begin formatting the disk. A series of blue boxes at the bottom of the Format window show you how the format is progressing.

When the format is complete, the Format Results dialog box appears. See Figure 2-5.

Figure 2-5 ◀
The Format
Results dialog
box

Total disk
space

Total space available
to store data

Bad sectors are
defects on the disk
surface—no data
will be stored in
these sectors.

Your serial number
might differ.

10. Click [Close].

11. Close all the windows on the desktop.

TROUBLE? To close the windows click each Close button ☒.

Working with Text

To accomplish many computing tasks, you need to type text in documents and text boxes. Windows 95 facilitates basic text entry by providing a text-entry area, by showing you where your text will appear on the screen, by helping you move around on the screen, and by providing insert and delete functions.

When you type sentences and paragraphs of text, do *not* press the Enter key when you reach the right margin. The software contains a feature called **word wrap** that automatically continues your text on the next line. Therefore, you should press Enter only when you have completed a paragraph.

If you type the wrong character, press the Backspace key to backup and delete the character. You can also use the Delete key. What's the difference between the Backspace and the Delete keys? The Backspace key deletes the character to left. The Delete key deletes the character to the right.

Now you will type some text using WordPad to learn about text entry.

To type text in WordPad:

1. Start WordPad.

   TROUBLE? If the WordPad window does not fill the screen, click the Maximize button 🔲.

2. Notice the flashing vertical bar, called the **insertion point**, in the upper-left corner of the document window. The insertion point indicates where the characters you type will appear.

3. Type your name, using the Shift key to type uppercase letters and using the spacebar to type spaces, just like on a typewriter.

4. Press the **Enter** key to end the current paragraph and move the insertion point down to the next line.

5. As you type the following sentences, watch what happens when the insertion point reaches the right edge of the screen:

   This is a sample typed in WordPad. See what happens when the insertion point reaches the right edge of the screen.

   TROUBLE? If you make a mistake, delete the incorrect character(s) by pressing the Backspace key on your keyboard. Then type the correct character(s).

The Insertion Point versus the Pointer

The insertion point is not the same as the mouse pointer. When the mouse pointer is in the text-entry area, it is called the **I-beam pointer** and looks like I. Figure 2-6 explains the difference between the insertion point and the I-beam pointer.

Figure 2-6 ◄
The insertion point vs. the pointer

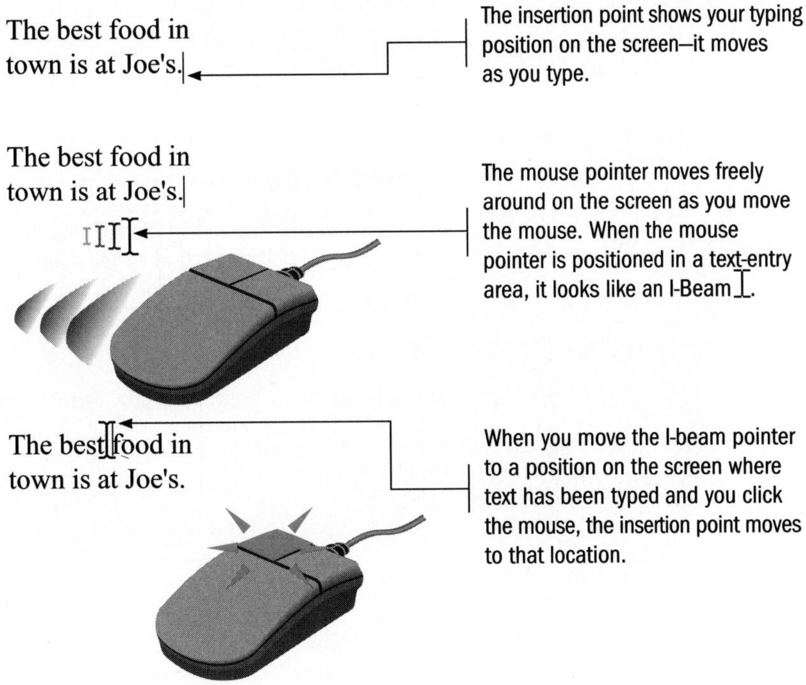

The best food in
town is at Joe's.|

The insertion point shows your typing position on the screen—it moves as you type.

The best food in
town is at Joe's.|

The mouse pointer moves freely around on the screen as you move the mouse. When the mouse pointer is positioned in a text-entry area, it looks like an I-Beam I.

The best food in
town is at Joe's.

When you move the I-beam pointer to a position on the screen where text has been typed and you click the mouse, the insertion point moves to that location.

To move the insertion point:

1. Check the location of the insertion point and the I-beam pointer. The insertion point should be at the end of the sentence you typed in the last set of steps.

   TROUBLE? If you don't see the I-beam pointer, move your mouse until you see it.

2. Use the mouse to move the I-beam pointer to the word "sample," then click the left mouse button. The insertion point jumps to the location of the I-beam pointer.

3. Move the I-beam pointer to a blank area near the bottom of the work space and click the left mouse button. *Notice that the insertion point does not jump to the location of the I-beam pointer.* Instead the insertion point jumps to the end of the last sentence. The insertion point can move only within existing text. It cannot be moved out of the existing text area.

Selecting Text

Many text operations are performed on a **block** of text, which is one or more consecutive words, sentences, or paragraphs. Once you select a block of text, you can delete it, move it, replace it, underline it, and so on. As you select a block of text, the computer highlights it. If you want to remove the highlighting, just click in the margin of your document.

Suppose you want to replace the phrase "See what happens" with "You can watch word wrap in action." You do not have to delete the text one character at a time. Instead you can highlight the entire phrase and begin to type the replacement text.

To select and replace a block of text:

1. Move the I-beam pointer just to the left of the word "See."

2. While holding down the left mouse button, drag the I-beam pointer over the text to the end of the word "happens." The phrase "See what happens" should now be highlighted. See Figure 2-7.

Figure 2-7 ◄
Highlighting
text

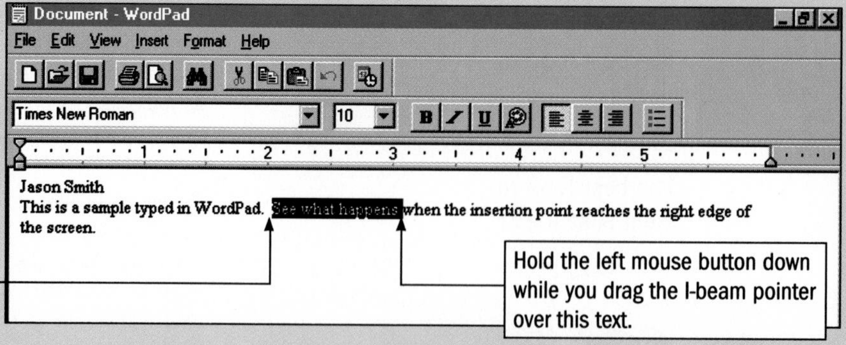

Position the
I-beam pointer here.

3. Release the left mouse button.

   TROUBLE? If the phrase is not highlighted correctly, repeat Steps 1 through 3.

4. Type: **You can watch word wrap in action**

   The text you typed replaces the highlighted text. Notice that you did not need to delete the highlighted text before you typed the replacement text.

Inserting a Character

Windows 95 programs usually operate in **insert mode**—when you type a new character, all characters to the right of the cursor are pushed over to make room.

Suppose you want to insert the word "sentence" before the word "typed."

To insert characters:

> **1.** Position the I-beam pointer just before the word "typed," then click.
>
> **2.** Type: **sentence**.
>
> **3.** Press the **spacebar**.

3.1 NOTE

When you save a file with a long filename, Windows 95 also creates an eight-character filename that can be used by Windows 3.1 applications. The eight-character filename is created by using the first six non-space characters from the long filename, then adding a tilde (~) and a number. For example, the filename Car Sales for 1997 would be converted to Carsal~1.

Notice how the letters in the first line are pushed to the right to make room for the new characters. When a word gets pushed past the right margin, the word-wrap feature pushes it down to the beginning of the next line.

Saving a File

As you type text, it is held temporarily in the computer's memory. For permanent storage, you need to save your work on a disk. In the computer lab, you will probably save your work on a floppy disk in drive A.

When you save a file, you must give it a name. Windows 95 allows you to use filenames containing up to 255 characters, and you may use spaces and punctuation symbols. You cannot use the symbols \ ? : * " < > | in a filename, but other symbols such as &, -, and $ are allowed.

Most filenames have an extension. An **extension** is a suffix of up to three characters that is separated from the filename by a period, as shown in Figure 2-8.

Figure 2-8 ◀
Filename and
extension

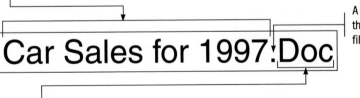

The filename can contain up to 255 characters. You may use letters, numbers, spaces, and certain punctuation marks.

A period separates the filename from the filename extension.

A filename extension can contain up to three characters. The filename extension helps to categorize the file by type or by the software with which it was created. You can customize Windows 95 to show the filename extension or to hide it.

The file extension indicates which application you used to create the file. For example, files created with Microsoft Word software have a .Doc extension. In general, you will not add an extension to your filenames, because the application software automatically does this for you.

Windows 95 keeps track of file extensions, but does not always display them. The steps in these tutorials refer to files using the filename, but not its extension. So if you see the filename Sample Text in the steps, but "Sample Text.Doc" on your screen, don't worry—these are the same files.

Now you can save the document you typed.

To save a document:

1. Click the **Save** button  on the toolbar. Figure 2-9 shows the location of this button and the Save As dialog box that appears after you click it.

Figure 2-9 ◄
The Save button

Save button ——

Save As
dialog box
appears after
you click the
Save button

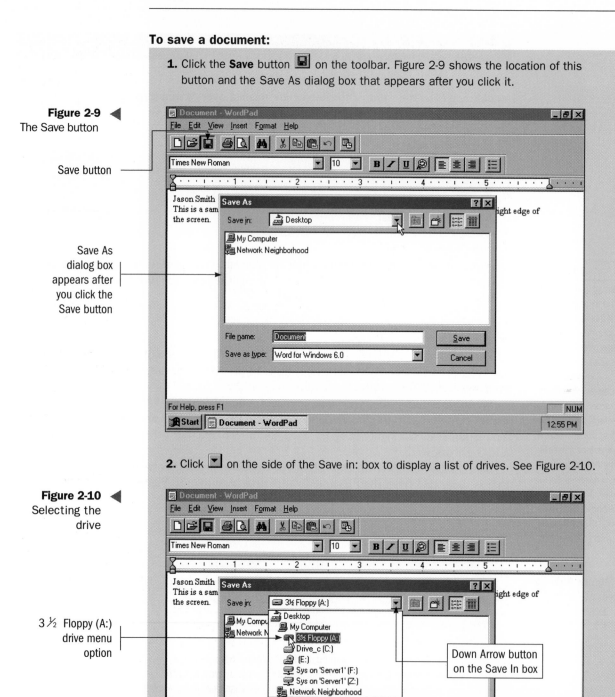

2. Click ▼ on the side of the Save in: box to display a list of drives. See Figure 2-10.

Figure 2-10 ◄
Selecting the
drive

3 ½ Floppy (A:)
drive menu
option

Down Arrow button
on the Save In box

3. Click **3½ Floppy (A:)**.

4. Select the text in the File Name box.

   TROUBLE? To select the text, position the I-beam pointer at the beginning of the word "Document." While you hold down the mouse button, drag the I-beam pointer to the end of the word.

5. Type **Sample Text** in the File Name box.

6. Click the **Save** button. Your file is saved on your Student Disk and the document title, "Sample Text," appears on the WordPad title bar.

What if you tried to close WordPad *before* you saved your file? Windows 95 would display a message—"Save changes to Document?" If you answer "Yes," Windows displays the Save As dialog box so you can give the document a name. If you answer "No," Windows 95 closes WordPad without saving the document.

After you save a file, you can work on another document or close WordPad. Since you have already saved your Sample Text document, you should continue this tutorial by closing WordPad.

To close WordPad:

1. Click the **Close** button ☒ to close the WordPad window.

Opening a File

Suppose you save and close the Sample Text file, then later you want to revise it. To revise a file you must first open it. When you **open** a file, its contents are copied into the computer's memory. If you revise the file, you need to save the changes before you close the application or work on a different file. If you close a revised file without saving your changes, you will lose the revisions.

Typically, you would use one of two methods to open a file. You could select the file from the Documents list or the My Computer window, or you could start an application program and then use the Open button to open the file. Each method has advantages and disadvantages. You will have an opportunity to try both methods.

The first method for opening the Sample Text file simply requires you to select the file from the Documents list or the My Computer window. With this method the document, not the application program, is central to the task; hence this method is sometimes referred to as *document-centric*. You only need to remember the name of your document or file—you do not need to remember which application you used to create the document.

The Documents list contains the names of the last 15 documents used. You access this list from the Start menu. When you have your own computer, the Documents list is very handy. In a computer lab, however, the files other students use quickly replace yours on the list.

If your file is not in the Documents list, you can open the file by selecting it from the My Computer window. Windows 95 starts an application program that you can use to revise the file, then automatically opens the file. The advantage of this method is its simplicity. The disadvantage is that Windows 95 might not start the application you expect. For example, when you select Sample Text, you might expect Windows 95 to start WordPad because you used WordPad to type the text of the document. Depending on the software installed on your computer system, however, Windows 95 might start the Microsoft Word application instead. Usually this is not a problem. Although the application might not be the one you expect, you can still use it to revise your file.

3.1 NOTE

Document-centric features are advertised as an advantage of Windows 95. But you can still successfully use the application-centric approach you used with Windows 3.1 by opening your application, then opening your document.

To open the Sample Text file by selecting it from My Computer:

1. Click the **My Computer** icon. Press the **Enter** key. The My Computer window opens.

2. Click the **3½ Floppy (A:)** icon, then press the **Enter** key. The 3½ Floppy (A:) window opens.

TROUBLE? If the My Computer window disappears when you open the 3½ floppy (A:) window, click View, click Options, then click the Folder tab, if necessary. Click the radio button labelled "Browse Folders using a separate window for each folder." Then click the OK button.

3. Click the **Sample Text** file icon, then press the **Enter** key. Windows 95 starts an application program, then automatically opens the Sample Text file.

TROUBLE? If Windows 95 starts Microsoft Word instead of WordPad, don't worry. You can use Microsoft Word to revise the Sample Text document.

Now that Windows 95 has started an application and opened the Sample Text file, you could make revisions to the document. Instead, you should close all the windows on your desktop so you can try the other method for opening files.

To close all the windows on the desktop:

1. Click ☒ on each of the windows.

   TROUBLE? If you see a message, "Save changes to Document?" click the No button.

The second method for opening the Sample Text file requires you to open WordPad, then use the Open button to select the Sample Text file. The advantage of this method is that you can specify the application program you want to use—WordPad in this case. This method, however, involves more steps than the method you tried previously.

To start WordPad and open the Sample Text file using the Open button:

1. Start WordPad.

2. Click the **Open** button 🗁 on the toolbar. Figure 2-11 shows the location of this button and the dialog box that appears after you click it.

Figure 2-11 ◀
The Open button
and dialog box

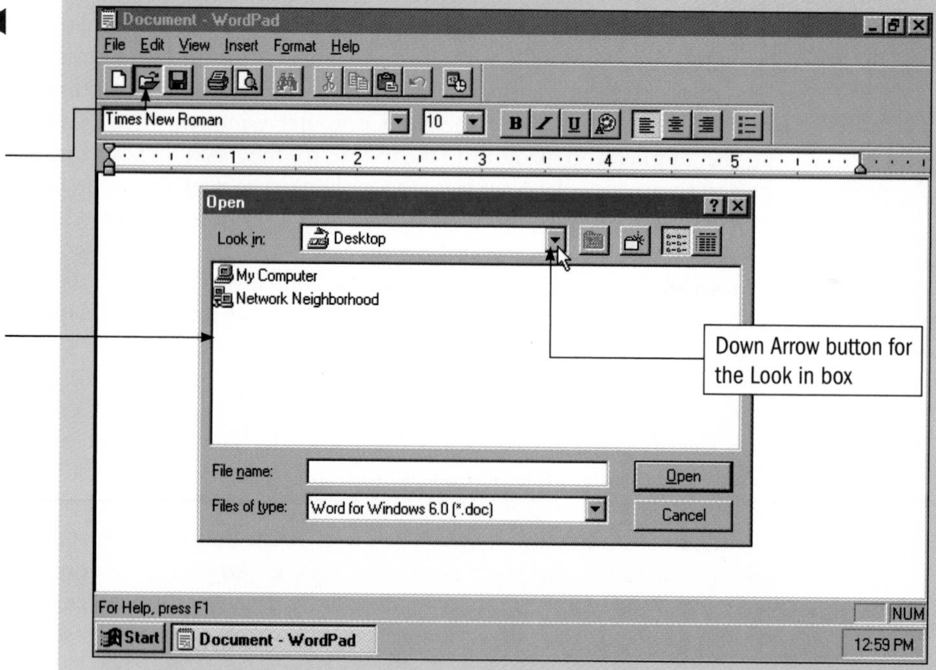

Open button

Open dialog box

3. Click ▼ on the side of the Look in: box to display a list of drives. See Figure 2-11.

4. Click **3½ Floppy (A:)** from the list. See Figure 2-12.

5. Click **Sample Text** to make sure it is highlighted. See Figure 2-12.

Figure 2-12 ◀
Opening the
Sample Text file

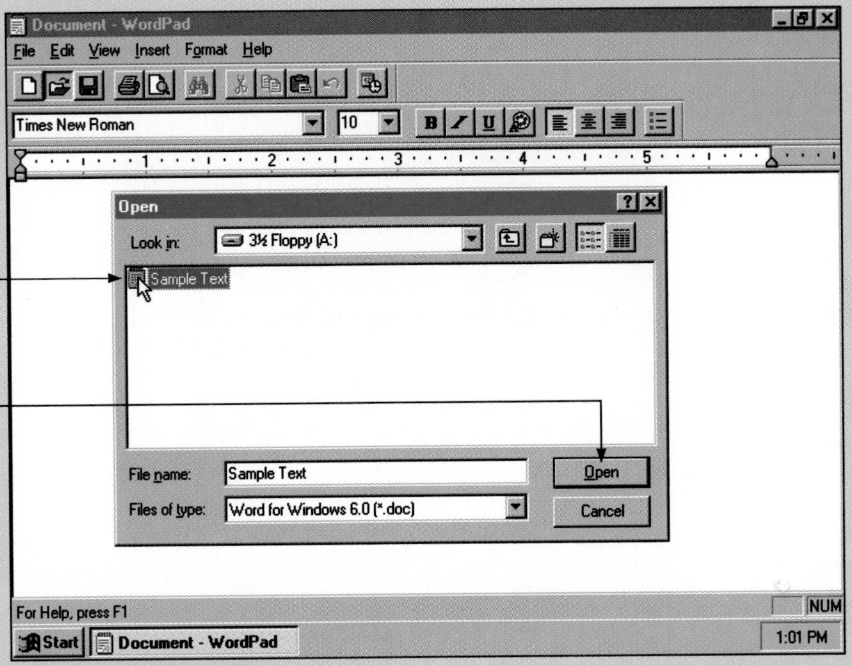

Sample Text
icon

Open button

6. Click [Open] in the lower right corner of the dialog box. Your document should appear in the WordPad work area.

Printing a File

Now that the Sample Text file is open, you can print it. It is a good idea to use Print Preview before you send your document to the printer. **Print Preview** shows on screen exactly how your document will appear on paper. You can check your page layout so you don't waste paper printing a document that is not quite the way you want it. Your instructor or technical support person might supply you with additional instructions for printing in your school's computer lab.

To preview, then print the Sample Text file:

1. Click the **Print Preview** button 🔍 on the toolbar.

2. Look at your print preview. Before you print the document and use paper, you should make sure that the font, margins, and other document features look the way you want them to.

TROUBLE? If you can't read the document text on screen, click the Zoom In button.

3. Click the **Print** button. A Print dialog box appears.

4. Study Figure 2-13 to familiarize yourself with the controls in the Print dialog box.

This is the name of the printer that Windows 95 will use for this printout. If you are using a network, you might have a choice of printers. If you need to select a different printer, ask your instructor or your technical support person for help.

The Properties button lets you modify the way your printer is set up. Do not change any of the settings on your school printer without the consent of your instructor or technical support person.

When you click this check box, your printout will go on your disk instead of to the printer.

You can specify how many copies you want by typing the number in this box. Alternatively, you can use the arrow buttons to increase or decrease the number in the box.

Figure 2-13 ◀
The Print
dialog box

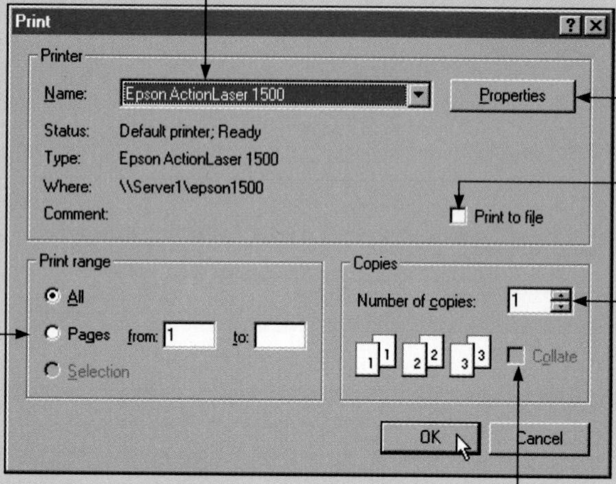

In the Print range box, you specify how much of the document you want to print. If you want to print only part of a document, click the Pages radio button and then enter the starting and ending pages for the printout.

If you print more than one copy of a multi-page document, you can specify that you want the printout collated, so you don't have to collate the pages manually.

5. Make sure your screen shows the Print range set to "All" and the number of copies set to "1."

6. Click the **OK** button to print your document. If a message appears telling you printing is complete, click the **OK** button.

TROUBLE? If your document does not print, make sure the printer has paper and the printer on-line light is on. If your document still doesn't print, ask your instructor or technical support person for help.

7. Close WordPad.

TROUBLE? If you see the message "Save changes to Document?" click the "No" button.

Quick Check

1 A(n) _____ is a collection of data that has a name and is stored on a disk or other storage medium.

2 _____ erases all the data on a disk and arranges the magnetic particles on the disk surface so the disk can store data.

3 When you are working in a text box, the pointer shape changes to a(n) _____.

4 The _____ shows you where each character you type will appear.

5 _____ automatically moves text down to the beginning of the next line when you reach the right margin.

6 Explain how you select a block of text: _____.

7 Which of these characters are not allowed in Windows 95 file names: \ ? : * " < > | ! @ # $ % ^ & ; + - ( ) /

8 In the filename New Equipment.Doc, .Doc is a(n) _____.

9 Suppose you created a graph using the Harvard Graphics software and then you stored the graph on your floppy disk under the name Projected 1997 Sales - Graph. The next day, you use Harvard Graphics to open the file and change the graph. If you want the new version of the file on your disk, you need to _____.

10 You can save _____ by using the Print Preview feature.

SESSION 2.2

In this session, you will learn how to manage the files on your disk—a skill that can prevent you from losing important documents. You will learn how to list information about the files on your disk; organize the files into folders; and move, delete, copy, and rename files.

Creating Your Student Disk

For this session of the tutorial, you must create a Student Disk that contains some sample files. *You can use the disk you formatted in the previous session.*

If you are using your own computer, the CTI Windows 95 Applications menu selection will not be available. Before you proceed, you must go to your school's computer lab and find a computer that has the CTI Windows 95 Applications installed. Once you have made your own Student Disk, you can use it to complete this tutorial on any computer you choose.

To add the sample files to your Student Disk:

1. Write "Windows 95 Student Disk" on the label of your formatted disk.

2. Place the disk in Drive A.

> **TROUBLE?** If your 3½-inch disk drive is B, place your formatted disk in that drive instead, and for the rest of this session substitute Drive B where ever you see Drive A.

3. Click the **Start** button [Start]. See Figure 2-14.

Figure 2-14 ◀
Making your
Student Disk

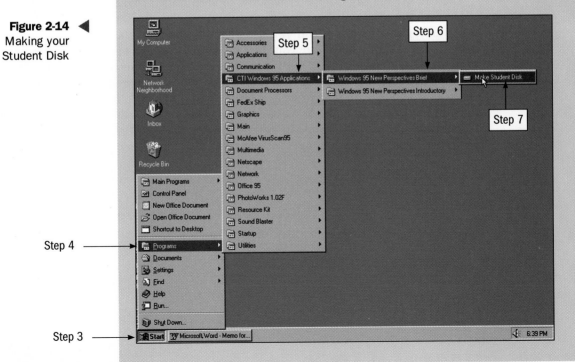

4. Point to **Programs**.

5. Point to **CTI Windows 95 Applications**.

TROUBLE? If CTI Windows 95 Applications is not listed, contact your instructor or technical support person.

6. Point to **Windows 95 New Perspectives Brief**.

7. Select **Make Student Disk**.

A dialog box opens, asking you to indicate the drive that contains your formatted disk.

8. If it is not already selected, click the Drive radio button that corresponds to the drive containing your student disk.

9. Click the **OK** button.

The sample files are copied to your formatted disk. A message tells you when all the files have been copied.

10. Click **OK.**

11. If necessary, close all the open windows on your screen.

Your Student Disk now contains sample files that you will use throughout the rest of this tutorial.

My Computer

The **My Computer** icon represents your computer, its storage devices, and its printers. The My Computer icon opens into the My Computer window, which contains an icon for each of the storage devices on your computer. On most computer systems the My Computer window also contains Control Panel and Printers folders, which help you add printers, control peripheral devices, and customize your Windows 95 work environment. Figure 2-15 on the following page explains more about the My Computer window.

You can use the My Computer window to keep track of where your files are stored and to organize your files. In this section of the tutorial you will move and delete files on your Student Disk in drive A. If you use your own computer at home or computer at work, you would probably store your files on drive C, instead of drive A. However, in a school lab environment you usually don't know which computer you will use, so you need to carry your files with you on a floppy disk that you use in drive A. In this session, therefore, you will learn how to work with the files on drive A. Most of what you learn will also work on your home or work computer when you use drive C.

In this session you will work with several icons, including My Computer. As a general procedure, when you want to open an icon, you click it and then press the Enter key.

Figure 2-15 ◀
Information
about My
Computer

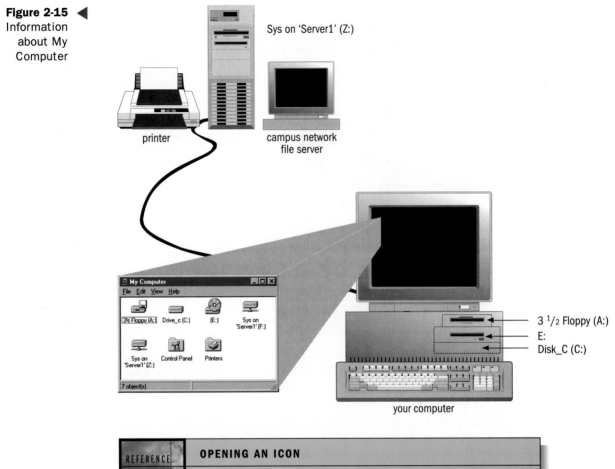

REFERENCE
window

OPENING AN ICON

■ Click the icon you want to open.
■ Press the Enter key.

Now you should open the My Computer icon.

To open the My Computer icon:

1. Click the **My Computer** icon to select it.

2. Press the **Enter** key. The My Computer window opens.

Now that you have opened the My Computer window, you can find out what is on
your Student Disk in drive A.

To find out what is on your Student Disk:

1. Open the **3½ Floppy (A:)** icon by clicking it, then pressing the **Enter** key. A window appears showing the contents of drive A:. See Figure 2-16.

Figure 2-16 ◀
Contents of
Student Disk

Icons show contents
of drive A

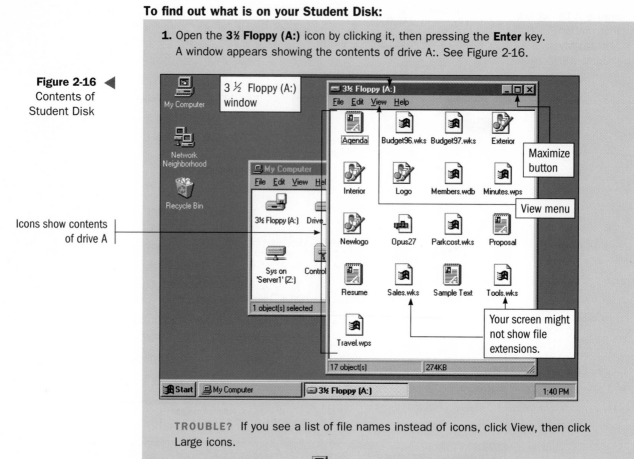

TROUBLE? If you see a list of file names instead of icons, click View, then click Large icons.

2. Click the **Maximize** button ▢ if the window is not maximized.

Windows 95 provides four ways to view the contents of a disk—large icons, small icons, list, or details. The standard view, shown on your screen, displays a large icon and title for each file. The icon provides a visual cue to the type and contents of the file, as Figure 2-17 illustrates.

Figure 2-17 ◀
Program and
file icons

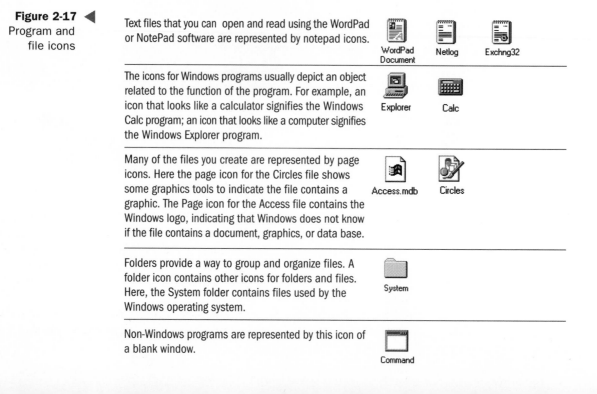

Text files that you can open and read using the WordPad or NotePad software are represented by notepad icons.

The icons for Windows programs usually depict an object related to the function of the program. For example, an icon that looks like a calculator signifies the Windows Calc program; an icon that looks like a computer signifies the Windows Explorer program.

Many of the files you create are represented by page icons. Here the page icon for the Circles file shows some graphics tools to indicate the file contains a graphic. The Page icon for the Access file contains the Windows logo, indicating that Windows does not know if the file contains a document, graphics, or data base.

Folders provide a way to group and organize files. A folder icon contains other icons for folders and files. Here, the System folder contains files used by the Windows operating system.

Non-Windows programs are represented by this icon of a blank window.

The **Details** view shows more information than the large icon, small icon, and list views. Details view shows the file icon, the filename, the file size, the application you used to create the file, and the date/time the file was created or last modified.

To view a detailed list of files:

1. Click **View** then click **Details** to display details for the files on your disk as shown in Figure 2-18.

Figure 2-18 ◄
Detailed file list

File icon

Filename

Your screen might not
show file extensions

Total number of
files and folders
in the window

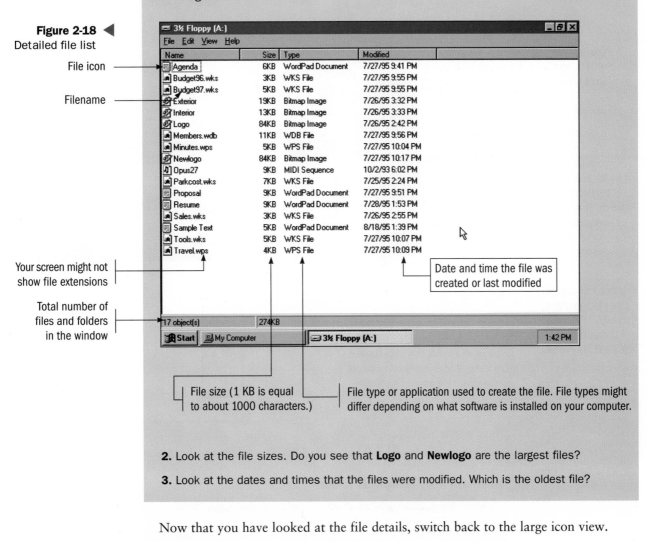

File size (1 KB is equal
to about 1000 characters.)

File type or application used to create the file. File types might
differ depending on what software is installed on your computer.

Date and time the file was
created or last modified

2. Look at the file sizes. Do you see that **Logo** and **Newlogo** are the largest files?

3. Look at the dates and times that the files were modified. Which is the oldest file?

Now that you have looked at the file details, switch back to the large icon view.

To switch to the large icon view:

1. Click **View** then click **Large Icons** to return to the large icon display.

Folders and Directories

A list of files is referred to as a **directory**. The main directory of a disk is sometimes called the **root directory**. The root directory is created when you format a disk and is shown in parentheses at the top of the window. For example, at the top of your screen you should see "3 ½ Floppy (A:)." The root directory is A:. In some situations, the root directory is indicated by a backslash after the drive letter and colon, such as A:\. All of the files on your Student Disk are currently in the root directory.

If too many files are stored in a directory, the directory list becomes very long and difficult to manage. A directory can be divided into **folders** (also called **subdirectories**), into which you group similar files. The directory of files for each folder then becomes much shorter and easier to manage. For example, you might create a folder for all the papers you write for an English 111 class as shown in Figure 2-19.

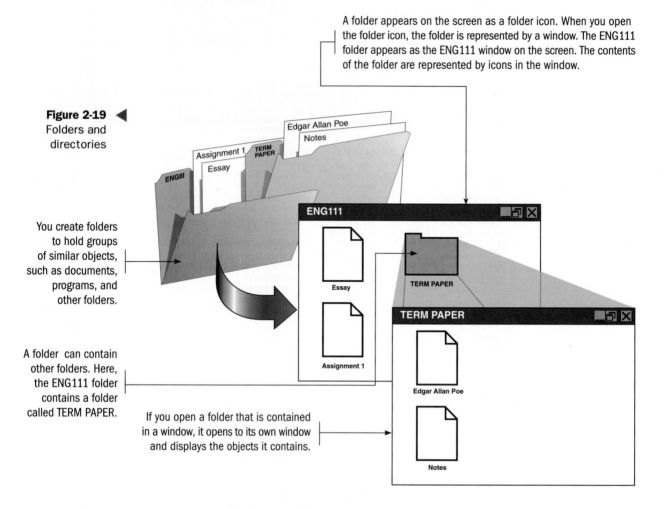

A folder appears on the screen as a folder icon. When you open the folder icon, the folder is represented by a window. The ENG111 folder appears as the ENG111 window on the screen. The contents of the folder are represented by icons in the window.

Figure 2-19 ◀
Folders and
directories

You create folders to hold groups of similar objects, such as documents, programs, and other folders.

A folder can contain other folders. Here, the ENG111 folder contains a folder called TERM PAPER.

If you open a folder that is contained in a window, it opens to its own window and displays the objects it contains.

Now, you'll create a folder called My Documents to hold your document files.

To create a My Documents folder:

1. Click **File** then point to **New** to display the submenu.

2. Click **Folder**. A folder icon with the label "New Folder" appears.

3. Type **My Documents** as the name of the folder.

4. Press the **Enter** key.

When you first create a folder, it doesn't contain any files. In the next set of steps you will move a file from the root directory to the My Documents folder.

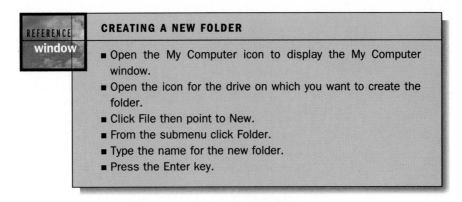

REFERENCE window

CREATING A NEW FOLDER

- Open the My Computer icon to display the My Computer window.
- Open the icon for the drive on which you want to create the folder.
- Click File then point to New.
- From the submenu click Folder.
- Type the name for the new folder.
- Press the Enter key.

Moving and Copying a File

You can move a file from one directory to another or from one disk to another. When you move a file it is copied to the new location you specify, then the version in the old location is erased. The move feature is handy for organizing or reorganizing the files on your disk by moving them into appropriate folders. The easiest way to move a file is to hold down the *right* mouse button and drag the file from the old location to the new location. A menu appears and you select Move Here.

You can also copy a file from one directory to another, or from one disk to another. When you copy a file, you create an exact duplicate of an existing file in whatever disk or folder you specify. To copy a file from one folder to another on your floppy disk, you use the same procedure as for moving a file, except that you select Copy Here from the menu.

Suppose you want to move the Minutes file from the root directory to the My Documents folder. Depending on the software applications installed on your computer, this file is either called Minutes or Minutes.wps. In the steps it is referred to simply as Minutes.

To move the Minutes file to the My Documents folder:

1. Click the **Minutes** icon to select it.

2. Press and hold the right mouse button while you drag the **Minutes** icon to the My Documents folder. See Figure 2-20.

Figure 2-20 ◀
Moving a file

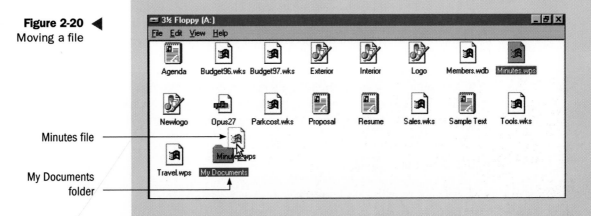

Minutes file ——

My Documents folder ——

3. Release the right mouse button. A menu appears.

4. Click **Move Here**. A short animation shows the Minutes file being moved to My Documents. The Minutes icon disappears from the window showing the files in the root directory.

> **REFERENCE window**
>
> **MOVING A FILE**
>
> - Open the My Computer icon to display the My Computer window.
> - If the document you want to move is in a folder, open the folder.
> - Hold down the *right* mouse button while you drag the file icon to its new folder or disk location.
> - Click Move Here.
> - If you want to move more than one file at a time, hold down the Ctrl key while you click the icons for all the files you want to move.

3.1 NOTE

Windows 3.1 users be careful! When you delete or move an icon in the Windows 95 My Computer window you are actually deleting or moving the file. This is quite different from the way the Windows 3.1 Program Manager worked.

Anything you do to an icon in the My Computer window is actually done to the file represented by that icon. If you move an icon, the file is moved; if you delete an icon, the file is deleted.

After you move a file, it is a good idea to make sure it was moved to the correct location. You can easily verify that a file is in its new folder by displaying the folder contents.

To verify that the Minutes file was moved to My Documents:

1. Click the **My Documents** folder, then press **Enter**. The My Documents window appears and it contains one file—Minutes.

2. Click the My Documents window **Close** button ☒.

   TROUBLE? If the My Computer window is no longer visible, click the My Computer icon, then press Enter. You might also need to open the 3 ½ Floppy (A:) icon.

Deleting a File

You delete a file or folder by deleting its icon. However, be careful when you delete a *folder*, because you also delete all the files it contains! When you delete a file from the hard drive, the filename is deleted from the directory but the file contents are held in the Recycle Bin. If you change your mind and want to retrieve the deleted file, you can recover it by clicking the Recycle Bin.

When you delete a file from a floppy disk, it does not go into the Recycle Bin. Instead it is deleted as soon as its icon disappears. Try deleting the file named Agenda from your Student Disk. Because this file is on the floppy disk and not on the hard disk, it will not go into the Recycle Bin.

To delete the file Agenda:

1. Click the icon for the file **Agenda**.

2. Press the **Delete** key.

3. If a message appears asking, "Are sure you want to delete Agenda?", click **Yes**. An animation, which might play too quickly to be seen, shows the file being deleted.

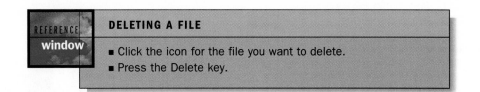

Renaming a File

You can easily change the name of a file using the Rename option on the File menu or by using the file's label. Remember that when you choose a filename it can contain up to 255 characters, including spaces, but it cannot contain \ ? : " < > | characters.

Practice using this feature by renaming the Sales file to give it a more descriptive filename.

To rename Sales:

1. Click the **Sales** file to select it.

2. Click the label "Sales". After a short pause a solid box outlines the label and an insertion point appears.

3. Type **Preliminary Sales Summary** as the new filename.

4. Press the **Enter key**.

5. Click the **Close** button ☒ to close the 3 ½-inch Floppy (A:) window.

REFERENCE window

RENAMING A FILE

- Click the icon for the file you want to rename.
- Click the label of the icon.
- Type the new name for the file.
- Press the Enter key.

Copying an Entire Floppy Disk

You can have trouble accessing the data on your floppy disk if the disk gets damaged, exposed to magnetic fields, or picks up a computer virus. If the damaged disk contains important files, you will have to spend many hours to try to reconstruct those files. To avoid losing all your data, it is a good idea to make a copy of your floppy disk. This copy is called a **backup** copy.

If you wanted to make a copy of an audio cassette, your cassette player would need two cassette drives. You might wonder, therefore, how your computer can make a copy of your disk if you have only one disk drive. Figure 2-21 illustrates how the computer uses only one disk drive to make a copy of a disk.

Figure 2-21 ◀
Using one disk
drive to make a
copy of a disk

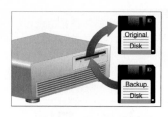

1. First, the computer
copies the data from your
original disk into memory.

2. Once the data is in
memory, you remove your
original disk from the drive
and replace it with your
backup disk.

3. The computer moves the
data from memory onto
your backup disk.

REFERENCE
window

MAKING A BACKUP OF YOUR FLOPPY DISK

- Click My Computer then press the Enter key.
- Insert the disk you want to copy in drive A.
- Click the 3 ½ Floppy (A:) icon   3½ Floppy (A:)   to select it.
- Click File then click Copy Disk to display the Copy Disk dialog box.
- Click Start to begin the copy process.
- When prompted, remove the disk you want to copy. Place your backup disk in drive A.
- Click OK.
- When the copy is complete, close the Copy Disk dialog box.
- Close the My Computer dialog box.

If you have two floppy disks, you can make a backup of your Student Disk now. Make sure you periodically follow the backup procedure, so your backup is up-to-date.

To back up your Student Disk:

1. Write your name and "Backup" on the label of your second disk. This will be your backup disk.

2. Make sure your Student Disk is in drive A.

3. Make sure the My Computer window is open. See Figure 2-22.

Figure 2-22 ◀
The My
Computer
window

4. Click the **3 ½ Floppy (A:)** icon to select it.

> **TROUBLE?** If you mistakenly open the 3½ Floppy (A:) *window*, click ☒.

5. Click **File**.

6. Click **Copy Disk** to display the Copy Disk dialog box as shown in Figure 2-23.

Figure 2-23 ◀
The Copy Disk
dialog box

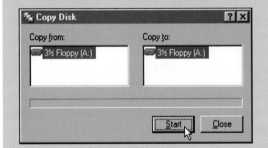

7. On the lower right side of the dialog box, you'll see a Start button. Click this **Start** button to begin the copy process.

8. When the message, "Insert the disk you want to copy from (source disk)..." appears, click the **OK** button.

9. When the message, "Insert the disk you want to copy to (destination disk)..." appears, insert your backup disk in drive A.

10. Click the **OK** button. When the copy is complete, you will see the message "Copy completed successfully."

11. After the data is copied to your backup disk, click ☒ on the blue title bar of the Copy Disk dialog box.

12. Click ☒ on the My Computer window to close the My Computer window.

13. Remove your disk from the drive.

Each time you make a backup, the data on your backup disk is erased, and replaced with the data from your updated Student Disk. Now that you know how to copy an entire disk, make a backup whenever you have completed a tutorial or you have spent a long time working on a file.

Quick Check

1. If you want to find out about the storage devices and printers connected to your computer, click the _____ icon.

2. If you have only one floppy disk drive on your computer, it is identified by the letter _____.

3. The letter C: is typically used for the _____ drive of a computer.

4. What are the five pieces of information that the Details view supplies about each of your files?

5. The main directory of a disk is referred to as the _____ directory.

6. You can divide a directory into _____.

7. If you delete the icon for a file, what happens to the file?

8. If you have one floppy disk drive, but you have two disks, can you copy a file from one floppy disk to another?

End Note

Just as you complete the Quick Check for Session 2.2, Steve appears. He asks how you are doing. You summarize what you remember from the tutorial, telling him that you learned how to insert, delete, and select text. You also learned how to work with files using Windows 95 software—you now know how to save, open, revise, and print a document. You tell him that you like the idea that these file operations are the same for almost all Windows 95 software. Steve agrees that this makes work a lot easier.

When Steve asks you if you have a supply of disks, you tell him you do, and that you just learned how to format a disk and view a list of files on your disk. Steve wants you to remember that you can use the Details view to see the filename, size, date, and time. You assure him that you remember that feature—and also how to move, delete, and rename a file.

Steve seems pleased with your progress and agrees that you're now ready to use software applications. But he can't resist giving you one last warning—don't forget to back up your files frequently!

Tutorial Assignments

1. Opening, Editing, and Printing a Document In this tutorial you learned how to create a document using WordPad. You also learned how to save, open, and print a document. Practice these skills by opening the document on your Student Disk called Resume, which is a résumé for Jamie Woods. Make the changes shown in Figure 2-24, and then print the document. After you print, save your revisions.

Figure 2-24 ◀

Change this to your name, address, and phone number. If you don't have an office number delete this.

Change this to the name of your university or college.

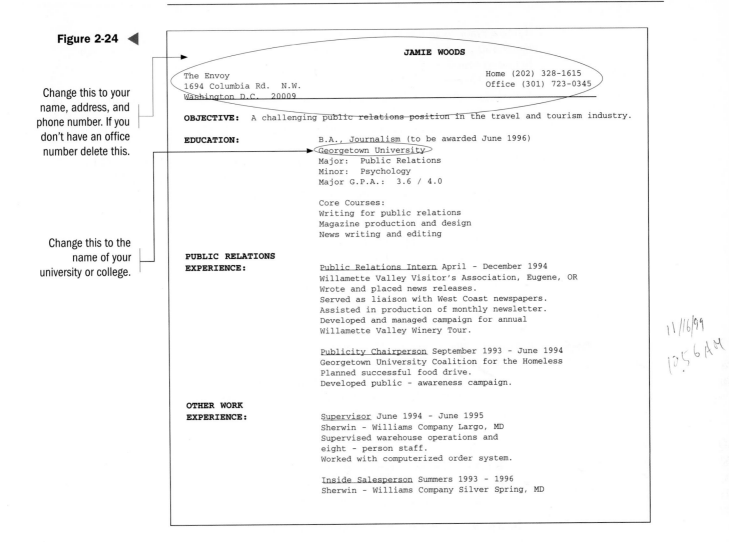

JAMIE WOODS

The Envoy   Home (202) 328-1615
1694 Columbia Rd. N.W.   Office (301) 723-0345
Washington D.C. 20009

OBJECTIVE: A challenging public relations position in the travel and tourism industry.

EDUCATION: B.A., Journalism (to be awarded June 1996)
                                        Georgetown University
                                        Major: Public Relations
                                        Minor: Psychology
                                        Major G.P.A.: 3.6 / 4.0

                                        Core Courses:
                                        Writing for public relations
                                        Magazine production and design
                                        News writing and editing

PUBLIC RELATIONS
EXPERIENCE: Public Relations Intern April - December 1994
                                        Willamette Valley Visitor's Association, Eugene, OR
                                        Wrote and placed news releases.
                                        Served as liaison with West Coast newspapers.
                                        Assisted in production of monthly newsletter.
                                        Developed and managed campaign for annual
                                        Willamette Valley Winery Tour.

                                        Publicity Chairperson September 1993 - June 1994
                                        Georgetown University Coalition for the Homeless
                                        Planned successful food drive.
                                        Developed public - awareness campaign.

OTHER WORK
EXPERIENCE: Supervisor June 1994 - June 1995
                                        Sherwin - Williams Company Largo, MD
                                        Supervised warehouse operations and
                                        eight - person staff.
                                        Worked with computerized order system.

                                        Inside Salesperson Summers 1993 - 1996
                                        Sherwin - Williams Company Silver Spring, MD

2. Creating, Saving, and Printing a Letter Use WordPad to write a one-page letter to a relative or a friend. Save the document in the My Documents folder with the name "Letter." Use the Print Preview feature to look at the format of your finished letter, then print it, and be sure you sign it.

3. Managing Files and Folders Earlier in this tutorial you created a folder and moved the file called Minutes into it. Now complete a through g below to practice your file management skills.

   a. Create a folder called Spreadsheets on your Student Disk.
   b. Move the files ParkCost, Budget96, Budget97, and Sales into the Spreadsheets folder.
   c. Create a folder called Park Project.
   d. Move the files Proposal, Members, Tools, Logo, and Newlogo into the Park Project folder.
   e. Move the ParkCost file from the Spreadsheets folder to the Park Project folder.
   f. Delete the file called Travel.
   g. Switch to the Details view and answer the following questions:
Write out your answers to questions a through e.
   a. What is the largest file in the Park Project folder?
   b. What is the newest file in the Spreadsheets folder?
   c. How many files are in the root directory?
   d. How are the Members and Resume icons different?
   e. What is the file with the most recent date on the entire disk?

4. More Practice with Files and Folders For this assignment, you will format your disk again and put a fresh version of the Student Disk files on it. Complete a through h below to practice your file management skills.

    a. Format a disk.

    b. Create a Student Disk. Refer to the section "Creating Your Student Disk" in Session 2.2.

    c. Create three folders on your new Student Disk: Documents, Budgets, and Graphics.

    d. Move the files Interior, Exterior, Logo, and Newlogo to the Graphics folder.

    e. Move the files Travel, Members and Minutes to the Documents folder.

    f. Move Budget96 and Budget97 to the Budgets folder.

    g. Switch to the Details view.

Answer questions a through f.

    a. What is the largest file in the Graphics folder?

    b. How many WordPad documents are in the root directory?

    c. What is the newest file in the root directory?

    d. How many files in all folders are 5KB in size?

    e. How many files in the Documents folder are WKS files?

    f. Do all the files in the Graphics folder have the same icon?

5. Finding a File Microsoft Windows 95 contains an on-line Tour that explains how to find files on a disk without looking through all the folders. Start the Windows 95 Tour (if you don't remember how, look at the instructions for Tutorial Assignment 1 in Tutorial 1), then click Finding a File, and answer the following questions:

    a. To display the Find dialog box, you must click the _____ button, then select _____ from the menu, and finally click _____ from the submenu.

    b. Do you need to type in the entire filename to find the file?

    c. When the computer has found your file, what are the steps you have to follow if you want to display the contents of the file?

6. Help with Files and Folders In Tutorial 2 you learned how to work with Windows 95 files and folders. What additional information on this topic does Windows 95 Help provide? Use the Start button to access Help. Use the Index tab to locate topics related to files and folders. Find at least two tips or procedures for working with files and folders that were not covered in the tutorial. Write out the tip in your own words and indicate the title of the Help screen that contains the information.

Lab Assignments

1. Using Files Lab In Tutorial 2 you learned how to create, save, open, and print files. The Using Files Lab will help you review what happens in the computer when you perform these file tasks. To start the Lab, follow these steps:

    a. Click the Start button.

    b. Point to Programs, then point to CTI Windows 95 Applications.

    c. Point to Windows 95 New Perspectives Brief.

    d. Click Using Files. If you can't find Windows 95 New Perspectives Brief or Using Files, ask for help from your instructor or technical support person.

Answer the Quick Check questions that appear as you work through the Lab. You can print your answers at the end of the Lab.

Answers to Quick Check Questions

SESSION 1.1

1. a. icon b. Start button c. taskbar d. Date/Time control e. desktop f. pointer

2. Multitasking

3. Start menu

4. Lift up the mouse, move it to the right, then put it down, and slide it left until the pointer reaches the left edge of the screen.

5. Highlighting

6. If a program is running, its button is displayed on the taskbar.

7. Each program that is running uses system resources, so Windows 95 runs more efficiently when only the programs you are using are open.

8. Answer: If you do not perform the shut down procedure, you might lose data.

SESSION 1.2

1. a. title bar b. program title c. Minimize button d. Restore button e. Close button f. menu bar g. toolbar h. formatting bar i. taskbar j. status bar k. workspace l. pointer

2. a. Minimize button—hides the program so only its button is showing on the taskbar.
   b. Maximize button—enlarges the program to fill the entire screen.
   c. Restore button—sets the program to a pre-defined size.
   d. Close button—stops the program and removes its button from the taskbar.

3. a. Ellipses—indicate a dialog box will appear.
   b. Grayed out—the menu option is not currently available.
   c. Submenu—indicates a submenu will appear.
   d. Check mark—indicates a menu option is currently in effect.

4. Toolbar

5. a. scroll bar b. scroll box c. Cancel button d. down arrow button e. list box f. radio button g. check box

6. one, check boxes

7. On-line Help

SESSION 2.1

1. file

2. formatting

3. I-beam

4. insertion point

5. word wrap

6 You drag the I-beam pointer over
the text to highlight it.

7 \ ? : * < > | "

8 extension

9 save the file again

10 paper

SESSION 2.2

1 My Computer

2 A (or A:)

3 Hard (or hard disk)

4 Filename, file type, file size, date, time

5 Root

6 Folders (or subdirectories)

7 It is deleted from the disk.

8 Yes

Organizing Files with Windows Explorer

OBJECTIVES

In this tutorial you will:

- "Quick" format a floppy disk

- View the structure of folders and files in Windows Explorer

- Select, create, and rename folders in Windows Explorer

- Change the view

- Arrange files by name, date modified, size, and type, using both ascending and descending order

- Select a single file, group of files, or all files

- Create a printout showing the structure of folders and files

- Move and copy one or more files from one folder to another

- Move and copy one or more files from one disk to another

- Delete files and folders

LABS

Windows Directories, Folders and Files

CASE

Kolbe Climbing School

Bernard Kolbe knew how to climb before he could ride a bike. In college he started what is now one of the most popular guide services in the Front Range, the Kolbe Climbing School, known to locals as "KCS." KCS offers guided climbs in the Front Range area, especially in Rocky Mountain National Park and nearby climbing areas such as Lumpy Ridge. While most clients simply want to learn rock and sport climbing, there are a few who want guides for longer alpine climbs and ice climbing.

Since he started his business, Bernard has handled the paperwork using yellow pads, clipboards, and manila folders. Recent conversations with his insurance agent and accountant, though, convinced him that he needs to keep better records on his employees, clients, and the use and condition of his equipment. The KCS offices adjoin a business services office, so Bernard for the first time rented some computer time and began creating the files he needs, storing them on a floppy disk.

Not too long ago, Bernard asked if you could help him out with KCS record-keeping. You agreed (in exchange for some free climbing lessons) and got to work by updating the client files on his floppy disk. When Bernard first gave you the disk he warned you that it could use a little organization, so you began by creating a folder structure on the disk.

This morning, though, you walked into the office to find that Bernard had spent yesterday evening at the rented computer adding new files to his disk. When you discover that he didn't bother to organize his work, you point out that an important part of computerized record-keeping is creating and using a system that makes it easy to find important information. Bernard is willing to learn more (it's too cold to climb anyway), so the two of you head over to the business services office to spend some time looking over Bernard's files.

In this session, you will learn how Windows Explorer displays the devices and folders that your computer can access. Understanding how to manipulate this display of devices and folders is the first Step toward using Windows Explorer to organize the files on your disks. In this tutorial you will work with the files and folders on a floppy disk. When you have your own computer or are in a business environment, you will more likely work with files and folders on a hard disk drive. You will discover that file management techniques are the same for floppy disks and hard disks.

Preparing Your Student Disk with Quick Format

Before you begin, you need to create a new Student Disk that contains the sample files you will work with in Tutorials 3 and 4. You can make your Student Disk using the CTI Windows 95 Applications menu.

If you are using your own computer, the CTI Windows 95 Applications menu will *not* be available. Before you proceed, you must go to your school's computer lab and use the CTI Windows 95 Applications menu to make your new Student Disk. Once you have made the disk, you can use it to complete this tutorial on any computer that runs Windows 95.

If you still have the Student Disk from Tutorials 1 and 2 and don't need it any longer, you can reuse it for Tutorials 3 and 4. Otherwise, bring a blank, formatted disk to the lab.

When you want to erase the contents of a floppy disk, you can use the Quick format option rather than the Full format that you use on a new disk. A Quick format takes less time than a Full format because instead of preparing the entire disk surface, a Quick format erases something called the file allocation table. The **file allocation table (FAT)** stores the locations of all the files on the disk. By erasing the FAT, you erase all the information that tells the computer about the files on the disk and so the disk appears empty to the computer.

To Quick format your Student Disk:

1. Place your Student Disk in drive A.

   TROUBLE? If your 3½-inch disk drive is B, place your formatted disk in that drive instead, and for the rest of this tutorial substitute drive B wherever you see drive A.

2. Click the **My Computer** icon, then press **Enter** to open the My Computer window.

3. Click the **3½ Floppy (A:)** icon.

4. Click **File**, then click **Format** to display the Format dialog box.

5. Make sure the **Quick (erase)** button and other settings in the dialog box match those shown in Figure 3-1.

Figure 3-1 ◀
Format
dialog box

click to Quick
format a disk

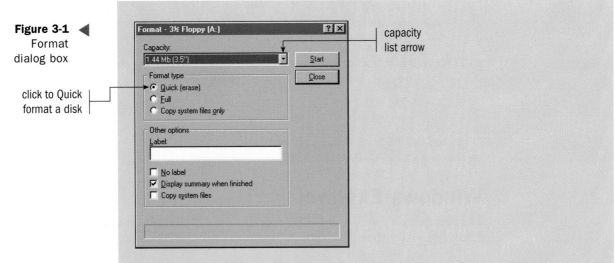

capacity
list arrow

6. Click the **Start** button to begin the Quick format.

TROUBLE? If an error message appears, it is possible your disk capacity is double-density instead of high-density. Click the Capacity list arrow, click 720 KB (3.5"), then repeat Step 6.

7. When the Format Results dialog box appears, click the **Close** button.

8. Click the **Close** button to close the Format dialog box.

Now that you have formatted your disk, you can make a Student Disk for Tutorials 3 and 4.

To create your Student Disk:

1. Click the **Start** button , point to **Programs**, point to **CTI Windows 95 Applications**, point to **Windows 95 New Perspectives Introductory**, then click **Make Student Disk**. Figure 3-2 shows the Start menu structure you need to navigate.

Figure 3-2 ◀
Making your
Student Disk

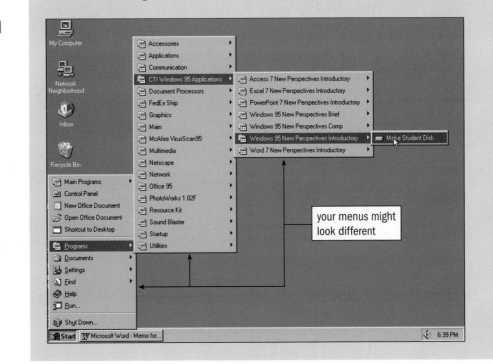

your menus might
look different

A dialog box opens, asking you to indicate the drive that contains your formatted disk.

2. Follow the instructions on the screen. The files are copied to your formatted disk. A message tells you when all the files have been copied.

3. Click the **OK** button. Your Student Disk now contains files that you will use throughout the rest of this tutorial.

4. Close all the open windows on your screen.

Windows Explorer

The root directory of Bernard's disk contains three folders plus the files he hasn't yet organized. Figure 3-3 shows the three folders and their contents.

Figure 3-3 ◀
Folders on
Bernard's disk

Folder name	Contents
Clients	Text files that contain client addresses, along with basic medical and insurance information
Gear	Microsoft Excel spreadsheet files that track harness inventory and the daily use of each rope for insurance purposes
Guides	Microsoft Word files that contain information on the guides the Kolbe Climbing School employs

Windows Directories, Folders and Files

3.1 NOTE

In many ways Windows Explorer is similar to the File Manager in Windows 3.1.

The files Bernard needs to organize are also in the root directory. The ideal tool for file organization tasks, you tell Bernard, is Windows Explorer.

Windows Explorer is a program included with Windows 95 that is designed to simplify disk management tasks such as locating, viewing, moving, copying, and deleting files or folders. Using a single window divided into two sections, Windows Explorer provides an easy-to-navigate representation of disks, folders, and files.

Windows 95 provides more than one way to accomplish most tasks. Although you can use My Computer to look at the contents of a disk, Windows Explorer is a more powerful file management tool. When you're moving just a file or two, My Computer works fine, but using it to organize many files on several disks often results in a frustrating game of "hide and seek" as you try to navigate on a screen cluttered with files, folders, and windows. For more advanced file management tasks, many people prefer to use Windows Explorer.

To start Windows Explorer:

1. Click the **Start** button 🎛 Start .

2. Point to **Programs** then click **Windows Explorer** to open a window titled "Exploring."

3. If the Exploring window is not maximized, click the **Maximize** button 🔲. See Figure 3-4, but don't try to arrange the folders and files on your screen to match those in the figure.

   TROUBLE? If your Exploring window lists look different, your computer probably contains different devices and folders than the ones shown in Figure 3-4. Don't worry about it.

Study Figure 3-4 and notice how the Exploring window is divided into two sections: a Folders list and a Contents list.

Contents list displays contents of this highlighted folder, which also appears in the title bar

Figure 3-4 ◄
Windows Explorer overview

icon that represents your floppy drive

folder icon

use this scroll bar to scroll through the Folders list

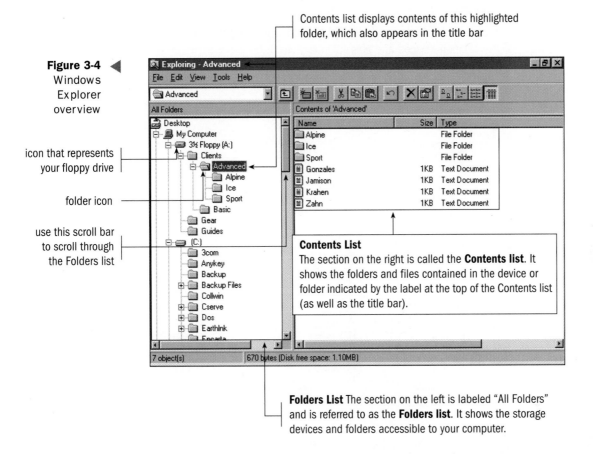

Contents List
The section on the right is called the **Contents list**. It shows the folders and files contained in the device or folder indicated by the label at the top of the Contents list (as well as the title bar).

Folders List The section on the left is labeled "All Folders" and is referred to as the **Folders list**. It shows the storage devices and folders accessible to your computer.

Notice the folders called Advanced and Basic in Figure 3-4. These two folders are contained in the folder called Clients. Folders that are contained in other folders are referred to as **subfolders**. The Advanced folder itself has subfolders: Alpine, Ice, and Sport. You might have noticed that both the Folders list and the Contents list display the Alpine, Ice, and Sport folders. To some people it is confusing that these folders are shown in both the Folders list and the Contents list. However, they are not duplicate folders; they are just shown twice. The Folders list displays a device's *structure*, that is, its levels of folders and subfolders. The Contents list, on the other hand, displays the *contents* of a device or folder, including its folders and its files.

To see the devices—drives, printers, and other objects—connected to your computer, you scroll through the Folders list. Each object in the list has a small icon next to it. Explorer uses the icons shown in Figure 3-5 to represent different types of storage devices.

Figure 3-5 ◄
Storage device icons

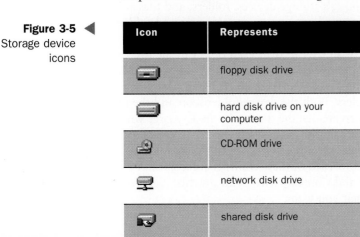

Icon	Represents
	floppy disk drive
	hard disk drive on your computer
	CD-ROM drive
	network disk drive
	shared disk drive

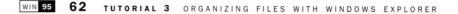

To see a list of storage devices connected to your computer:

1. Drag the Folders list scroll box until you can see the 🖳 Desktop icon at the top. Refer to Figure 3-6 for the location of this scroll box.

> **TROUBLE?** If you don't have a scroll box, you don't have more than one screen of open devices and files. Skip to Step 3.

2. Scroll to the bottom of the Folders list. See Figure 3-6.

Figure 3-6 ◀
Devices and
folders in the
Folders list

Folders list shows the
devices and folders
accessible to your
computer system

drag to scroll through
the Folders list

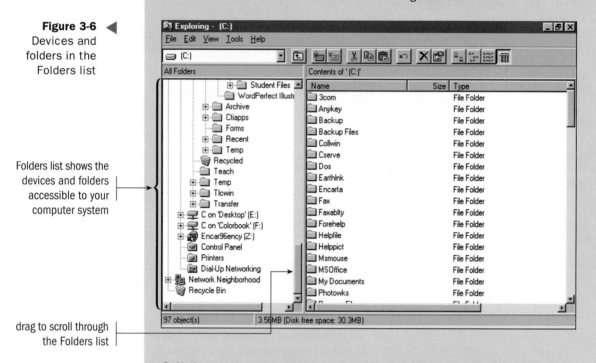

3. Notice whether your computer has a CD-ROM drive or access to network storage devices.

> **TROUBLE?** Although the computer Bernard is using, shown in Figure 3-6, has both a CD-ROM drive and network disk drive, your list is probably different.

4. After you look at the list of devices and folders, scroll back to the top of the Folders list so you can see the Desktop icon at the top of the list.

Viewing the Folders on a Disk Drive

Like a file cabinet, a typical storage device on your computer contains files and folders. These folders can contain additional files and one or more levels of subfolders. If Explorer displayed all your computer's storage devices, folders, and files at once, it could be a very long list. Instead, Explorer allows you to open devices and folders only when you want to see what they contain. Otherwise, you can keep them closed.

As you've seen, the small icon next to each object in the list, called the device icon or folder icon, represents the device or folder in the Folders list. Many of these icons also have a plus box or minus box next to them that indicates whether the device or folder contains additional folders. Both the device/folder icon and the plus/minus box are controls that you can click to change the display in the Explorer window. You click the plus box to display folders or subfolders, and you click the minus box to hide them. You click the device/folder icon to control the display in the Contents list.

Figure 3-7 explains how each of these controls accomplishes a different task to change the view in the Folders and Contents lists. With practice you'll see how to use these controls to display only what you want.

3.1 NOTE

File Manager showed a separate window for each storage device. With Windows Explorer, you can see all the devices in a single list.

Selecting a Device or Folder

To work with a device or folder, you first click it to select it, and Windows highlights it. It is important to understand that using the plus/minus box does not select a device or folder. To select a device or folder, you must click its *icon*, not its plus/minus box. When you select a device or folder, it becomes active. The **active** device or folder is the one the computer uses when you take an action.

REFERENCE window	**SELECTING A DEVICE OR FOLDER**
	■ Click the icon that represents the device or folder to select it and highlight it.

For example, if you want to create a new folder on drive A, you first need to select drive A. It then becomes the active drive. If you don't first activate drive A, the new folder you create would be placed in whatever device or folder was currently active—it could be a folder on the hard drive or network drive. How do you know which device or folder is active? Two ways. First, it is highlighted. Second, its name appears at the top of the Contents list and in the title bar, as shown in Figure 3-10.

name of active device
appears at top of Contents
list and in title bar

Figure 3-10 ◀
Active device

active device
is highlighted

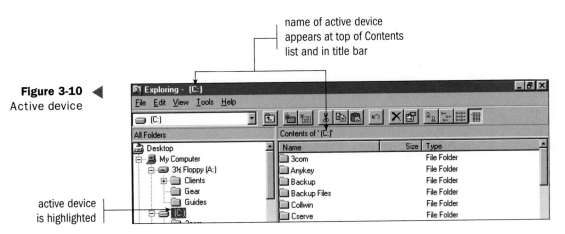

You can experiment with changing the active device and folder by selecting drive A and then selecting the Clients folder.

To select devices and folders:

1. Click ▭ **drive A**. To show that drive A is selected, the computer highlights the label, usually "3½ Floppy (A:)," and displays it in both the title bar and at the top of the Contents list. See Figure 3-11 on the next page.

Figure 3-11 ◄
Drive A is the
active device

click drive A device
icon to activate it

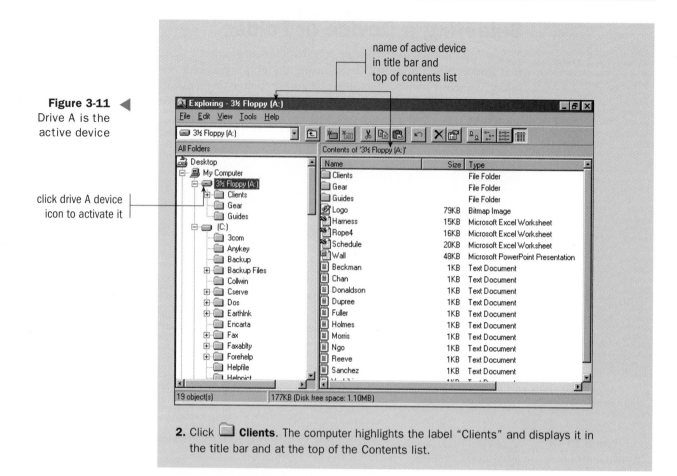

name of active device
in title bar and
top of contents list

2. Click 📁 **Clients**. The computer highlights the label "Clients" and displays it in
   the title bar and at the top of the Contents list.

Creating New Folders

Bernard tracks gear usage for both ropes and harnesses. Climbers wear harnesses to
attach themselves to the rope for protection in case they fall, and Bernard owns a number
of harnesses that his clients use on guided climbs. There is already a folder named "Gear"
that contains files for each of the KCS ropes. You decide to create two new subfolders
within the Gear folder: one for all files having to do with harnesses, and the other for the
ropes files.

REFERENCE window	**CREATING A FOLDER IN WINDOWS EXPLORER**
	▪ Click the device or folder that will contain the new folder in the Folders list.
	▪ Click File, then click New.
	▪ Click Folder.
	▪ Type a name for the new folder.
	▪ Press the Enter key.

The Clients folder is currently active. If you create a new folder now, it will become a
subfolder of Clients. Because you want to create the two subfolders in the Gear folder,
you must make the Gear folder active.

To create the new Gear subfolders on Bernard's disk:

1. Click 📁 **Gear** in the Folders list to activate the Gear folder.

   TROUBLE? If you clicked ➕ instead of the folder icon 📁 you did not activate the folder. Be sure you click the folder icon. The Gear folder should appear high-lighted and the icon should change to 📂.

2. Click **File** to open the File menu, point to **New**, then click **Folder**. A folder icon labeled "New Folder" appears at the end of the Contents list.

3. Type **Harnesses** as the title of the new folder.

4. Press the **Enter** key. Now create the second subfolder of the Gear folder for all the rope files.

5. Click **File**, point to **New**, click **Folder**, type **Ropes** as the name of the second folder, then press the **Enter** key.

6. Click ➕ next to the Gear folder to see the new folders in the Folders list. See Figure 3-12.

Figure 3-12 ◀
Creating
new folders

new folders
in Folders list

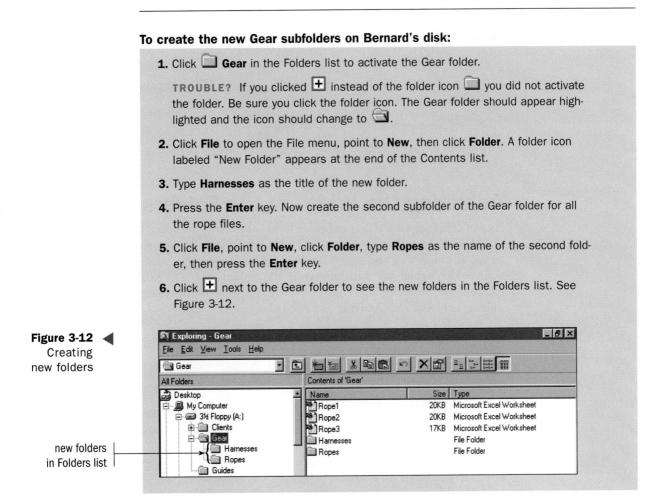

Renaming a Folder

As you and Bernard talk over the current folder structure, you realize that a complete inventory of the KCS gear includes not just ropes and harnesses but many other types of equipment: carabiners, belay plates, chalk bags, runners, and so on. Therefore, the two of you decide to rename the Harnesses folder as "Equipment," so you can store files on just the ropes in the Ropes folder and files for all the other gear in the Equipment folder.

REFERENCE window	**RENAMING A FOLDER**
	■ Click the folder you want to rename to activate it if necessary.
	■ Click the folder label.
	■ Type the new name.
	■ Press the Enter key.

3.1 NOTE

In Explorer you can rename a folder by simply clicking its label, rather than having to use a menu command.

The easiest way to rename a folder is to select the folder, click the folder label (not the plus/minus box or the folder icon), then type the new name.

To change the name of the Harnesses folder to "Equipment":

1. Click 📁 **Harnesses**.

2. Click the *label* **Harnesses**. After a short pause, a flashing insertion point appears at the end of the folder name.

3. Type **Equipment** as the new folder name.

4. Press the **Enter** key.

Adjusting the Width of the Folders List

As you create or view more and more levels of folders, the space for the Folders list might not be wide enough to display all the levels of folders. As a result, you might not be able to see all the device and folder icons. Whether or not this occurs depends on how long your folder names are and how wide the Folders list was in the first place. You can increase the width of the Folders list by dragging the dividing bar that separates the Folders list from the Contents list.

REFERENCE window	**ADJUSTING THE WIDTH OF THE FOLDERS LIST**
	▪ Move the mouse pointer to the dividing bar between the Folders list and the Contents list. ▪ When the arrow-shaped pointer ⌖ changes to a double-ended arrow ◀▮▶, hold down the left mouse button and drag the dividing line right or left as necessary. ▪ When the dividing bar is in its new position, release the mouse button.

To increase the width of the Folders list:

1. Move the mouse pointer to the dividing bar between the Folders list and the Contents list. The ⌖ pointer changes to a ◀▮▶ pointer.

2. Hold down the left mouse button while you drag the dividing bar to the right about one-half inch, as shown in Figure 3-13.

Figure 3-13 ◀
Adjusting the
width of the
Windows
Explorer lists

double-ended arrow
appears when you
point at dividing bar

gray bar shows new
location as you drag

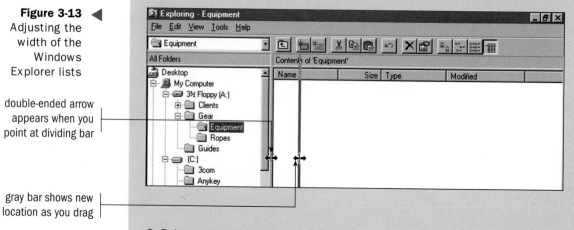

3. Release the mouse button. Use this method as necessary when you work with Windows Explorer to adjust the Folders list width.

Closing Windows Explorer

You have now properly restructured the folders on Bernard's disk. In the next session, you will work with the files on his disk. You can close Windows Explorer by using the Close button on the Exploring window.

To close Windows Explorer:

1. Click the **Close** button ☒ to close the Exploring window. You return to the Windows 95 desktop.

Quick Check

1. _____ is an alternative to using My Computer for file management tasks.

2. The Exploring window is divided into two parts: the _____ list and the _____ list.

3. True or false: If you see folders with the same names on both the right and left sides of the Exploring window, the folders are duplicates and you should erase those on the right side of the screen.

4. True or false: The Folders list displays all the files in a folder.

5. A folder that is contained in another folder is referred to as a(n) _____.

6. You click the _____ to expand the display of folders in the Folders list.

7. If you want to create a new folder on drive A, what should you click in the Folders list?

8. True or false: To adjust the width of the Folders list, be sure the mouse pointer looks like ⇱ before you start to drag the dividing bar.

SESSION 3.2

In Session 3.2 you will work with the right side of the Exploring window, which displays folders and files. You will learn how to switch between icon views and list views of the files, and how to arrange files by name, date, size, and file type. You will also learn how to select multiple files. These skills will help you find, move, copy, and delete files in the process of organizing your disks.

Viewing the Explorer Toolbar

To continue, you need to restart Windows Explorer. Windows Explorer has a toolbar that provides quick access to many Explorer commands. You will use the toolbar shortly, so you should make sure the toolbar is displayed on your screen.

To display the Explorer toolbar:

1. Make sure your Student Disk is in drive A, then start Windows Explorer and scroll the Folders list, if necessary, so you can see drive A.

2. Maximize the Exploring window if necessary.

3. Check your screen to see if the Explorer toolbar is displayed. See Figure 3-14.

4. If the toolbar is not visible on the screen, click **View** on the menu bar, then click **Toolbar** to display it. Figure 3-14 shows the Explorer toolbar.

Figure 3-14 ◀
Explorer toolbar

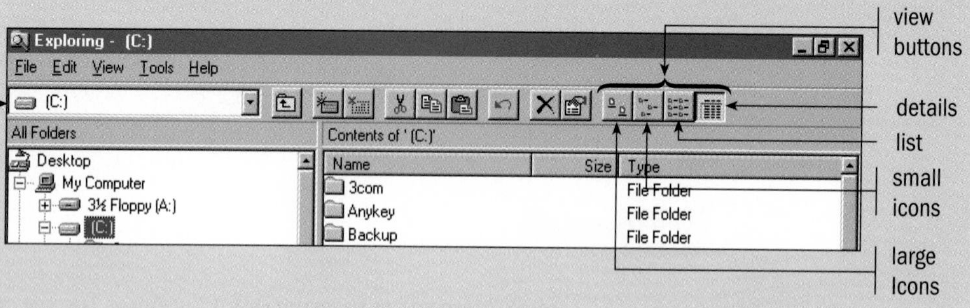

Explorer toolbar ──→

view buttons

details

list

small icons

large Icons

If you forget the function of a toolbar button, you can always point to the button. After a short pause a ToolTip will appear, telling you what the button does.

Viewing the Contents List

The right side of the Exploring window shows the Contents list, which lists the contents, both folders and files, of the active device or folder. Clicking a plus/minus box does not affect the Contents list. To change the Contents list, you must activate a device or folder by clicking its corresponding device or folder icon. Explorer highlights the icon, and the Contents list changes to display the contents of the device or folder you clicked.

REFERENCE window	**VIEWING A LIST OF FILES**
	▪ Adjust the Folders list to display the device or folder whose contents you want to view.
	▪ Click the icon next to the device or folder that contains the files you want to view.

You and Bernard now examine the contents of drive A.

To view the contents of drive A:

1. Click 🖫 **drive A** in the Folders list. See Figure 3-15 if you have trouble locating this icon. The Contents list changes to show the contents of drive A.

TROUBLE? If nothing happened in your Contents list, it probably already showed the contents of drive A. If this is true, the label at the top of the Contents list will read "Contents of '3½ Floppy (A:)'." Continue to Step 2.

2. Click **View**, then click **Details** so that your Contents list looks like the one in Figure 3-15.

Figure 3-15 ◄
Contents
of drive A

drive A ———

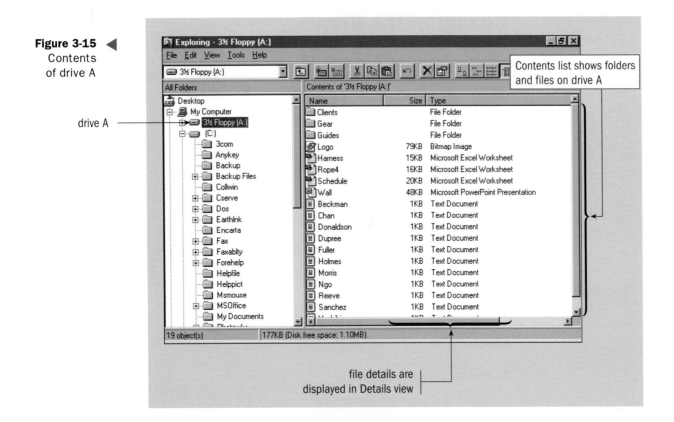

Contents list shows folders
and files on drive A

file details are
displayed in Details view

You can see that the root directory of drive A contains three folders and a number of files; however, you cannot see the contents of the folders in this list. To see the contents of a folder, you must select the folder by clicking it. When the Steps tell you to click a folder icon, click it in the Folders list and not in the Contents list. You want to view the contents of the Gear folder.

To view folder contents:

1. Click ⊞ in front of drive A to display its folders.

2. Click 📁 **Gear** (not the plus box) in the Folders list. The Contents list on the right side of the window changes to display the files in the Gear folder. In addition to the two subfolders you created earlier, there are three files, one for each rope KCS owns. See Figure 3-16.

Figure 3-16 ◄
Contents of
Gear folder

Gear folder ———

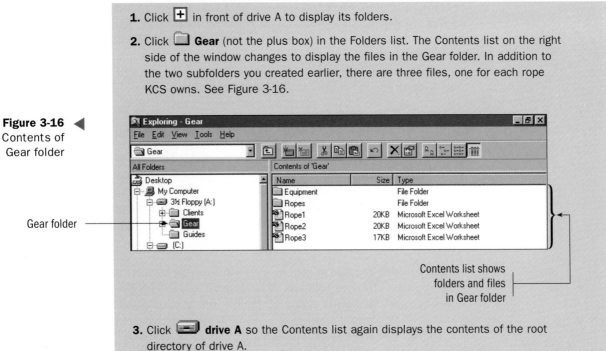

Contents list shows
folders and files
in Gear folder

3. Click 💾 **drive A** so the Contents list again displays the contents of the root directory of drive A.

Changing the View

Explorer provides four different view options for the Contents list: Large Icons, Small Icons, List, and Details, similar to the view options available in My Computer. Most users prefer to use the Details view because it shows the file size and the date when the file was created or last modified. This information is often useful when making decisions about which files to move and delete.

REFERENCE window

CHANGING THE WAY FILES ARE DISPLAYED IN THE CONTENTS LIST

- Click one of the four View buttons on the right side of the toolbar.
  or
- Click View, then click Large Icons, Small Icons, List, or Details.

You can use the four buttons on the right side of the toolbar to change the way the files are displayed in the Contents list.

To change the file display:

1. Click the **Large Icons** button to view the files as large icons.

2. Click the **Small Icons** button to view the files as small icons.

3. Click the **List** button to view the files as a list.

4. Click the **Details** button to view all file details.

Arranging Files in the Contents List

For many file management tasks, one of your first Steps is to locate one or more files that you want to delete, copy, or move. To help you locate files, Explorer provides you with the option to arrange files by name, size, date, or type. The arrangement you use will depend on the file management task you are doing. For example, arranging files by name is useful if you are looking for a particular file to move, copy, or delete and you know its name. If there are any folders in the Contents list, Explorer displays those first.

REFERENCE window

ARRANGING FILES BY NAME, SIZE, DATE, OR TYPE

- Make sure the files you want to arrange are displayed in the Contents list.
- Click the Name, Size, Type, or Modified button once to view files in ascending order and twice to view files in descending order.

When you view the files in the Contents list using the Details button, a button appears at the top of each of the four columns: Name, Size, Type, and Modified, as shown in Figure 3-17. You can click the button to arrange the files by the corresponding column. For example, clicking the Name button arranges the files by name in ascending order (from A to Z). If you click the Name button a second time, the files appear in descending order (from Z to A).

To arrange the files by name:

1. Click the **Name** button. See Figure 3-17.

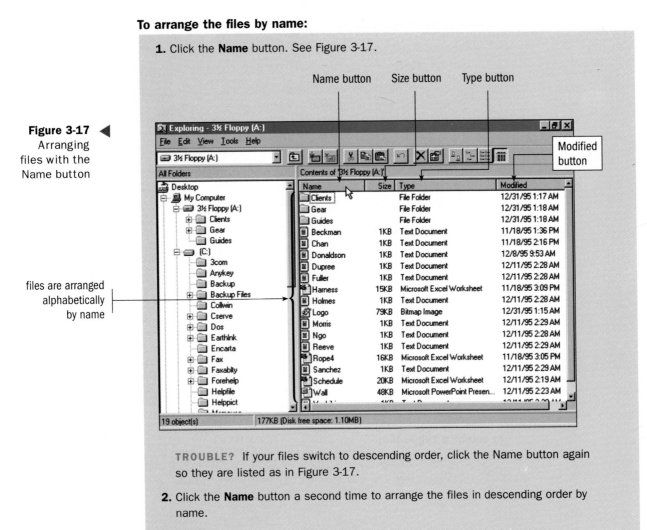

Figure 3-17 ◀
Arranging
files with the
Name button

files are arranged
alphabetically
by name

TROUBLE? If your files switch to descending order, click the Name button again so they are listed as in Figure 3-17.

2. Click the **Name** button a second time to arrange the files in descending order by name.

3. Click the **Name** button once again to return to ascending order by name.

Clicking the Size button displays the files in order according to the number of bytes or characters each contains. This is helpful when you need to make more space available on a disk and are trying to decide which files to delete or move to another disk. When the files are arranged in descending order by size, the largest files appear at the top. You can delete those first when you need more disk space.

To arrange the files by size:

1. Click the **Size** button to arrange the files in ascending order by size.

2. Click the **Size** button a second time to arrange the files in descending order by size. The Logo file is the largest file on the disk.

Clicking the Modified button displays the files in order by the date they were modified. This arrangement is useful, for example, if you are looking for a file you know you created yesterday but whose name you have forgotten.

To arrange the files by date:

1. Click the **Modified** button. The files are now listed with the newest or most recently modified file at the top of the list.

TROUBLE? Depending on the width of the columns in the Contents list, you might have to scroll to the right to see the Modified button.

Sometimes you want to locate all files of a particular type. For example, you might want to quickly locate all the files created with WordPad. This sorting arrangement is useful when you know you created a file using a particular application. Explorer identifies the application that created the file in the Type column.

To arrange the files by type:

1. Click the **Type** button. Explorer now groups the files by application type.

2. Click the **Name** button to restore ascending alphabetical order.

Selecting Files

After you locate the file or files you need for a file management task, you have to tell Explorer which specific file(s) you want to work with. If you want to delete, move or copy a single file, you must first select the file. Take a moment to learn some file selection techniques before working with the files on Bernard's disk.

To select a single file:

1. Click the **Beckman** file to select it. As shown in Figure 3-18, the file is highlighted to show that it is selected, and the status bar indicates that one object is selected (170 bytes in size).

Figure 3-18 ◀
Selecting a single file

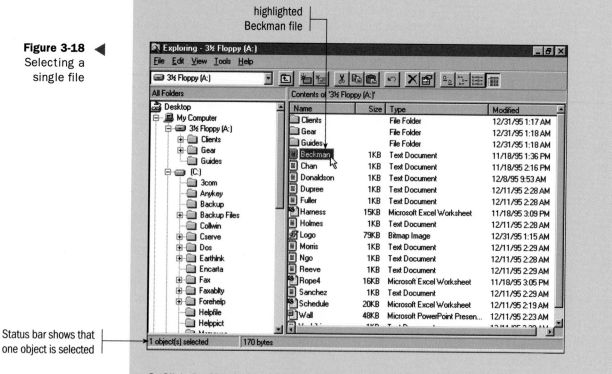

Status bar shows that one object is selected

2. Click the **Morris** file. The Morris file is highlighted to show that it is selected, and Beckman is no longer highlighted.

You can select all the files and folders in a folder or device in a single Step.

To select all files and folders on drive A:

1. Click **Edit**, then click **Select All**. Explorer highlights the files and folders to show they are selected. The status bar now tells you that 19 objects are selected. See Figure 3-19.

Figure 3-19 ◀
Selecting
all files

all files in drive A
(including folders)
are selected

Status bar updates to
show number of
objects that are
selected and size of
cumulative selection
(your size might
be different)

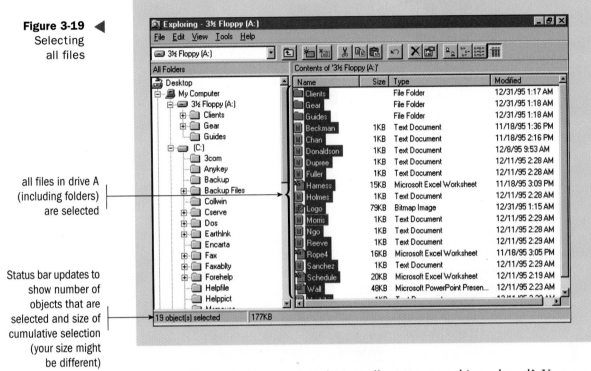

What if you decide that you don't really want everything selected? You can always deselect the objects you have selected by clicking any blank area in the Contents list window.

To deselect the range of files:

1. Click any blank area in the Contents list. The highlighting is removed from all the files to indicate that none are currently selected.

What if you want to work with more than one file, but not all the files in a folder? For example, suppose Bernard wants to delete three of the files in a folder. In Explorer there are two ways to select a group of files. You can select files listed consecutively or you can select files scattered throughout the Contents list. Figure 3-20 on the next page explains the two different ways to select a group of files.

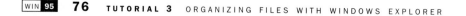

Figure 3-20 ◀
Two ways
to select a
group of files

Consecutive files   Non-consecutive files

📁 Clients   📁 Clients
📁 Gear   📁 Gear
📁 Guides   📁 Guides
📄 Beckman   📄 Beckman
📄 Chan   📄 Chan
📄 Donaldson   📄 Donaldson
📄 Dupree   📄 Dupree
📄 Fuller   📄 Fuller
📄 Harness   📄 Harness
📄 Holmes   📄 Holmes
📄 Logo   📄 Logo

SHIFT   CTRL

The Shift key lets you select consecutive files, whereas the Ctrl key lets you select non-consecutive files.

REFERENCE
window

SELECTING FILES

- Make sure the files you want to select are displayed in the Contents list.
- To select a single file, click it.
- To select consecutive files, hold down the Shift key while you click the first and last files you want to select.
- To select non-consecutive files, hold down the Ctrl key while you click each of the files you want to select.
- To select all the files in the active device or folder, click Edit, then click Select All.

You can use the Shift key along with the mouse to select consecutive files. When you are holding down the Shift key, all the files between the first file you click and the second file you click will be selected.

To select consecutive files:

1. Click the **Beckman** file.

2. Hold down the **Shift** key while you click the **Fuller** file. All files from Beckman to Fuller are highlighted. See Figure 3-21.

Figure 3-21 ◀
Selecting
consecutive
files

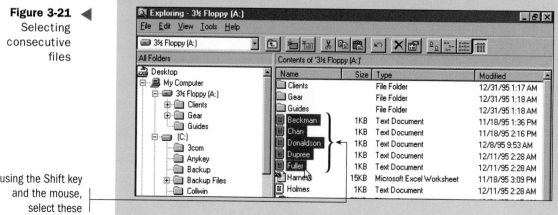

using the Shift key
and the mouse,
select these
consecutive files

3. Release the **Shift** key.

When you want to select non-consecutive files scattered within a folder, you hold down the Ctrl key while you click the individual files.

To select multiple files using the Ctrl key:

1. Click the **Morris** file. Notice that clicking this file automatically deselects any selected files.

2. Hold down the **Ctrl** key and click the **Reeve** file.

3. Keep holding down the **Ctrl** key and click the **Sanchez** file. All three files should be highlighted. See Figure 3-22.

TROUBLE? If you released the Ctrl key after Step 1, don't worry. Press it again and click Reeve and Sanchez.

Figure 3-22 ◀
Selecting non-consecutive files

using the Ctrl key and the mouse, select these non-consecutive files

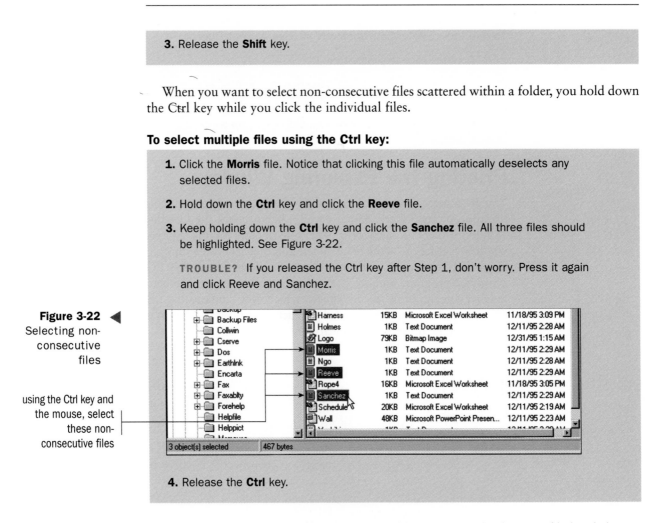

4. Release the **Ctrl** key.

While selecting multiple files with the Ctrl key, you can deselect any file by clicking it again. You can also select more files by holding down the Ctrl key again, then selecting the additional files.

To select and deselect additional files:

1. Hold down the **Ctrl** key and click the **Chan** file to select it. Four files are now selected.

2. Keep holding down the **Ctrl** key and click the **Sanchez** file to deselect it. Now three files are selected: Chan, Morris, and Reeve.

Suppose you want to select all the files *except one* in a folder? You can use the Invert Selection menu option to select all the files that are *not* highlighted.

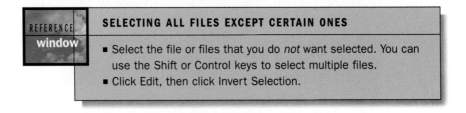

REFERENCE
window

SELECTING ALL FILES EXCEPT CERTAIN ONES

■ Select the file or files that you do *not* want selected. You can use the Shift or Control keys to select multiple files.
■ Click Edit, then click Invert Selection.

To use Invert Selection to select all files except Dupree:

1. Click the **Dupree** file to select it.

2. Click **Edit**, then click **Invert Selection**. All the files *except* Dupree are now selected.

3. Click a blank area to remove the highlighting for all the files on drive A.

Printing the Exploring Window

You are almost ready to move the new files Bernard created from the root directory into the appropriate folders. Bernard would like to mark the files that need to be moved. He wonders if there's a quick way to get a hard copy (that is, a paper copy) of the Exploring window that he can write on. You tell him that you can temporarily store an image of the Exploring window in memory using the Print Screen key. Then, you can start the WordPad program and paste the Exploring image into a blank WordPad document. Finally, you can print the document (which now contains the Exploring window). It can be handy to have a printout of the structures of certain important devices for reference, so this is a good procedure to learn.

REFERENCE window	**PRINTING THE EXPLORING WINDOW**
	■ Adjust the Exploring window so you see the files and folders you want on the printout. ■ Press the Print Screen key. ■ Click the Start button, click Accessories, then click WordPad. ■ Type your name, date, or any other text you want on the print-out of the Exploring window. ■ Click Edit, then click Paste to paste the Exploring image into WordPad. ■ Click File, then click Print to display the Print dialog box. ■ Click OK to print the document. ■ Close WordPad, clicking No when asked if you want to save. It is not necessary to save the document you just printed.

The Exploring window is a graphical image, so it can take a fairly long time to print, especially on a dot-matrix printer. If your lab has a dot matrix printer, make sure you preview before you print so you do not have to print multiple copies.

To print the Exploring window:

1. Click ⊞ next to Clients, Advanced, and Gear so that all the folders and subfolders on Bernard's disk are visible.

2. Press the **Print Screen** key. Although it seems as if nothing happened, an image of the Exploring window was stored in memory.

3. Click the **Start** button ⬛Start, point to **Programs**, point to **Accessories**, then click **WordPad**. The WordPad window opens.

4. Maximize the WordPad window, type **Bernard Kolbe, 8/22/97** at the top of the WordPad window, then press the **Enter** key twice.

5. Click **Edit**, click **Paste**, then scroll to the top of the document. The Exploring screen image appears in the WordPad document. See Figure 3-23.

WordPad window

Figure 3-23
Exploring
screen image in
a WordPad
document

Print Preview button

image of Exploring
window pasted
into WordPad

WordPad scroll bars
scroll the image up,
down, right, and left

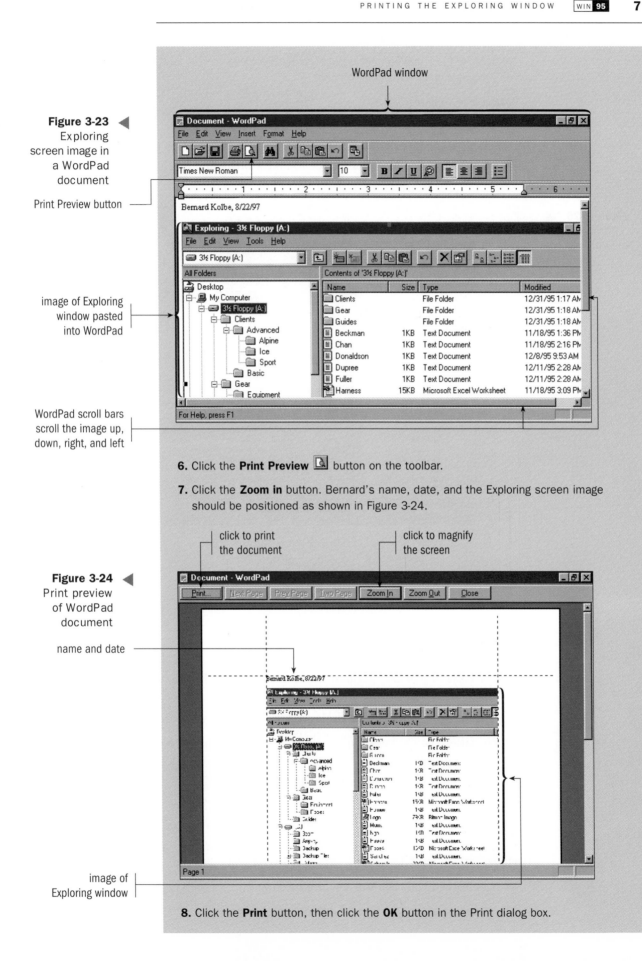

6. Click the **Print Preview** 🔍 button on the toolbar.

7. Click the **Zoom in** button. Bernard's name, date, and the Exploring screen image should be positioned as shown in Figure 3-24.

click to print
the document

click to magnify
the screen

Figure 3-24
Print preview
of WordPad
document

name and date

image of
Exploring window

8. Click the **Print** button, then click the **OK** button in the Print dialog box.

9. Close the WordPad window. When you see a message asking if you want to save the document, click the **No** button.

10. Close Windows Explorer.

Bernard annotates the printout, shown in Figure 3-25, so you know where to move the files in the root directory. You decide to take a break and finish working with Bernard's files tomorrow.

Figure 3-25 ◄
Bernard's
printout

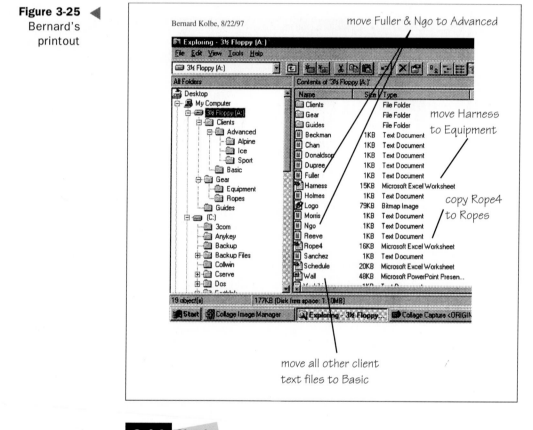

Quick Check

1 True or False: If you click ⊞ next to the Clients folder, Explorer displays a list of files in the Clients folder.

2 You click the _____ to display a device's or folder's contents in the Contents list.

3 True or false: The Explorer toolbar contains buttons you use to select consecutive files in the Contents list.

4 Most Windows 95 users prefer to use the _____ view because it shows the file size and the date when the file was created or last modified.

5 The Arrange Icons menu gives you the option to sort files by ____, _____, _____, or ____.

6 If you hold down the _____ key when you select files, you will select consecutive files, whereas if you hold down the _____ key you will select non-consecutive files.

7 What button do you click to view files by date?

8 What happens when you press the Print Screen key?

SESSION

3.3

So far in this tutorial you have learned how to use the Folders list to view the structure of folders on a disk. You have also learned how to view and select files in the Contents list. In Session 3.3, you put these skills to use in the procedures for copying, moving, and deleting files or folders.

Moving a Single File Between Folders

To organize his disk, Bernard needs to move a number of files to different folders. The basic procedure for moving a file is to open the folder that contains the file, select the file, and use the *right* mouse button to drag the file to its new location.

REFERENCE window	**MOVING ONE OR MORE FILES BETWEEN FOLDERS**
	■ Make sure the Contents list shows the files you want to move and the Folders list shows the folders to which you want to move the file(s).
	■ Click the file(s) you want to move. For multiple files, you can use the Shift or Ctrl keys when you select the files to be moved.
	■ Hold down the *right* mouse button while you drag the file(s) to the new location.
	■ Make sure the new location is highlighted before you release the mouse button.
	■ Click Move Here from the menu.

Bernard has marked the files you need to move on the printout you created in the previous session. You begin by moving the Harness file from the root directory to the Equipment folder.

To move the Harness file:

1. Start Windows Explorer.

2. Click ▭ **drive A**, then click ⊞ in front of drive A to display its folders.

3. Click ⊞ next to the Gear folder to display its subfolders.

4. Click the **Harness** file in the Contents list, then hold down the *right* mouse button while you drag **Harness** to the Equipment folder as shown in Figure 3-26 on the next page.

   TROUBLE? Don't worry if the filename is displayed as Harness.xls.

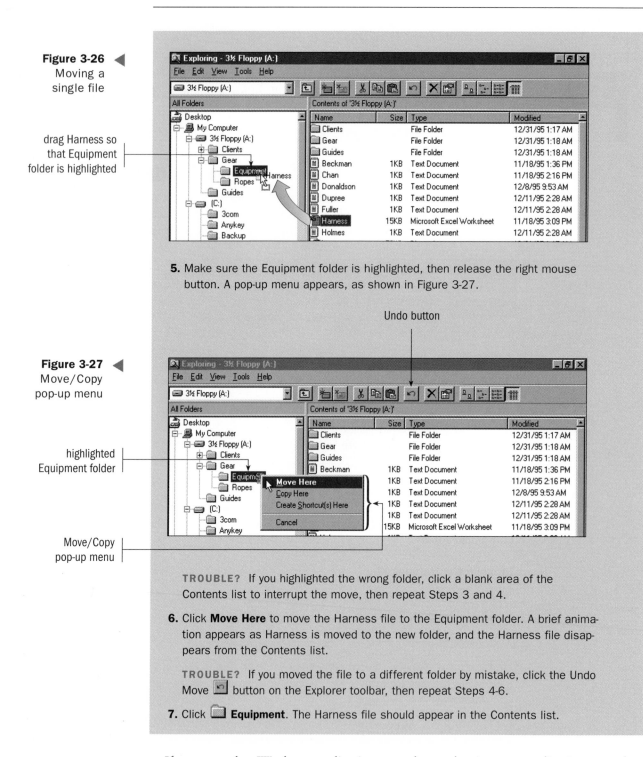

Figure 3-26 ◀
Moving a
single file

drag Harness so
that Equipment
folder is highlighted

5. Make sure the Equipment folder is highlighted, then release the right mouse button. A pop-up menu appears, as shown in Figure 3-27.

Undo button

Figure 3-27 ◀
Move/Copy
pop-up menu

highlighted
Equipment folder

Move/Copy
pop-up menu

TROUBLE? If you highlighted the wrong folder, click a blank area of the Contents list to interrupt the move, then repeat Steps 3 and 4.

6. Click **Move Here** to move the Harness file to the Equipment folder. A brief animation appears as Harness is moved to the new folder, and the Harness file disappears from the Contents list.

TROUBLE? If you moved the file to a different folder by mistake, click the Undo Move 🔄 button on the Explorer toolbar, then repeat Steps 4-6.

7. Click 📁 **Equipment**. The Harness file should appear in the Contents list.

If you use other Windows applications, you know that in most applications you drag objects with the left mouse button. Although you can drag files in Windows Explorer with the left mouse button, you need to be careful. When you use the left mouse button, Windows Explorer will not open the pop-up menu. Instead, it simply moves or copies the file to the folder you highlight, depending on the circumstances. When you drag a file from one folder to another *on the same drive*, Explorer moves the file. However, when you drag a file from a folder on one drive to a folder *on a different drive*, Explorer copies the file; it does not move it. Therefore, to prevent mistakes, most beginners should use the right mouse button to drag files.

Copying a Single File to a Folder

The procedure for copying a file is similar to the procedure for moving, except that you select Copy Here instead of Move Here from the pop-up menu. Bernard recently purchased a fourth rope, and he is tracking its use in the file Rope4. He wants a copy of the Rope4 file in the Ropes folder.

REFERENCE window

COPYING ONE OR MORE FILES

- Make sure the folder that contains the file(s) you want to copy is active in the Folders list and the folder to which you want to copy the file(s) is visible.
- Click the file(s) you want to copy. You can use the Shift or Ctrl keys to select more than one file to copy.
- Hold down the *right* mouse button while you drag the file(s) to a new location.
- Make sure the new location is highlighted before you release the mouse button.
- Click Copy Here from the menu.

To copy the Rope4 file into the Ropes folder:

1. Click ⬛ **drive A** to view the files in the root directory once again.

2. Click **Rope4** to select it.

3. Hold down the *right* mouse button while you drag Rope4 to the Ropes folder.

4. Make sure the Ropes folder is highlighted, then release the right mouse button.

5. Click **Copy Here** from the pop-up menu. An animation shows Rope4 being copied from the root directory to the Ropes folder.

   Notice that Rope4 is still displayed in the Contents list for drive A, because you copied the file rather than moved it.

6. Click ⬛ **Ropes** and notice that Rope4 appears in the Contents list for this folder.

Moving or Copying Multiple Files Between Folders

You can move or copy more than one file at a time by selecting multiple files before you drag. Remember that you can use the Ctrl key, the Shift key, or the Select All command on the Edit menu to select more than one file. Bernard wants to move the three rope files from the Gear folder to the Ropes folder. The rope files are listed consecutively, so you should use the Shift key to quickly select these three files before you move them as a group.

To move the rope files to the Ropes folder:

1. Click ⬛ **Gear** to activate the Gear folder and view the other rope files, which also need to be moved into the Ropes folder.

2. Click the **Rope1** file.

3. Hold down the **Shift** key and click the **Rope3** file to select all three rope files.

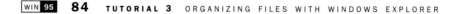

4. With the pointer over one of the selected files, hold down the *right* mouse button while you drag the selected files to the **Ropes** folder. See Figure 3-28.

Figure 3-28 ◀
Moving a
group of files

outline of the files
you want to move

highlight shows
the destination
for the files

Exploring - Gear

File Edit View Tools Help

Gear

All Folders | **Contents of 'Gear'**

Desktop
└ My Computer
  └ 3½ Floppy (A:)
    ├ Clients
    ├ Gear
    │   ├ Equipment
    │   ├ Ropes
    │   └ Guides
    └ (C:)
        └ 3com

Name	Size	Type	Modified
Equipment		File Folder	12/31/95 1:49 AM
Ropes		File Folder	12/31/95 1:49 AM
Rope1	20KB	Microsoft Excel Worksheet	11/18/95 2:56 PM
Rope2	20KB	Microsoft Excel Worksheet	11/18/95 2:58 PM
Rope3	17KB	Microsoft Excel Worksheet	11/18/95 3:01 PM

files selected to move
to the Ropes folder

TROUBLE? How can you tell when the files have reached the Ropes folder? Watch for the highlight to appear on the Ropes folder.

5. Make sure the Ropes folder is highlighted, then release the right mouse button.

6. Click **Move Here** to move the files to the Ropes folder.

7. Click ▭ **Ropes** to display the files in the Ropes folder. Rope1, Rope2, Rope3, and Rope4 should appear in the Contents list.

You've got Bernard's gear files organized, so now it's time to look at the new client files he added. Mark Fuller and George Ngo are interested exclusively in alpine climbing, so you decide to move the Fuller and Ngo client files into the Alpine folder.

To move non-consecutive files from one folder to another:

1. Click ▭ **drive A** to display the files it contains in the Contents list, then click ⊞ in front of Clients and Advanced.

2. Click the **Fuller** file.

3. Hold down the **Ctrl** key while you click the **Ngo** file.

4. Release the **Ctrl** key.

5. Drag the files to the Alpine folder using the *right* mouse button.

6. Click **Move Here**.

7. Click ▭ **Alpine**. The Contents list should include the files you just moved, plus the ones that were already there. See Figure 3-29.

Figure 3-29 ◀
Alpine folder
with moved
files

Exploring - Alpine

File Edit View Tools Help

Alpine

All Folders | **Contents of 'Alpine'**

Desktop
└ My Computer
  └ 3½ Floppy (A:)
    └ Clients
      └ Advanced
        ├ Alpine
        └ Ice

Name	Size	Type	Modified
Alora	1KB	Text Document	11/18/95 2:15 PM
Birkley	1KB	Text Document	12/10/95 10:19 AM
Fuller	1KB	Text Document	12/11/95 2:28 AM
Ngo	1KB	Text Document	12/11/95 2:28 AM
Tucker	1KB	Text Document	12/10/95 10:27 AM

files you moved
from root directory
to Alpine folder

You need to move the remaining client files from the root directory into the Basic folder. You can combine some of the methods you have already learned to complete this task most efficiently. For instance, notice that the client files are all text files. If you arrange these files by type, they'll all be next to each other, so you can select them as a group and drag them together to the Basic folder.

To move a group of related files to a new folder:

1. Click ⬜ **drive A** to view the contents of the root directory.

2. Click the **Type** button. The client text files are now grouped together at the bottom of the Contents list.

   TROUBLE? The Type button is at the top of the third column in the Contents list.

3. Click the **Beckman** file, hold down the **Shift** key, then click the **Yoshiki** file.

4. Move the client files into the **Basic** folder.

Bernard's disk is now restructured, with the gear and client files in the correct folders.

Moving or Copying Files Between a Floppy Disk and a Hard Disk

In the business world, companies use floppy disks to share files and information with clients and project members; telecommuters (workers who work on both an office computer and a home computer) use floppy disks to take files to and from the office, and software companies distribute programs and files on floppy disks. In your school computer lab, in contrast, you will rarely find yourself in a situation where you need to copy a file from your floppy disk to the hard disk of a lab computer. However, if you have a computer at home, you might want to move or copy files from your floppy disk to your hard disk to take advantage of its speed and large storage capacity.

Moving or copying files from a floppy disk to a hard disk is similar to the procedure for moving or copying files between folders. To practice this task, copy the Excel spreadsheet file named Schedule.xls to the hard disk.

To copy a file from a floppy disk to the hard disk:

1. If necessary, use the scroll bar to position the All Folders list so you can see the icon for drive C.

2. Click ⬜ **drive C** in the Folders list.

3. Click **File**, point to **New**, then click **Folder** to create a new folder on drive C.

   TROUBLE? If you receive a warning message telling you that you can't create a folder on drive C, you might be on a network that restricts hard-drive access. Ask your instructor or technical support person about other options for working on a hard drive, and read through the rest of this section to learn how you would work on a hard drive if you had the opportunity.

4. Type **Climbing** as the name of the new folder, then press **Enter** to finalize the name.

   TROUBLE? If there is already a Climbing folder on the hard disk, you must specify a different name. Use the name "Climb" with your initials, such as "ClimbJP." Substitute this folder name for the Climbing folder for the rest of the tutorial.

5. Click ⬜ **drive A** to display its contents in the Contents list.

6. Click the **Schedule** file to select it.

7. Hold down the *right* mouse button while you drag the **Schedule** file to the **Climbing** folder on drive C. See Figure 3-30.

Figure 3-30 ◄
Copying a file
from a floppy
disk to a
hard disk

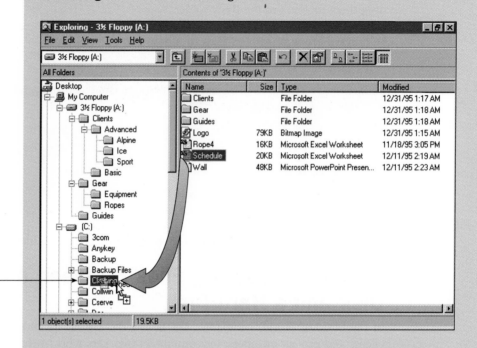

folder you created
on hard drive

8. Make sure the Climbing folder is highlighted, release the right mouse button, then click **Copy Here** to copy the file to the new folder. The original Schedule file remains in the root directory of drive A. An identical copy of the file has been placed in the Climbing folder on drive C.

9. Click ▭ **Climbing** on drive C to display the Schedule file in the Contents list, then click ▭ **drive A** so you can see its contents in the Contents list.

Copying a File From One Floppy Disk to Another Floppy Disk

You notice that Bernard has a PowerPoint file on his disk called Wall; you ask him about it. He explains that he is putting together a slide presentation for civic leaders that proposes building an artificial climbing wall in the area. You tell Bernard that you would love to help him develop the slide show; if he gave you a copy of the file you could work on it on your computer at home. He agrees, but says he doesn't know how to make you a copy because there is only one disk drive on the computer.

If your computer has only one floppy disk drive, you can't just drag a file from one floppy disk to another because you can't put both floppy disks in the drive at the same time. So how do you copy the file from one floppy to another? You first copy the file to a temporary location on the hard drive, then insert the destination floppy disk into drive A and finally move the file from the hard disk to the floppy disk. Figure 3-31 shows how this procedure works.

Figure 3-31 ◀
Copying a file
to the hard disk
and then to
a different
floppy disk

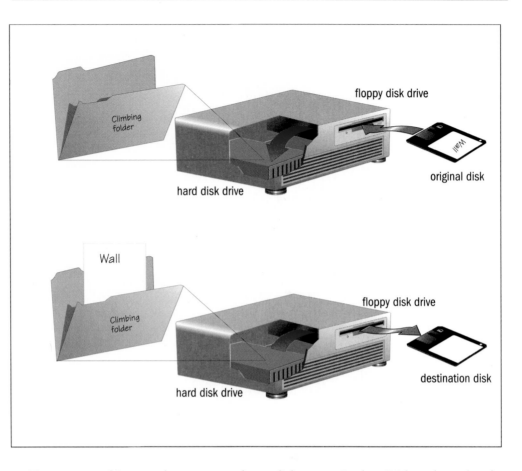

To carry out this procedure, you need two disks: your Student Disk and another formatted floppy disk. You can use the Backup disk you created in Tutorial 2 or any other formatted disk.

REFERENCE window	**COPYING A FILE FROM ONE FLOPPY DISK TO ANOTHER USING A SINGLE FLOPPY DISK DRIVE**

- Make sure you have a folder on the hard drive to which you can copy a file. If necessary, create a new folder on the hard drive.
- Copy the file to the hard drive.
- Take your Student Disk out of the floppy drive and insert the floppy disk on which you want the file copied.
- Click View, then click Refresh to tell the computer you switched disks.
- *Move* the file from the hard disk to the floppy that is now in the floppy disk drive.
- If you created a temporary file on the hard drive, delete it.

To copy one file from your Student Disk to a different floppy disk:

1. Click the **Wall** file to select it.

2. Hold down the *right* mouse button while you drag the **Wall** file to the **Climbing** folder on drive C, release the mouse button when the Climbing folder is highlighted, then click **Copy Here** to copy the file to drive C.

3. Remove your Student Disk and insert the other formatted floppy disk into drive A.

4. Click **View**, then click **Refresh** to indicate that you switched disks. The Refresh command examines the contents of the disk again and updates the Contents list accordingly.

5. Click the **Climbing** folder on drive C.

6. Click the **Wall** file to select it, then hold down the *right* mouse button while you drag the **Wall** file to drive A. See Figure 3-32.

Figure 3-32
Dragging the Wall file from the hard drive to the floppy disk

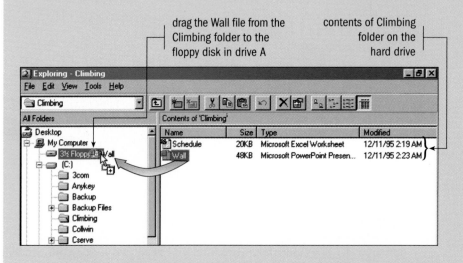

7. Release the right mouse button, then click **Move Here** to move the file to drive A.

8. Click ▭ **drive A** and make sure the Wall file is displayed in its Contents list, then remove the floppy disk from drive A.

9. Place your Student Disk back in drive A, click **View**, then click **Refresh** to view the files on the Student Disk.

Deleting Files and Folders

Looking over the Contents list of the drive A root directory of Bernard's disk, you realize that you could delete the Rope4 file since there's a copy of it in the Equipment folder.

When you delete a file or folder from the hard drive, recall that it goes into the Recycle Bin, so if you make a mistake you can always recover the file or folder. Once you delete a file from a floppy disk, though, there is no easy way of recovering it, so be sure before deleting that you are doing the right thing.

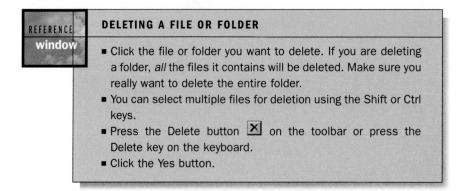

REFERENCE window

DELETING A FILE OR FOLDER

- Click the file or folder you want to delete. If you are deleting a folder, *all* the files it contains will be deleted. Make sure you really want to delete the entire folder.
- You can select multiple files for deletion using the Shift or Ctrl keys.
- Press the Delete button ☒ on the toolbar or press the Delete key on the keyboard.
- Click the Yes button.

To delete the Rope4 file:

1. Make sure the Contents list displays the files in the root directory.

   TROUBLE? Click 🖭 drive A in the Folders list.

2. Click **Rope4**.

3. Press the **Delete** key, then click the **Yes** button.

Two recent ice-climbing accidents have convinced Bernard to stop offering ice climbing because it's simply too unpredictable and dangerous. This business decision affects the folder structure on Bernard's disk. You decide to move the client files in the Ice folder into the Advanced folder and then delete the Ice folder altogether.

To move the files from Ice to Advanced, then delete the Ice folder:

1. If the folder structure of drive A is no longer displayed in the Folders list, click ⊞ next to drive A.

2. Click ⊞ next to Clients and Advanced so you can see the Ice folder in the Folders list.

3. Click 📁 **Ice**.

4. Click **Edit** on the menu bar, then click **Select All** to select the Kranmer and Wei files.

5. Drag the selection to the Advanced folder using the *right* mouse button, then click **Move Here**.

6. Click 📁 **Ice**.

7. Click the **Delete** button ☒.

8. When you see the message, "Are you sure you want to remove the folder 'Ice' and all its contents?" click the **Yes** button.

9. Click 📁 **Advanced** so you can verify that the Kranmer and Wei files have been correctly moved here from the Ice folder.

You've finished organizing Bernard's disk, and as you're getting ready to go, the attendant at the business services center reminds you to be sure to delete any work from the hard drive so it doesn't get cluttered. You should always "clean up" after a session on a computer that doesn't belong to you. You can do so easily by simply removing the Climbing folder from drive C.

To delete the Climbing folder from drive C:

1. Click the **Climbing** folder on drive C, scrolling as necessary to locate it in the Folders list.

2. Click the **Delete** button ☒ to display the Confirm Folder Delete dialog box. See Figure 3-33 on the next page.

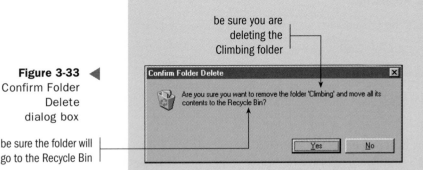

be sure you are
deleting the
Climbing folder

Figure 3-33 ◄
Confirm Folder
Delete
dialog box

be sure the folder will
go to the Recycle Bin

TROUBLE? If a message appears telling you you can't perform this operation, your system administrator might have restricted deletion privileges from the hard drive. Continue reading the rest of the tutorial.

3. Make sure that the message indicates the Climbing folder will be moved to the Recycle Bin.

TROUBLE? If a different filename appears in the Confirm Folder Delete dialog box, click the No button and go back to Step 1.

4. Click the **Yes** button to delete the folder from drive C.

5. Close Explorer.

Quick Check

1. Why is it wise to use the right mouse button rather than the left to drag files in Windows Explorer?

2. When you take one floppy disk out of the disk drive and put another disk in, you should use the _____ command to tell the computer about the switch.

3. True or False: You can copy a file from one floppy disk to another even if you only have one floppy disk drive in your computer and access to a hard drive.

4. True or False: When you delete a folder, you should first move out any files that you don't want to delete.

5. True or False: When you delete files or folders from the floppy disk, they go into the Recycle Bin.

End Note

You look over the structure of folders and files on Bernard's disk and realize that as his business increases the structure will be increasingly more useful. You've used the power of Windows Explorer to simplify tasks such as locating, moving, copying, and deleting files. You can apply these skills to larger file management challenges when you are using a computer of your own and need to organize and work with the files on your hard drive.

Tutorial Assignments

1. Preparing a File Listing Bernard would like a list of all the gear KCS owns. Use the skills you learned in this tutorial to place all the gear files in the Gear folder, delete the Gear subfolders, and then print out the folder's contents.

    a. Start Windows Explorer, place your Student Disk in drive A, then click the drive A device icon. Open the Gear folder and its subfolders in the Folders list, and then move the rope and harness files from each subfolder into the Gear folder.

    b. Delete the Ropes and Equipment folders.

    c. View the files in the Gear folder by date in descending order (the newest first), then print the Exploring screen using the techniques you learned in this tutorial.

2. Copying Files to the Hard Drive Bernard wants to place his sport-climbing client files on the hard drive to work with them on an advertisement campaign. The Sport folder is a subfolder of Advanced, which is itself a subfolder of Clients.

    a. Create a new folder on drive C called "Advertise."

    b. Copy the client files in the Sport folder on your Student Disk to the Advertise folder on the hard drive.

    c. Open the Advertise folder on the hard drive to display the files it contains.

    d. Print the Exploring screen.

    e. Delete the Advertise folder from the hard drive when your printout is complete.

3. Creating a New Folder and Copying Files Use the Quick Format option to format your Student Disk, then make a new Student Disk. Use the Windows 95 New Perspectives Introductory option on the CTI Windows 95 Applications menu. Bernard now wants a folder that contains all the clients he has because he'd like to do a general mailing to everyone advertising an expedition to the Tetons. (*Hint:* The client files are all text files, so consider viewing the files in the root directory by type. Don't forget that there are also client files in the Client folder and its subfolders.)

    a. Create a folder called "All Clients" on the drive A root directory and copy all the text files into the All Clients folder.

    b. Open the Clients folder and all its subfolders one at a time, and copy the text files from those folders into the new All Clients folder.

    c. Print out the Exploring screen showing the All Clients folder *arranged by name.*

    d. Delete the All Clients folder and all its contents. (*Hint:* You don't have to delete the files one at a time. You can simply click the All Clients folder and use the Delete command.)

4. Restructuring a Disk Use Quick Format to format your Student Disk, then make a new Student Disk. This time use the Windows 95 New Perspectives Brief option on the CTI Windows 95 Applications menu (the files you worked with in Tutorial 2). Rearrange the files on the disk so they correspond to Figure 3-34. Create the new folders shown in Figure 3-34. Delete any files or folders that are not shown in the figure. Print out the Explorer screen that shows your new organization and the files in the Yellowstone Park folder *arranged by size.*

Figure 3-34

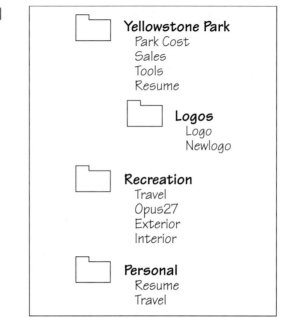

5. Copying Between Floppy Disks Suppose someone who doesn't know how to use the Windows Explorer (she missed class) wants to copy the Guides folder from her Student Disk to another floppy disk. Try this yourself, and as you go through the procedure, write down each Step so this student would be able to follow the Steps and make a copy of Guides without knowing how to use Explorer.

6. Creating a Folder Structure When you complete your computer class, you are likely to use a computer for other courses in your major and for general education requirements such as English and Math. Think about how you would organize the floppy disk that would hold the files for your courses, then prepare a disk to contain your files.

    a. Make a sketch of this organization.

    b. Use Quick Format to erase the contents of your Student Disk.

    c. Create the folder structure on your Student Disk (even though you don't have any files to place in the folders right now). Use subfolders to help sort files for class projects (your composition course, for example, might have a midterm and final paper).

    d. Place an image of the Exploring screen into WordPad using the Print screen key and the methods described in this tutorial.

    e. Use WordPad to write one or two paragraphs explaining your plan. Your explanation should include information about your major, the courses you plan to take, and how you might use computers in those courses.

    f. Print your WordPad document, then close WordPad. You don't need to save this file.

7. Exploring Your Computer's Devices, Folders, and Files Answer each of the following questions about the devices, folders, and files on your lab computers. You can find all the answers using the Exploring window and its menus.

    a. How many folders (not subfolders) are on drive C?

    b. How many of these folders on drive C have subfolders? What is the easiest way to find the answer to this question?

    c. Which folder on drive C contains the most subfolders?

d. Which folder or subfolder on drive C contains the most files? How could you tell?

e. Do you have a Windows folder on drive C? If so, how many objects does it contain?

f. Do you have a DOS folder on your disk? If so, what is the size of the largest file in this folder?

g. Does your computer have a CD-ROM drive? If so, what drive letter is assigned to the CD-ROM?

h. Does your computer have access to a network storage device? If so, indicate the letter(s) of the network storage device(s).

i. How much space on drive C do the files and folders occupy?

8. Separating Program and Data Files Hard-disk management differs from floppy-disk management because a hard disk contains programs and data, whereas a floppy disk (unless it is an installation disk that you got from a software company) generally only contains data files. On a hard disk, a good management practice is to keep programs in folders separate from data files. Keeping this in mind, read the following description, draw a sketch of the folder structure described, then make a sketch of how the current structure could be improved.

The Marquette Chamber of Commerce uses a computer to maintain its membership list and to track dues. It also uses the computer for most correspondence. All the programs and data used by the Chamber of Commerce are on drive C. The membership application software is in a folder called Members. The data file for the membership is in a subfolder of Members called Member Data. The accounting program used to track income and expenditures is in a folder called Accounting Programs. The data for the current year is in a folder directly under the drive C icon called Accounting Data 1997. The accounting data from 1995 and 1996 are stored in two subfolders of the folder called Accounting Programs. The word-processing program is in a folder called Word. The documents created with Word are stored in the Member Data folder. Finally, Windows 95 is stored in a folder called Windows, which has ten subfolders.

Lab Assignments

Windows Directories, Folders, and Files Graphical user interfaces such as MacOS, Windows 3.1, and Windows 95 use a filing system metaphor for file management. In this Lab, you will learn the basic concepts of these file system metaphors. With this background, you will find it easy to understand how to manage files with graphical user interfaces.

1. Click the Steps button to learn how to manipulate directories, folders and files. As you proceed through the Steps, answer all of the Quick Check questions that appear. After you complete the Steps, you will see a Quick Check Summary Report. Follow the instructions on the screen to print this report.

2. Click the Explore button. Make sure drive a: is the default drive. Double-click the a:\ folder to display the folder contents, then answer the following questions:

a. How many files are in the root directory of drive a:?

b. Are the files on drive a: data files or program files? How can you tell?

c. Does the root directory of drive a: contain any subdirectories? How can you tell?

3. Make sure you are in Explore. Change to drive c: as the default drive. Double-click the c:\ folder to display its contents, then answer the following questions:

a. How many data files are in the root directory of drive c:?

b. How many program files are in the root directory of drive c:?

c. Does the root directory of drive c: contain any subdirectories? How can you tell?

d. How many files are in the dos folder?

e. Complete the diagram in Figure 3-35 to show the arrangement of folders on drive c:. Do not include files.

Figure 3-35 ◀

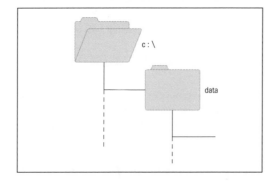

4. Open and close folders, and change drives as necessary to locate the following files. After you find the file, write out its file specification:
   a. config.sys, b.win.ini, c.toolkit.wks, d.meeting.doc
   b. newlogo3.bmp, f.todo.doc

Customizing Windows 95 for Increased Productivity

In this tutorial you will:

- Place a document icon on the desktop and use Notepad's time-date stamp

- Create and delete shortcuts to a drive, a document, and a printer

- Change desktop properties, including background and wallpaper

- Activate a screen saver

- Select monitor color and resolution

- Check energy-saving features

- Use the Control Panel to access system settings

- Customize the mouse, including pointer trails and pointer speed

- Activate accessibility options such as MouseKeys, StickyKeys, and high contrast

- Turn off accessibility options automatically

CASE

Companions, Inc.

Bow Falls, Arizona, is a popular Sun Belt retirement mecca that is at the same time a college town with several distinguished universities and colleges. Beth Yuan, a graduate of Bow Falls University, realized that the unusual mix of the old and young in her town might be perfectly suited to a services business. She formed Companions, Inc. to provide older area residents with trained personal care assistants and to help with housecleaning, home maintenance, and running errands. Beth's company now includes employees who work directly with clients and an office staff that help her manage the day-to-day tasks of running a business. Many of Beth's employees are students at local colleges who like the flexible hours and who enjoy spending time with the elderly residents.

The offices of Companions, Inc. are equipped with computers that maintain client records, schedule employees, manage company finances, develop training materials, and create informational documents about Beth's business. Beth recently upgraded her computers to Windows 95. She has heard that it's easy to change Windows 95 settings to reflect the needs of her office staff. She asks you to find a way to make it easier to access documents and computer resources. She would also like you to give the desktop a corporate look and feel. Finally, she wonders if you can customize Windows 95 to adapt it to users with special needs.

In this session, you will learn how to use the right mouse button to place a Notepad document icon on the desktop and to stamp the document with the time and date. You will create shortcuts to the objects you use most often, including your computer's floppy disk drive, a document, and a printer. You will learn how to use the icons you create and to restore your desktop to its original state.

Right-clicking to Open an Object's Menu

Your mouse device usually has two buttons: one on the left and one on the right. You already know how to use the left mouse button to select an object. You can also click an object with the right mouse button, which is called right-clicking. **Right-clicking** both selects the object and opens a menu that shows the most common commands for that object.

Figure 4-1 ◀
Clicking with the left and right mouse buttons

clicking with left mouse button selects object

click with left mouse button

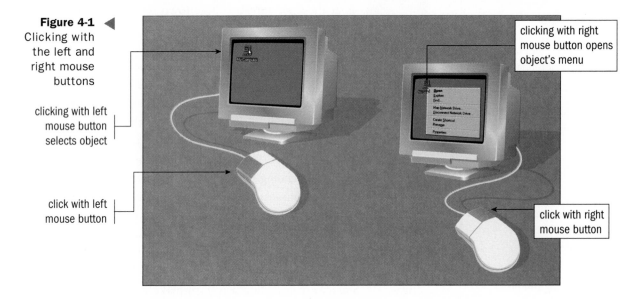

clicking with right mouse button opens object's menu

click with right mouse button

3.1 NOTE

In some Windows 3.1 applications, right-clicking an object opens a menu. In Windows 95, right-clicking has become a standard feature of the operating system so that right-clicking any object opens a menu of common commands and properties.

The left mouse button in Figure 4-1 clicks the My Computer icon to select it. The right mouse button clicks the My Computer icon to open its menu. One of the most important commands on this menu is the Properties command, which gives you access to an object's settings. You'll learn how to use the Properties command in Session 4.2. For now, try opening the My Computer menu by right-clicking its icon.

To open the My Computer menu:

1. Start Windows 95, if necessary.

2. Position the pointer over the My Computer icon.

3. Click the **My Computer** icon with the *right* mouse button. Figure 4-2 shows the menu that opens.

TROUBLE? If you are using a trackball instead of a mouse there might be a third button in the middle of the device. Be sure you click with the button on the far right.

TROUBLE? If your menu looks slightly different from the one shown in Figure 4-2, don't worry. Different computers have different commands, depending on their configuration.

Figure 4-2 ◀
Menu that opens when you right-click the My Computer icon

click the My Computer icon with the right mouse button

Properties command accesses an object's properties

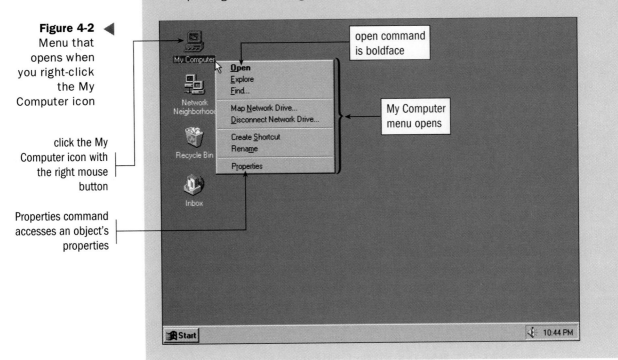

3.1 NOTE

Right-clicking and then selecting Open accomplishes the same result as double-clicking.

Take a look at the My Computer menu that opens when you right-click. The first command for objects on the desktop is usually Open. Clicking Open on this menu accomplishes the same result as left-clicking the object and pressing Enter. For example, in earlier tutorials you opened My Computer by left-clicking and pressing Enter. The Properties command is usually at the bottom of the menu. You'll use this command later in the tutorial.

In the rest of this tutorial, the steps tell you to "right-click" whenever you need to click with the right mouse button. You can right-click almost anything in Windows 95: a file, a folder, a drive, the taskbar, and even the desktop itself.

To close the My Computer menu:

1. Click an empty area of the desktop with the *left* mouse button to close the My Computer menu.

Document-centric Desktops

Windows 95 automatically places several icons on your desktop, such as the My Computer and the Recycle Bin. You can place additional icons on the desktop that represent objects such as printers, disk drives, programs, and documents. For example, you can create an icon right on your desktop that represents your resume. To open this document, you use its icon. You no longer have to navigate menus or windows or even locate the program you used to create the document. A desktop that gives this kind of immediate access to documents is called **document-centric**.

Creating a Document Icon on the Desktop

Employees in the Companions offices keep a log of their telephone calls using Notepad. The Notepad accessory that comes with Windows 95 includes a **time-date stamp** that automatically inserts the date every time you open the document. Figure 4-3 shows you a Notepad document with automatic time-date stamps.

Figure 4-3 ◀
Notepad document with time-date stamp

time and date automatically inserted each time you open document

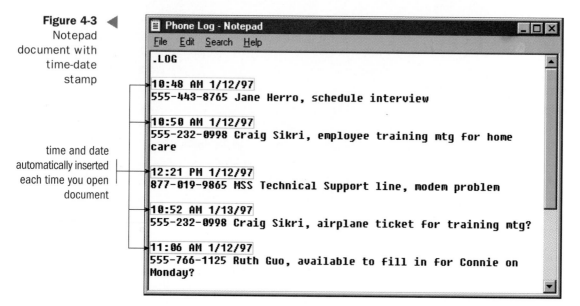

You create a new document on the desktop by right-clicking the desktop and then selecting the type of document you want from a list. An icon, called a **document icon**, appears on the desktop that represents your document.

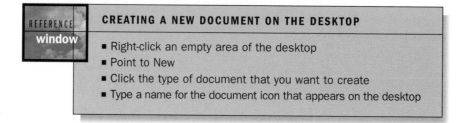

REFERENCE **window**

CREATING A NEW DOCUMENT ON THE DESKTOP

- Right-click an empty area of the desktop
- Point to New
- Click the type of document that you want to create
- Type a name for the document icon that appears on the desktop

The phone log is a perfect candidate for a document on the desktop because employees use it so frequently. When you use the document icon to open the document, Windows 95 locates and starts the appropriate software program for you. To create a Notepad document, you choose the Text Document option.

To create a Notepad document icon on the desktop:

1. Right-click a blank area of the desktop, then point to **New**. The menu shown in Figure 4-4 opens.

TROUBLE? If no menu appears, you might have clicked with the left mouse button instead of the right. Repeat Step 1.

TROUBLE? If your New menu looks different from the one shown in Figure 4-4, don't worry. The document types that appear on the New menu depend on what software is loaded on your computer.

Figure 4-4 ◄
Creating a new
text document

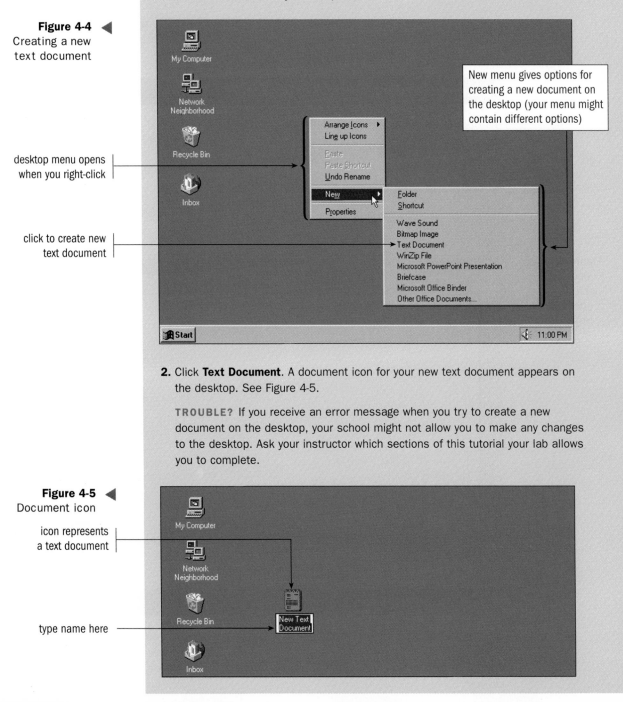

New menu gives options for creating a new document on the desktop (your menu might contain different options)

desktop menu opens
when you right-click

click to create new
text document

2. Click **Text Document**. A document icon for your new text document appears on the desktop. See Figure 4-5.

TROUBLE? If you receive an error message when you try to create a new document on the desktop, your school might not allow you to make any changes to the desktop. Ask your instructor which sections of this tutorial your lab allows you to complete.

Figure 4-5 ◄
Document icon

icon represents
a text document

type name here

3. Type **Phone Log** as the name of your document.

4. Press the **Enter** key. See Figure 4-6.

TROUBLE? If you see a message about changing the filename extension, click No and type Phone Log.txt.

Figure 4-6 ◀
Phone Log
document icon

new name —————

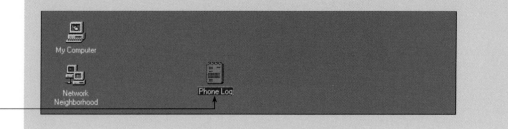

You can often identify an object's type by its icon. The Phone Log document icon 🖼 identifies a Notepad text document. Later in this tutorial you'll see other icons that represent other object types.

Opening a Document on the Desktop

To open a document on your desktop, you click the document icon and then press the Enter key. Windows 95 starts the appropriate program, which in this case is Notepad, and opens the document so you can edit it.

To open the Phone Log:

1. Click the **Phone Log** icon, then press the **Enter** key. Windows 95 starts Notepad. See Figure 4-7.

Figure 4-7 ◀
Phone Log
document
opens in
Notepad

```
📄 Phone Log - Notepad                              _ □ ✕
File   Edit   Search   Help
```

Creating a LOG File

Notepad automatically inserts the date when you open a document only if the document begins with .LOG, in uppercase letters. Your next step is to set up a document with .LOG at the beginning and enter some initial information. Then you will save the document and close it.

To set up the Phone Log document:

1. Type **.LOG**. *You must use uppercase letters.*

2. Press the **Enter** key to move to the next line.

3. Type **Phone Log for Beth Yuan**, then press the **Enter** key.

4. Click the **Close** button ![X] to close Notepad.

5. Click **Yes** to save the changes.

Now you should test the Phone Log document to see if an automatic date-time stamp appears when you open it.

To test the .LOG feature:

1. Open the **Phone Log** document.

TROUBLE? To open the Phone Log document, click it and press Enter or double-click it.

2. Make sure your document contains a date and time stamp. See Figure 4-8.

Figure 4-8 ◀
Time-date
stamp

typing .LOG in
uppercase letters tells
Notepad to insert
time-date stamp

Time-date stamp

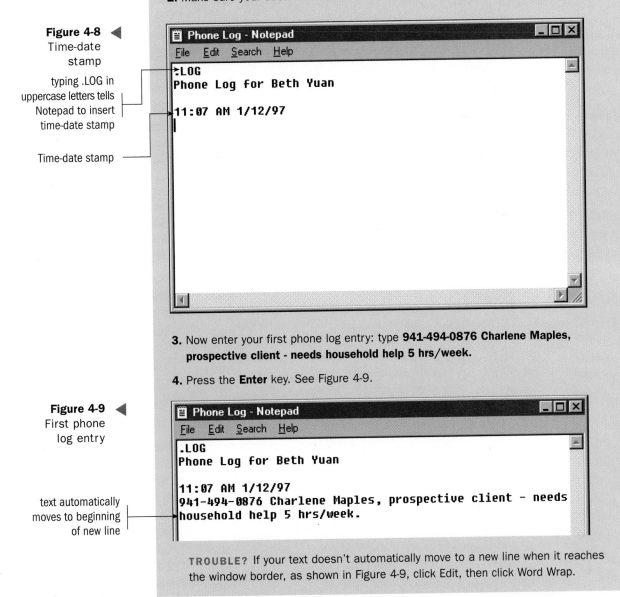

3. Now enter your first phone log entry: type **941-494-0876 Charlene Maples, prospective client - needs household help 5 hrs/week.**

4. Press the **Enter** key. See Figure 4-9.

Figure 4-9 ◀
First phone
log entry

text automatically
moves to beginning
of new line

TROUBLE? If your text doesn't automatically move to a new line when it reaches the window border, as shown in Figure 4-9, click Edit, then click Word Wrap.

5. Click the **Close** button ⊠ to close Notepad.

6. Click **Yes** to save the changes.

Creating Shortcuts to Objects

Beth uses her floppy drive regularly and would like an easier way to access it. It sounds like what she needs is a shortcut icon on the desktop to her floppy drive. A **shortcut icon** provides easy access to the objects on your computer you use most often. You can create shortcut icons for drives, documents, files, programs, or other computer resources such as a printer. These "shortcuts" reduce the number of mouse clicks needed to work with files, start programs, and print.

To create a shortcut, you use Windows Explorer to find the icon for the document, program, or resource for which you want a shortcut. Then you use the right mouse button to drag the icon onto the desktop.

As with other icons on the desktop, to activate a shortcut, you simply click it and press the Enter key or you double-click it. The shortcut locates and then opens the document, program, or resource specified by the shortcut icon. Shortcut icons are identified by the arrow in their lower-left corner, as shown in Figure 4-10.

Figure 4-10 ◀
Comparing
shortcut icon
to document
icon

shortcut icon has
small arrow in lower
left corner

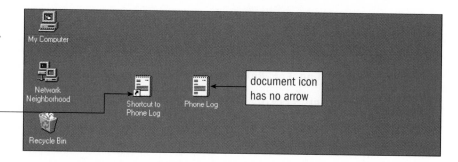

The shortcut icon on the left in Figure 4-10 is a shortcut to a document, whereas the document icon on the right is the *document itself*. You will learn more about this important distinction when you actually create a shortcut icon to a document later on.

REFERENCE window	CREATING A SHORTCUT
	▪ Use Windows Explorer to locate the icon that represents the program, document, or resource for which you want to create a shortcut.
	▪ Make sure you can see the Windows 95 desktop. You must make sure that none of the windows are maximized.
	▪ Hold down the *right* mouse button and drag the icon for the shortcut to the desktop.
	▪ Release the mouse button to display the menu.
	▪ Click Create Shortcuts Here.

Creating a Shortcut to a Drive

Now you will create a shortcut to your floppy drive. Once this shortcut is on the desktop, you can open it to view the contents of your Student Disk, or you can move or copy documents to it without having to start Windows Explorer.

To create a shortcut to your floppy drive:

1. Start the Windows Explorer program.

   TROUBLE? To start Windows Explorer, click the Start button, point to Programs, then click Windows Explorer.

2. Make sure the Exploring window is open, but not maximized.

   TROUBLE? If the Exploring window is maximized, click 🗗.

3. Place your Student Disk in drive A.

   TROUBLE? If your 3½-inch disk drive is B, place your Student Disk in that drive instead, and for the rest of the tutorial substitute drive B wherever you see drive A.

4. Locate the device icon 💾 for 3½ Floppy (A:) in the Folders list on the left side of the Exploring window.

5. Hold down the *right* mouse button while you drag the device icon 💾 for 3½ Floppy (A:) into an empty area of the desktop. The pointer looks like 🗂.

6. Release the mouse button. Notice the menu that appears, as shown in Figure 4-11.

Figure 4-11 ◀
Creating a
shortcut to
drive A

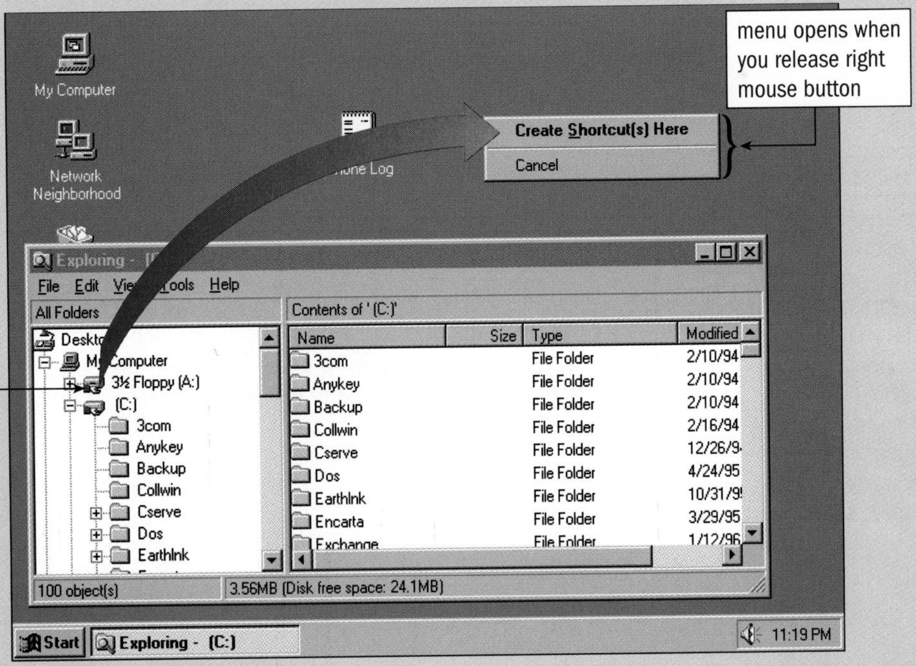

drag icon to an empty
area of the desktop
using the right
mouse button

menu opens when
you release right
mouse button

7. Click **Create Shortcut(s) Here**.

8. Click the **Close** button ❌ to close Windows Explorer. A shortcut labeled "Shortcut to 3½ Floppy (A:)" now appears on the desktop. See Figure 4-12.

Figure 4-12 ◀
Shortcut to
drive A

shortcut icon (notice
the small arrow)

Now you can test the shortcut to see if it gives you immediate access to your Student Disk.

To test the 3½ Floppy (A:) shortcut:

1. Open **3½ Floppy (A:)** using the shortcut icon. A window showing the contents of your 3½ Floppy (A:) drive opens.

2. Click the **Close** button ❌ to close the 3½ Floppy (A:) window.

Using a Shortcut Icon

Beth often works out of her home office and needs to be able to take the phone log with her. You tell her the shortcut makes this easy. All she has to do is move the phone log from the desktop to a floppy disk using the shortcut.

You move a document from your desktop to your Student Disk by dragging it to the shortcut.

3.1 NOTE

Although Windows 3.1 allows dragging in a few isolated circumstances, such as moving a file from one open window to another, Windows 95 allows dragging in many more situations as you'll see in this tutorial.

To move the document from the desktop to a floppy disk:

1. Hold down the *right* mouse button and drag the **Phone Log** icon on the desktop to the 3½ Floppy (A:) shortcut you just created. When you release the right mouse button, a menu opens, as shown in Figure 4-13.

TROUBLE? If the Shortcut to 3½ Floppy (A:) icon is not highlighted, the Phone Log document will not move to drive A. Be sure the Shortcut to 3½ Floppy (A:) icon is highlighted, as shown in Figure 4-13, before you proceed to Step 2.

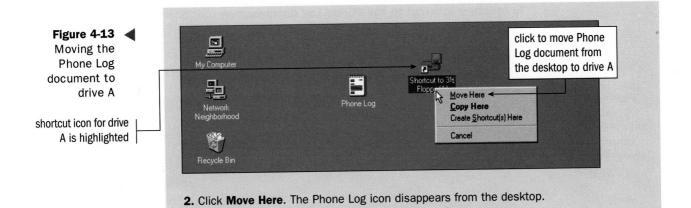

Figure 4-13
Moving the
Phone Log
document to
drive A

shortcut icon for drive
A is highlighted

click to move Phone
Log document from
the desktop to drive A

Move Here
Copy Here
Create Shortcut(s) Here

Cancel

2. Click **Move Here**. The Phone Log icon disappears from the desktop.

When you moved the document icon to the drive A shortcut, the file itself was moved to drive A and off your desktop. You must access the Phone Log by opening drive A. You could open drive A from My Computer or Windows Explorer, but it is handier to use the drive A shortcut. Try using the shortcut method as you add an entry for another phone call.

To open the Phone Log document from the new 3½ Floppy (A:) window and add a new entry:

1. Open **3½ Floppy (A:)** using the shortcut icon to verify that the Phone Log document is on your Student Disk.

   TROUBLE? If you don't see the Phone Log document on your Student Disk, click the Undo Move button 🔄 (or click Edit, then click Undo Move if the toolbar isn't displayed), then repeat the previous set of steps for moving a document to a floppy disk.

2. Open the **Phone Log** document from the 3½ Floppy (A:) window. Windows 95 starts Notepad.

3. Click the last line of the phone log so you can type a new entry.

4. Type **555-885-0876 Frank Meyers, next week's home care schedule.**

5. Click the **Close** button ☒ to close Notepad.

6. Click **Yes** to save the changes.

Creating a Shortcut to a Document

The Phone Log document is now on a floppy disk, as Beth requested, but it no longer has an icon on the desktop. If you want to access the Phone Log document directly from the desktop, you can create a shortcut that automatically starts Notepad and opens the Phone Log from your Student Disk.

To create a shortcut to the Phone Log document on your Student Disk:

1. Hold down the *right* mouse button while you drag the Phone Log icon from the 3½ Floppy (A:) window onto the desktop, as shown in Figure 4-14, then release the mouse button.

Figure 4-14 ◀
Creating a shortcut to the Phone Log document on drive A

your Student Disk might show different folders and files

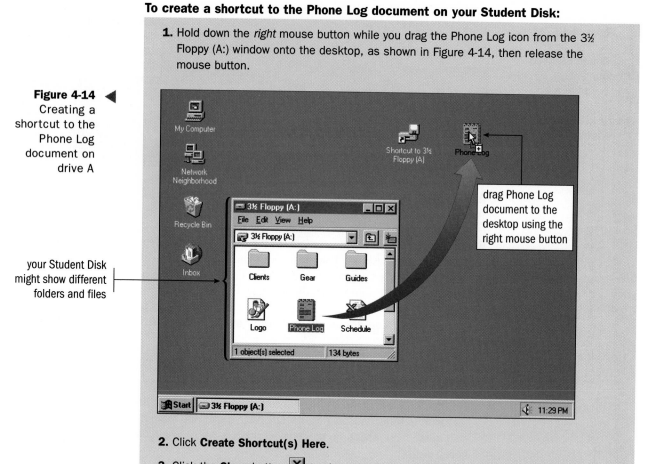

2. Click **Create Shortcut(s) Here**.

3. Click the **Close** button ⊠ to close the 3½ Floppy (A:) window. An icon labeled "Shortcut to Phone Log" now appears on the desktop.

You might wonder if dragging with the left mouse button creates a shortcut icon in the same way as dragging with the right mouse button. The answer is no. If you drag an icon onto the desktop using the left mouse button, you create a *copy* of the document on the desktop, not a *shortcut* to the document. This distinction is important to remember so that you don't find yourself working with a copy when you want to be working with the original. Now you can test the shortcut to see if it automatically opens the Phone Log.

To test the Phone Log shortcut:

1. Open the **Shortcut to Phone Log**. Windows 95 starts the Notepad program, then opens the Phone Log document.

2. Type: **313-892-7766 Trinity River Accounting** at the end of the list of calls.

3. Click the **Close** button ⊠ to close Notepad.

4. Click **Yes** to save the changes.

The shortcut icon you just created is different from the Phone Log icon you created at the beginning of this tutorial. That icon was not a shortcut icon. It was a document icon representing a document that was actually located right on the desktop. A shortcut icon, on the other hand, can represent a document located anywhere. The shortcut icon currently on your desktop represents a document located on your Student Disk. You can tell the difference between an actual document icon and a shortcut icon by looking for a small arrow in the corner of the icon. If there is no arrow, that icon represents the document. Glance back at Figure 4-10 to see this important difference.

If you delete a document icon, you also delete the document. If you delete a shortcut icon (with the arrow) you don't delete the document itself, you are just deleting the shortcut.

Creating a Shortcut to a Printer

You now have a very efficient way to open the Phone Log and to access your floppy drive. You're sure that Beth will be pleased when you tell her. But first you decide to add a printer shortcut to your growing collection of desktop icons so employees can easily print their phone logs and other documents.

You create a printer shortcut in much the same way as you created a shortcut for the floppy drive. First, you locate the printer icon in Windows Explorer. Then you use the right mouse button to drag the icon onto the desktop.

To create a Printer Shortcut:

1. Open Windows Explorer.

   TROUBLE? To open Windows Explorer, click the Start button, click Programs, then click Windows Explorer.

2. If the Exploring window is maximized, click the **Restore** button 🗗 so you can see part of the desktop.

3. Locate and then click the **Printers** folder. It is usually located at the bottom of the Folders list. See Figure 4-15.

Figure 4-15 ◀
Printers folder
in Windows
Explorer

Printers is highlighted ⎯⎯⎯

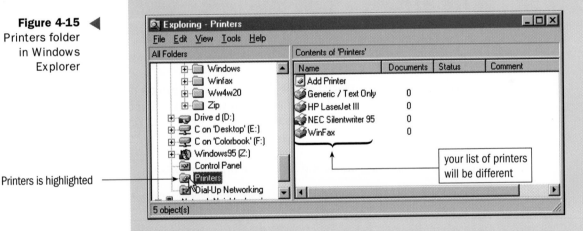

4. Position the pointer over the icon of the printer for which you want to create a shortcut.

   TROUBLE? If more than one printer is listed and you do not know which printer you usually use, ask your instructor or technical support person.

5. Hold down the *right* mouse button while you drag the printer icon to the desktop.

6. Release the right mouse button to drop the printer icon on the desktop.

7. Click **Create Shortcut(s) Here** on the menu. The printer shortcut appears. See Figure 4-16.

Figure 4-16 ◀
Creating a
shortcut to
a printer

drag printer to
desktop with the right
mouse button

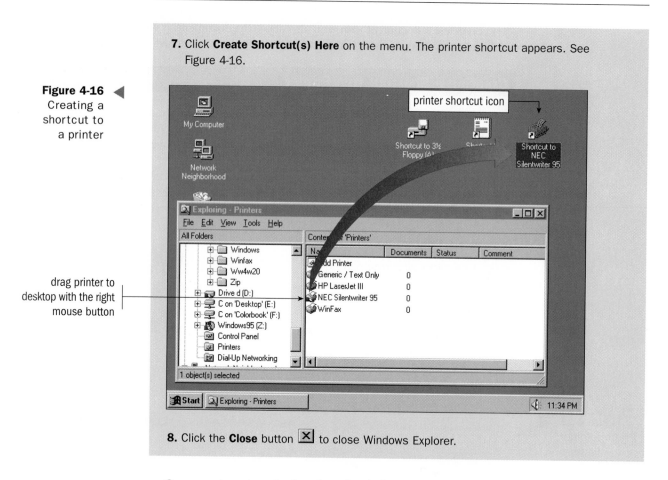

8. Click the **Close** button ☒ to close Windows Explorer.

Once a printer icon is placed on the desktop, you can print a document by dragging its icon to the printer icon. Think of the steps you save by printing this way: you don't have to open any programs or search through menus to locate and open the document or the Print dialog box.

To print the Phone Log document using the printer shortcut:

1. Drag the **Phone Log** shortcut icon using the *left* mouse button to the Printers shortcut icon. See Figure 4-17.

Figure 4-17 ◀
Printing a
document
using shortcuts

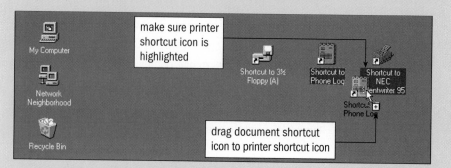

2. When you release the mouse button, watch as Windows 95 starts the Notepad program, opens the Phone Log, prints Phone Log, then closes Notepad. Because your document has an automatic time-date stamp, Windows 95 asks if you want to save the document before closing it. You don't need to save it because you don't have any phone entries to log.

3. Click **No**. Windows 95 closes Notepad without saving the time-date stamp.

Identifying Icons on the Desktop

Your desktop now has three new shortcut icons. Although the names of the shortcut icons help you identify what they are, the icons themselves help you identify the shortcut type. Figure 4-18 shows typical icons you might see on a desktop and the objects they represent.

Figure 4-18 ◀
Types of short-
cut icons you
might see on
the desktop

Icon	Object the icon represents
	Text document
	Floppy drive
	Hard drive
	CD-ROM drive
	Printer
	Folder
	Microsoft Word program
	Microsoft Excel program

When you are opening a document represented by a desktop icon you can usually identify which program Windows 95 will start by looking at the icon representing the document.

Deleting Shortcut Icons

If you are working on your own computer you can leave the printer and drive icons in place if you think you'll find them useful. Otherwise, you should delete all the shortcuts you created so the desktop is clean for the next user. You can delete them one at a time by clicking a shortcut and then pressing the Delete key.

To delete your shortcuts:

1. Click the printer shortcut icon with the *left* mouse button so that it is highlighted.

2. Press the **Delete** key, then click **Yes** to delete the printer icon.

3. Repeat Steps 1 and 2 with the floppy drive shortcut icon.

4. Repeat Steps 1 and 2 with the phone log shortcut icon.

Your desktop is restored to its original appearance.

Quick Check

1. True or false? In a document-centric desktop, the quickest way to open a document is by locating the program that created the document, starting the program, and then using the Open command to locate and open the document.

2. True or false? You can create a document with an automatic time-date stamp in Notepad by typing "log" at the beginning of the document.

3. Name two ways to open a document on the desktop.

4. What happens if you delete a document icon that does not have an arrow on it?

5. What happens if you delete a shortcut icon?

6. What happens if you try to create a shortcut icon by dragging with the left mouse button instead of the right?

SESSION

4.2

In this session you'll change the appearance of your desktop by working with the desktop's property sheets. You'll experiment with patterns and wallpaper, enable a screen saver, try different colors to see how they look, and modify desktop settings to explore your monitor's capabilities.

Viewing Desktop Properties

In Windows 95, you can think of all the parts of your computer—the operating system, the programs, and the documents—as individual objects. For example, the desktop is an object, the taskbar is an object, a drive is an object, a program is an object, and a document is an object. Each object has **properties**, or characteristics, that you can examine and sometimes change. The desktop itself has many properties, including its color, its size, and the font it uses. Most objects in Windows 95 have property sheets associated with them. A **property sheet** is a dialog box that you open to work with an object's properties. To open an object's property sheet, you right-click the object and then click Properties on the menu.

3.1 NOTE

Property sheets are new with Windows 95. They offer easier, more intuitive, and more consistent access to object properties than Windows 3.1.

REFERENCE window

VIEWING AND CHANGING OBJECT PROPERTIES

- Right-click the object whose properties you want to view.
- Click Properties on the menu that opens.
- Click the tab for the property sheet you want to view.
- Change the appropriate settings.
- Click the Apply button to apply the changes and leave the property sheet open, or click the OK button to apply the changes and close the property sheet.

To view desktop properties:

1. Right-click an empty area of the desktop to open the menu. See Figure 4-19.

Figure 4-19 ◀
Desktop menu

right-click to view
desktop properties

menu opens when
you right-click empty
area of the desktop

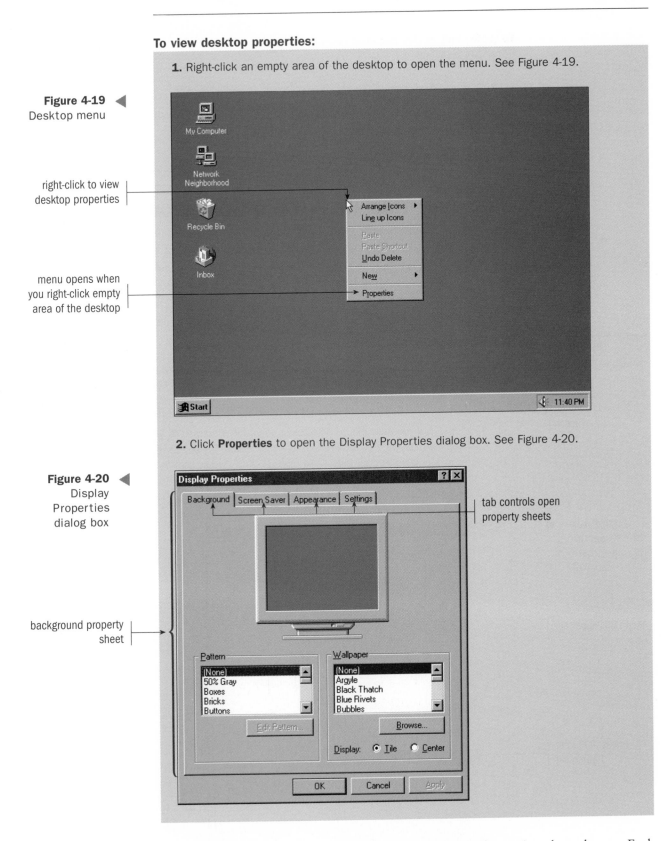

2. Click **Properties** to open the Display Properties dialog box. See Figure 4-20.

Figure 4-20 ◀
Display
Properties
dialog box

tab controls open
property sheets

background property
sheet

The Display Properties dialog box has four tab controls running along the top. Each tab corresponds to a property sheet. Some objects require only one property sheet, but the desktop has so many properties associated with it that there are four tabs. The Background tab appears first, displaying list boxes for the desktop background's pattern and wallpaper. To view a different property sheet, you click its tab.

To view each of the desktop property sheets:

1. Click the **Screen Saver** tab to view options for enabling a screen saver.

2. Click the **Appearance** tab to view options that affect the desktop's appearance.

3. Click the **Settings** tab to view options for the color palette, desktop fonts, and monitor resolution.

4. Click the **Background** tab to return to the first property sheet.

Changing Your Desktop's Background

Beth wants the staff computers in the Companions offices to have a corporate look. You can change the desktop background, which by default is a light forest green with no pattern. Alternatively, you can select a pattern or a graphic, called **wallpaper,** as a background design for your screen using the Pattern and Wallpaper lists on the Background property sheet. The image of a monitor at the top of the Background property sheet lets you preview the pattern or wallpaper you choose.

3.1 NOTE

Windows 95 can use any patterns installed previously by Windows 3.1, and also adds some new ones.

To select a pattern:

1. Click the **Bricks** pattern in the Pattern list. The monitor preview changes to show the Bricks pattern. See Figure 4-21.

   TROUBLE? If the Bricks pattern isn't available, choose a different one.

   TROUBLE? If you have installed Microsoft Plus! for Windows 95, you might have the Desktop Themes feature. You need to turn this feature off before you can work with patterns and backgrounds. Click Start, click Settings, then click Control Panel. Locate and open Desktop Themes, click the Theme list arrow, then click Windows Default. Close the Desktop Themes dialog box and the Control Panel, and repeat Step 1.

Figure 4-21 ◀
Bricks pattern in monitor preview

monitor preview shows Bricks pattern

bricks pattern in Pattern list

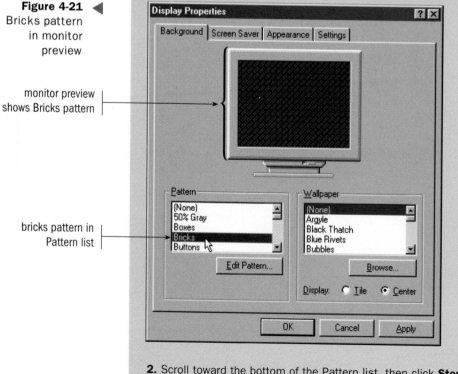

2. Scroll toward the bottom of the Pattern list, then click **Stone**. The monitor preview now shows the Stone pattern.

3. Click the **Apply** button to see how this pattern appears on the entire desktop. See Figure 4-22.

Figure 4-22
Stone pattern applied to desktop

monitor preview shows Stone pattern

Stone pattern in Pattern list

Stone pattern on desktop

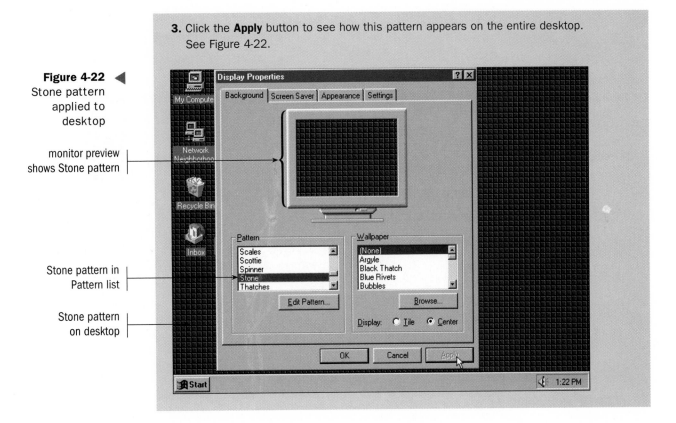

This pattern is not really what Beth wants. You decide to experiment with the Windows 95 wallpapers. Perhaps you can find one that matches Companions' corporate look.

To select a wallpaper:

1. Scroll to the top of the Pattern list, then click **(None)** to deselect the pattern.

2. Click **Bubbles** in the Wallpaper list. The monitor preview displays bubbles.

TROUBLE? If the Bubbles wallpaper isn't available, choose a different one.

3. Click the **Center** radio button to display one copy of the wallpaper image centered on the screen.

4. Click the **Tile** radio button to display multiple copies of the wallpaper image repeated across the entire screen.

5. Click the **OK** button. The resulting wallpaper, shown in Figure 4-23, is a little overwhelming. You know Beth wouldn't want this look, so you return to the Background property sheet to make a different selection.

Figure 4-23 ◄
Bubbles
wallpaper
applied to
desktop

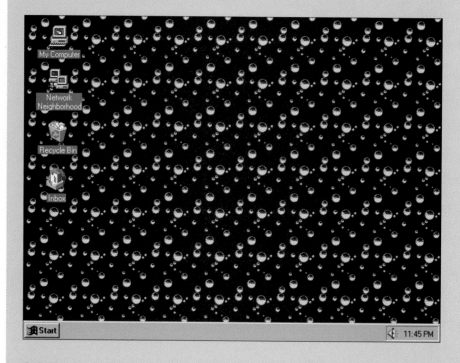

6. Right-click an empty area of the desktop, then click **Properties**.

7. Experiment with the wallpapers available on your computer by clicking them in the Wallpaper list and viewing them in the monitor preview.

8. Click **(None)** when you have exhausted the list, then click the **Apply** button.

None of the wallpapers that come with Windows 95 would suit Beth's corporate image, so you ask her if she would like to use the bitmap image of her company logo. She is enthusiastic; it would be great if clients who come to the offices could see the company logo on office computers.

REFERENCE
window

USING A BITMAP IMAGE AS CUSTOM WALLPAPER

- Right-click an empty area of the desktop, then click Properties.
- Click the Background tab.
- Click the Browse button.
- Locate the folder containing the bitmap image you want to use as wallpaper, then click the bitmap image.
- Click the OK button.
- Click the Center radio button to center the image on the screen or the Tile radio button to display duplicate images.
- Click the OK button.

To use a bitmap image as custom wallpaper:

1. Place your Student Disk in **drive A**, then click the **Browse** button on the Background property sheet.

2. Click the **Drives** list arrow, click drive A, click the file **Logo.bmp**, then click the **OK** button. See Figure 4-24.

   TROUBLE? If your Student Disk does not contain the Logo file, use Quick Format to erase your Student Disk. Then click the Start button, point to Programs, point to CTI Windows 95 Applications, point to Windows 95 New Perspectives Introductory, then click Make Student Disk.

Figure 4-24 ◀
Locating the bitmap image

Logo file ⟶

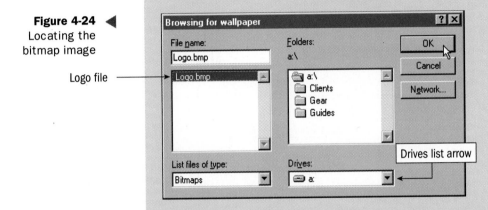

3. Click the **Center** radio button to center the image on the screen, then click the **OK** button to close the Display Properties dialog box. See Figure 4-25.

Figure 4-25 ◀
Companions logo applied as wallpaper

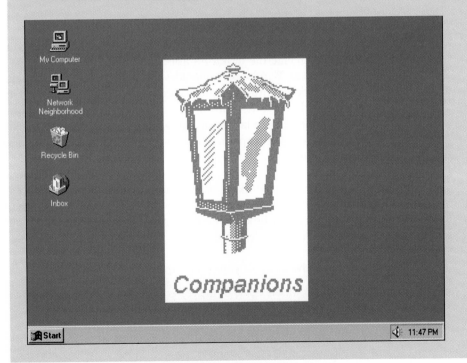

Changing Your Desktop's Appearance

Beth looks over your shoulder and comments that the red of the logo doesn't go very well with the green of the screen background, and she asks if you can try other background colors. The Appearance property sheet gives you control over the color not only of the desktop background but also of all the items on the screen: icons, title bars, borders, menus, scroll bars, and so on.

To view the Appearance property sheet:

1. Right-click an empty area of the desktop, then click **Properties**.

2. Click the **Appearance** tab. The Appearance property sheet is shown in Figure 4-26.

Figure 4-26 ◀
Appearance
property sheet

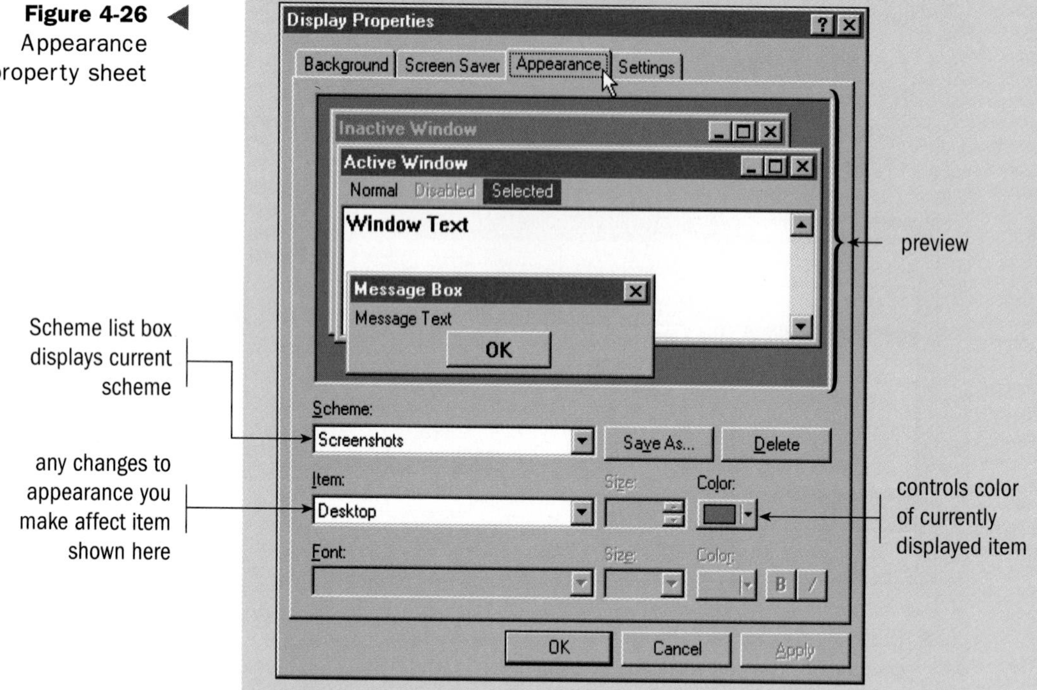

Scheme list box
displays current
scheme

any changes to
appearance you
make affect item
shown here

preview

controls color
of currently
displayed item

The Appearance property sheet includes several list boxes from which you choose options to change the desktop's appearance. Notice the Scheme list box. A **scheme** is a desktop design. Windows 95 includes a collection of design schemes. You can create your own by working with the Appearance property sheet until you arrive at a look you like, then using the Save As button. The default scheme is Windows Standard. However, if your computer is in a lab, your lab manager might have designed and selected a different scheme. Before you experiment with the appearance of your desktop, you should write down the current scheme so you can restore it later.

The preview in the Appearance property sheet displays many of the elements you are likely to see when working with Windows 95. You can click an item in the preview to change its color, and sometimes its font or size. You want to change the desktop itself to red. The Item list box currently displays "Desktop," so any changes you make in the Color list affect the desktop.

To change the color of your desktop to red:

1. Write down the name of the current scheme, which is displayed in the Scheme list box.

TROUBLE? If your Scheme list box is empty, your lab manager might have changed scheme settings without saving the scheme. You should check with your lab manager before making any changes to the Appearance property sheet. If you get permission to change the scheme, make sure you record the original colors so you can restore them when you are finished.

2. Make sure the Item list box displays "Desktop."

TROUBLE? If the Item list box does not display "Desktop," click the Item list arrow, scroll until you see "Desktop," then click Desktop.

3. Click the **Color** list arrow ▾, then click **red**, the first box in the second row. See Figure 4-27.

Figure 4-27 Changing the color of the desktop

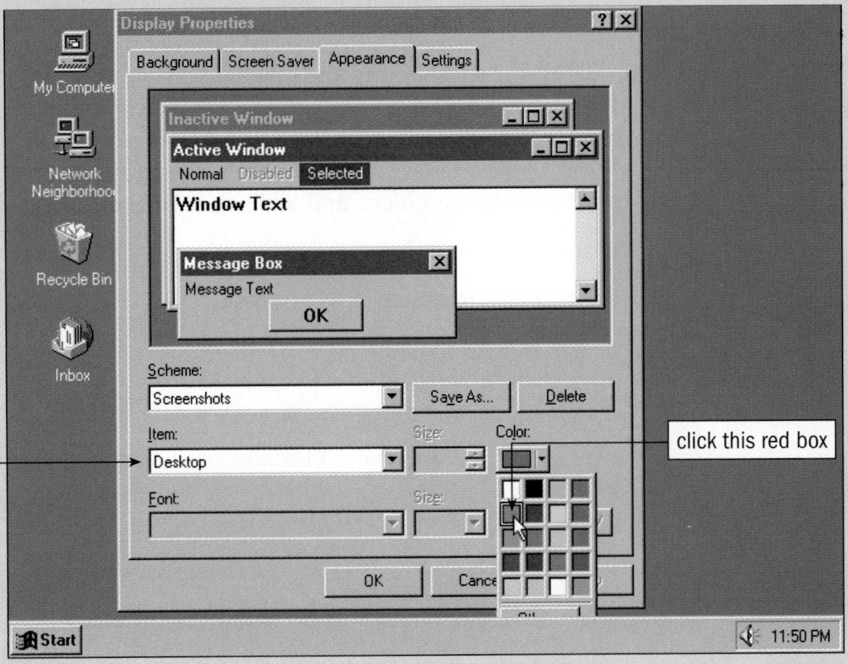

Desktop is item you are changing

The desktop color in the preview changes to red. Notice that the Scheme list box is now empty because you are no longer using the current scheme. You notice that blue title bars looks strange in contrast to the red desktop. You decide to change the title bars to red as well. To change an element, you either click it in the preview or select it from the Item list.

To change the title bars to red:

1. Click the **Message Box title bar** in the preview. See Figure 4-28 for the location of this title bar. Note that the Item list box now displays "Active Title Bar."
2. Click the **Color** list arrow, then click **red**. See Figure 4-28.

Figure 4-28 Desktop with the new color applied

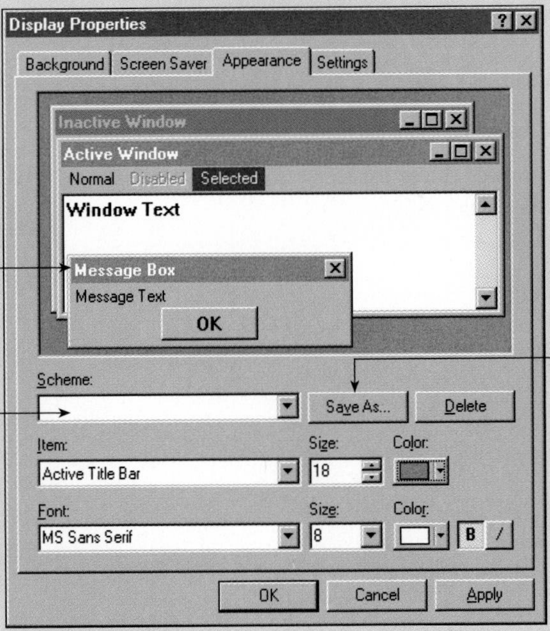

click this title bar to change color of active title bar

Scheme list box is empty

clicking this would let you save the new color scheme

3. Click the **OK** button to see how the desktop looks with a red background.

The next time you open a dialog box, you'll see a red title bar. Open the desktop property sheet to observe this. Then you should restore the desktop to its original settings. You can do this by simply selecting the scheme you wrote down earlier. You could save the colors that match Beth's logo as a scheme if you wanted to. You would click the Save As button, type a name for your scheme, and then click the OK button.

To restore the desktop colors and wallpaper to their original settings:

1. Right-click an empty area of the desktop, then click **Properties**.

2. Click the **Appearance** tab.

3. Click the **Scheme** list arrow, then locate and click the scheme you wrote down earlier. Most likely this is Windows Standard, which you will find at the bottom of the list.

TROUBLE? If your Scheme list box was blank when you began working with the Appearance property sheet, skip Step 3 and instead restore each setting you changed to its original color. Then proceed to Step 4.

4. Click the **Background** tab to open the Background property sheet.

5. Scroll to the top of the Wallpaper list, then click **(None)**.

6. Click the **Apply** button. The original desktop is restored.

Activating a Screen Saver

A **screen saver** blanks the screen or displays a moving design whenever the system sits idle for a specified period of time. In older monitors, a screen saver can help prevent 'burn-in' or the permanent etching of an image that is caused by the same image being displayed for long periods of time. This is not a concern with newer VGA monitors, but if you step away from your computer, the screen saver is handy for hiding your data from the eyes of passers-by.

You can determine how long you want the computer to sit idle before the screen saver activates. Most users find settings between 3 and 10 minutes to be the most convenient. You can change the setting by clicking the up or down arrow on the Wait box.

3.1 NOTE

You can use Windows 3.1 screen savers in Windows 95 but you do not see a preview of what they look like in the Screen Saver property sheet.

To activate a screen saver:

1. Click the **Screen Saver** tab.

2. Click the **Screen Saver** list arrow ▾ to display the list of available screen savers. See Figure 4-29.

Figure 4-29 ◀
Viewing
available
screen savers

available screen
savers; your list
might be different

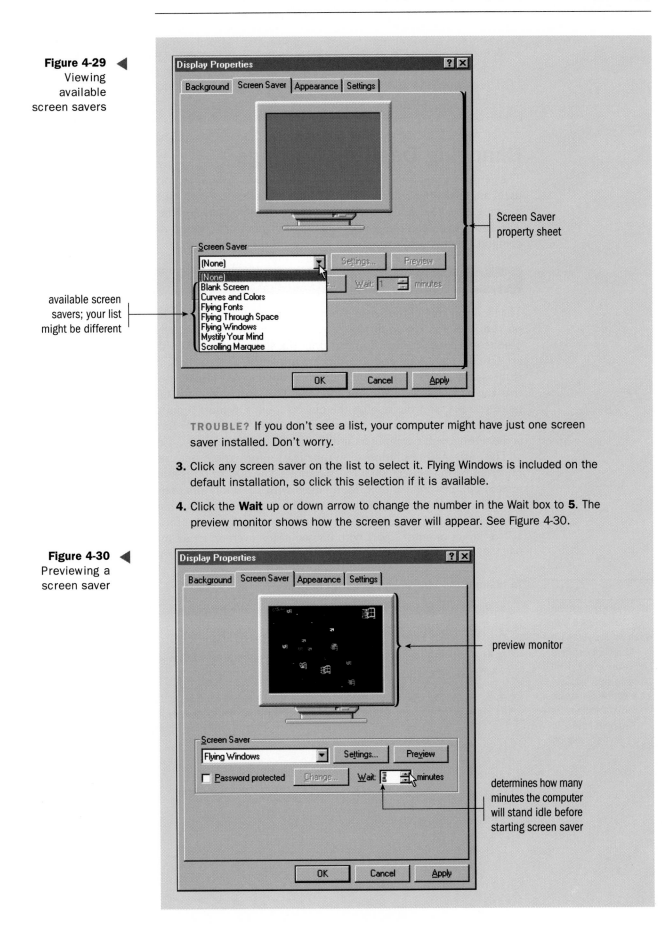

Screen Saver
property sheet

TROUBLE? If you don't see a list, your computer might have just one screen
saver installed. Don't worry.

3. Click any screen saver on the list to select it. Flying Windows is included on the
default installation, so click this selection if it is available.

4. Click the **Wait** up or down arrow to change the number in the Wait box to **5**. The
preview monitor shows how the screen saver will appear. See Figure 4-30.

Figure 4-30 ◀
Previewing a
screen saver

preview monitor

determines how many
minutes the computer
will stand idle before
starting screen saver

5. Click the **Cancel** button to cancel your screen saver changes. If you were working on your own computer and wanted to save the changes, you would click the Apply button to save the changes or the OK button to save the changes and close the Display Properties dialog box.

Changing Desktop Settings

The Settings property sheet gives you control over several important settings that casual users might never need to consider. However, if you want to take full advantage of your monitor type, you should be aware of the options you have on the Settings property sheet. The settings you can change depend on your monitor type and the **video card** inside your computer that controls the image you see on the screen.

Changing the Size of the Desktop Area

The Desktop area of the Settings property sheet lets you display less or more of the screen on your monitor. If you display less, objects will look bigger, while if you display more, objects will look smaller. You can drag the slider bar between these two extremes. You are actually increasing or decreasing the **resolution**, or sharpness, of the image. Resolution is measured by the number of individual dots, called **pixels**, short for picture elements, that run across and down your monitor. The more pixels the higher the resolution, the more you see, and the smaller the objects look. On most monitors in today's computer labs, the standard monitor resolution is 640×480: 640 pixels across and 480 down. This is the setting Beth's computers use.

The 640×480 resolution shows the least information, but uses the largest text and is preferred by most users with 14" monitors. The 800×600 resolution shows more information but uses smaller text. Many users with 15" monitors prefer the 800×600 resolution. The 1024×768 resolution shows the most information but uses the smallest text. Most users find the 1024×768 resolution too small for comfort unless they are using a 17" or larger monitor. Users with limited vision even on larger monitors might prefer the 640×480 setting because objects and text are bigger and easier to see.

3.1 NOTE

When you change the resolution with Windows 3.1 you have to reboot before it takes effect. With Windows 95, you can change the resolution on many monitors without having to reboot.

To change the size of the desktop area:

1. Right-click an empty area of the desktop, then click **Properties**.

2. Click the **Settings** tab to display the Settings properties.

3. Make a note of the original setting in the Desktop area so that you can restore it after experimenting with it.

4. To select the 640×480 resolution, drag the **Desktop area** slider to the left. The preview monitor shows the relative size of the 640×480 display. See Figure 4-31.

Figure 4-31 ◀
640×480
resolution

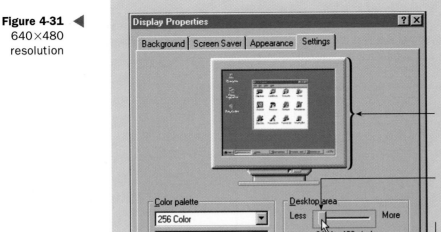

preview monitor

Desktop area slider

resolution shown
in preview monitor

5. To select the intermediate 800×600 resolution, drag the **Desktop area** slider to the center or all the way to the right. The preview monitor shows the relative size of the 800×600 display. See Figure 4-32.

Figure 4-32 ◀
800×600
resolution

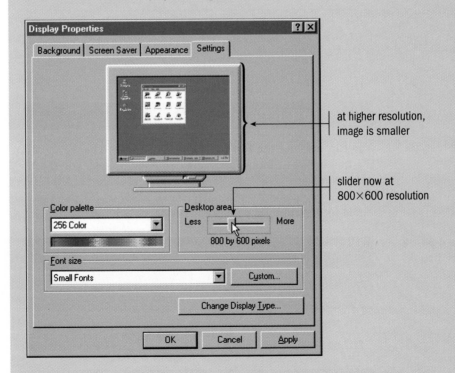

at higher resolution,
image is smaller

slider now at
800×600 resolution

6. To select the 1024×768 resolution, drag the **Desktop area** slider to the right. The preview monitor shows the relative size of the 1024×768 display as shown in Figure 4-33.

TROUBLE? If the 1024×768 resolution doesn't appear, your monitor might not support this setting. Skip Step 6. You also might have higher resolutions available. You can test them yourself by selecting them the same way you selected the resolutions in the preceding Steps.

Figure 4-33 ◀
1024×768
resolution

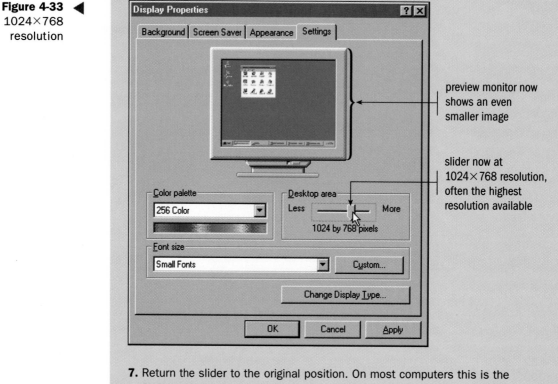

preview monitor now shows an even smaller image

slider now at 1024×768 resolution, often the highest resolution available

7. Return the slider to the original position. On most computers this is the 640×480 resolution.

Changing the Color Palette

You can also use the Settings property sheet to change the **color palette**, which specifies the number of colors available to your computer. For most video cards, the available palettes include 16 colors, 256 colors, High Color (32,000 colors), and True Color (16.7 million colors). Beth's computers have a 256-color palette. Figure 4-34 provides additional information on common palettes.

Figure 4-34 ◀
Color palettes

Palette	Description
16 colors	Very fast, requires the least video memory, sufficient for use with most programs but not adequate for most graphics.
256 colors	Relatively fast, requires a moderate amount of video memory, sufficient for most programs and adequate for the graphics in most games and educational programs. This is a good setting for general use.
High Color (32,000 colors)	Requires an accelerated video card and additional video memory. This setting is useful for sophisticated painting, drawing, and graphics manipulation tasks.
True Color (16.7 million colors)	Requires the most video memory and runs the slowest. This setting is useful for professional graphics tasks, but might not be available or might be too slow on many computer systems.

To view the color palette options:

1. Click the **Color palette** list arrow ▾ to display the list of color palettes. See Figure 4-35.

Figure 4-35 ◀
Available color palettes

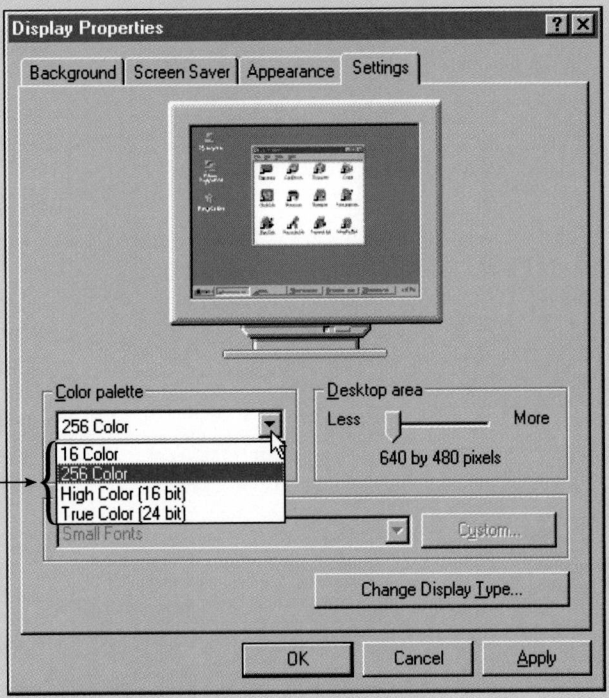

available color palettes; your list might be different (band is hidden underneath)

2. Click each option on the list and watch the color band below the Color palette list box change.

TROUBLE? If the band does not change when you select a different color palette, your monitor or video card doesn't support the selected color palette.

3. Click the **Color palette** list arrow again to close the list.

If you actually wanted to change the Color palette, you would have to reboot Windows 95. You should not change the Color palette setting in a computer lab.

Using Energy-saving Features

Some computer systems come with energy-saving features that power down components of your computer automatically when they've been idle for a specified time period. Computer components such as monitors that support energy-saving features are called **Energy Star compliant** and are often identified by a special Energy Star compliant sticker . Windows 95 includes two energy-saving features for Energy Star compliant monitors. You can find these features on the Screen Saver property sheet, if your monitor is Energy Star compliant. The first, called Low-power standby, switches your monitor to a mode that requires less power. The second feature, called Shut off monitor, shuts off your monitor after a specified period of idleness. When you tell Beth about these features, she is eager to implement them on the Companions computers, because they conserve both energy and money.

If you are in a computer lab, you can take a look at the property sheet to see if these features are available, but *do not* change them.

To view energy-saving features:

1. Click the **Screen Saver** tab. The energy-saving features appear at the bottom of the dialog box. See Figure 4-36.

Figure 4-36 ◀
Energy-saving
features

sticker that looks like this appears on Energy Star compliant components

switches your monitor to a mode requiring less power

energy-saving features might not appear on your computer if your monitor doesn't support them

shuts your monitor off

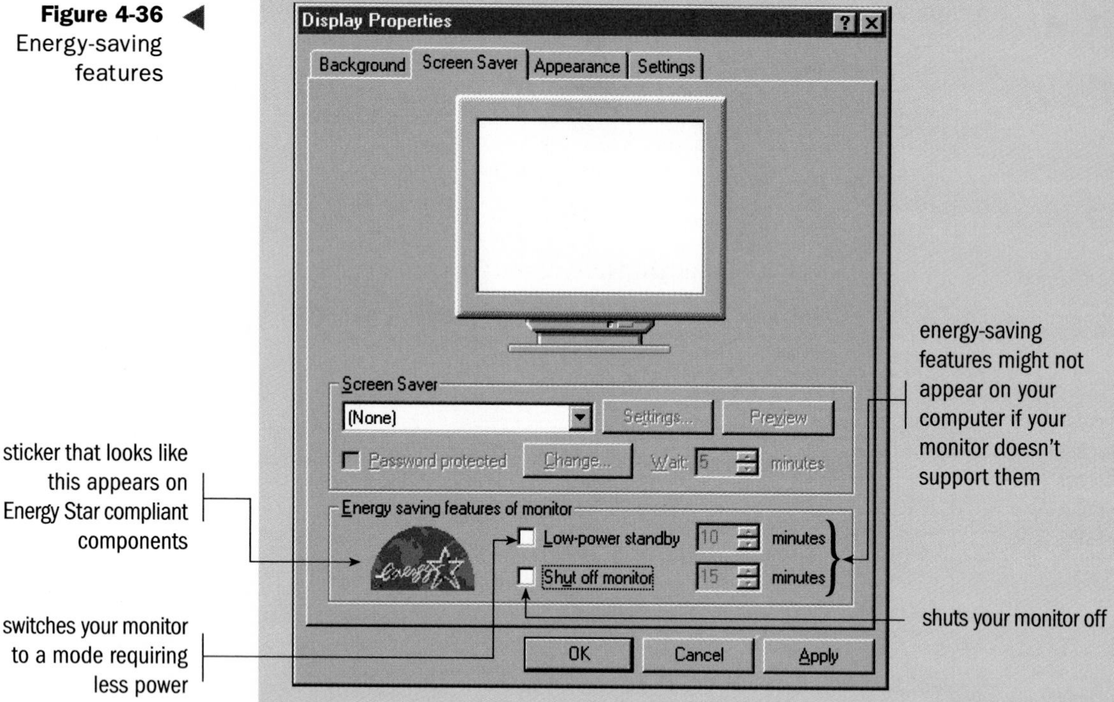

TROUBLE? If there is no Energy saving features area in your Screen Saver property sheet, your monitor might not be Energy Star compliant. If you think your monitor does support these features but the Energy saving features don't appear, click the Settings tab, and then click Change Display Type. Make sure the Monitor is Energy Star compliant check box is checked. Return to the Settings property sheet. If the area still doesn't appear, you might have the wrong monitor or adapter type selected. You can check this setting in the Change Display Type dialog box, but you should change this setting only if you are sure what monitor and adapter type you have.

2. If you are on your own computer and you want to enable this feature, click the **Low-power standby** check box to switch your monitor to standby after the period of time specified in the corresponding spin box.

3. If you are on your own computer and you want to enable this feature, click the **Shut off monitor** check box to turn off your monitor after the period of time specified in the corresponding spin box.

4. Click the **Cancel** button to close the Display Properties dialog box without making any further changes to your desktop.

If you have your own computer, you can combine screen-saver and energy-saving features. For example, you could specify five minute intervals for the three features: after five minutes your screen saver turns on, after 10 minutes your monitor goes into standby mode, and after 15 minutes your monitor shuts off.

Quick Check

1. True or false? Although a document is an object, and so is a drive, the desktop is not an object.

2. How do you open an object's property sheet?

3. Name three desktop properties you can change with the desktop property sheets.

4. If you have an older monitor and you want to protect it from harm caused by the same image being displayed for a long time, what can you do?

5. What does it mean to say a monitor's resolution is 640×480?

6. Users with limited vision might want to use which resolution: 640×480, 800×600, or 1024×768? Why?

7. What is the disadvantage of using a color palette with the most possible colors, like True Color, which can display 16.7 million colors on a monitor?

8. If you are shopping for a new monitor and want to make sure you can use the Windows 95 power-saving features on it, what sticker should you look for on the package?

SESSION 4.3

Windows 95 lets you further increase productivity by giving you control over your working environment. Customizing mouse settings can make some operations, especially graphics operations, easier. Depending on whether you are left- or right-handed, you might want to change other mouse settings. You might also want to take advantage of a variety of accessibility options, depending on your circumstances. In this session, you'll use the Control Panel to locate and adjust some of these settings.

Using the Control Panel

Windows 95 includes a **Control Panel**, available through the Start menu, that centralizes many of your computer's operations and customization features. You'll find the property sheets for many objects, including the desktop, on the Control Panel, as well as other tools that help you control your computer's settings. The Control Panel is so useful that you might want to place a shortcut to it on your desktop.

REFERENCE window

USING THE CONTROL PANEL TO CUSTOMIZE SETTINGS

- Click Start, point to Settings, then click Control Panel.
- Click the setting you want to work with, then press Enter.
- Change the settings in the dialog box that opens.
- Click OK.

To open the Control Panel:

1. Make sure you are at the Windows 95 desktop and no windows are open.

2. Click the **Start** button [Start], point to **Settings**, then click **Control Panel**.

    TROUBLE? If a message appears indicating that the Control Panel is not available, you might be in a computer lab with limited customization access. Ask your instructor or lab manager for options.

3. Click **View**, then click **List** to display the icons as in Figure 4-37.

    TROUBLE? Because some tools are optional, your Control Panel might display different tools than the ones shown in Figure 4-37.

Figure 4-37 ◄
Control Panel

list of available tools;
yours might be
different

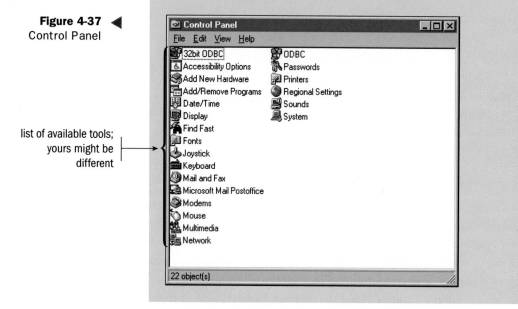

Customizing the Mouse

The Mouse Properties dialog box, available through the Control Panel, lets you customize the mouse settings. You can configure it for the right or left hand, you can adjust the double-click speed, you can turn on pointer trails to make it easier to locate the pointer, and you can adjust the pointer speed. Beth, and two of her employees, are left-handed, so one of the first things you want to do is experiment with the left-handed mouse settings.

Configuring the Mouse for the Right or Left Hand

You can configure the mouse for either right-handed or left-handed users. If you select the left-handed setting, the operations of the left and right mouse buttons are reversed. If you are instructed to click the *right* mouse button, you must click the *left* mouse button, and vice versa. *Check with your instructor or lab manager before you change this setting on a school lab computer, and make sure to change it back before you leave.*

To configure the mouse for right-handed or left-handed users:

1. Click the **Mouse** icon in the Control Panel, then press the **Enter** key to display the Mouse Properties dialog box. You can set the mouse for right-handed users or left-handed users by clicking the appropriate radio button. See Figure 4-38.

Figure 4-38 ◀
Buttons
property sheet

options that
determine left-
handed or right-
handed mouse
operations

descriptions of
mouse operations

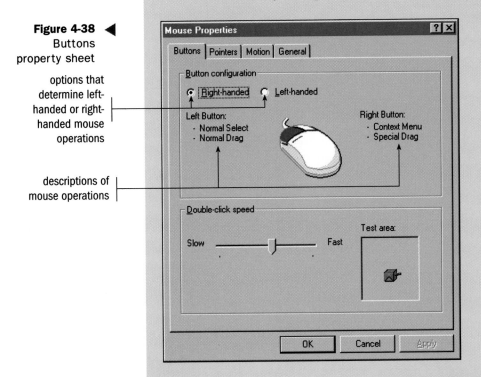

2. Click the **Right-handed** radio button if you are right-handed; click the **Left-handed** radio button if you are left-handed. Notice that as you change this setting the descriptions of mouse operations in the preview change.

3. If you are working on your own computer, click the **Apply** button to apply your changes, then test the new mouse setting by dragging the **Mouse Properties** dialog box with the appropriate mouse button.

4. Return this setting to its original state, then click the **Apply** button.

   TROUBLE? If clicking Apply doesn't seem to work, try using the other mouse button!

Adjusting Double-Click Speed

Double-clicking is equivalent to clicking an object and pressing Enter, or right-clicking an object and clicking Open. Many new users have difficulty double-clicking, which is why Microsoft designed Windows 95 to work without double-clicking. However, some users find double-clicking the quickest way to work. Beth wants you to experiment with slowing down the double-click speed.

To test the current double-click speed:

1. Position the pointer over the purple box in the Test area of the Mouse Properties dialog box, as shown in Figure 4-39.

Figure 4-39 ◀
Testing double-click speed

double-click slider ————

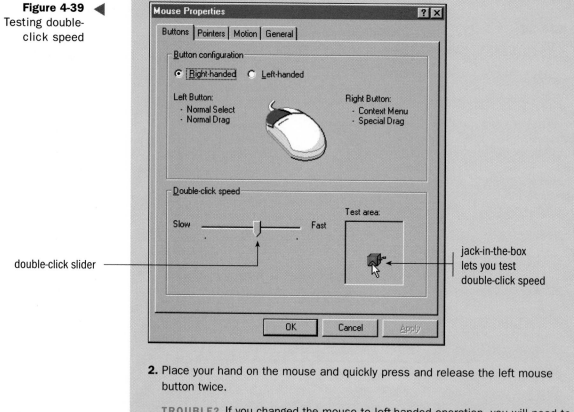

jack-in-the-box
lets you test
double-click speed

2. Place your hand on the mouse and quickly press and release the left mouse button twice.

   TROUBLE? If you changed the mouse to left-handed operation, you will need to double-click by quickly pressing and releasing the *right* mouse button twice.

3. If you double-click successfully, the jack-in-the-box pops out of the box.

4. Double-click the **purple box** again to close it.

   TROUBLE? Don't worry if you can't open the jack-in-the-box. In the next series of steps you'll learn how to adjust the double-click speed for your convenience.

If you have trouble double-clicking, you can slow down the double-click speed using the Double-click speed slider bar. *Check with your instructor or lab manager before you change this setting on a school lab computer, and make sure to change it back before you leave.*

To slow down the double-click speed:

1. Drag the **Double-click speed** slider toward Slow. This lets you take more time between the two clicks.

2. Double-click the **jack-in-the-box** to see if you can make it pop up.

3. If you still cannot successfully double-click, drag the **Double-click speed** slider even farther toward Slow, then repeat Step 2.

4. Once you can successfully double-click, try increasing or decreasing the double-click speed to find the most comfortable speed for you.

5. If you are using your own computer, click the **Apply** button to change the double-click speed to the new setting.

Using Pointer Trails

A **pointer trail** is a trail of pointers that appears on the screen in the wake of the pointer as you move it, like the wake of a boat. Locating the pointer is sometimes difficult, especially on some notebook computer displays. You might find the pointer trail helpful if you occasionally have trouble locating the pointer on your screen. For example, if Beth is on a business trip, she might enable the pointer trail while she uses her notebook computer in a dimly lit hotel room. Users with vision problems might also find this feature helpful. *Check with your instructor or lab manager before you change this setting on a school lab computer, and make sure to change it back before you leave.*

3.1 NOTE

Pointer trails are the same thing as Mouse Trails in Windows 3.1.

To turn on the pointer trail:

1. From the Mouse Properties dialog box, click the **Motion** tab to display the Motion property sheet. See Figure 4-40.

Figure 4-40 ◀
Motion property sheet

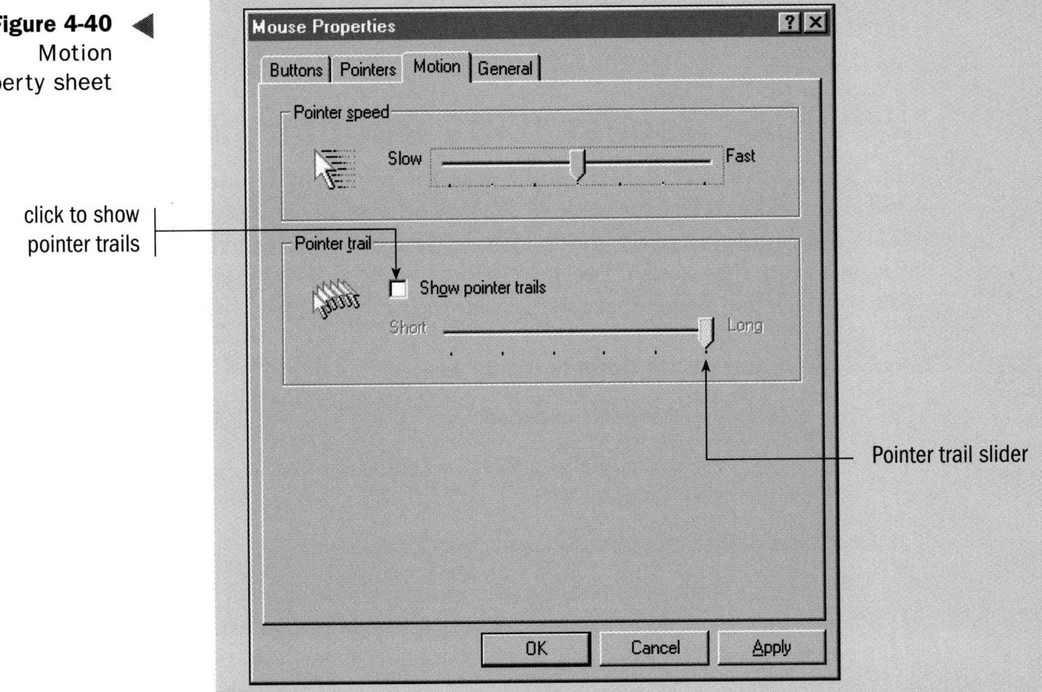

click to show
pointer trails

Pointer trail slider

2. Click the **Show pointer trails** check box.

3. Move the mouse. A trail of pointers follows the pointer when you move it.

4. To increase the length of the trail, drag the **Pointer trail slider** toward Long.

5. To decrease the length of the trail, drag the **Pointer trail slider** toward Short.

6. Click the **Apply** button if you want to leave pointer trails on, or, if you prefer to work without pointer trails, click the **Show pointer trails** check box again to remove the check mark.

Adjusting Pointer Speed

You can also adjust the pointer speed or the relative distance that the pointer moves on the screen when you move the mouse. *Check with your instructor or lab manager before you change this setting on a school lab computer, and make sure to change it back before you leave.*

To adjust the pointer speed:

1. Make sure the the Motion tab of the Mouse Properties dialog box is displayed.

2. To decrease the pointer speed, drag the **Pointer speed slider** toward Slow.

3. To increase the pointer speed, drag the **Pointer speed slider** toward Fast.

4. Adjust the pointer speed to the setting that is most comfortable for you, then click the **Apply** button.

5. Click the **OK** button to close the Mouse Properties dialog box.

Activating Accessibility Options

There is one other way you can customize the mouse in Windows 95: you can set the numeric keypad to take over some of the functions of the mouse. This option is not available on the Mouse property sheet. Instead, you need to open the Accessibility Options dialog box from the Control Panel. In this dialog box, Windows 95 includes many accessibility options that make computers easier to use for people with disabilities.

3.1 NOTE

Accessibility options are new with Windows 95.

To open the Accessibility Options dialog box:

1. Make sure the Control Panel is open.

   TROUBLE? If the Control Panel is not open, click the Start button, click Settings, then click Control Panel.

2. Click the **Accessibility Options** icon in the Control Panel.

   TROUBLE? If the Accessibility Options icon does not appear in the Control Panel, you might need to ask your lab manager to install Accessibility Options. If you are working on your own computer, you can install it yourself. Click the Add/Remove Programs icon in the Control Panel, click Windows Setup, then click Accessibility Options, click the OK button, then follow the instructions on the screen to install Accessibility Options from the original disks.

3. Press **Enter** to display the Accessibility Options dialog box. See Figure 4-41.

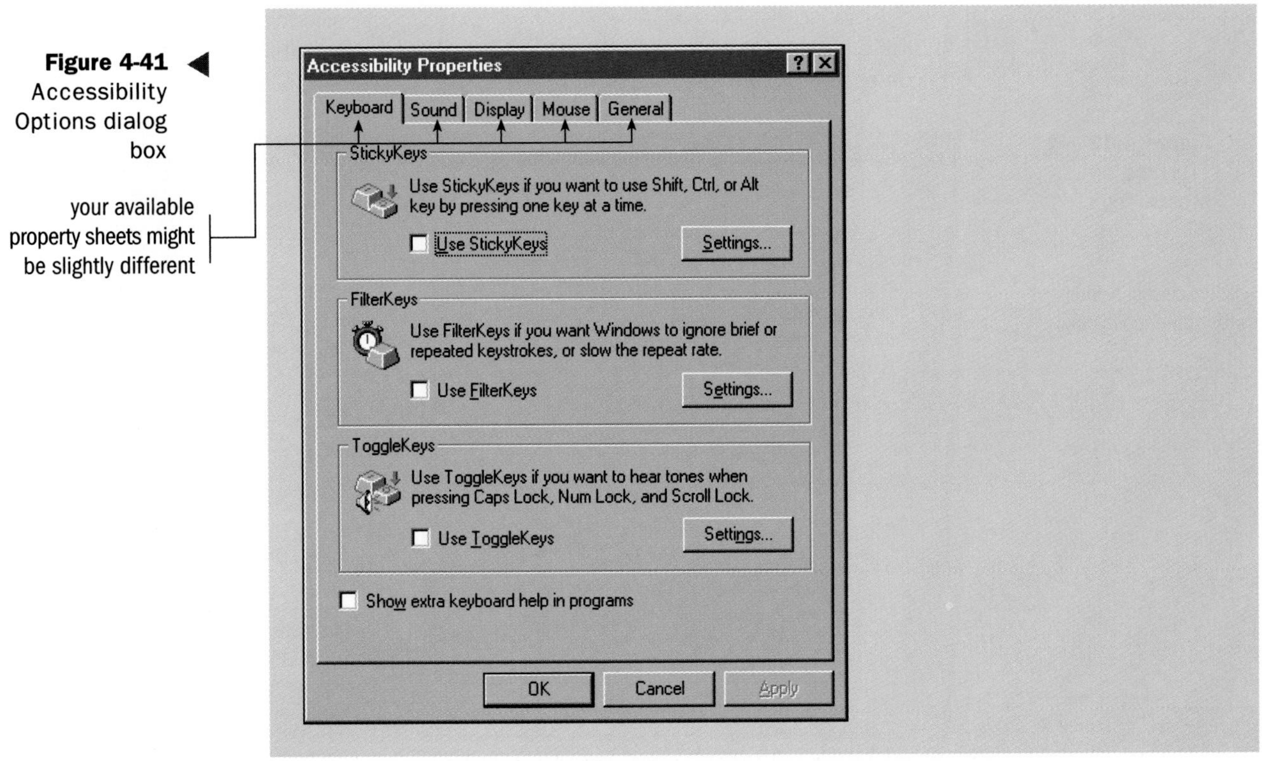

Figure 4-41 ◄
Accessibility
Options dialog
box

your available
property sheets might
be slightly different

There are five property sheets available through the Accessibility Options dialog box: Keyboard, Sound, Display, Mouse, and General. Don't worry if you don't have all these tabs. In this session you explore some of the most helpful accessibility options. For example, if you have restricted movement, you can use the keyboard instead of the mouse and can simplify some key press sequences. If you have limited vision, you can select high-contrast mode to make it easier to see the objects and text on the screen.

Using Keys to Control the Pointer

All users occasionally have trouble using the mouse to precisely control the pointer when using programs such as Paint or other drawing or graphics programs. You can turn on MouseKeys to control the pointer with the numeric keypad as well as with the mouse. This is also a useful feature if you have a temporary or permanent hand injury.

To turn on MouseKeys:

1. Click the **Mouse** tab in the Accessibility Properties dialog box.

2. Click the **Use MouseKeys** check box to place a check mark in it.

3. Click the **Apply** button to activate MouseKeys. After a short time, the MouseKeys icon appears at the right end of the taskbar. See Figure 4-42.

Figure 4-42 ◀
Turning on
MouseKeys

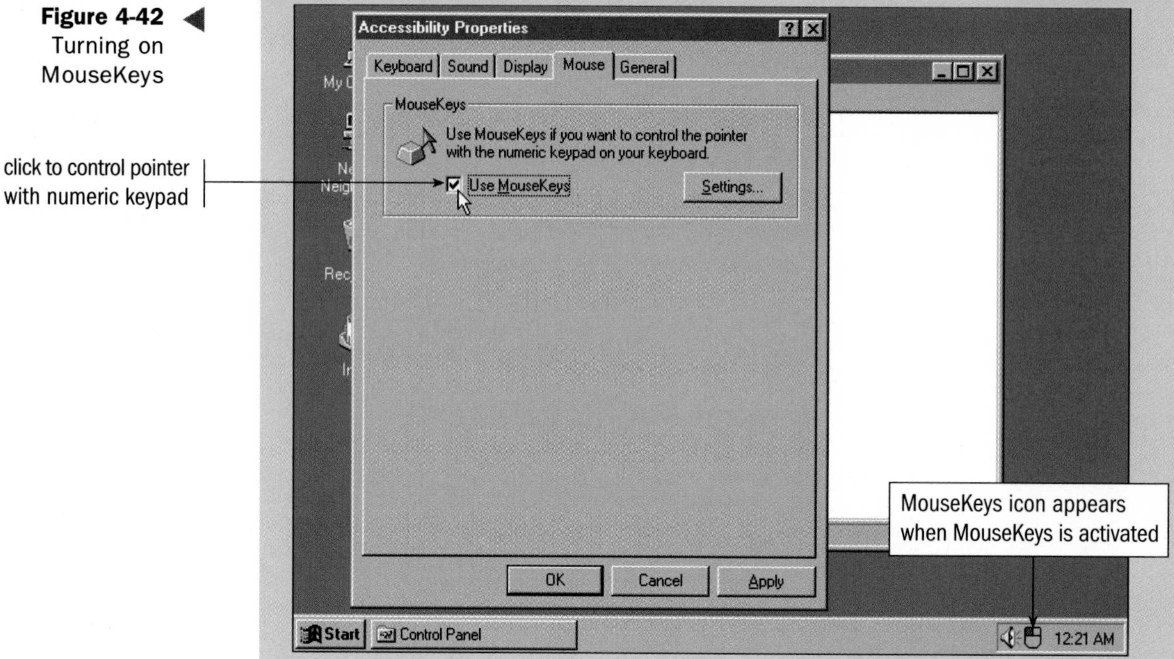

click to control pointer
with numeric keypad

MouseKeys icon appears
when MouseKeys is activated

When the MouseKeys feature is active, you can control the pointer using either the mouse or the keys on the numeric keypad. Before you try working with MouseKeys, study Figure 4-43, which summarizes the mouse actions you can duplicate using keys on the numeric keypad.

Figure 4-43 ◀
MouseKeys
actions and
corresponding
keys

Mouse Action	Corresponding Numeric Keypad Key
Move pointer horizontally	Press 4 to move left, 6 to move right
Move pointer vertically	Press 8 to move up, 2 to move down
Move pointer diagonally	Press 7, 1, 9, and 3
Click	Press 5
Double-click	Press + (plus)
Right-click	Press – (minus), then press 5
Begin dragging after pointing to object	Press 0
End dragging	Del
Move a single pixel at a time	Press and hold Shift, then use directional keys

To practice using MouseKeys:

1. Use the numeric keypad to move the pointer over the **Start** button. The End key moves you to the lower left.

TROUBLE? Most keyboards have two keypads: one with only arrows and one with numbers and arrows. Make sure you are using the keypad with numbers. If the pointer doesn't move when you press the number keys, press the NumLock key on the keyboard.

TROUBLE? If you waited very long to start using MouseKeys, it's possible that Windows 95 is set to reset accessibility options after a specified amount of time. Return to the Mouse property sheet, and then reset MouseKeys by clicking Apply. Then click the General tab, and check if Automatic reset is enabled. If it is, click the check box to turn it off for now.

2. Press **5** once the pointer is over the Start button.

3. Hold down the **8** key to move the pointer to **Programs**, then press **5**.

4. Move the pointer to **Accessories**, then press **5**.

5. Move the pointer to **Paint**, then press **5** to start the Paint program.

6. Practice moving the pointer by pressing the **7 8 9**, **4 6**, and **1 2 3** number keys on the numeric keypad.

7. Press the **0** key on the numeric keypad to start drawing. Press the number keys to move the pointer and draw precise vertical, horizontal, and diagonal lines. See Figure 4-44.

Figure 4-44 ◀
Drawing in
Paint using
MouseKeys

draw any shape
you want

pressing number keys
moves this pointer

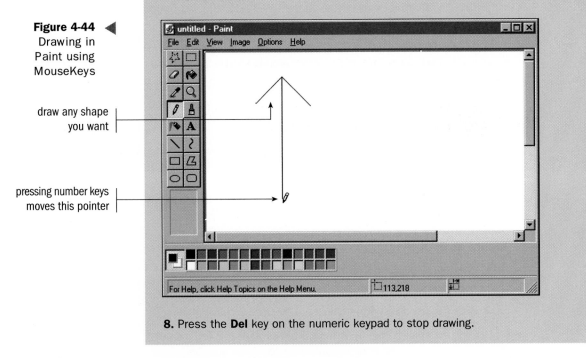

8. Press the **Del** key on the numeric keypad to stop drawing.

MouseKeys is especially useful for drawing precise diagonal lines in a graphics package like Paint, although, as you've probably discovered, it is slower. Now close Paint and deactivate MouseKeys.

To use MouseKeys to close the Paint window:

1. Use the keys on the numeric keypad to move the pointer over the **Close** button ⊠ on the Paint window.

2. Press the **5** key to click ⊠.

3. Use the keys on the numeric keypad to move the pointer over the **No** button on the Paint dialog box, then press the **5** key to close Paint.

4. Click the **Use MouseKeys** check box to turn this feature off.

Simplifying Key Operation with StickyKeys

StickyKeys is a feature that makes Windows 95 easier for users who have trouble holding down one key while pressing another key. Three keys typically used in conjunction with other keys are the Shift key, the Ctrl key, and the Alt key. These keys are also known as **modifier keys**—you hold them down while pressing another key to modify the action of the second key. Many actions that you perform with the mouse can also be performed with modifier keys. For example, instead of clicking the Start button to open the Start menu, you can use Ctrl+Esc. Keys combinations such as these are often called **keyboard shortcuts**. To more clearly show the effect of StickyKeys, you'll start by using a keyboard shortcut without StickyKeys enabled.

To test the normal behavior of a modifier key:

1. Click the **Control Panel** button on the taskbar to bring the Control Panel window to the foreground.

2. Notice the underlined character in each word on the menu bar. For example, notice the underlined F in File and the underlined V in View. You can use the underlined character with a modifier key to open the menu in a single step.

3. Press and hold the **Alt** key, then press **F** to display the File menu.

4. Press **Esc** to close the File menu.

5. Click the **Minimize** button ▬ to minimize the Control Panel window.

Now try enabling StickyKeys to see how it affects the way you use key combinations such as Alt+F.

To turn on StickyKeys:

1. Click the **Keyboard** tab in the Accessibility Properties dialog box to display the Keyboard properties.

2. Click the **Use StickyKeys** check box to place a check mark in it.

3. Click the **Apply** button to activate StickyKeys. After a few moments the StickyKeys icon appears in the bottom right corner of the taskbar. See Figure 4-45.

Figure 4-45 ◀
Activating
StickyKeys

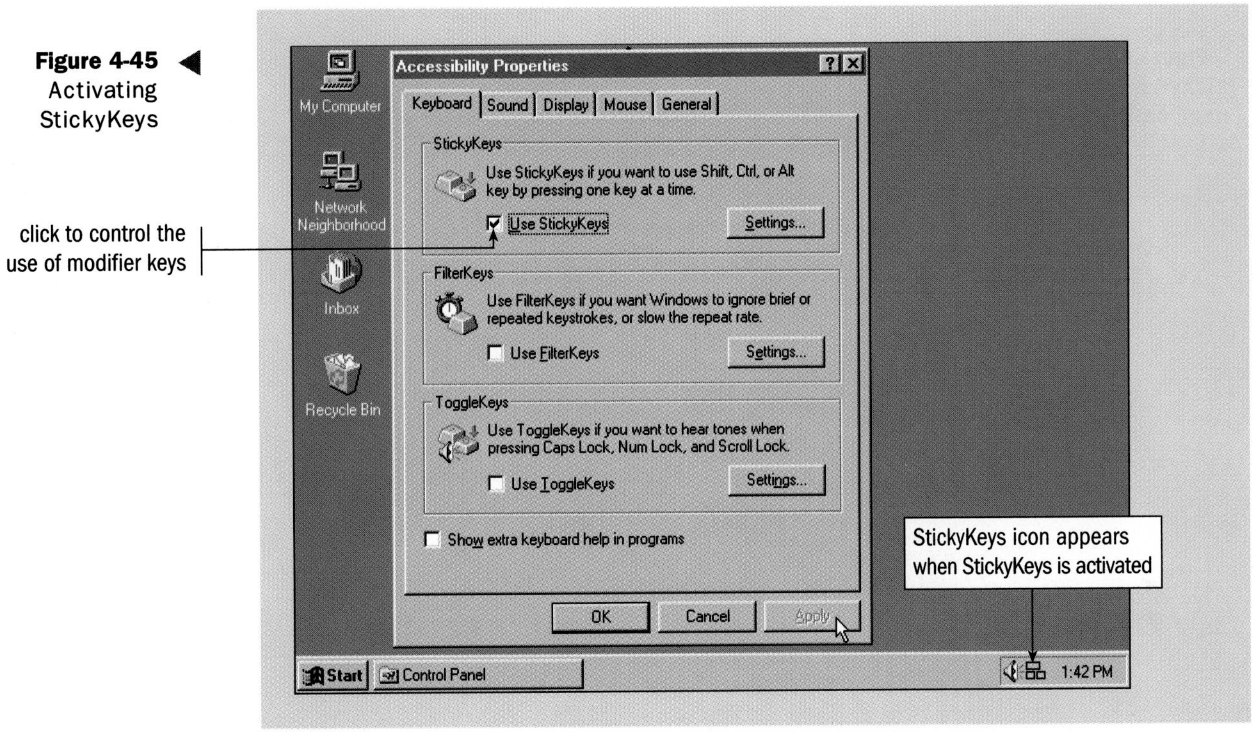

click to control the
use of modifier keys

StickyKeys icon appears
when StickyKeys is activated

Once StickyKeys is enabled, you can press and release the modifier key and then press the action key to take the place of the keyboard shortcut. When you press the modifier key, the lower-right key in the StickyKeys icon is shaded.

To test the effect of StickyKeys:

1. Click the **Control Panel** button on the taskbar to bring the Control Panel window to the foreground.

2. Press and release the **Alt** key. A sound indicates that a StickyKey has been pressed and the bottom right box in the StickyKeys icon is filled in. See Figure 4-46. The sound and the icon indicate that the next key you press will be combined with the Alt StickyKey.

    TROUBLE? If you didn't hear a sound, sounds might not be enabled on your StickyKeys settings. You can enable sounds by clicking the Settings button in the Keyboard property sheet and selecting the sound settings you want.

Figure 4-46 ◀
StickyKey has
been pressed

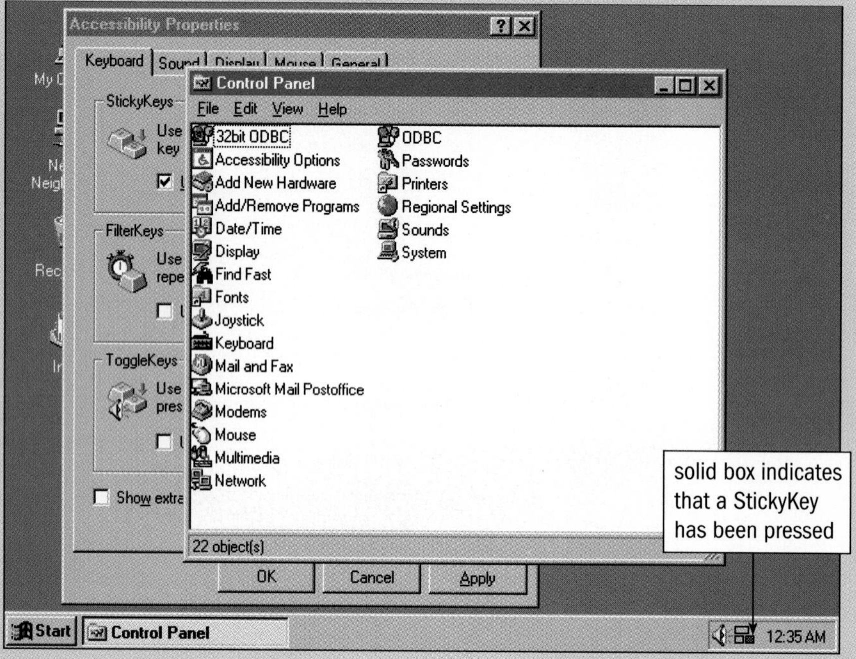

3. Press the **F** key. Because StickyKeys was activated, you did not have to hold down the Alt key while you pressed the F.

4. Press **Esc** to close the File menu.

5. Click the **Minimize** button 🗕 to minimize the Control Panel window.

6. Click the **Use StickyKeys** check box to remove the check mark, then click the **Apply** button to deactivate StickyKeys. The StickyKeys icon disappears from the right end of the task bar.

StickyKeys can be very helpful for users who want to use shortcut keys but have difficulty holding down one key while pressing another.

Enabling High Contrast

The Display property sheet lets you set the screen display to high contrast. **High contrast** uses large white letters on a black background and greatly increases the size of the title bar and window control buttons. In high-contrast mode, objects and text stand out more visibly. If you have limited vision, a dark office, or you're not wearing your glasses, high-contrast mode can make it much easier to see what's on your screen.

To turn on high contrast:

1. Click the **Display** tab to see the display properties.

2. Click the **Use High Contrast** check box to place a check mark in it.

3. Click the **Apply** button to activate the high-contrast settings. After a short time, the screen changes to the high-contrast display. See Figure 4-47.

Figure 4-47 ◀
Applying high contrast

larger letters

color contrast is
more intense

The high-contrast setting affects all programs, but it does not affect the contents of the document window in a program. Try opening WordPad to see how high contrast works in a program.

To run WordPad with high contrast active:

1. Click the **Start** button [Start], point to **Programs**, then point to **Accessories**.

2. Click **WordPad** to start the WordPad program. WordPad appears as shown in Figure 4-48.

Figure 4-48 ◀
Opening a
program in high
contrast

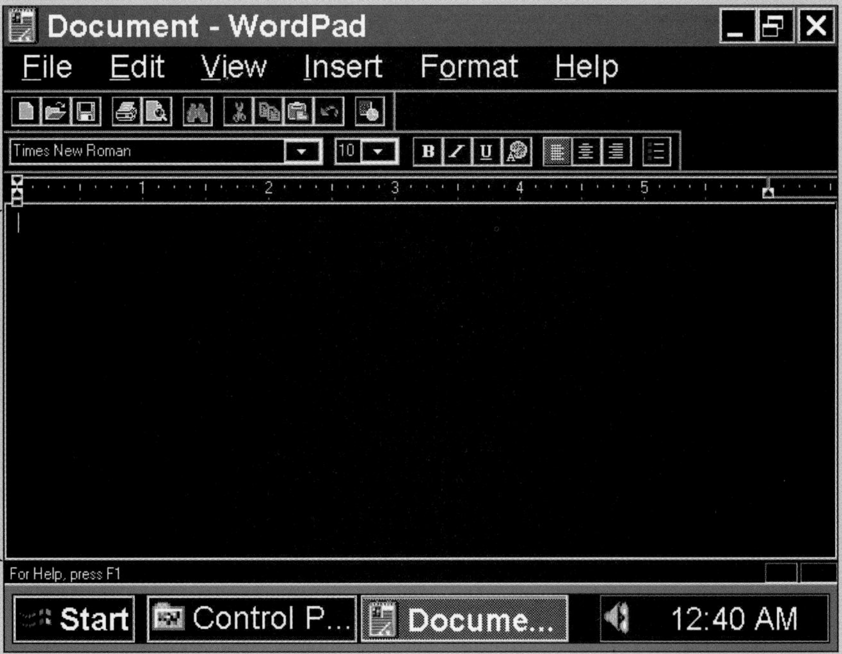

default font in
WordPad will not
change when you
type something

3. Type your name, and notice that the default font in WordPad itself does not change when high contrast is active.

4. Click the **Close** button ⊠ to close WordPad.

5. Click the **No** button when you are asked if you want to save the document.

You shouldn't leave the desktop display in high-contrast mode if you are in a computer lab at your school. Restore the desktop to its original appearance. When you turn off high contrast, you'll find that the taskbar is larger than it should be. You can easily restore it to its normal size by dragging its top border down.

To turn off the high-contrast setting:

1. Click the **Use High Contrast** check box to remove the check mark.

2. Click the **Apply** button to apply the new setting. After a short time the screen returns to the normal display.

   TROUBLE? If the Apply button is hidden behind the taskbar, drag the title bar of the Accessibility window up until you can see the Apply button.

3. To return the taskbar to its normal height, position the pointer over the top edge of the taskbar as shown in Figure 4-49, then drag the top edge of the task bar down to the normal height and release the mouse button.

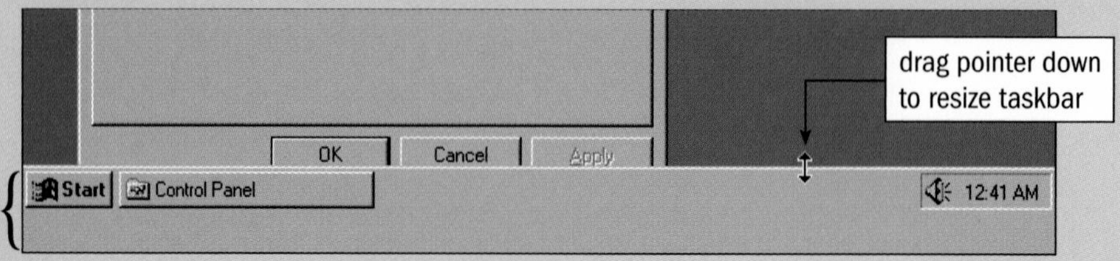

Figure 4-49 ◀
Resizing the
taskbar

taskbar is twice its
normal size

drag pointer down
to resize taskbar

OK   Cancel   Apply

Start   Control Panel   12:41 AM

You might not notice it, but the Start menu has also been affected by the high-contrast settings. To return it to its original size, you use the property sheet for the taskbar.

To restore the Start menu to its original size:

1. Right-click a blank area of the taskbar, then click Properties.

2. Click the **Show small icons in Start menu** check box, then click the **Apply** button. See Figure 4-50.

Figure 4-50 ◀
Restoring Start
menu icons

changes to small
icons when selected

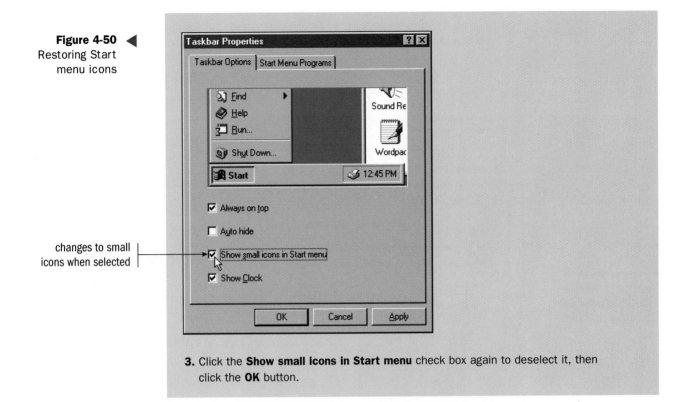

3. Click the **Show small icons in Start menu** check box again to deselect it, then click the **OK** button.

It might seem strange that you must first reduce the icons to their smallest size before you can return them to the default size. There is no other easy way to restore the Start menu to its original size.

Turning Off Accessibility Options Automatically

You can set Accessibility Options to turn off automatically after the computer sits idle for a specified period of time. This is ideal for situations such as computer labs where you want to use accessibility options but other users don't. You can activate an accessibilty option, and when you're done, Windows 95 automatically turns it off if the computer sits idle for a period of time.

To make sure that Accessibility Options turn off after a specified period of time:

1. Click the **General** tab in the Accessibility Properties dialog box.

2. If the **Turn off accessibility features after idle for:** check box is not checked, click it to activate this feature.

3. You can click the **minutes** list arrow to select a period of time from 5 to 30 minutes after which the accessibility features automatically turn off. Study Figure 4-51 to see how you would make sure that the accessibility features turn off after a specified period of time. Don't make this change, however, if you are using a lab computer.

Figure 4-51 ◀
Idling
accessibility
options

turns accessibility
options off when
selected

select number of
minutes of idle time
before accessibility
options disengage

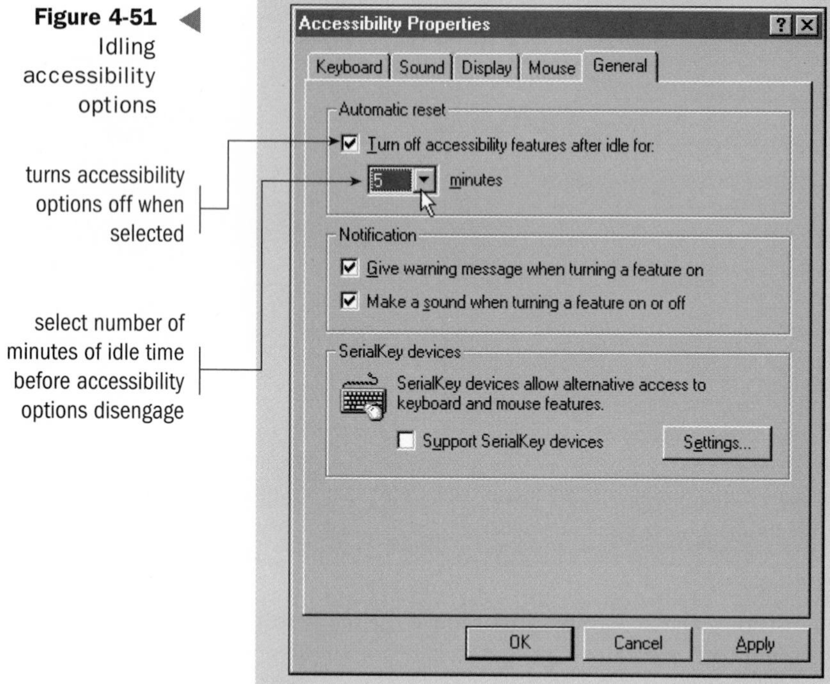

4. Click the **OK** button to close the Accessibility Properties dialog box.

5. Click the Control Panel button in the taskbar, then close the Control Panel window.

Quick Check

1 You change most mouse settings using the Control Panel mouse icon. What mouse setting can you change using the Mouse property sheet in the Accessibility Options dialog box?

2 If you set the mouse for left-handed use, what happens when you click an icon with the left mouse button?

3 Name two settings you can change to make it easier to use Windows 95 if you have limited vision.

4 If you are using MouseKeys, what number on the numeric keypad should you press when you want to select an object?

5 What keyboard shortcut opens the Start menu?

6 What modifier key do you use to open a menu?

End Note

Beth is impressed with the degree of customization possible with Windows 95. After working with the document-centric desktop she created for herself, she realizes that trivial as they may seem, the icons on the desktop increase productivity enormously. She never fails to log a phone call because the phone log is immediately available. She can access her drives, documents, and printer more easily than ever. Moreover, clients have commented on the professional look of the office desktops, and with her new skills Beth plans to use a bitmap of a favorite mountain scene as her home computer desktop background. She's also confident that she could customize one of the Companions computers for any of her employees with special needs.

One of the most exciting features of Windows 95 is the way it lends itself to the needs of its users. Although your ability to customize Windows 95 in a lab setting is limited, and is most likely to be changed by the next user, if you are running Windows 95 on your own computer, you will find that designing a desktop that reflects your needs is time well spent. In creating a document-centric desktop you should keep one thing in mind: too many icons on the desktop defeats the purpose of giving quick access to your documents. If you have icons crowded all over the desktop, it is difficult to locate quickly the one you want.

Tutorial Assignments

1. **Creating Shortcuts** Use Quick Format to format your Student Disk, then make a new Student Disk. Use the Windows 95 New Perspectives Introductory option on the CTI Windows 95 Applications menu (the files you worked with in Tutorial 3). Start Windows Explorer. First create a shortcut to the printer you use regularly. Then create a shortcut to the Beckman text document on your Student Disk. Drag the Beckman shortcut icon to the printer shortcut to print the Beckman document. When you are finished, delete both icons from your desktop.

2. **Customizing a Desktop at Highland Yearbooks** You provide computer support at Highland Yearbooks, a company that publishes high school and college yearbooks. Highland has just upgraded to Windows 95, and you'd like to get right to work customizing the desktops of Highland employees for optimal performance. You start with the computer belonging to John McPhee, one of the sales representatives. Create a desktop for John that takes the following circumstances into account. When you are done, print an image of the desktop using the techniques you learned in the previous tutorial. Then make sure you remove any shortcuts you created and restore the desktop to its original settings. Write down which options you changed to meet John's needs on the back of your printout.
   a. John keeps a Notepad file with a time-date stamp of long-distance phone calls stored on a floppy disk.
   b. John wants to be able to print the phone log file quickly without having to open it first.
   c. The company colors at Highland Yearbooks are blue and gold. John would like a blue desktop with gold title bars.
   d. John recently slammed the car door on his fingers and would like to avoid using the mouse until the bruises have healed.

3. **Create a Shortcut to a Folder** Beth recently assigned an undergraduate at one of the local colleges, Sally Hanson, to provide housekeeping for three clients. Sally plans to be out of the area over spring break, so Beth needs to write a memo to each client asking if they need replacement help. Beth would like to be able to get at the correspondence for Sally Hanson more easily.
   a. Start Windows Explorer, then create a new folder called "Sally" on your Student Disk.
   b. Start Notepad, then compose the three memos, typing in your own message as the text. Save the memos to the Sally folder on your Student Disk with the names "Smith," "Arruga," and "Kosta" (the names of the three clients). Close Notepad when you are finished.

c. Drag the Sally folder from Windows Explorer to the desktop using the right mouse button, then click Create Shortcut(s) Here.

d. Name the shortcut icon "Sally."

e. Test the shortcut icon by opening the Sally folder, then open one of the memos. Use two different methods to open these two objects, and write down which methods you used.

f. Arrange your desktop so you can see the open memo in Notepad, the open folder window, and the shortcut icon. You might need to resize the windows to make them smaller. Then print an image of the desktop using the techniques you learned in the previous tutorial.

g. Remove the shortcut to the folder when you are done.

4. **Customizing the Mouse** One of Beth's older clients, Antonio Castagna, would like part-time work at the offices of Companions, Inc. helping prepare client schedules. Beth wants to make the mouse easier for him to use. She asks you to adjust the double-click speed and pointer speed to their lowest settings. Print images of the two property sheets you use to do this using the techniques you learned in Tutorial 3. Restore the settings to their original speed when you are finished.

5. **Exploring Accessibility Options** This tutorial didn't use the FilterKeys and ToggleKeys options on the Keyboard property sheet in the Accessibility Options dialog box. Explore these options. Click the Help button (the question mark ? in the upper-right corner of the dialog box) and then click these two items on the property sheet to discover what they do. Write a paragraph describing the circumstances under which you'd use these settings.

6. **Create a New Bitmap on the Desktop** In this tutorial you created a new text document directly on the desktop. In this tutorial assignment, you'll create an icon on the desktop for a new bitmap image. Once you've created the icon, you'll open the bitmap image and use the mouse to write your signature. Then you'll use this bitmap image as the wallpaper on your desktop.

a. Right-click an empty area of the desktop, point to New, then click Bitmap Image.

b. Name the new icon "My Signature."

c. Open My Signature. What program does Windows 95 use to open this file?

d. Drag the mouse over the empty canvas to write your signature, as shown in Figure 4-52.

Figure 4-52 ◀

e. Exit the program, and save your changes.

f. Right-click an empty area of the desktop, click Properties, then make sure the Background property sheet is visible. Arrange the dialog box so you can see the My Signature icon.

g. Drag the My Signature icon into the Wallpaper list box, as shown in Figure 4-53.

Figure 4-53 ◀

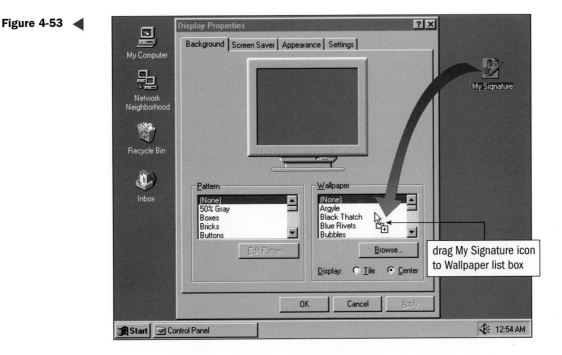

drag My Signature icon to Wallpaper list box

h. Click the OK button. Your signature appears as the wallpaper. Print an image of the screen using the techniques you learned in Tutorial 3.

i. Restore the desktop to its original appearance by returning the Wallpaper setting to None in the Background property sheet (make sure you click OK), and then deleting the My Signature icon from the desktop.

7. **Explore Your Computer's Desktop Properties** Answer each of the following questions about the desktop properties on your lab computers. You can find all the answers in the Display Properties dialog box, which you can reach by right-clicking an empty area of the desktop and then clicking Properties.

a. What is your monitor type? Click the Change Display Type button on the Settings property sheet to find out. Is your monitor Energy Star compliant?

b. If your monitor is Energy Star compliant, is it running any of the Windows 95 energy-saving features? Which ones?

c. What is the setting for monitor resolution? What other resolution settings are available? Drag the slider to find out. If it's an older monitor, it might not have higher resolutions available.

d. What color palette are you using?

e. Is Windows 95 using a screen saver? Which one? After how many minutes of idle time does it engage?

f. What is your desktop's default color scheme?

g. Does your desktop display a pattern or wallpaper? Which one?

EXPLORE

8. **Customizing Your Desktop** The ability to place icons directly on the desktop gives you the opportunity to create a truly document-centric desktop. Figure 4-54 shows Beth's desktop after she's had a chance to create all the shortcuts you recommended and add additional shortcuts for programs, folders, files, and other resources she uses regularly.

Figure 4-54 ◀

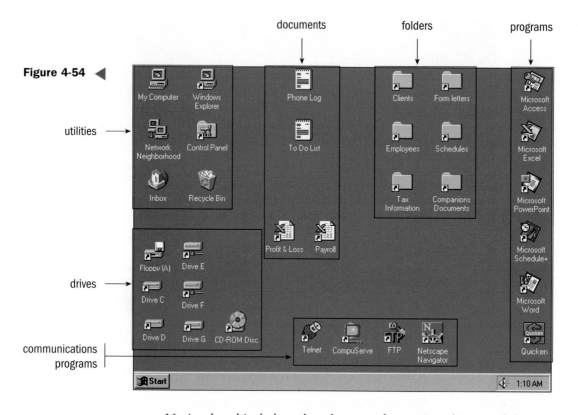

Notice that this desktop has shortcuts for not just drives and documents, but also for programs, utilities, and other Windows 95 objects. The amount of time you save by arranging your desktop in this manner cannot be overestimated if you spend a lot of time at the computer. If you have your own computer, create a desktop that meets your needs.

Use the following strategy:
a. Use Windows Explorer to locate the drives on your computer, then create a shortcut to each drive.
b. If you haven't already, use Windows Explorer to create folders for the work you usually do on your computer. You might want a folder for each class you're taking, letters you write, projects, or hobbies. Then create a shortcut to each folder you use regularly.
c. Create shortcuts for each document you use repeatedly. Remember not to overcrowd your desktop.
d. If you know how to locate program and utility files, create shortcuts to the programs and utilities you use most often.
e. Group the icons on your desktop so that similar objects are in the same location.

NEW
PERSPECTIVES
SERIES

Microsoft® Windows® 95

INTERMEDIATE

TUTORIALS

Read This **Before You Begin**

STUDENT DISKS

To complete the Intermediate tutorials and Tutorial Assignments you need three Student Disks. Your instructor will either provide you with Student Disks or will ask you to make your own.

If you are supposed to make your own Student Disks, you will need three blank, formatted high-density disks. Follow the instructions in Intermediate Tutorial 1 to use the Make Student Disk program to make your own Student Disks. The following table shows you which disk you should use with each tutorial.

Student Disk	Write this on the label
1	Student Disk: Intermediate Tutorial 1
2	Student Disk: Intermediate Tutorial 2
3	Student Disk: Intermediate Tutorials 3-6

When you begin each tutorial, be sure you are using the correct Student Disk. See the inside front or inside back cover of this book for more information on Student Disk files, or ask your instructor or technical support person for assistance.

COURSE LABS

Intermediate Tutorial 6 features two interactive Course Labs to help you understand disk maintenance concepts. There are Lab Assignments at the end of this tutorial that relate to these Labs. To launch the Labs, follow the instructions at the beginning of the first Lab Assignment.

USING YOUR OWN COMPUTER

If you are going to work through this book using your own computer, you need:

- **Computer System** Windows 95 must be installed on your computer. This book assumes a complete installation of Windows 95.

- **Student Disks** Ask your instructor or lab manager for details on how to get the Student Disks. You will not be able to complete the tutorials or exercises in this book using your own computer until you have Student Disks. The student files may also be obtained electronically over the Internet. See the inside front or inside back cover of this book for more details.

- **Course Labs** See your instructor or technical support person to obtain the Course Lab software for use on your own computer.

VISIT OUR WORLD WIDE WEB SITE

Additional materials designed especially for you are available on the World Wide Web. Go to **http://coursetools.com**.

To complete the tutorials in this book, your students must use a set of files on Student Disks. The Instructor's Resource Kit CD-ROM for this text contains setup software that generates the Student Disks. To install this software on your server or on standalone computers, follow the instructions in the Readme file. Your students can then use the Windows 95 Start menu to run the program that will create their Student Disks. Intermediate Tutorial 1 contains steps that instruct your students on how to generate Student Disks.

If you prefer to provide Student Disks rather than letting students generate them, you can run the program that will create Student Disks yourself, following the instructions in Intermediate Tutorial 1.

COURSE LAB SOFTWARE

Intermediate Tutorial 6 features online, interactive Course Labs that introduce basic disk maintenance concepts. This software is distributed on a CD-ROM included in the Instructor's Resource Kit. To install the Course Lab software, follow the setup instructions in the Readme file on the CD-ROM. Once you have installed the Course Lab software, your students can start the Labs following the instructions in the Lab Assignments in Intermediate Tutorial 6.

CTI COURSE LAB SOFTWARE AND STUDENT FILES

You are granted a license to copy the Student Files and Course Labs to any computer or computer network used by students who have purchased this book.

Finding Files and Data

CASE

Speechwriter's Aide

Like thousands of other college students who are graduating soon, you've been dropping in at the campus job center regularly. Today, you notice that Senator Susannah Bernstein's speechwriter needs an aide. During your freshman year you campaigned vigorously for Senator Bernstein and were part of a committee that brought her to speak at your college. When you call to inquire, Carolyn King, the senator's speechwriter, asks you to come by the next morning. Carolyn explains that her aide left rather suddenly, and she needs an immediate replacement.

Your interview goes very well. Carolyn is interested to hear that you are familiar with Windows 95, because all of Senator Bernstein's staff use Windows 95 on their computers. Carolyn explains that the aide collects and organizes information in a filing cabinet—newspaper clippings, articles, old speeches, political briefings, and so on. The aide builds and maintains this archive and then uses it to provide material for Senator Bernstein's speeches. Another source of speech material is an electronic "quotations archive" that the previous aide started. The electronic archive includes close to a hundred files on a floppy disk. These files contain anecdotes, jokes, and "quotable quotes."

You tell Carolyn you know you can handle the job, and she hires you on the spot. You report for work early the next day and start browsing through the filing cabinet to familiarize yourself with the paper archives. Your first task is to look for appropriate material for a speech on the effect of gender on politics that the Senator will deliver next week at Stanton College. You find a very funny Dave Barry column on "the battle of the sexes" in the *Washington Post* that you clip, but by late afternoon you haven't found much else in the filing cabinet. You start browsing through the quotations archive disk. You discover that the disk is organized into several folders. You open a few files and find quotes from a wide variety of people—historical figures such as Eleanor Roosevelt and Gandhi, as well as modern celebrities like Jay Leno and Martina Navratilova. You ask Carolyn if it's okay to take the quotations archive disk home for further exploration. She praises your enthusiasm and tells you not to work too late. You copy the archive files onto a floppy disk, and home you go.

SESSION

1.1

In this session you learn how to start a Windows 95 feature called Find and perform simple searches for files by their filenames. You experiment with different search words and techniques, including wildcards. You also work with the Results list in order to display the files in the most convenient format.

Preparing Your Student Disks

Before you can begin working, you need to bring three **blank, formatted disks** to the computer lab to create the Student Disks containing the sample files you will work with in Tutorials 1 through 6. As you go through the tutorials, refer to the Read This Before You Begin page to make sure you are using the correct disk.

In the computer lab, you will make your Student Disks using the CTI Windows 95 Applications menu. If you are using your own computer, however, the CTI Windows 95 Applications menu will *not* be available. Before you proceed, you must go to your school's computer lab and use the CTI Windows 95 Applications menu to make your Student Disks. Once you have made the disks, you can use them to complete these tutorials on any computer that runs Windows 95.

To make your Student Disks:

1. Place the first blank, formatted 3½-inch disk in drive A.

   TROUBLE? If your 3½-inch disk drive is B, place your formatted disk in that drive instead, and for the rest of this tutorial substitute drive B wherever you see drive A.

2. Click the **Start** button [Start].

3. Point to **Programs**, point to **CTI Windows 95 Applications**, point to **Windows 95 New Perspectives Intermediate**, then click **Make Student Disk**. Figure 1-1 shows this menu option.

Figure 1-1 ◀
Making your
Student Disk

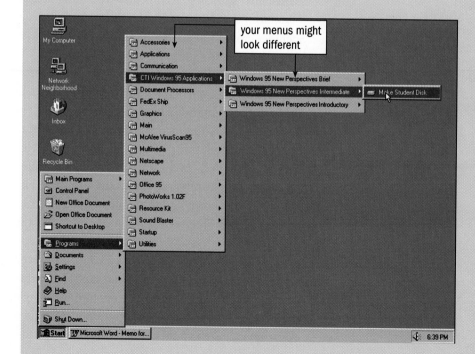

A dialog box opens, asking you to indicate the drive that contains your first formatted disk.

4. Follow the instructions on the screen. The files are copied to your formatted disk. Insert new disks as prompted. A message tells you when all the files have been copied.

5. Click the **OK** button. Your Student Disks now contain files that you will use throughout the rest of these tutorials.

6. Close all the open windows on your screen.

Search Strategies

At home, you sit down at your computer and place the quotations archives disk in the drive. You hope to find a few good quotes for Senator Bernstein's gender and politics speech before you quit for the night. From the short time you spent at work with the quotations archives disk, you know there are so many files on the disk that opening and reading through every one of them would be time consuming. You learned at school that the Windows 95 **Find** utility helps you locate files, data, folders, computers on your network, and other network and online resources.

You are most likely to use Find when you are working on someone else's computer, a network computer, a computer with multiple users who share documents, or you have a disk with someone else's data, as is the case with the quotations archive disk. On your own computer, the best way to make sure you can find your files quickly and easily is to start with a well-organized folder structure. Chances are then you might not need to use Find very often. But even on your own computer, you might forget the names or locations of certain files. Find can help you avoid searching manually through the hundreds of files your hard disk contains.

To search for a file, you provide Find with **search criteria**, one or more conditions you want Find to match. For example, you could provide search criteria specifying all or part of a filename and the drive you think the file might be on. Find then locates and displays every file that matches those criteria. Find groups search criteria into three categories—Name & Location, Date Modified, and Advanced—as shown in Figure 1-2.

Figure 1-2 ◀
Search criteria
available in Find

Tab	Search Criteria
Name & Location	• All or part of a filename • The location (computer, drive, or folder) in which you want Windows 95 to search
Date Modified	• The date or range of dates on which the file was created or modified
Advanced	• File type • Any words or phrases in the file • File size

In Session 1.1 you'll search for files using criteria in the first category, Name & Location. In Session 1.2 you'll search for files using criteria from the other two categories, Date Modified and Advanced.

Starting Find

You didn't create the quotations files and you know very little about them, so Find is just the tool to help you locate quotations for Senator Bernstein's speech. You begin thinking about how you will perform searches to find the quotations you need. Find is one of the options on the Start menu, so you can begin a search any time during a computer session: while you are working on the desktop or in a program. When you select the Find option, a menu opens that lets you specify what you are looking for: files or folders, a computer, or other online resources. You decide to start Find.

3.1 NOTE

In Windows 3.1 you can search for files only from File Manager. In Windows 95 you can search from anywhere.

To start Find and specify that you want to search for files or folders:

1. Click the **Start** button .

2. Point to **Find**. The Find menu opens. Your Find menu might not show all the options in Figure 1-3. The Computer option appears only if your computer is on a network. It helps you locate another computer on the network. The On The Microsoft Network option appears only if you have access to The Microsoft Network, either over your lab network or over a modem. Because you are looking for files, you'll choose the first option, Files or Folders.

Figure 1-3 ◀
Find menu

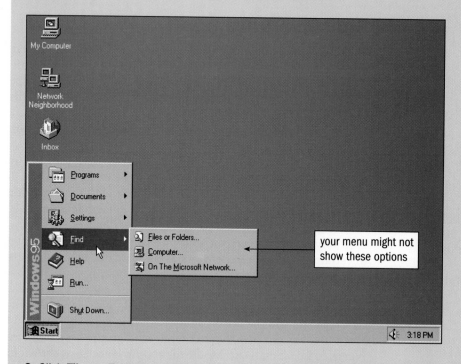

3. Click **Files or Folders** on the Find menu. A dialog box opens that lets you specify criteria for the file you are looking for. See Figure 1-4.

Figure 1-4 ◀
Find: All Files
dialog box

your Look in box
might show a
different drive

    The title of the dialog box that opens when you first start Find is Find: All Files. As you will see as you go through this session, when you specify search criteria, the title changes to describe the kind of search you are performing.

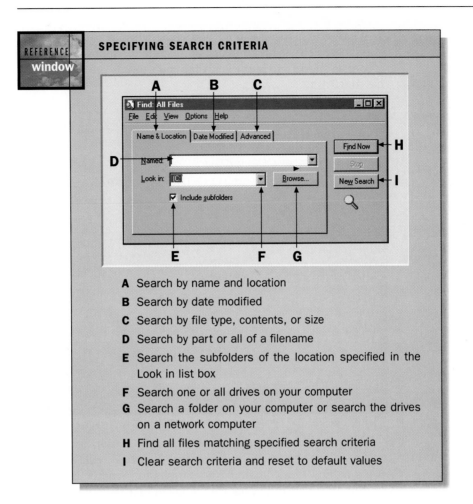

SPECIFYING SEARCH CRITERIA

REFERENCE window

A   Search by name and location

B   Search by date modified

C   Search by file type, contents, or size

D   Search by part or all of a filename

E   Search the subfolders of the location specified in the Look in list box

F   Search one or all drives on your computer

G   Search a folder on your computer or search the drives on a network computer

H   Find all files matching specified search criteria

I   Clear search criteria and reset to default values

The Find: All Files dialog box helps you locate a file by entering search criteria. The three tabs at the top of the Find: All Files dialog box correspond to the three search criteria categories shown in Figure 1-2. The active tab, Name & Location, lets you specify all or part of a filename and a location in which Find should search.

Searching by Name and Location

To find a specific file, you type as much of the filename as you know in the Named box. The letters you type are called a **search string**. Because Find is not case sensitive, you can type the search string in either uppercase or lowercase letters. After you enter the search string, you select the drive or folder where you think the file might be located. Then you click the Find Now button. Find locates and then lists any files or folders whose names contain the search string.

REFERENCE window

SEARCHING FOR A FILE BY NAME

- Click the Start button, point to Find, then click Files or Folders.
- Type a search string in the Named box.
- Click the Look in list arrow, then click the drive you want to search or click My Computer to select all the drives on your computer.
- Use the Include subfolders check box to indicate whether you want to search subfolders of the drive or folder in the Look in box.
- Click the Find Now button.

What search string should you enter when you don't know the filename? You can guess, based on the file contents. For example, suppose you want to find a particular quotation, as shown in Figure 1-5, that you think is on the disk but you don't know which file contains it.

Figure 1-5 ◀
Ideas for
search strings

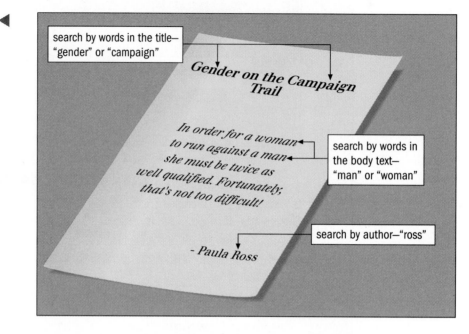

The quotation itself suggests several likely search strings: "gender," "politics," "man" or "men," and "woman" or "women." You could use any of these words as your search string to find files containing quotations for Senator Bernstein's speech. You decide to start by looking for files named "women." Later you can try other search strings.

To search for files containing "women" in the filename:

1. Click the **Named** box.

2. Type **women** in the Named box.

You've entered a criterion for the filename, and now you need to specify a file location. When you first start Find, drive C usually appears in the Look in box. This means Find will search only on drive C. If your computer has multiple drives and you aren't sure which drive contains the file you're looking for, you can search your entire computer by clicking My Computer on the Look in list. However, if you know which drive contains the file, you can speed up your search by limiting the search to that drive.

All the files you are looking for are located on the disk in drive A, so you specify drive A as your search location.

To specify drive A as the file location:

1. Click the **Look in** list arrow. The Look in list opens, showing the drives available on your computer. See Figure 1-6.

Figure 1-6 ◄
Available drives
to search

Look in list arrow ——

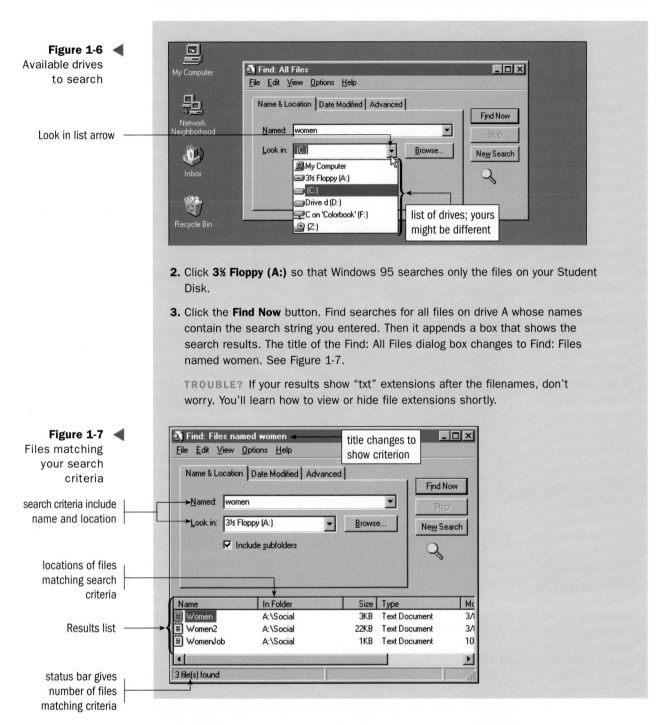

list of drives; yours
might be different

2. Click **3½ Floppy (A:)** so that Windows 95 searches only the files on your Student Disk.

3. Click the **Find Now** button. Find searches for all files on drive A whose names contain the search string you entered. Then it appends a box that shows the search results. The title of the Find: All Files dialog box changes to Find: Files named women. See Figure 1-7.

TROUBLE? If your results show "txt" extensions after the filenames, don't worry. You'll learn how to view or hide file extensions shortly.

Figure 1-7 ◄
Files matching
your search
criteria

search criteria include
name and location

locations of files
matching search
criteria

Results list ——

status bar gives
number of files
matching criteria

The **Results list,** the box Find appends that shows search results, shows three files that contain quotations about women: Women, Women2, and WomenJob. The In Folder column provides the file locations, A:\Social. The location begins with the drive, in this case, A:. If the file is in a folder, a backslash (\) separates the drive from the folder name.

Therefore, files in A:\Social are in the Social folder on drive A. If there are subfolders, additional backslashes separate the folders from one another. Figure 1-8 shows how this notation works on a drive A that contains two folders, Politics and Speeches, both of which have subfolders.

Figure 1-8 ◀
File locations

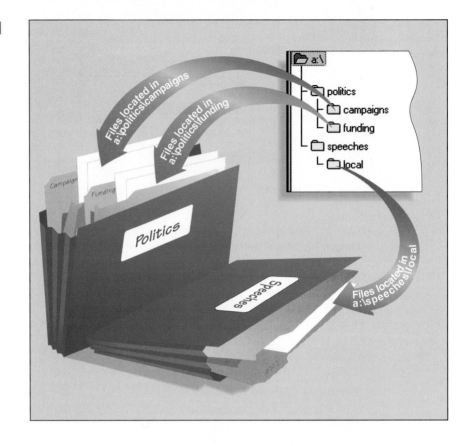

Experimenting with Search Strings

3.1 NOTE

With Windows 3.1, you have to reopen the Search dialog box and retype your search string each time you start a new search. Windows 95 makes it much easier to experiment with different search strings—and it also places previous searches in the Named list box so you can click to repeat a search.

Now that you know there are files containing quotations specifically about women, you decide to look for files on men, using "men" as your search string. To perform a new search, you can change the existing criteria, add new criterion, or click the **New Search** button, which returns all settings to their defaults. You decide to change the search string "women" to "men" in the Named box. Drive A is still specified in the Look in box.

To search for files containing the search string "men" on drive A:

1. Change the entry in the Named box from **women** to **men**.

2. Click the **Find Now** button. The Results list again shows a successful search.

3. Resize the Find dialog box to show the entire Results list. See Figure 1-9.

   TROUBLE? To resize a dialog box, you drag its border.

Figure 1-9 ◄
Updated
Results list

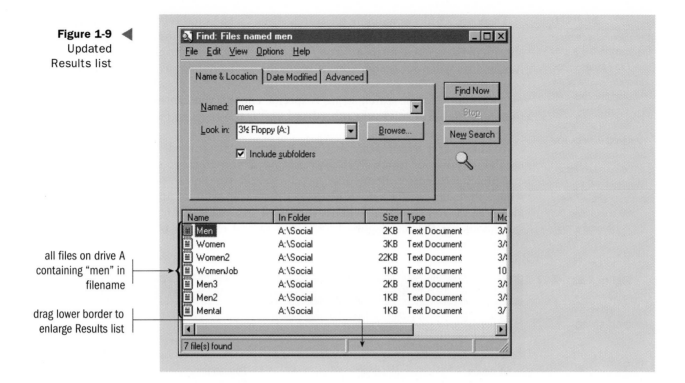

all files on drive A
containing "men" in
filename

drag lower border to
enlarge Results list

You notice that the Results list contains files with names such as Mental and Women in addition to Men. Then you remember that the search string "men" can be any part of a filename. You could have saved yourself the work of an extra search by using "men" as your search string at the outset, because files about both men and women would have appeared in the Results list. However, sometimes using a shorter search string causes Find to locate a large number of files that aren't applicable. Consider Figure 1-10, which shows what might happen if you search for "men" on a computer with multiple drives.

Figure 1-10 ◄
Search strings
appear in any
part of filename

searching a
computer named
"Bob"

search string "men"
is colored red to
illustrate how search
string can appear
anywhere in the
filename

large number of files
found

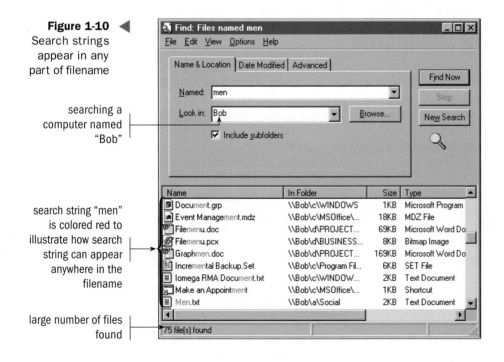

3.I NOTE

When you search for a file in Windows 3.1 in File Manager, the search results show only the files that match the exact search string you entered (unless you use wildcards, which are discussed later). Windows 95 Find, in contrast, shows every file containing the search string.

There are 75 files containing the search string "men" on this computer. Imagine if you were searching a network! Your search might have yielded hundreds of files whose names contain the search string "men." You need to think ahead to prevent an impractically long Results list. Will your search criteria result in too many files, as in Figure 1-10? Will it omit important ones, as "women" omitted files named "men" whereas "men" included files for both? If your search string is specific enough you can minimize the number of files in the Results list. On the other hand, if it is too specific, Find might not locate the file you need.

To construct a search string that will find the files you need, one rule of thumb is to use the *root* of your search word. For example, if you decide to search for files on political topics for Senator Bernstein's speech, should you enter "politics" as your search string? Probably not, because a file named Politician will not appear in the Results list. However, the root "politic," without the added "s," yields files named Politician, Political Quotations, or Politics. Figure 1-11 shows several examples of constructing a search string using a root.

Figure 1-11 ◀
Choosing effective search strings

Topic	Use this search string:	Finds these filenames:
politics	politic	Politics Politicians Political Quotations
education	educ	Education Educative Issues Educators
computers	comput	Computers Computing Computerization

Of course the root of the word, if it is very general, might also let in unwanted files, as the root "men" did in Figure 1-10. Fortunately, with Find it's easy to adjust your search string until you find only those files you want.

Using Wildcards

As you have seen, using the root of a word as your search string is useful in some situations but impractical in others. In situations where you want to locate a group of files whose names follow certain specific patterns, such as all files beginning with "men" or all files ending with the letter "s," you can use wildcards. **Wildcards** are characters that you can substitute for all or part of a filename in a search string. Find recognizes two wildcards: the asterisk and the question mark.

The * (asterisk) wildcard stands in place of any number of consecutive characters in a filename. For example, with the search string "m*n" Find could locate the following files:

Men
Malign
Mourn

but not

Male
Mental
Women

Here, the files that Find locates have a common characteristic: they all begin with "m" and end with "n." You might wonder why the Results list excludes the file named Women. After all, the search string "men" located the Women file, so why wouldn't the more general "m*n"? The answer is that when Find encounters the asterisk wildcard in a search string, it allows additional characters only in those places indicated by the wildcard. Find does not include, as it does in the "men" search, filenames with characters before the "m" or after the "n." If this is not what you had in mind, you can use additional wildcards. If you specify the search string "*m*n*" then Find includes:

Men
Malign
Mourn
Women
Mental

but not

Male

These files have the letter "m" in common, which appears somewhere in the name, followed at a later point by the letter "n."

You decide to search for only those files beginning with "men." To do this, you use "men*" as your search string. Try this search now.

To locate files using the asterisk wildcard:

1. Click the **Named** box.

2. Type **men*** then click the **Find Now** button. Find locates files whose names start with "men," followed by any number of characters. Files that don't begin with "men" are not included. The Results list is now a more manageable size. See Figure 1-12.

Figure 1-12 ◀
Asterisk
wildcard

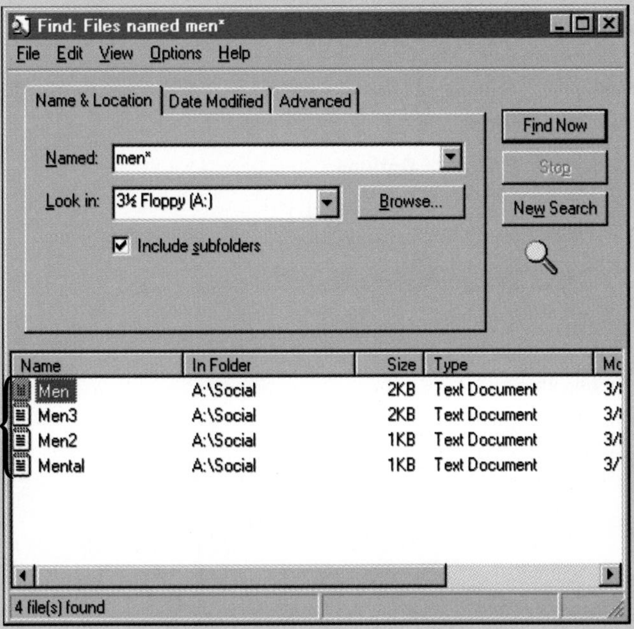

only files beginning
with "men" appear →

3. Return the Find dialog box to its original size.

You can also control the Results list with the ? (question mark) wildcard, which lets you select files when one character in the filename varies. For example, the search string "m?n" locates

Men
Min
Man

but not

Mourn
Mistaken
Moon

Files that match the "m?n" criteria must have the letters "m" and "n" in their file-names, separated by a single character. Unlike the asterisk wildcard, however, the question mark wildcard does not cause Find to exclude files with characters before or after the "m" or "n." So although "m*n" excludes Women and Mental, "m?n" does not, because both of these files contain "m" and "n" separated by a single character.

The question mark wildcard is often used to locate files whose names include version numbers or dates, such as Sales1, Sales2, and Sales3, or Tax94, Tax95, Tax96, and Tax97. You've already seen that the quotations archive disk contains files named Men2 and Men3. What search string can you use to produce just those files in the Results list? "Men?" might seem the obvious answer, but you would find that "men?" includes files such as Womenjob. To eliminate those kinds of files from the Results list, you can include a file extension (the three letter suffix that identifies the file type) in your search string, either as a wildcard or as a particular type. When Find encounters a file extension, it does not search for additional characters besides those indicated by the wildcards. For example, the search string "men?.*" allows only one character between the "men" string and the start of the file extension. Thus the criteria "men?.*" will locate files like Men2.txt, but not Women1.txt.

To perform searches that include the file extension, you might want to set your computer to show extensions as part of the filename. Windows 95 lets you specify whether or not the extension appears on the screen. You decide to change the settings on your computer so you can view file extensions. Then you search for all files beginning with "men," followed by a single character, followed by the extension "txt," the extension Windows 95 uses for text files. To do this, you enter the search string "men?.txt."

To set your computer's view options so that file extensions appear:

1. Open My Computer on the desktop (you might need to move the Find dialog box to view this icon).

2. Click **View** then click **Options**.

3. Click the **View** tab. See Figure 1-13.

Figure 1-13
Viewing file extensions

View tab

if check box is selected, file extensions do not appear

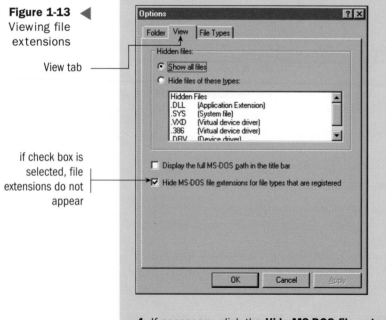

4. If necessary, click the **Hide MS-DOS file extensions for file types that are registered** check box to remove the check mark. Make a note of the original setting so you can change it back at the end of the session.

5. Click the **OK** button, then click the My Computer **Close** button ☒. The next time you perform a search, Find will display file extensions as part of the filenames.

Now you can use the question mark wildcard to display only files that begin with "men" followed by a single character.

To locate files using the question mark wildcard:

1. Click the **Named** text box.

2. Type **men?.txt** then click the **Find Now** button. See Figure 1-14.

Figure 1-14 ◀
Question mark
wildcard

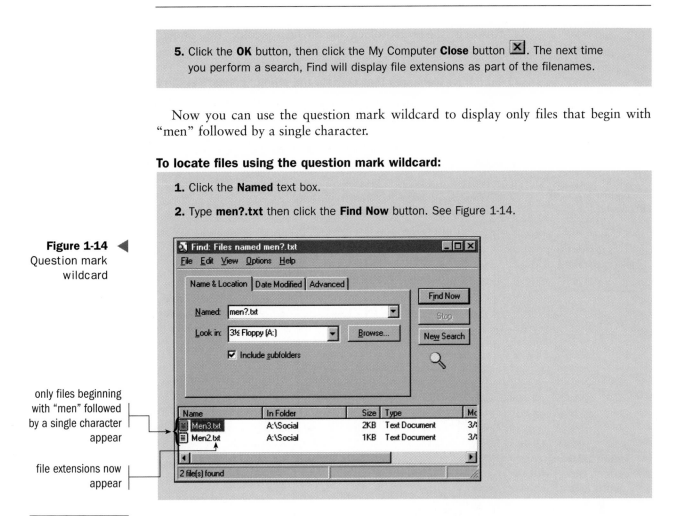

only files beginning
with "men" followed
by a single character
appear

file extensions now
appear

3.1 NOTE

Wildcards are necessary with the Windows 3.1 File Manager because the Search command finds only exact matches to search strings. The Windows 95 Find utility eliminates the need for wildcards in some situations where they were needed in 3.1. For example, 3.1 the string ".txt" (pronounced "star dot t-x-t") locates all text files. The string "*.*" (pronounced "star dot star") locates all files. However, with Windows 95 Find, you can find all text files using the Type criteria, as you'll see in Session 1.2, and you can display all files by leaving the Named box blank.*

The disadvantage of the question mark wildcard in this example is that while it eliminated the Mental file, it also eliminated the Men file.

As you can see, the rules governing wildcards can be complex. The examples in this section have shown you ways you are most likely to use wildcards. You'll get an opportunity to explore wildcards further in the Tutorial Assignments.

Searching for Files in a Specific Folder

You have now identified a batch of files containing quotations about men and women that are likely to be useful for Senator Bernstein's speech. You are ready to try another search string, such as "gender." You notice the files you've found so far are all in the Social folder. Any files on gender are probably in that folder too. Hoping for really quick results, you decide to tell Find to search only that folder.

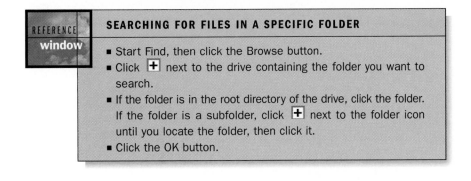

REFERENCE
window

SEARCHING FOR FILES IN A SPECIFIC FOLDER

- Start Find, then click the Browse button.
- Click ⊞ next to the drive containing the folder you want to search.
- If the folder is in the root directory of the drive, click the folder. If the folder is a subfolder, click ⊞ next to the folder icon until you locate the folder, then click it.
- Click the OK button.

To specify the Social folder, you navigate a folder tree similar to the one in Windows Explorer.

To search for filenames that contain the string "gender" in the Social folder on drive A:

1. Click the **Browse** button. A list of devices, drives, and folders appears. See Figure 1-15.

   TROUBLE? Your list of devices, drives, and folders might look different, depending on your computer's drives and network.

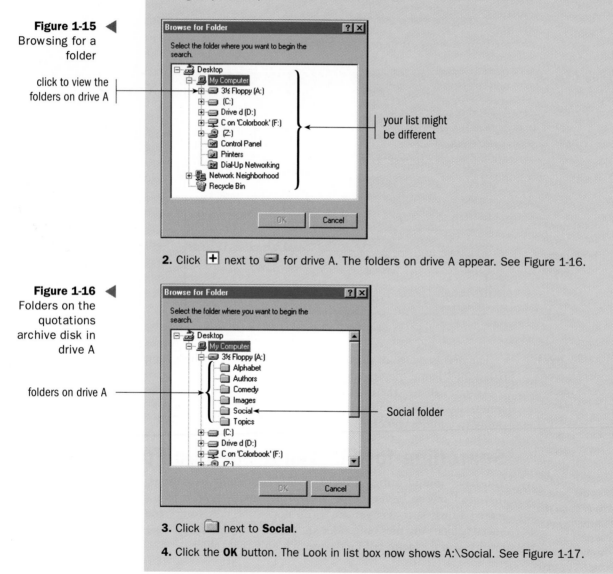

Figure 1-15 ◀
Browsing for a folder

click to view the folders on drive A

your list might be different

2. Click ⊞ next to ▭ for drive A. The folders on drive A appear. See Figure 1-16.

Figure 1-16 ◀
Folders on the quotations archive disk in drive A

folders on drive A

Social folder

3. Click ▭ next to **Social**.

4. Click the **OK** button. The Look in list box now shows A:\Social. See Figure 1-17.

Figure 1-17 ◀
Searching a
folder

Social folder is
specified

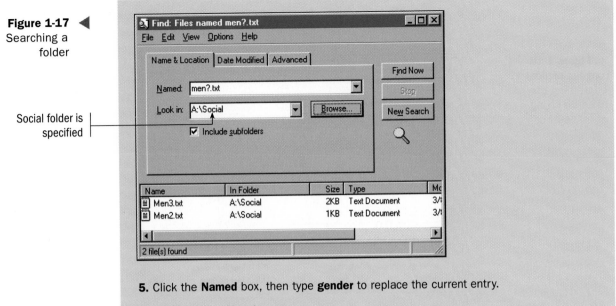

5. Click the **Named** box, then type **gender** to replace the current entry.

6. Click the **Find Now** button.

This search procedure tells Find to look only in the Social folder on drive A and to include any subfolders it might contain as it searches for files whose names include the string "gender." Find locates five such files. You add them to your growing collection of files that might contain quotes for Senator Bernstein's speech.

Working with the Results List

Up until now, the Results lists that you've examined have been short and manageable. When your search yields a large number of files, you can adjust the Results list to display the information in a more suitable and organized format.

You wonder whether there is a way to find quotations by author. You decide to search the disk for any files or folders that contain the term "author."

To search for files and folders named "author" on drive A:

1. Click the **Named** text box, then type **author**.

2. Click the **Look in** list arrow ▼, then click **3½ Floppy (A:)** to search all the folders on drive A.

3. Click the **Find Now** button. The Results list displays all files and folders that have the word "author" in their filenames. There are 28 such files. See Figure 1-18.

Figure 1-18 ◀
Long list of files containing the search string "author"

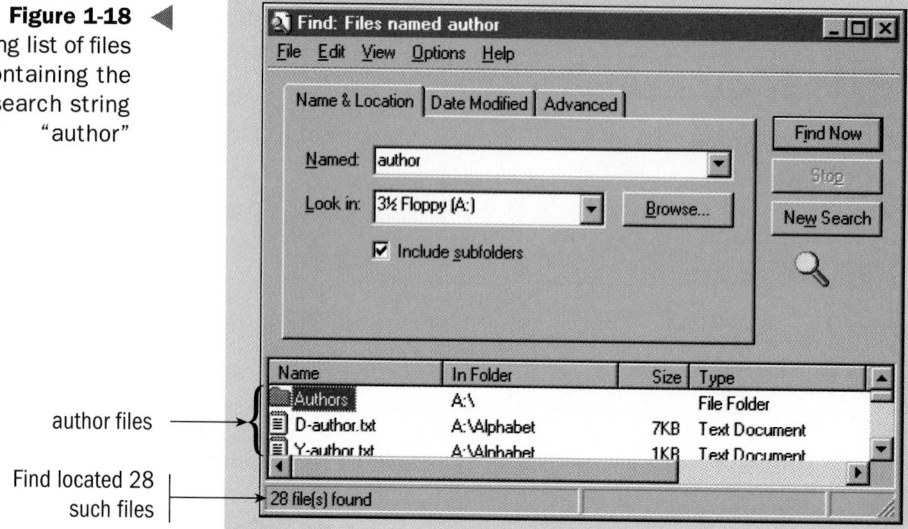

author files →

Find located 28 such files

You display files in the Results list the same way you do in My Computer or Windows Explorer. You can view the files in the list by Large Icons, Small Icons, List, or Details, and you can resize columns by dragging their borders. Even though you probably already know how these options work, let's practice using them to organize the Results list of author files.

To change the view in the Results list:

1. Click **View** then click **Large Icons**.

2. Click **View** then click **Small Icons**.

3. Click **View** then click **List**.

4. Click **View** then click **Details**.

The Details view is probably the most useful view because it gives you all the information you need to verify that you've found the file you want. However, you might need to resize the column widths to view all the information.

To change the column widths in Details view:

1. Move the mouse pointer to the dividing bar between the **Name** button and the **In Folder** button. The pointer changes to ←|→.

2. Drag the dividing bar to the right about one-half inch, as shown in Figure 1-19. This widens the Name column.

Figure 1-19 ◄
Widening the
Name column

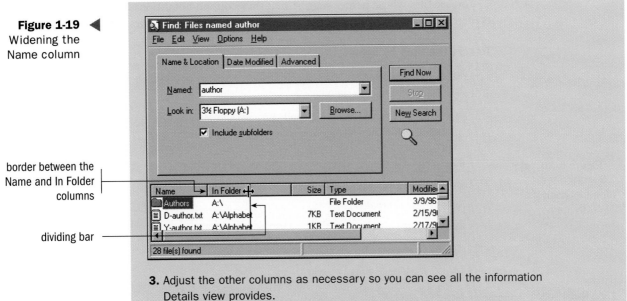

border between the
Name and In Folder
columns

dividing bar

3. Adjust the other columns as necessary so you can see all the information
Details view provides.

TROUBLE? If information is still hidden, you might need to enlarge the Find dialog box first, and then readjust the column widths.

In Details view, Find shows you the name, location, size, type, and date modified of
each file. Just as in My Computer and Windows Explorer, you can sort the files in the
Results list by any of these criteria.

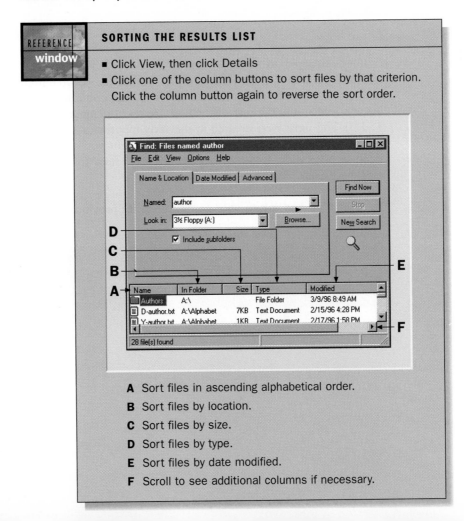

REFERENCE window

SORTING THE RESULTS LIST

- Click View, then click Details
- Click one of the column buttons to sort files by that criterion.
  Click the column button again to reverse the sort order.

A Sort files in ascending alphabetical order.

B Sort files by location.

C Sort files by size.

D Sort files by type.

E Sort files by date modified.

F Scroll to see additional columns if necessary.

You see files whose names suggest that they contain quotations for authors by last name. Is there a file for each letter of the alphabet? You can sort the files by name to find out.

To sort the files by name:

1. Click the **Name** button, as shown in Figure 1-20, to arrange the files in ascending alphabetical order by name.

   TROUBLE? If your files are already arranged in alphabetical order, Step 1 might place them in descending order. Click the Name button again.

Figure 1-20 ◀
Sorting files
alphabetically
by name

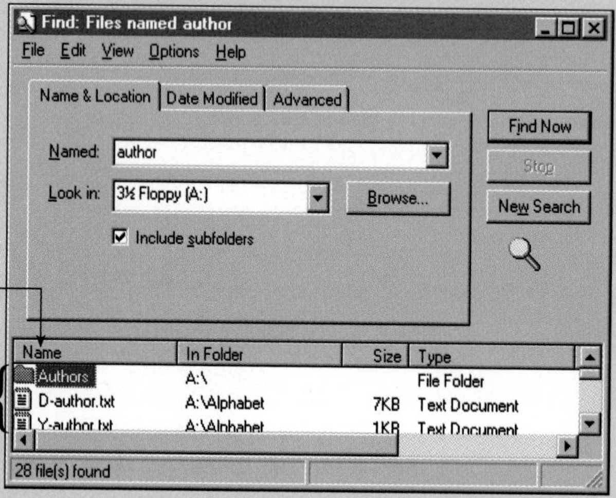

Name button

folders are
alphabetized first,
then files

2. Scroll down the Results list and observe that there are files for most letters of the alphabet.

If you wanted to find quotations by one of Senator Bernstein's favorite authors, Flannery O'Connor, you could try the O-Author file, located in the Alphabet folder. What else can you learn from the Results list? The Type column shows that the first item on the list is a folder, and the rest of the files are text documents. All the files are small (under 15 KB), and most were created in the early months of 1996.

The judicious use of search strings has taught you a lot about the files in the quotations archives disk. In Session 1.2 you'll learn how to use additional criteria, like date, type, and size.

To close Find and return your computer to its previous settings:

1. Click the Find **Close** button ☒.

2. If necessary, open **My Computer**, click **View**, click **Options**, click the **View** tab, and change the **Hide MS-DOS file extensions for file types that are registered** check box to its original setting. Then click the **OK** button and close My Computer.

Quick Check

1. True or false: You can start Find while editing a document in your word processor.

2. When searching for a file only on drive A, what criterion must you specify?

3. True or false: You can type uppercase or lowercase letters when searching for a filename.

4. True or false: The Results list displays only the files whose names exactly match the search string you entered.

5. What is a wildcard? What is the difference between the asterisk wildcard and the question mark wildcard?

6. What files appear in the Results list if you enter *.* in the Named box?

7. Interpret this notation using plain English: D:\Work\Current.

8. What view should you use in the Results list to see information such as file size and date?

SESSION

1.2

In this session you will work with file type, size, and date as your search criteria, you'll search for text within a file, and then you'll combine these criteria for more effective searches. You'll learn to delete and open files directly from the Results list, and to save and clear searches. Finally, you'll examine the Documents list to explore another way of locating a file.

Descriptive Search Criteria

In Session 1.1 you searched for files with particular filenames on the quotations archive disk. When you don't know the filename, you can locate a file using other criteria other than the filename—criteria such as size, date, and type—using the other tabs in the Find dialog box. These criteria are "descriptive" in that they help you identify files that share common characteristics. You can answer questions such as: Are any files more than a few years old? What programs created the files? How large are they? You enter the characteristic you want to study, and then Find lists all files that share that characteristic, such as all files created before 1996, all Microsoft Word files, or all files larger than 50 KB.

You can use these descriptive search criteria on their own or in combination with filename search strings. The specifications you select on any one tab are added to any criteria you specify on the other tabs. If your disk contains files created by DOS or Windows 3.1, you might find these filenames difficult to remember and locate, because in these operating environments filenames are restricted to eight characters. A first-quarter 1996 budget analysis might have the filename Bdgt1q96, while a memo to a CD company for a return might be called Retcdmem. Descriptive search criteria can help you wade through the alphabet soup of eight-character filenames.

3.1 NOTE

In Windows 3.1 you specify only one search criterion in File Manager's Search command: the filename. Windows 95 offers much broader search criteria possibilities.

To prepare to search for files on the quotations archive disk:

1. Make sure your Student Disk is in drive A.

2. Click the **Start** button ⊞Start, point to **Find**, then click **Files or Folders**.

3. Click the **Look in** list arrow ▼, then click the drive containing your Student Disk.

Finding a File by Date

In your new job as archivist, you want to know how up to date the quotations on your disk are. When did the previous aide begin collecting files? Before 1996? Before 1997? Are some dates missing? To search for files by date, you can use the **Date Modified** tab. Searching for files by date is also useful when you want a file that you know you were working with on a given date but you can't remember where you stored it.

REFERENCE window

LOCATING FILES BY DATE

A Search for all files regardless of date.

B Search a range of dates, specified by one of the three options below.

C Enter a start date and an end date. If you leave the start date blank, Find looks for all files previous to the end date. If you leave the end date blank, Find looks for all files after the start date.

D Specify the number of months prior to the search.

E Search for files modified in the previous day or days, as specified in the spin box for days.

You decide to check if any files were created before 1996. You'll need to change the Date setting from its default of All files to All files created before 1/1/96.

To search for files created before 1/1/96:

1. Click the **Date Modified** tab.

2. Click the **between** radio button.

3. Press **Tab** then press the **Delete** key to clear the contents of the start date box. By leaving the start date box blank, Find uses an unrestricted start date.

4. Press **Tab** then type **1/1/96** in the end date box. See Figure 1-21.

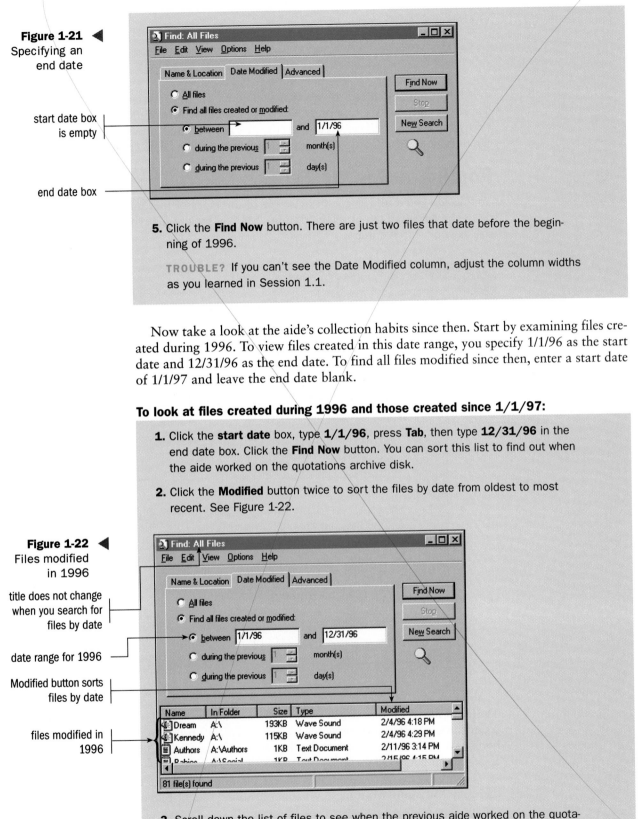

Figure 1-21 ◀
Specifying an
end date

start date box
is empty

end date box

5. Click the **Find Now** button. There are just two files that date before the beginning of 1996.

> TROUBLE? If you can't see the Date Modified column, adjust the column widths as you learned in Session 1.1.

Now take a look at the aide's collection habits since then. Start by examining files created during 1996. To view files created in this date range, you specify 1/1/96 as the start date and 12/31/96 as the end date. To find all files modified since then, enter a start date of 1/1/97 and leave the end date blank.

To look at files created during 1996 and those created since 1/1/97:

1. Click the **start date** box, type **1/1/96**, press **Tab**, then type **12/31/96** in the end date box. Click the **Find Now** button. You can sort this list to find out when the aide worked on the quotations archive disk.

2. Click the **Modified** button twice to sort the files by date from oldest to most recent. See Figure 1-22.

Figure 1-22 ◀
Files modified
in 1996

title does not change
when you search for
files by date

date range for 1996

Modified button sorts
files by date

files modified in
1996

3. Scroll down the list of files to see when the previous aide worked on the quotations files; notice there are large time gaps. Now view the files created since 12/31/96.

4. Change the start date to **1/1/97** and delete the entry in the end date, then click the **Find Now** button to perform an open-ended search.

5. Click the **Modified** button to see that the aide's last entries were in February 1998.

6. Click the **All files** radio button to display all the files again.

It might have occurred to you that you could get information about file dates more quickly by opening My Computer and sorting the files by date. You'd be right if the files were all in one folder. However, when the files are scattered among multiple folders, Find can display files from any of those folders that meet your date criteria.

Finding a File by Type

You decide you'd like to get an overview of the types of files on the quotations archive disk. The **Advanced tab** of the Find utility lets you specify file type, file contents, and file size as your search criteria.

REFERENCE window

USING ADVANCED SEARCH CRITERIA

A Search for files by type. Click the Of type list arrow, click the type you want, then click Find Now.

B Search for files that contain a specific text string. Type the text string in the Containing text box, then click Find Now.

C Search for files by size. Click the Size is list arrow, then click either At least or At most. Enter a size in the KB box by typing it or using the spin arrows. Click the Find Now button.

You can look for files by their general file type or by the program that created them. The list of file types from which you can choose includes text files, MIDI sound files, wave sound files, Quick Time movie clips, bitmaps, DOS program files, Quattro Pro notebooks, Word documents, Access databases, Web documents, and so on depending on the resources on your computer.

You already know there are lots of text files, but you'd like to know how many. Are there any Microsoft Word files? What about sound files or bitmap images? You decide to use file type criteria to answer these questions.

To view files by type:

1. Click the **Advanced** tab.

2. Click the **Of type** list arrow ▼, then scroll down the list to locate "Text Document." See Figure 1-23.

Figure 1-23 ◄
Selecting a
file type

Of type list arrow ───

available file types;
your list might be
different

Text Document
file type

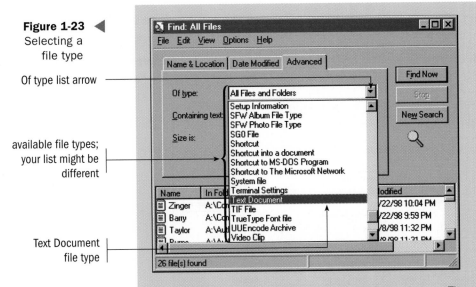

3. Click **Text Document**, then click the **Find Now** button. The status bar reports that there are 89 text files on your disk.

   TROUBLE? If your list is much shorter, you might have forgotten to return the Date Modified setting back to All files. Forgetting to reset criteria to their original settings can confuse your search efforts.

4. Next you want to look for Word files created by Microsoft Word. Click the **Of type** list arrow ▾. Scroll to and then click **Microsoft Word Document**. Click the **Find Now** button. Notice that the quotations archive disk contains 11 Word documents.

   TROUBLE? If you do not find the Microsoft Word Document option on your list, choose a similar option such as "Microsoft Word 6.0 Document" if there is one. If there is no similar option, skip Step 4 and proceed to Step 5.

5. Next you want to look for sound files. Click the **Of type** list arrow ▾. Scroll to and then click **Wave Sound**. Click the **Find Now** button. There are two such files.

   TROUBLE? If Wave Sound is not on the list, look for Sound and click it instead.

6. What about bitmap image files? Click the **Of type** list arrow ▾. Scroll to and then click **Bitmap Image**. Click the **Find Now** button. There is only one bitmap graphics file.

7. Return the type to its default setting: click the **Of type** list arrow ▾, scroll to the top, then click **All Files and Folders**.

Finding a File by Size

In searching for files by type, you found several image and sound files. You know these files are usually bigger than text files or word processed documents. If you are short on disk space, you'll want to identify the largest files so you can delete or move them to free up space. You can find this information by looking for a file by its size. You specify either "at least" or "at most" and then pick the number of kilobytes you want. If disk space is a problem, you might want to look for all files that are at least 25 KB in size. Try that search now.

To search for files by size:

1. Click the **Size is** list arrow ▾, then click **At least**.

2. Click the **KB** box, then type **25**. (You could also use the spin arrows to enter a number.)

3. Click the **Find Now** button. The Results list shows five such files. You can sort these files to more easily identify the largest.

4. Click the **Size** button twice to sort the files by size, with the largest files first. Not surprisingly, the largest files are the two sound files. See Figure 1-24.

Figure 1-24 ◄
Searching for
files by size

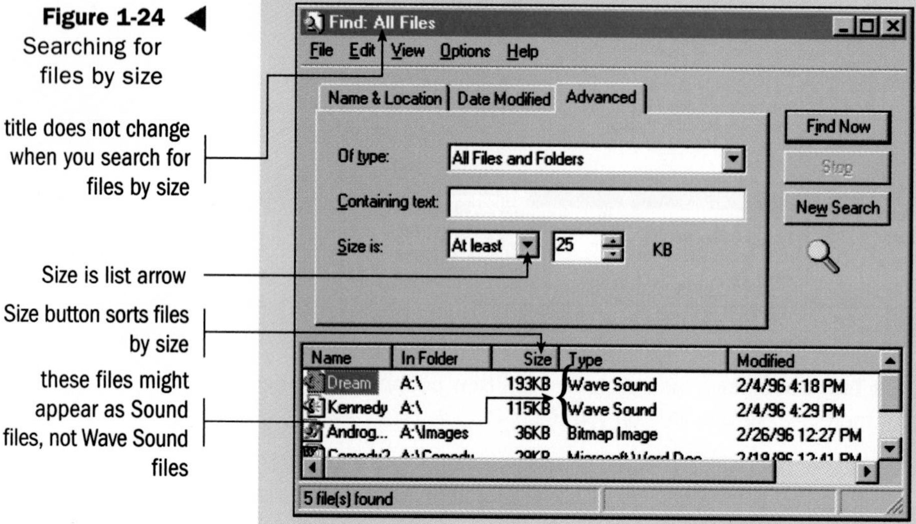

title does not change
when you search for
files by size

Size is list arrow

Size button sorts files
by size

these files might
appear as Sound
files, not Wave Sound
files

5. Click the **Size Is** list arrow, then click the blank entry at the top of the list so the Size is box is empty.

TROUBLE? Don't worry that 25 KB still appears in the spin box. Find ignores the entry for future searches because the Size is box is blank.

Deleting a File from Find

You decide to delete the sound files from the quotations archive disk because they take up so much room. You have copies of them at work, and later on you can create a new disk just for sound files. In Find you can use many of the My Computer and Windows Explorer file manipulation techniques that you've already learned, such as file deletion. To delete one or more files, you select the files in the Results list and then press the Delete key. You can use the Ctrl key or the Shift key to select more than one file at a time.

To delete the sound files:

1. Click the **Dream** file in the Results list.

2. Press and hold down **Ctrl**, then click the **Kennedy** file. Both Dream and Kennedy are selected. See Figure 1-25.

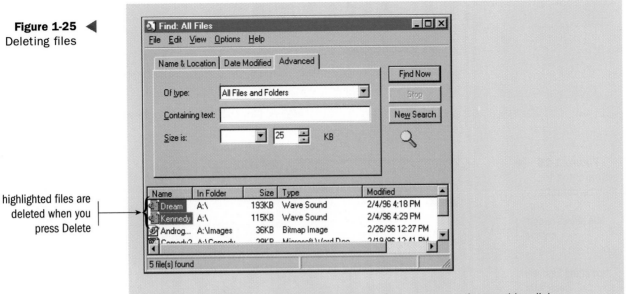

Figure 1-25 ◀
Deleting files

highlighted files are
deleted when you
press Delete

3. Press the **Delete** key. The files are deleted from your quotations archive disk.

TROUBLE? If a message box asks if you are sure you want to delete these files,
click Yes.

Finding a Text String in a File

Over the course of the evening you've been trying to think of who said "Men and women.
Women and men. It will never work." This quote might be a good lead-in to Senator
Bernstein's speech. A very useful feature of the Windows 95 Find utility is its ability to
search for a word or phrase within a file. To use this feature, you enter a text string. A
text string is a series of characters, such as a word or a phrase. Find searches through the
entire text of every file to find the specified text string. If you use this option on a hard
disk, be prepared to wait, because searching file contents, one file at a time, is time consuming. If you can narrow the search range using other criteria so that Find searches
fewer files, you will speed things up.

When you use the text string feature of the Find utility you can specify whether your
search is case-sensitive. For example, if you wanted to find a letter you wrote to Brenda
Wolf, you could enter "Wolf" as your text string, and then choose the Case Sensitive command on the Options menu to locate only files containing Wolf with an initial capital letter.
The Case Sensitive option affects only the case of letters in the Containing text box—not
those in the Named box on the Name & Location tab.

You decide to search for the text string "it will never work" because there might be too
many files containing the string "men and women."

To look for the text string "it will never work" within a file:

1. Click the **Containing text** box, then type **it will never work** but *do not* press the
   Enter key. Because you aren't sure what case the quote might be in, you want to
   make sure Find isn't set to perform case-sensitive searches.

2. Click **Options** on the menu bar, then make sure **Case Sensitive** is not checked. If
   it is, click it to remove the check mark. Otherwise Find might not locate the file if
   the case of the search string is different.

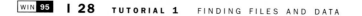

3. Click the **Find Now** button. Find locates only one file, as shown in Figure 1-26. The name of the file is Jong. You suddenly remember that Erica Jong is the source of that quote.

TROUBLE? Don't worry if Find takes longer than usual. Searching for file contents even on a floppy disk is time consuming.

TROUBLE? If Find did not locate any file, check to make sure you didn't type the text string "it will never work" incorrectly.

Figure 1-26 ◀
Searching for
files by content

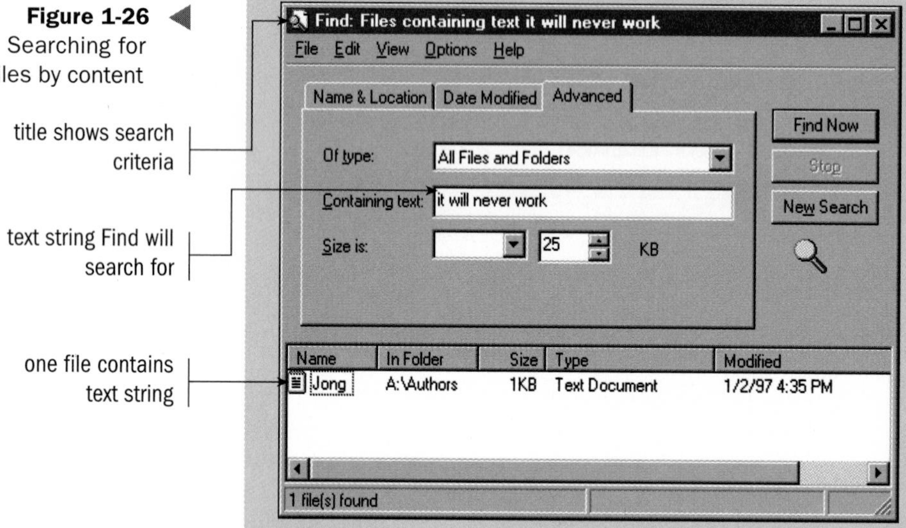

title shows search
criteria ──────┐

text string Find will
search for ────┐

one file contains
text string ───┐

> **Find: Files containing text it will never work**
> File Edit View Options Help
>
> | Name & Location | Date Modified | Advanced |
>
> Of type: All Files and Folders ▾
>
> Containing text: it will never work
>
> Size is: ▾ 25 ▾ KB
>
> [Find Now]
> [Stop]
> [New Search]
>
> | Name | In Folder | Size | Type | Modified |
> | Jong | A:\Authors | 1KB | Text Document | 1/2/97 4:35 PM |
>
> 1 file(s) found

4. Delete the entry in the **Containing text** box to clear that search criterion.

Finding a File Using Multiple Criteria

As you're thinking about quotations suitable for Senator Bernstein's speech, you recall that in February 1996 your local public radio station rebroadcast a speech on gender and politics that was given a few years ago on England's BBC radio. The station also posted the text of the speech on the Internet. You wonder if any part of the speech is included in a file on the quotations archives disk. You have no idea what such a file might be named, but if you specify multiple criteria, such as the date, a likely filename, and a likely text string, you might be able to pinpoint it.

As you consider how to specify this search, you reason as follows: you already know there are files on the archive disk whose filenames contain the search string "gender." You guess that the speech probably used the word "politics," so you could specify the root "politic" as your text string on the Advanced tab. Moreover, the file would probably have been created in February or March of 1996. You decide to specify these three criteria and see if you can find an excerpt from the speech. Find uses the criteria from all the tabs to perform the search.

To find a file with multiple criteria:

1. Click the **Name & Location** tab.

2. Click the **Named** box, then type **gender**.

3. Click the **Date Modified** tab.

4. Click the **between** radio button, press **Tab**, type **2/1/96**, press **Tab**, then type **3/31/96**.

5. Click the **Advanced** tab.

6. Click the **Containing text** box, type **politic**, then click the **Find Now** button. See Figure 1-27.

Figure 1-27 ◀
Finding a file using multiple criteria

title shows multiple criteria

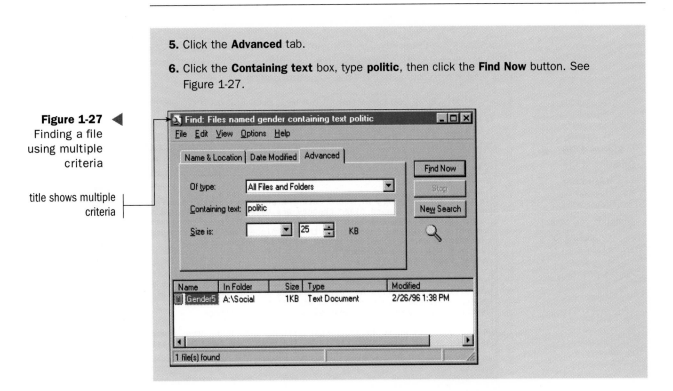

The combined search criteria produce a single file: Gender5. Does this file contain excerpts from the speech you're looking for? You decide to open it and see.

Opening a File from Find

Once you locate a file using the Find utility, you can open it directly from Find. In the document-centric environment of Windows 95, you don't have to start a program before you can open a file. You can use one of the three standard methods to open a file: click the file in the Results list then press the Enter key, right-click the file then click Open, or double-click the file. Windows 95 locates and starts the program for you. If Windows 95 cannot open your file, it is possible that you don't have the necessary program installed on your computer. If this is the case, the Open With dialog box opens and gives you the opportunity to specify the program you want Windows 95 to open for that file.

You want to open the Gender5 file to see if it contains any part of the speech you remember.

To open a file from the Results list:

1. Click the file **Gender5** in the Results list.

   TROUBLE? If your file appears as Gender5.txt, don't worry. You can hide file extensions using the techniques covered in Session 1.1.

2. Press the **Enter** key. The file opens in Notepad. See Figure 1-28. You recognize the first quotation as being from the speech. The names of the speakers are there too. You've found what you were looking for.

TROUBLE? If you can't see all the text, click Edit on the Notepad menu bar, then click Word Wrap.

Figure 1-28 ◀
Opening a file
from Find

quotation you were
looking for

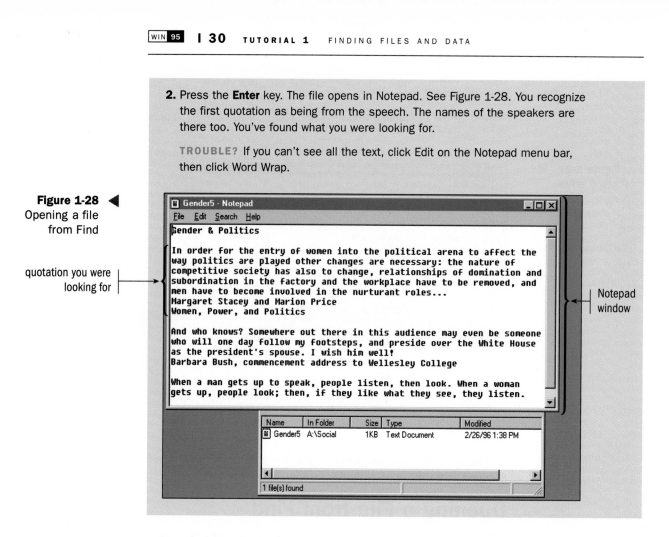

Notepad
window

You decide to print the contents of this file so that you can start assembling a collection of quotations to give to Carolyn in the morning.

To print the file and close Notepad:

1. Click **File** then click **Print**. You retrieve the hard copy and put it in your briefcase.

2. Click the Notepad **Close** button ☒ to close Notepad. Click **No** if you are prompted to save your changes.

Saving a Search

For more complicated searches like the one you just performed or for searches you are likely to perform again and again, it can be helpful to save the search so you can open it again later. Find includes a Save Search command that places an icon representing the search on your desktop. To reopen the search, you simply activate the icon.

REFERENCE window	**SAVING A SEARCH**
	▪ Run the search you want to save.
	▪ Click File then click Save Search.
	▪ To open the search later, click the search icon on the desktop and press the Enter key.

You decide to save the search you performed to locate the Gender5 file.

To save and then reopen a search:

1. Click **File** then click **Save Search**. It might seem that nothing happens, but if you check the desktop you'll see the search is there.

2. Click the Find **Close** button ☒ to close Find. See Figure 1-29. The search is on the desktop.

   TROUBLE? If you don't see a search icon similar to the one in Figure 1-29, it's possible that you are on a network computer that doesn't allow users to save anything to the hard drive. If so, read Step 3 without performing it.

Figure 1-29 ◀
Saved search icon

your desktop might look different

search icon appears on the desktop; might be on a different location on your desktop

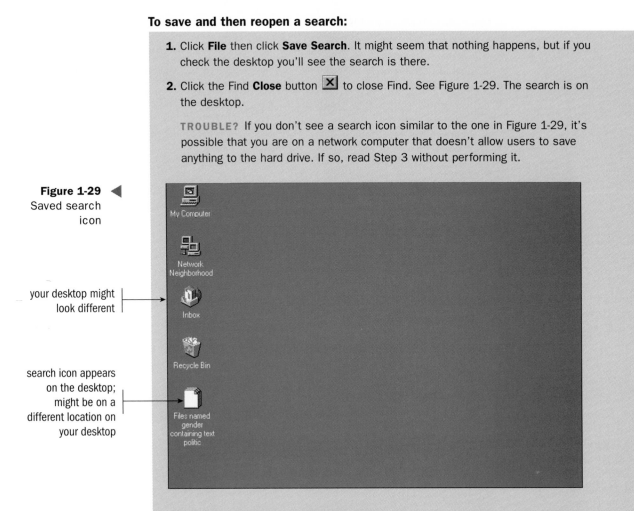

3. Click the **saved search icon**, as shown in Figure 1-29, then press the **Enter** key to reopen Find to the same criteria and Results list. The old search results appear in the Results list, so you need to click Find Now to update the results.

4. Click the **Find Now** button.

   TROUBLE? If you have removed the floppy disk from the drive or moved the Gender file somewhere else since creating the search, the Results list will change.

Clearing a Search

Throughout this tutorial you've returned each criterion setting to its default so it wouldn't affect subsequent searches. You could do the same for the multiple criteria you just set up, although that would take several steps. To save you time, Windows 95 provides the New Search button to clear the search criteria from all tabs at once. However, you should be aware that there is a possible drawback to using the New Search button—if you want to search your Student Disk any further, you must return to the Name & Location tab and reset the Look in list box to drive A.

To clear all criteria and close Find:

1. Click the **New Search** button.

2. Click the **OK** button to acknowledge the message that this will clear your current search. Find returns all settings to their defaults.

3. Click the Find **Close** button ☒.

4. Return to the desktop and delete the saved search icon.

   TROUBLE? To delete an icon, you click it, press the Delete key, then click Yes if prompted.

Opening Recent Documents

3.1 NOTE

The Documents menu is new to Windows 95. There is no equivalent in Windows 3.1.

So far in this tutorial you have used Find to locate files. There is another way to locate a file you've worked on recently. You can view a list of recently opened documents using the Documents command on the Start menu. If you click one of the documents on the Documents menu, Windows 95 locates and starts the program that created the document and then opens the document.

To view the most recent documents list:

1. Click the **Start** button 🅁 Start.

2. Point to **Documents**. The Documents menu opens. See Figure 1-30. Don't do this now, but to open a file from the Documents menu, you would click it.

Figure 1-30 ◄
Most recent documents on the Documents menu

most recent documents; your list will be different

Documents option

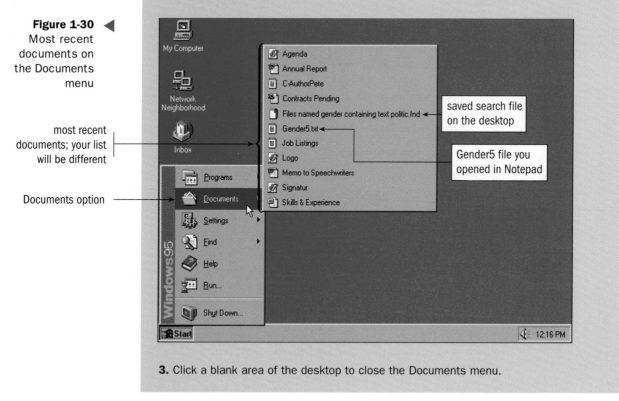

3. Click a blank area of the desktop to close the Documents menu.

The Documents command is useful only when you have recently worked on a file. It can be the quickest way to find and open such a file.

Quick Check

1. To find all files modified before the year 1997, what dates should you enter in the start date and end date boxes?

2. If you want the Find utility to display only the bitmapped images on your floppy disk, what tab should you click in Find and what criterion should you specify?

3. True or false: When you choose the Case Sensitive option, Find looks for files whose names match the case of the entry in the Named box on the Name & Location tab.

4. What search criteria might you specify in Find if you want to find a paper you wrote yesterday in WordPerfect on how rap music is used commercially? List four possible criteria.

5. If the Results list displays the file you were looking for, how do you open the file for editing?

6. Something seems to be wrong with Notepad. You can see only the first ten words or so of each paragraph. What should you do?

7. You want to find a file that you know is exactly 48 KB in size. What should you do: Click "Exactly" in the Size is list and then type 48, or click "At least" in the Size is list and then type 47?

8. Where can you find a saved search?

9. You're looking for a file named Resume that you created last week. You know it's on the hard drive that you've specified in the Look in list, but your searches aren't successful. You're sure you have the right name in the Named box. You wonder if something is wrong with Find. What might be the problem?

SESSION

1.3

In this session you will learn about Quick View, a utility that lets you look at the contents of files without actually opening them. You will learn how to check whether Quick View is installed, how to view one or more files in Quick View, and how to work with the Quick View window's appearance.

Viewing a File Using Quick View

3.1 NOTE

Quick View is a new Windows 95 feature. There is no Windows 3.1 equivalent.

In Session 1.2 you saw how to open files directly from Find. However, if you don't have the program that created the file, you won't be able to open it. Windows 95 provides a useful utility called **Quick View** that lets you view a file without opening its corresponding program. Quick View is also useful when you want to view a batch of files quickly. For example, the searches you performed in Sessions 1.1 and 1.2 yielded a list of files on men, women, and gender. You'd like to take a look at the contents of some of these files to see if they might contain material for Senator Bernstein's speech on gender and politics. Because you have at least ten files to look through, you decide to use Quick View rather than open each file individually.

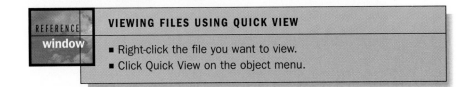

REFERENCE window

VIEWING FILES USING QUICK VIEW

- Right-click the file you want to view.
- Click Quick View on the object menu.

Note that Quick View is not included in the typical installation of Windows 95. You'll know if Quick View is installed by looking at a file's object menu. Use "men" as your search string, then right-click one of the files in the Results list to open the file's object menu and see if Quick View appears.

To check whether Quick View is installed and then to start Quick View:

1. Place your Student Disk in drive A if necessary, start Find, click the **Look in** list arrow, and select drive A.

2. Type **men** in the Named box.

3. Click the **Find Now** button, then click the **Name** button to sort the files alphabetically by last name so the file named "Men" is visible at the top of the Results list.

   TROUBLE? If clicking the Name button orders the files in descending alphabetical order, click the Name button again.

4. Right-click **Men**, then look at the object menu that opens. If Quick View is installed, it appears as an option on the object menu. See Figure 1-31.

   TROUBLE? If Quick View appears as an option on the menu, as shown in Figure 1-31, then Quick View is installed on your computer and you can proceed. If Quick View does not appear, then you cannot complete this session until Quick View is installed. Check with your instructor or technical support person for directions. If you are using your own computer and you have the installation disks, online Help can help you install Quick View. Search for "installing" in the Index, then choose "Windows components." The topic that opens is called "To install a Windows component after Windows has been installed." If you still can't install Quick View, read through this session without doing the steps.

Figure 1-31 ◀
Opening a text file's object menu from Find

Quick View on the object menu; yours might look different

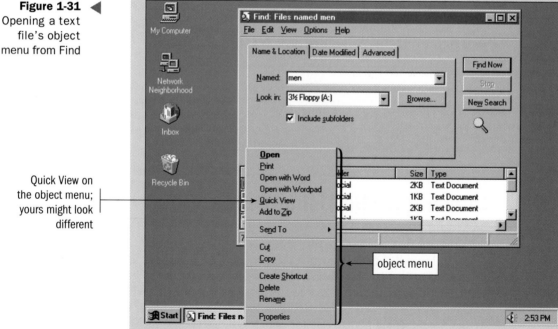

5. Click **Quick View**. The Quick View window opens. See Figure 1-32.

   TROUBLE? If your document does not appear as a page, click View, then click Page View. If necessary, click the Increase Font Size button to increase the size of the text to match Figure 1-32.

Figure 1-32 ◀
Quick View
window

Increase Font
Size button

page in Quick
View window

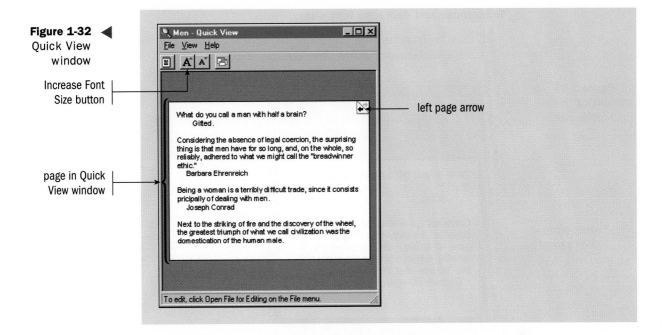

left page arrow

Quick View displays the contents of a file in the document window either in Page or Normal view. **Page view**, as shown in Figure 1-32, displays the document in pages. **Normal view** displays the text as a continuous document and supplies scroll bars you can use to view it. In Page view, if the document is more than one page, page arrows appear in the upper-right corner.

The degree of accuracy with which Quick View displays your documents depends on the type of file you are viewing. If you are viewing a word processed document, for example, Quick View doesn't duplicate your document's fonts and keeps formatting to a minimum (bold and italic only; no lines or bullets). If there are objects such as graphics or charts in the text document, Quick View represents them with shaded boxes. If you are viewing a document such as a bitmap image or a PowerPoint slide presentation, however, Quick View shows the actual drawing.

Changing the Font Size

For a simple text document, the Quick View window in Page view shows your file in "pages"—not the actual pages of your document if you were to print it, but pages that show a portion of the file. Quick View uses a **font**, or typeface style, that is easy to read. The amount of text on the page depends on the font size of the letters. The larger the letters, the less of the file that fits on a page.

The page in Figure 1-32 shows several quotations about men, some of which might interest Senator Bernstein. You decide to experiment with the font size to see more or less of the document. Changing the font size in Quick View does not affect the formatting of the document itself.

To increase and decrease font size:

1. Click the **Increase Font Size** button [A] several times. The text is easier to read, but fewer quotes fit on the page. See Figure 1-33.

Figure 1-33 ◀
Increasing the font size

fewer quotes
fit on a page

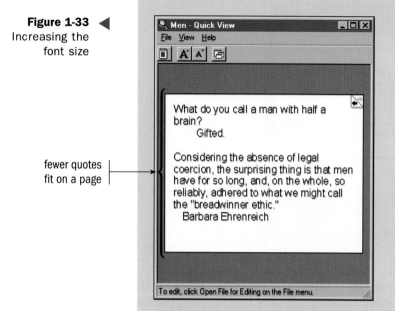

2. Click the **Decrease Font Size** button [A] several times. Now more quotations fit on the page, but they are harder to read. See Figure 1-34.

Figure 1-34 ◀
Decreasing the font size

more quotes
fit on a page

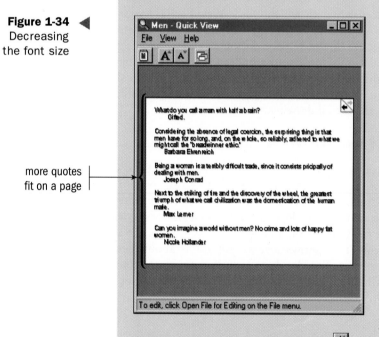

3. Click the **Increase Font Size** button [A] until the font size is just right for you.

Navigating Quick View Pages

You realize you're only seeing the first few quotations in the file, and you wonder if there are any others that might work for Senator Bernstein's speech. You'd like to scroll through the entire document. Unless your document is very short, it cannot be displayed on a single page in Quick View. To do so, you can "turn the pages" by clicking the page arrows in the upper-right corner of the document.

To view more pages of a document in Quick View:

1. Click the **left page arrow** ⬅. The next page of text appears. See Figure 1-35.

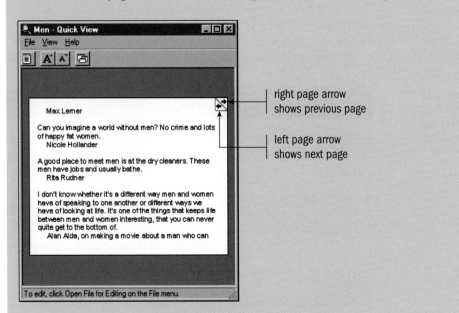

right page arrow
shows previous page

left page arrow
shows next page

TROUBLE? If you don't see a page arrow, you might not be in Page view. Click View, then click Page view.

2. Continue clicking the **left page arrow** ⬅ until you reach the end of the document. The left page arrow turns gray when you have reached the end. See Figure 1-36.

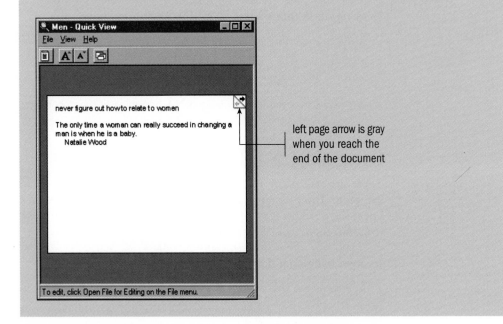

left page arrow is gray
when you reach the
end of the document

To go back to the beginning of the document, you can click the right page arrow ➡ repeatedly or you can use your keyboard's navigation keys. **Navigation keys** are keys that you press to move through a document, including Page Up, Page Down, Home, End, and the arrow keys →, ←, ↑, ↓. These keys have standard functions in most software packages. Figure 1-37 shows the function of each key, along with a few standard key combinations.

Try navigating your document in Quick View using the navigation keys.

Figure 1-37 ◀
Navigation keys
and key
combinations

Key	Function
Page Up	Moves up one screen or page
Page Down	Moves down one screen or page
Home	Moves to the beginning of the current line or page
End	Moves to the end of the current line or page
Arrow Keys	Moves through the document one line or one character at a time in the direction of the arrow
Ctrl + Home	Moves to beginning of document
Ctrl + End	Moves to end of document

To navigate in Quick View using the navigation keys:

1. Press **Page Up** two or three times. You move up in the document one page at a time.

2. Press **Ctrl + End**. You move to the end of the document.

3. Press **Ctrl + Home**. You move to the beginning of the document.

Dragging a File into Quick View

There are still many interesting files listed in the Find Results list that you've not yet explored. You'd like to take a look at one of the files on women. Once Quick View is open, the quickest way to look at another of the files in the Results list is to drag the file icon into the Quick View window.

To open additional documents in Quick View:

1. Arrange the Find and Quick View windows so parts of both are visible.

   TROUBLE? To arrange the windows, make sure they are not maximized, then drag their title bars to a new location.

2. Using the left mouse button, drag the file **Women** into the Quick View window (scroll the Results list to see it if necessary). See Figure 1-38. The contents of this file appear.

Figure 1-38 ◄
Dragging a file
into Quick
View window

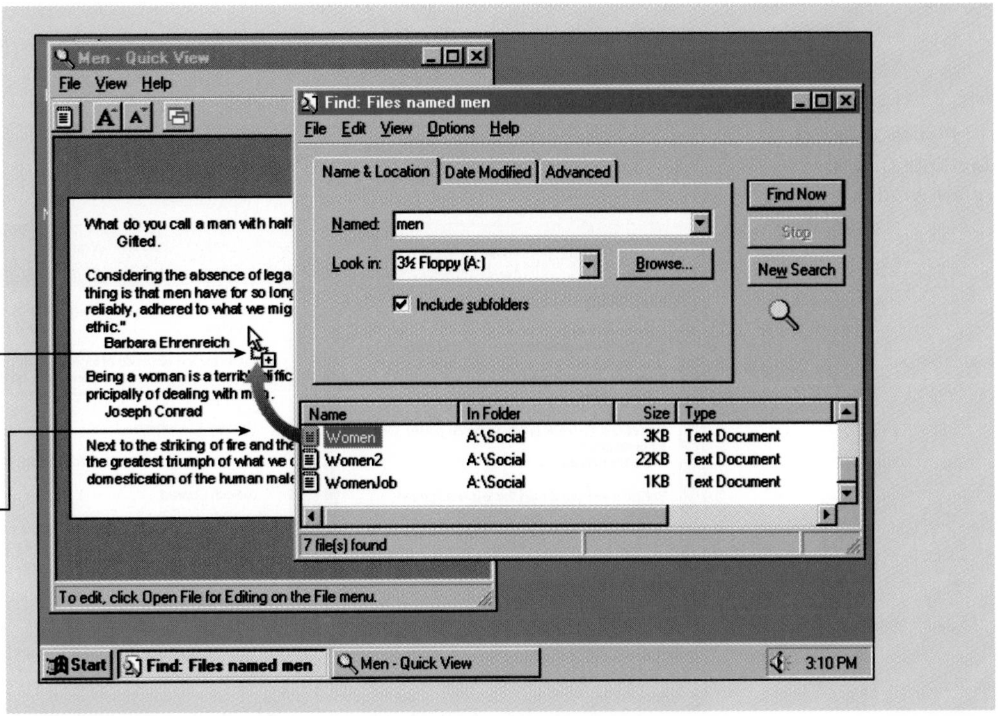

pointer when
you drag file

drag file from
Find to Quick View

If you want to compare files while in Quick View, you can open two Quick View windows at a time. You decide to compare the quotations in the Women file to the ones in the Men file so you have a balanced view of the quotations available for both genders.

To open two files in Quick View:

1. Right-click **Men** in the Find window.

2. Click **Quick View**. The Men file opens in a new Quick View window. You decide to arrange the windows so you can see both quotations files at the same time.

   TROUBLE? If only one Quick View window is open, Quick View on your computer might be set to replace the file in the open Quick View window with the new file. Click the Replace Window button ⊡ so it is not selected, then repeat Steps 1 and 2 with the Women file.

3. Minimize the **Find** window, then move the two open Quick View windows so they are side by side. See Figure 1-39.

Figure 1-39 ◀
Multiple Quick
View windows

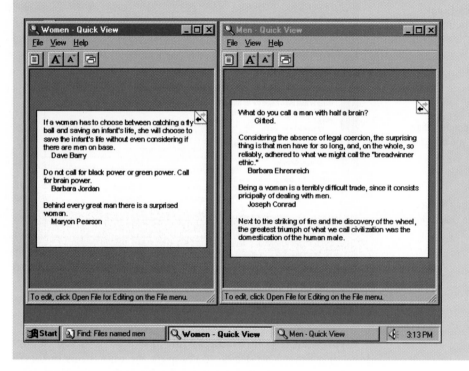

After looking at the two Quick View windows, you decide to print both these files because they contain good material. However, you can't print a file directly from Quick View. You must close the Quick View windows, and print the files directly from Find using the Print command on the object menu.

To close the Quick View windows and print the files from Find:

1. Click the **Close** button ☒ on both Quick View windows.

2. Click the **Find** button on the taskbar.

3. Right-click the **Men** file, then click **Print**.

4. Right-click the **Women** file (scroll to see it if necessary), then click **Print**. You retrieve these printouts and staple them together with the one you made earlier.

5. Click the Find **Close** button ☒.

Quick Check

1 How can you look at a file's contents if the program that created it is not loaded on your computer?

2 Does Quick View display the pages of your file exactly as they would appear if you printed them? Explain your answer.

3 Can you use Quick View to view a bitmap image, or is it useful only for text files?

4 You can barely read the words in the Quick View window. What button should you click?

5 You're using Quick View to examine a large file. Describe two ways to get to the end of the file.

End Note

With the printouts of the BBC speech excerpt and the quotations on men and women, you have the beginnings of a list of recommendations for Carolyn. It's late, so you shut down your computer. You look forward to giving the quotations you've found so far to Carolyn, and you feel confident about managing the quotations archive disk. Because you can search for files by name, location, date, type, size, and contents, you're sure that you'll always be able to find the files you need. Once you've found them, you know how to get at them quickly, either by opening them or viewing them in Quick View.

Tutorial Assignments

1. Locating Folders on a Hard Disk On which drive is your Windows folder? Specify My Computer in the Look in list, then search for "Windows" in the Named box. Write the answer on a piece of paper. If there are too many files in the Results list, sort the files by name so folders appear at the top.

2. Finding a File Using a Search String The governor has asked Senator Bernstein to represent the state in upcoming negotiations with Taiwan for exporting dairy products. Senator Bernstein is preparing a staff briefing on the special issues she expects to arise during these negotiations. Carolyn wants you to start searching for good material for Senator Bernstein's opening remarks. In any international negotiation, language is always an issue. You remember a very funny story about the translation of an ad for Coca-Cola into another language. Might that anecdote be somewhere on the quotations archive disk?

    a. To find out, start Find and enter likely search strings into the Named box. Make sure you select drive A.

    b. Once you find a file you think looks promising, open it from Find.

    c. When you've found what you want, print it, then close Notepad and Find.

3. Learning More About Files On a sheet of paper, write the answers to the following questions about the files on the Student Disk. You can answer all the questions by examining the filenames.

    a. How many files are there with the search string "comedy" in the filename?

    b. How many files and folders are on the disk? Use Find to answer this question. What did you do to find the answer?

    c. Which letters of the alphabet are missing in the filenames of the alphabetically organized Author files?

    d. How many files are there on inspirational topics? What search string did you use to find this answer?

4. Using Wildcards What search strings could you use to produce the following Results lists? Write the search strings on a piece of paper. Use a wildcard for each one. For example, a Results list of Budget96.xls, Budget97.xls, and Budget98.xls could come from the search string "Budget9?.xls."

    a. Comedy1.doc, Comedy2.doc, Comedy3.doc

    b. Social.txt, Society.txt, Socratic Method.txt

    c. PhotoWorks, Network, Files for Work

5. Generalizing About Wildcards Specify the following search strings in the Named box, and examine the Results list for each search string very carefully. What generalizations about wildcards can you make from your observations?

    men

    men.*

    men.

    men*.*

    men?

    men?.*

6. Searching for Files by Date You can answer these questions about the Student Disk by using the Date Modified tab. Write the answers on a sheet of paper. Return all settings to their defaults when you are done.

    a. What files did Carolyn's previous aide enter on April 2, 1997?

    b. Over what period of time did Carolyn's previous aide enter all author files in the Alphabet folder?

    c. What is the oldest file on the Student Disk?

7. Searching a Hard Drive for Types of Files You can use Find to learn about the files on your hard drive. Record how many files of each of the following type exist on your hard drive. Return the file type to its default of All Files and Folders when you are done.

    a. Application. Write down the names of five application files in the Windows folder of your hard drive.

    b. Bitmap Image. What folders on your hard drive seem to store the most bitmap images?

    c. Screen Saver. Write the locations of some of the screen savers on your hard drive.

    d. Text Document. Once the Results list shows all the text documents on your hard drive, order them by Name. Are there any files named Readme? Write down the locations of two of them. Software programs often come with a Readme text file that lists known software problems and answers to common questions.

8. Locating Files by Size How many files of 1 KB or less are on the Student Disk? How many files of 15 KB or more? Return this setting to its default when you are done.

9. Locating Files by Contents You still have that Dave Barry column you clipped from the *Washington Post*. Search the contents of the files on the Student Disk to see how many of them contain the text string "barry," then record that number. Write down the name of the file that looks like it contains the most Dave Barry quotations. Open the file from Find and read through its contents. When you are done, delete the criteria you entered.

10. Experimenting with Search Criteria You look over Senator Bernstein's speech topics for the next several months and decide to search for appropriate quotations. For each speech topic, write down the criteria you used to locate a file, and then write down the file location as displayed in the In Folder column of the Results list. If you find more than one file, write down the first one in the list.

    a. Senator Bernstein has been invited to give the toast at a football brunch hosted by the President of Stanton College.

    b. The family of a deceased friend has asked Senator Bernstein if she'd like to contribute a few lines to an obituary in the local newspaper.

    c. Senator Bernstein is cochairing this year's Renaissance Festival downtown. The Festival will feature outdoor performances of three of Shakespeare's plays, including one by the Young Shakespeare's Guild, a troupe of children under age 18. She's promised to give the opening remarks at the Festival.

11. Saving a Search Search for a file with a quotation by Bill Cosby.

    a. Save this search.

    b. Right-click the saved search icon on the desktop and click Properties.

    c. Move the Properties dialog box so you can see both the icon and the dialog box, then use the Print Screen key to store an image of the screen. Paste the image into WordPad, then print the image.

    d. On the printout, write the file type of the saved search. Circle its file extension.

    e. Close the Properties dialog box and delete the saved search icon when you are done.

12. Opening Files from Find You learned how to open a text document from Find in Session 1.2. You can open other types of files the same way, as long as your computer contains the application that created the file.

    a. Use Quick Format in Windows Explorer to format your Student Disk, then make a new Student Disk for this tutorial as described in the beginning of Session 1.1.

    b. Search for Bitmap Image files on your Student Disk. There should be only one. Click it, then press the Enter key. It opens in Paint. Click File, then click Print to print the image.

    c. Search for Wave Sound files on your Student Disk (this object might appear as Sound). Right-click one of them, click Play, then click the Play button. What did you hear? Click the Close button when the sound file is done playing. If you don't hear anything, your computer might not have speakers, or they might be off.

    d. Search for Video Clip files on your computer's hard drive. If you found any, right-click one of them, click Play, then click the Play button. Describe what you see. Click the Close button when the video clip is done playing.

13. Viewing Recent Documents Write down the names of 10 documents recently accessed on the hard disk.

14. Searching and Viewing File Contents Use Quick View to find the answers to the questions below. You will probably need to search for a text string in the file's contents using the Advanced tab. If Quick View isn't installed on your computer, open the files from Find to find the answers. For each answer, write the name of the file you used to find the answer. (*Hint:* Once you've located and opened the file, you can either scroll through it to find the answer, or, if the file is a long one, click Search on the Notepad menu bar then click Find.) Type the text string in the Find what box, then click the Find Next button.

    a. What did Elsa Einstein think about her husband Albert's theory of relativity?

    b. Do you think cartoonist Jim Borgman is an optimist or a pessimist? Why?

    c. What was Helen Keller's opinion of college?

    d. How many children does Erma Bombeck recommend? (Look carefully at the filenames in the Results list so you don't open more files than necessary.)

    e. What is the dry cleaners really good for?

    f. What did Elbert Hubbard have to say about books? (Look carefully at the filenames in the Results list so you don't open more files than necessary.)

Working with Graphics

CASE

Kiana Ski Shop

Cross-country ski enthusiast Joe Nitka owns Kiana Ski Shop in the heart of the northern Wisconsin Chequamegon National Forest, near the site of the world-class Birkebeiner cross-country ski race. Joe is one of the local promoters of the race. He gathers and releases information on lodging and transportation for competitors, the media, and spectators. You recently moved to the area, and you and Joe have become friends. An avid cross-country skier yourself, you volunteer to help Joe create his Birkebeiner promotions to make them look more professional. Currently Joe types race information on a typewriter, copies it on colored paper, and distributes these flyers to interested parties. You tell him his promotions would capture more attention if they included a few graphics, such as a skier or a picture of the race logo.

Joe agrees, and says he could photocopy some drawings from a clip art collection of images and pictures at the library. You tell him there are advantages to using a computer instead: clip art can be resized more easily, pasted seamlessly into a word-processed document, and edited. Joe doesn't have a computer, but you do; so you invite him to your house to work with you. You think you can find some eye-catching clip art on the Internet that you can customize, or you could even create a graphic or two from scratch. Joe wants to learn about computer graphics, so he accepts your invitation. He explains that his first priority is the announcement that he'll send to local motel and hotel owners asking if they'd like to advertise their services in his promotions.

You spend a little time on the Internet before Joe arrives, and you find a graphic file called Sports that includes several sports-related images. When Joe arrives, you explain that if you decide to use computer clip art, you'll need to make sure it is not copyrighted. Only clip art that is in the public domain may be downloaded and used freely.

SESSION 2.1

In this session you open a graphic in the Windows 95 graphics accessory, Paint. You will crop a portion of the graphic and save it in a new file. Then you will edit the graphic to meet your needs and save it in a monochrome and color bitmapped graphic format.

Starting Paint

Joe comments how great it is that you can draw things on your computer. You tell him that drawings on a computer are called **graphics**. Some graphics are created using a **scanner** to convert an existing paper image to an electronic file that you can open and work with on your computer, as shown in Figure 2-1.

Figure 2-1 ◀
Using a
scanner to
create a
graphic

scanner takes a
picture of the image

scanner saves the
image as a file

you open the file in a
graphics program on
your computer

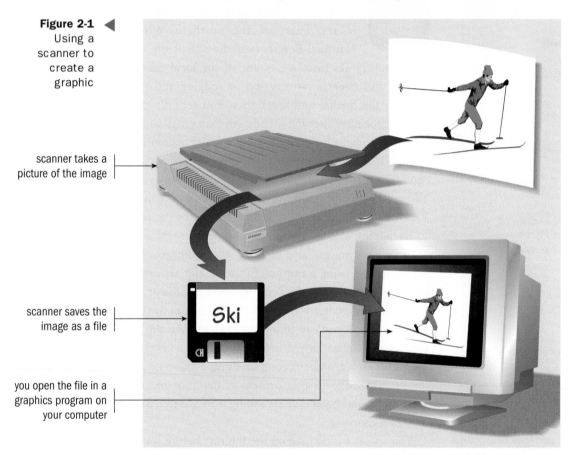

3.1 NOTE

Paint replaces the Windows 3.1 Paintbrush accessory. Many of the tools are the same, although they are arranged slightly differently in the tool box.

You can also create a graphic from scratch using a **graphics program**. Popular graphics programs include, among an ever-growing market, CorelDraw, Freehand, and Photoshop. Windows 95 includes a basic graphics program in its Accessories group called **Paint**, which lets you create, edit, and manipulate graphics. Graphics come in two fundamental types: bitmapped and vector. A **bitmapped graphic** is made up of small dots, whereas a **vector graphic** is created by mathematical formulas. Computer clip art can come in either graphic type, although vector clip art is more precise because of its mathematical nature. Paint, however, handles only bitmapped graphics. Because the Sports graphic you found is a bitmapped graphic, for Joe's purpose Paint will work fine. In this session you'll work with an existing graphic, and in Session 2.2 you'll create one from scratch.

You decide to start Paint and introduce Joe to the world of computer graphics.

To start Paint:

1. Click the **Start** button ![Start].

2. Point to **Programs** then point to **Accessories**. The Accessories menu opens.

3. Click **Paint**. The Paint window opens. See Figure 2-2.

   TROUBLE? If Paint doesn't appear, it might not be installed on your system. Ask your instructor or lab manager for assistance.

Figure 2-2 ◀
Paint window

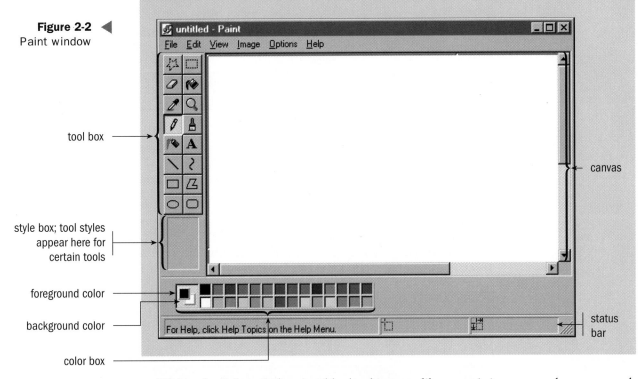

tool box

style box; tool styles appear here for certain tools

foreground color

background color

color box

canvas

status bar

Within the Paint window is a blank white area like an artist's canvas, where you work with your graphic. At the bottom of the window is the color box, which displays available colors or shades for the foreground and background of your graphic. To the left of the color box are two additional boxes, the top for the foreground color and the bottom for the background color of any object you might draw. The status bar at the bottom of the window provides information about the location of the pointer.

To the left of the canvas is the **tool box**, a collection of tools that you use to draw and edit graphics. The tools all work the same way: You click a tool, the pointer changes to a shape representing the tool, and then you either click or drag on the canvas to draw with the tool. Some of the tools offer different widths or shapes, which are depicted in a style box that appears below the tool box, as you'll see in Session 2.2.

Figure 2-3 shows the available tools, along with the pointer shape that appears when you use the tool.

Figure 2-3 ◀
Paint tools

Tool	Button	Description	Pointer
Free-Form Select		Select a free-form portion of a graphic	
Select		Select a rectangular portion of a graphic	
Eraser/Color Eraser		Erase a portion of the graphic	
Fill With Color		Fill an enclosed area with the current color	
Pick Color		Pick up an existing color in the graphic	
Magnifier		Change the magnification	
Pencil		Draw a free-form line or draw one pixel at a time	
Brush		Draw using a brush in a variety of widths	
Airbrush		Draw using an airbrush in a variety of widths	
Text		Insert text into a graphic	
Line		Draw a line	
Curve		Draw a curve	
Rectangle		Draw a rectangle or square	
Polygon		Draw a polygon	
Ellipse		Draw an ellipse or circle	
Rounded Rectangle		Draw a rectangle or square with rounded corners	

REFERENCE window

USING THE TOOL BOX TOOLS

- Click one of the tool box tools.
- If applicable, click one of the tool styles in the style box that appears below the tool box.
- Drag the pointer over the canvas for drawing or selection tools, or click for fill, text, or view tools.

You'll work with some of the editing tools in this session, with the drawing tools in Session 2.2, and with the color and text tools in Session 2.3.

Opening a Graphic in Paint

Joe wants to take a look at the Sports graphic to see if there is anything that might work for his announcement. To open an existing graphic in Paint, you use the Open command on the File menu.

To open the Sports graphic:

1. Place your Student Disk in drive A. See the "Read This Before You Begin" page to make sure you are using the correct disk for this tutorial.

   TROUBLE? If your 3½-inch disk drive is B, place your Student Disk in that drive instead, and for the rest of this tutorial substitute drive B wherever you see drive A.

2. Click **File** then click **Open**.

3. Click the **Look in** list arrow ☑, then click the drive containing your Student Disk.

4. Click Sports then click the **Open** button.

   TROUBLE? If Sports appears as Sports.bmp, your computer is set to display file extensions as part of the filename. Click Sports.bmp, click Open, then continue with Step 5.

5. Click the **Maximize** button ☐ to maximize the Paint window.

6. Scroll to the bottom of the graphic and to the right side. See Figure 2-4. The Sports graphic contains a number of sporting figures.

Figure 2-4 ◀
Sports graphic

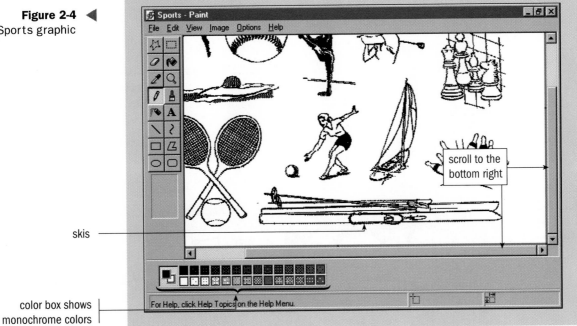

skis

color box shows
monochrome colors

Note the color box at the bottom of the Paint window. It no longer offers the array of colors in Figure 2-2. You tell Joe that the Sports graphic is a **monochrome graphic**, that is, a graphic with only two colors—black and white—available to it. Notice that the color box includes only black, white, and patterns of black and white that give the illusion of gray shading.

Cropping a Portion of a Graphic

Looking over the graphic, Joe notices the pair of skis at the bottom. He thinks the skis alone would look great at the bottom of the announcement. You tell Joe you can capture just that portion of the graphic by **cropping**, or cutting out, everything around it. To crop a graphic, you use either the Select tool or the Free-Form Select tool. With the **Select tool**, you draw a rectangle, called a **selection box**, around the area you want to crop. With the **Free-Form Select tool**, you draw any shaped line around the area. Once you have selected the graphic you need, you save that selection to a separate file. The separate file contains only the cropped area—in Joe's case, the pair of skis.

<table>
<tr><td>REFERENCE
window</td><td>CROPPING A GRAPHIC

■ Click the Select tool or the Free-Form Select tool.
■ Select the area you want to retain.
■ Click Edit, then click Copy To.
■ Enter a name and location in the Save As dialog box, then click the Save button.
■ Open the cropped graphic.</td></tr>
</table>

In this section you'll use the Select tool because it's easier to manipulate than the Free-Form Select tool. However, because the sailboat and the bowling ball images are so close to the skis, when you crop you will inadvertently include portions of those graphics. Don't worry; in the next section you'll learn how to erase parts of a graphic that you don't want. In the Tutorial Assignments, you'll have an opportunity to use the Free-Form Select tool to avoid the extra step of erasing. You're ready to select the skis.

To select the skis:

1. Locate and click the **Select** button ⬚ in the tool box.

2. Move the pointer over the canvas. The pointer looks like ┼.

3. Next you need to drag a selection box around the pair of skis. To do this, point to the white space to the upper-left of the skis. Press the left mouse button and hold it down while you drag to the lower-right corner of the skis. As you drag, a selection box appears. See Figure 2-5.

   TROUBLE? If you release the mouse button too early or your selection box doesn't include the entire pair of skis, click an area of the canvas outside the selection box and repeat step 3.

Figure 2-5 ◀
Selecting an
area to crop

Select tool —

selection box —

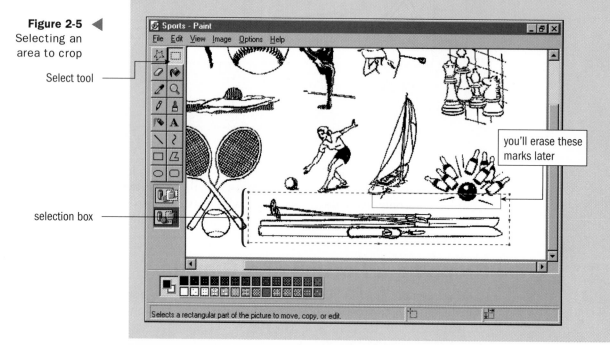

you'll erase these
marks later

Now that the skis are selected, you can use the Copy To command to save the selected area to a new file.

To save the selected area to a new file:

1. Click **Edit** then click **Copy To**.

2. Type **Skis** in the File name box. Make sure the Save in box shows your Student Disk. Notice that the file type is a Monochrome Bitmap because this is a monochrome graphic. You'll learn more about Paint's file types later in this session.

3. Click the **Save** button. The file is saved on your Student Disk with the filename Skis.

The Sports graphic is still open in Paint, and the Skis graphic is in a separate file. In Paint, you can work with only one graphic file at a time. If you try to open another graphic or create a new graphic, Paint closes the current one, prompting you to save it if necessary. If you want two Paint graphics open at the same time, you must start a separate Paint session so that there are actually two Paint windows open with one graphic in each.

To open the Skis graphic:

1. Click **File** then click **Open**.

2. Click Skis then click the **Open** button. If Paint asks if you want to save the changes to Sports, click the **No** button. The Skis graphic opens. See Figure 2-6.

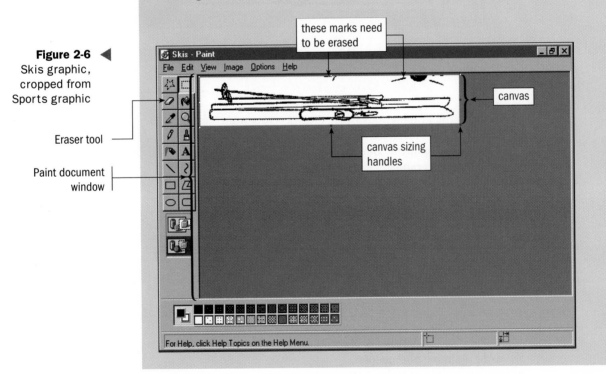

Figure 2-6
Skis graphic, cropped from Sports graphic

Eraser tool

Paint document window

Notice that the canvas now takes up only a small portion of the Paint document window. You can resize the canvas by dragging the canvas **sizing handles,** the small boxes shown in Figure 2-6. However, you don't need to do that now.

Erasing Parts of a Graphic

Joe notices the portions of the sailboat and bowling ball graphics at the top of the Skis graphic. You tell him it's easy to erase unneeded portions of a graphic. You use the **Eraser/Color Eraser tool**, which erases the area over which you drag the pointer. If you erase more than you intended, you can use the **Undo** command on the Edit menu, which reverses one or more of your last three actions, depending on how many times you click Undo.

To erase the portions of the graphic that you don't want:

1. Click the **Eraser/Color Eraser** tool 🖉. The pointer changes to □.

2. Drag the pointer □ over the areas at the top of the Skis graphic to erase them. As you drag, the unwanted black marks disappear. See Figure 2-7.

   TROUBLE? If the black marks aren't disappearing, make sure you press and hold the mouse button while you move the Eraser pointer over the black marks.

   TROUBLE? If you erase a portion of the graphic that you wanted to keep, click Edit, then click Undo.

Figure 2-7 ◀
Erasing
unwanted
marks

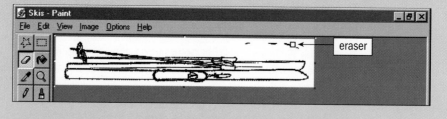

3. Click the **Pencil** tool 🖉 in the tool box so you don't inadvertently erase part of the graphic.

Now the graphic looks just the way you want. You tell Joe that he can use a word processor to create his announcement and insert the graphic directly into the word-processed document. But that's a project for another day. You decide to print and then save the Skis graphic.

To print and save the Skis graphic:

1. Click **File** then click **Print**. The Print dialog box opens.

2. Check the printer settings and make any necessary changes.

3. Click the **OK** button.

4. Click **File** then click **Save**.

Because the graphic is black and white, Joe will be able to reproduce it inexpensively using a simple photocopier.

Bitmapped Graphics

Joe wonders how easy it would be to add color to the Skis graphic if he decides to create an announcement in full color. You tell him you'd have to change the file type from Monochrome Bitmap to one of the color bitmapped graphic types. Joe asks you to explain.

You tell Joe that a computer screen is a gridwork of small dots of light called **pixels**, which is short for "picture elements." The pixels form images on the screen by displaying different colors, sort of like a television set. Buttons on the taskbar, for example, are formed by the pixels shown in Figure 2-8.

Figure 2-8 ◀
Pixels

each square
represents a pixel

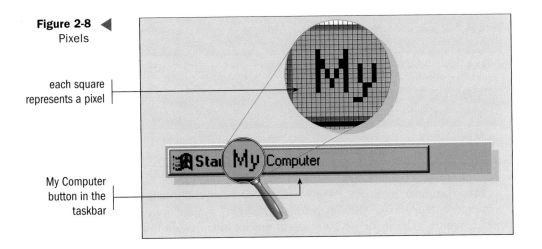

My Computer
button in the
taskbar

Each pixel has a color, and the individual colored pixels form the graphics you see on your screen. To understand how a graphic can be created from pixels, imagine a piece of graph paper where each square represents a pixel. To draw a straight line, you color in a row of squares, or to draw a circle you fill in the squares as best you can to approximate the curve, as shown in Figure 2-9. In this drawing, every pixel within the circle's border is black, and every pixel not in the circle is white. Your computer uses 0's and 1's as a code for the color of each pixel. Each 0 or 1 is called a **bit**. To determine the color of each pixel in a drawing that is only black and white, you need only one bit, because a bit can "take on" a value of either 0 or 1—that is, it can be either off or on.

Figure 2-9 ◀
Bits determine
pixel color

bit has value of "0"
so color is "off"

bit has value of "1"
so color is "on"

bits that are "on"
approximate the
shape of a circle

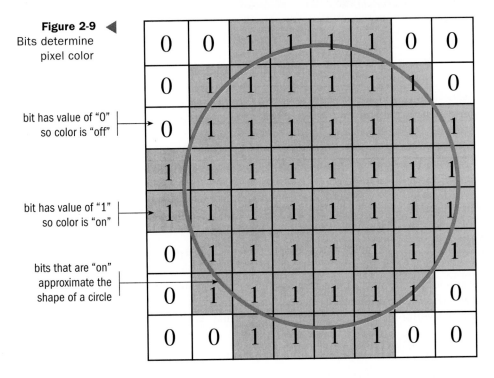

A 1-bit graphic, where each pixel is described by a single bit, is also known as **monochrome bitmap**. The Skis image is such a graphic. If your graphic contains more colors, the computer needs to use more bits for the code. For example, to code the colors black, white, blue, and red, you would need two bits—00 for black, 01 for white, 10 for red, and 11 for blue. There are four bitmap types available in Paint—1-bit, 4-bit, 8-bit, and 24-bit. The more bits you use, the more colors are available. Figure 2-10 shows the bit strings available with four bits.

Figure 2-10
Bit strings
available with
four bits

0000	0100	1000	1100
0001	0101	1001	1101
0010	0110	1010	1110
0011	0111	1011	1111

Your computer maps, or assigns a color, to each code, hence the term "bitmap." A sequence of four zeros, 0000, might mean "black;" a sequence of four ones, 1111, might mean "white." The sequence 1000 might mean "blue." With four bits there are 16 available colors, so in Paint a graphic that uses four bits is saved in the **16 Color Bitmap** file type. The other file types are Monochrome Bitmap, 256 Color Bitmap, and 24-bit Bitmap. The **256 Color Bitmap** type uses sequences of eight bits to represent 256 colors. Similarly, the **24-bit Bitmap** type uses sequences of 24 bits to represent 16.7 million colors—useful for working with color photos. Figure 2-11 summarizes the file types that Paint allows, the number of bits per pixel, the number of distinct colors each type can display, and the size of a file that starts out as a 4 KB monochrome bitmap and then is saved in each type.

Figure 2-11
Paint file
formats

File type	Number of bits	Number of colors	Sample file size
Monochrome	1	2	4 KB
16 Color Bitmap	4	16	13 KB
256 Color Bitmap	8	256	27 KB
24-bit Bitmap	24	16.7 million (also known as True Color)	77 KB

Note that as the number of bits increases, so does the number of available colors. This increases the size of the file. Therefore, you might not want to select a bitmap type with more colors than you need. For a simple black-and-white graphic, monochrome is the best choice.

Paint stores its graphics with the **BMP** file extension—the standard Windows 95 file format for bitmapped graphics. There are many additional graphic formats that Paint doesn't support, including TIFF, GIF, or JPEG. If you want Paint to work with graphics that have TIF, GIF, or JPG file extensions, you need to first use a software program called a **graphics converter** to change the file to BMP format, which Paint can then access.

Resizing Bitmapped Graphics

Joe comments that he's heard people complain about how bitmapped graphics can look rough around the edges. You agree. If the bitmapped graphic is sized correctly it looks fine, but if you try to resize it you might have problems. A bitmapped graphic is defined by pixels, but you can't change the size of an individual pixel. When you try to enlarge a bitmapped graphic, Paint duplicates the pixels to approximate the original shape as best it can—often resulting in jagged edges. On the other hand, when you shrink a bitmapped graphic, Paint removes pixels, and the drawing loses detail. In either case, you distort the original graphic. Sometimes the resized bitmapped graphic will look fine, as when there are many straight lines, but just as often the resized graphic's image quality suffers. For example, if you were to enlarge the Skis graphic, the result might look like Figure 2-12.

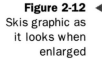

Figure 2-12 ◄
Skis graphic as it looks when enlarged

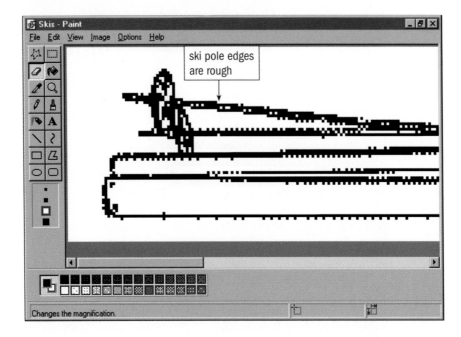

How do you get around this problem? In Paint, there is no easy solution to resizing graphics because they are all bitmapped. If your work with graphics requires resizing—for example, if you are a graphic designer who needs to create logos that must look good on a small business card and a large poster—vector graphics are a better choice. Because vector graphics are mathematically based, you can resize them as necessary without sacrificing image quality.

Saving a Paint Graphic

Joe decides he would like you to save the Skis graphic in a color file type so he can experiment later with adding color.

When you save a graphic in a different file type in Paint, the graphic's appearance doesn't change. The pixels that were black stay black, and those that were white stay white. However, the number of bits that defines each color changes, and so the file increases in size. When you are ready to color the graphic, you'll find a new set of colors available to you. Instead of the black, white, and pattern boxes that you see now in the color box, you will see colors. You decide to save the Skis graphic as a 256 Color Bitmap because it provides a wide array of colors but doesn't take up as much space as the 24-bit Bitmap format.

To save the graphic file as a 256 Color Bitmap:

1. Click **File** then click **Save As**.

2. Click the **Save as type** list arrow ⏷. See Figure 2-13.

Figure 2-13 ◀
Saving a
graphic in a
different file
type

file types available
in Paint

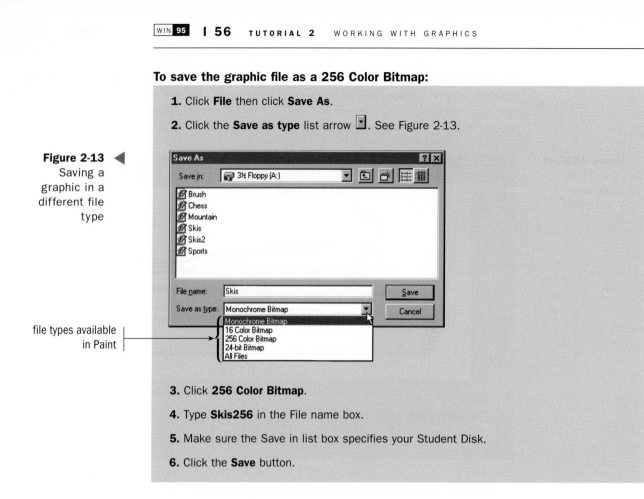

3. Click **256 Color Bitmap**.

4. Type **Skis256** in the File name box.

5. Make sure the Save in list box specifies your Student Disk.

6. Click the **Save** button.

The monochrome graphic closes. Paint now offers an array of colors in the color box. You decide to show Joe how the 256-color format affects the size of the graphics file.

To view the graphics files:

1. Minimize the Paint window.

2. Click the **My Computer** icon on the desktop, then press the **Enter** key.

3. Click 3½" **Floppy (A:)**, then press the **Enter** key.

4. Click **View** then click **Details** to view file sizes. The Skis graphic is a mere 4 KB, whereas the Skis256 graphic is 31 KB. See Figure 2-14.

   TROUBLE? Your graphic files might be sized differently, depending on the size of the canvas when you started.

Figure 2-14 ◀
Relative
file sizes of
Skis files

Monochrome Bitmap
is 4 KB; your size
might be different

256 Color Bitmap is
31 KB; your size might
be different

You tell Joe that if he wants to come back another time and add color to the Skis graphic, that's fine with you. But for now, you're ready for a break.

To finish the session:

1. Click the **Close** button to close the floppy drive window.

2. Click the **Skis256 - Paint** button on the taskbar to reopen the Paint window, then click the **Close** button .

Quick Check

1. Describe how you save a portion of a graphic to a separate file.

2. How do you resize the canvas?

3. True or false: You can open only one graphic in Paint at a time.

4. The small dots on your screen are called _____.

5. Why do color graphics use more file space than monochrome graphics?

6. Can you open a JPEG file in Paint? Why or why not?

SESSION 2.2

In this session you will learn to edit an existing graphic and draw new graphics with Paint's collection of drawing tools. You'll use the Pencil, Line, Brush, and Ellipse tools; and you'll look at options for flipping, rotating, sizing, and stretching your graphics. You'll learn techniques that make drawing easier, such as controlling the magnification, editing one pixel at a time, using the grid and a thumbnail, and copying and pasting parts of a graphic. You'll also learn how to correct mistakes.

Drawing with the Pencil Tool

Joe drops by a few days after your initial computer session with a problem: The Skis graphic isn't right for the Birkebeiner announcement because it shows a downhill ski, not a cross-country ski. The bindings for the two ski types are different, as shown in Figure 2-15.

Figure 2-15 ◄
Problem with the Skis graphic

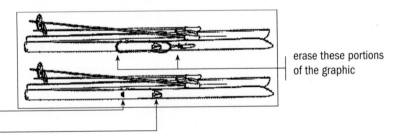

erase these portions of the graphic

add a heel plate

retain the toe clip

You tell Joe you can fix this problem by erasing unwanted portions and then using the **Pencil tool**, which draws free-form dots or lines. Once you have selected the Pencil tool, you click the canvas to draw pixel-size dots or you drag over the canvas to draw a line that is one pixel wide. You decide to show Joe these two methods of drawing with the Pencil tool before you fix the Skis graphic.

3.I NOTE

The Pencil tool is new with Windows 95. To draw one pixel at a time in the Windows 3.1 Paintbrush accessory, you used the Brush tool with the thinnest line width.

Figure 2-16 ◀
Drawing with
the Pencil tool

To experiment with the Pencil tool:

1. Start Paint and make sure your Student Disk is in drive A. Paint opens to an empty canvas.

2. If necessary, click the **Pencil** tool ✎ then move the pointer onto the canvas. The pointer looks like ✎ .

3. Hold the mouse button down and drag ✎ over the canvas. Your pointer leaves a trail as you drag it. See Figure 2-16. Practice drawing lines with the Pencil tool until you feel comfortable with its operation.

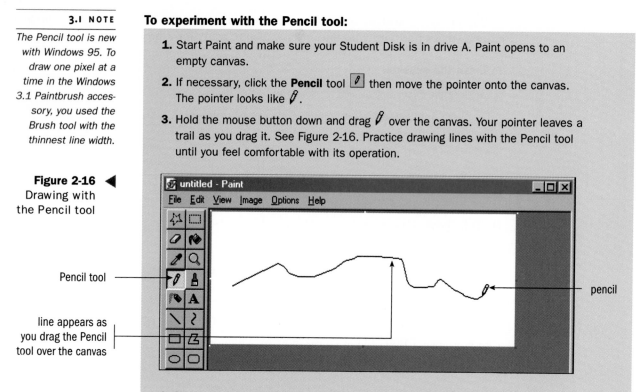

Pencil tool

line appears as you drag the Pencil tool over the canvas

pencil

4. Click a blank area of the canvas to draw a dot the size of a pixel.

Now that you've shown Joe how easy it is to draw lines or dots with the Pencil tool, you are ready to edit the Skis graphic. You first must erase the parts of the binding that are for downhill skis, and then you must add a heel plate for the cross-country ski binding.

Changing View Options

The changes you need to make to the Skis graphic require careful erasing and redrawing—a task made easier when the view is magnified. The **Magnifier tool** allows you to view a graphic at a number of different magnification levels. The default magnification is 100%, also called **Normal view**. If you click the Magnifier tool and then click the graphic, Paint displays it at 400%. You can select a different magnification using the box that appears below the tool box when you click 🔍: 1x (Normal view), 2x (200% magnification), 6x (600% magnification), and 8x (800% magnification). These and more magnification options are also available on the **Custom Zoom dialog box**. Increasing the magnification is called **zooming in**.

If you are magnifying the view to edit a few pixels at a time, the grid can help you navigate. The **grid** is a checkerboard background like a piece of graph paper where each square represents a pixel. The grid guides your drawing so your lines are straight and your shapes are precise.

REFERENCE window	**USING THE VIEW OPTIONS**
	▪ Click the Magnifier tool, then click the graphic to zoom to the default magnification of 400%, or click one of the magnifications in the box below the tool box. *or* ▪ Click View, point to Zoom, click Custom to open the Custom dialog box, select a magnification, then click the OK button. ▪ In a magnified view, click View, point to Zoom, then click Show Grid to view gridlines. ▪ In a magnified view, click View, point to Zoom, then click Show Thumbnail to view a portion of the magnified graphic in Normal view.

You decide to work with the monochrome Skis graphic because Joe's Birkebeiner announcement will be in black and white, not color. You need to open the Skis graphic, zoom in to the highest magnification, and then show the grid so you can more easily edit the graphic. So that your Skis graphic will match the one shown in the figures, you'll open a copy of the graphic, stored on your Student Disk as Skis2, and save it with the name Skis, replacing the original graphic.

To change the view for editing:

1. Click **File**, click **Open**, then locate and open the **Skis2** file on your Student Disk. Click **No** if you are prompted to save changes to the untitled graphic you were just working with.

2. Click **File** then click **Save As**. Make sure the Save in box displays the drive containing your Student Disk. Type **Skis** in the File name box, then click the **Save** button. Click **Yes** when you are asked whether you want to replace the existing file.

3. Click the **Magnifier** tool ⊕ and move the pointer over the canvas. The pointer changes to ⊕ and a box appears that shows the portion of the graphic Paint will magnify.

4. Click the left side of the graphic to use the default 400% magnification.

5. Click **View**, point to **Zoom**, then click **Show Grid**. You can see the individual pixels. See Figure 2-17. The boxes are too small to work with easily, so you decide to use the Custom dialog box to zoom in even more.

   TROUBLE? If your graphic shows a different portion of the skis, scroll all the way to the left.

Figure 2-17 ◀
Grid in a
magnified view

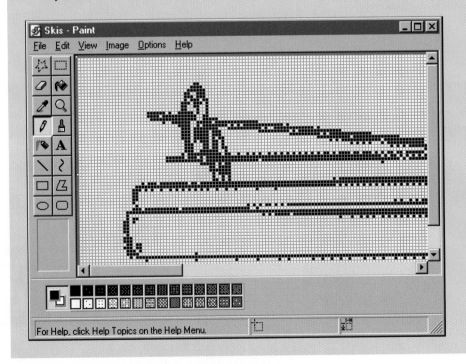

6. Click **View**, point to **Zoom**, then click **Custom**. The Custom Zoom dialog box opens. See Figure 2-18.

Figure 2-18 ◀
Choosing
a different
magnification

current magnification
is 400%

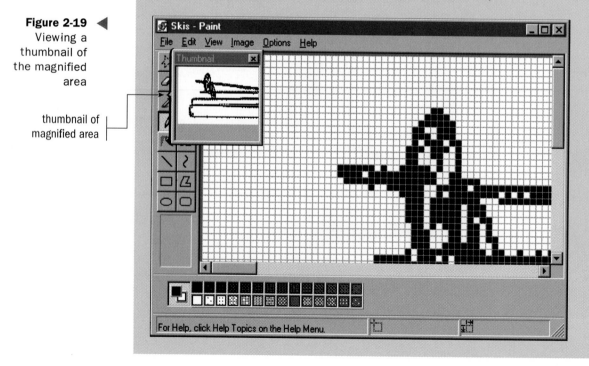

7. Click the **800%** radio button, then click the **OK** button. Now the boxes are larger, and you'll have no problem editing individual pixels.

When you're zoomed in this closely, you sometimes lose sight of the picture's appearance. You can view a **thumbnail**, a small box that shows in Normal view the area you're zooming in on. Thumbnails are especially handy for editing. You decide to view a thumbnail of the area you're working on.

To view a thumbnail:

1. Click **View** then point to **Zoom**.

   TROUBLE? If the thumbnail already appears, skip steps 1 and 2.

2. Click **Show Thumbnail**. A thumbnail of the area you're examining appears on the Paint window. See Figure 2-19.

   TROUBLE? If the thumbnail appears in a different area of the Paint window and it obscures an area you want to examine, drag it out of the way.

Figure 2-19 ◀
Viewing a
thumbnail of
the magnified
area

thumbnail of
magnified area

With the grid on, you can see each pixel, and you are viewing a thumbnail so you can see how your changes affect the larger picture. You're ready to start editing!

Erasing in a Magnified View

Once you are zoomed in, you can erase unwanted portions of the graphic a few pixels at a time. You need to erase the portions of the binding that are for downhill skis. To erase, you drag the Eraser tool over the appropriate pixels. The Eraser tool comes in several different sizes; select the size according to the number of pixels you need to erase. The largest size lets you erase large sections of a graphic in 10×10 boxes (100 pixels at a time). The smallest size lets you erase in 4×4 boxes (16 pixels at a time). There is no way to erase one pixel at a time using the Eraser tool. Figure 2-21 shows you exactly which pixels (the ones shown in red) you'll erase in the next set of steps.

To erase the parts of the ski binding you don't need:

1. Scroll until you see the binding. Watch the thumbnail to see where the binding is located.

2. Click the **Eraser** tool ▨ .

   TROUBLE? If the thumbnail is in the way, drag it to the lower-right corner of the screen.

3. Click the **smallest box** in the Eraser tool styles box. See Figure 2-20.

Figure 2-20 ◄
Selecting the
smallest size of
the Eraser tool

use Eraser tool to
erase pixels within the
ski and below the ski

smallest eraser size

drag thumbnail out of
the way, if necessary

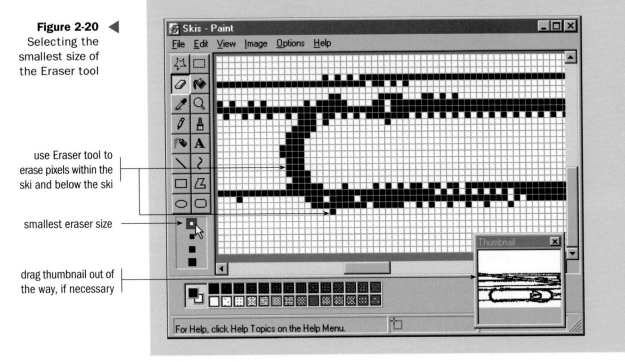

4. Drag the **Eraser** tool over the pixels inside the ski and below the ski, as shown in Figure 2-21. Scroll as necessary to complete the erasures. The pixels that you should erase are shown in red. Don't worry if you miss a few or erase a few extra. In a bitmapped graphic of this size, a few variations will not be noticeable.

TROUBLE? If you erased an area you didn't want to erase, click Edit, then click Undo. If you need to start over, do so without saving your changes.

Figure 2-21 ◄
Pixels that
need to be
erased

pixels you need
to erase are
shown in red

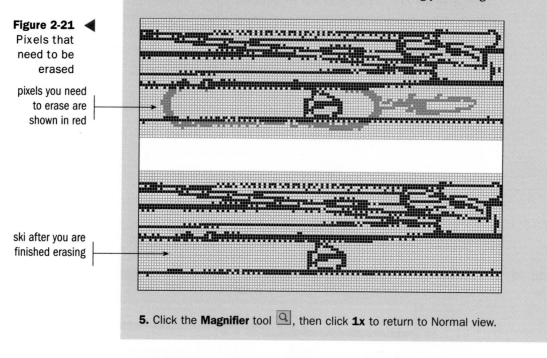

ski after you are
finished erasing

5. Click the **Magnifier** tool 🔍, then click **1x** to return to Normal view.

In Normal view you can see how your erasures have changed the look of the ski. It looks good.

Drawing in a Magnified View

You are now ready to draw the heel plate, which has a trapezoidal shape. You'll use the Pencil tool to draw it a few pixels at a time.

You've already seen how to use the thumbnail to "locate" yourself in the Paint window. Paint offers one other feature to help you control your location as you draw. The **pixel coordinates** in the status bar specify the exact location of the pointer on the canvas relative to the pixels on your screen. Paint displays the pixel coordinates in an (x,y) format (x representing the horizontal location and y the vertical location). Pixel coordinates of 138,25, for example, indicate that the pointer is 138 pixels from the *left* edge of the screen and 25 pixels from the *top*. The next set of steps uses pixel coordinates to help you add the heel plate in just the right location.

You'll use the Magnifier tool to zoom back in, this time to only 600% because the work isn't as meticulous. A lower magnification lets you view a little more of your graphic.

To create the heel plate:

1. Click the **Magnifier** tool 🔍, then click the **6x** magnification option in the box below the tool box.

2. Scroll to the binding area of the ski.

3. Click the **Pencil** tool 🖉, then position the pointer at pixel coordinate **155,57**. See Figure 2-22 for the location of this pixel.

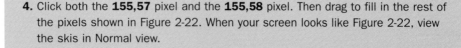

4. Click both the **155,57** pixel and the **155,58** pixel. Then drag to fill in the rest of the pixels shown in Figure 2-22. When your screen looks like Figure 2-22, view the skis in Normal view.

TROUBLE? If you draw in an area you didn't intend to, click Edit, then click Undo.

Figure 2-22 ◄
Using pixel coordinates to draw the heel plate

(155,57)

(155,58)

(159,60)

pixel coordinates of pointer

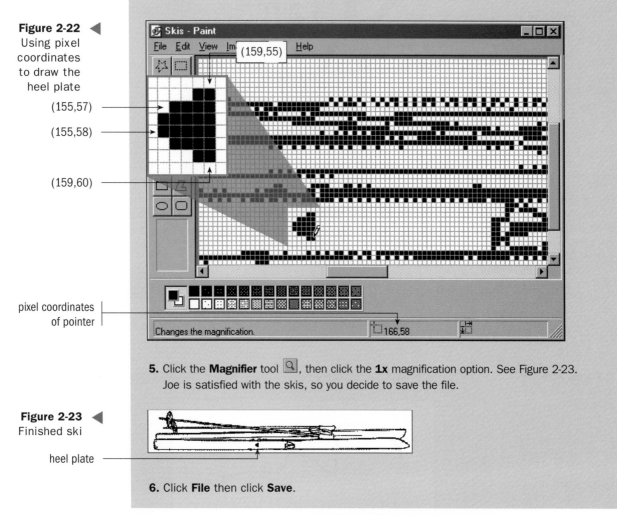

5. Click the **Magnifier** tool $\boxed{Q}$, then click the **1x** magnification option. See Figure 2-23. Joe is satisfied with the skis, so you decide to save the file.

Figure 2-23 ◄
Finished ski

heel plate

6. Click **File** then click **Save**.

Drawing with the Brush Tool

Joe sees how easy it is to draw and asks about creating some new graphics that he could use for advertising Kiana Ski Shop. You've already saved the Skis graphic, so you have three choices for creating a new graphic: you can erase the contents of the canvas using the Eraser tool and then save the file under a different filename, you can choose Clear Image from the Image menu to clear the canvas and then save the file under a different filename, or you can choose New from the File menu to open a new file. You decide to use the third option.

To create a new file:

1. Click **File** then click **New**. An empty canvas opens.

Joe sketches a few ideas, and you decide to draw the sketch in Figure 2-24.

Figure 2-24 ◄
Idea for a Kiana
graphic

. . . to create this ski

you'll draw this ski
and copy it . . .

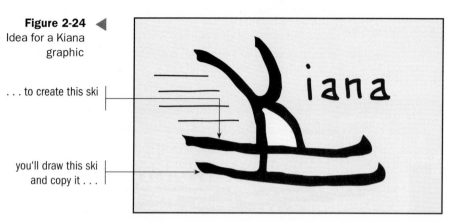

3.1 NOTE

*Although the Brush
tool in Windows 3.1
offers a variety of
brush widths, it does
not offer a variety of
styles, as does the
Windows 95
Brush tool.*

To create this graphic, you explain to Joe, you can use the Brush tool. Unlike the Pencil tool, the **Brush tool** offers a variety of widths and different brush styles to draw with. To create the skis, you can use an angular style brush. To create the letter "K" you can use a rounded brush. You can add the other letters with the Text tool, which you'll learn to use in Session 2.3. First you're going to show Joe how to use the Brush tool.

To draw with the Brush tool:

1. Click the **Brush** tool [A]. Notice the brush styles below the tool box. The current brush style is highlighted.

2. Drag the brush pointer over the canvas. A thick rounded line appears. See Figure 2-25.

Figure 2-25 ◄
Drawing with
the Brush tool

Brush tool

brush styles

angular brush

brush pointer

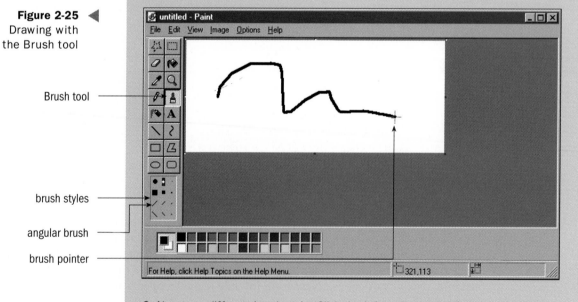

3. Now try a different brush style. Click the left-most **angular line** brush style in the third row, as shown in Figure 2-26, then drag the brush pointer over the screen. You create a line like the one in Figure 2-26. Now try drawing a ski using this tool.

Figure 2-26 ◄
Brush styles

line drawn with
rounded brush

line drawn with
angular brush

angular brush
style is selected

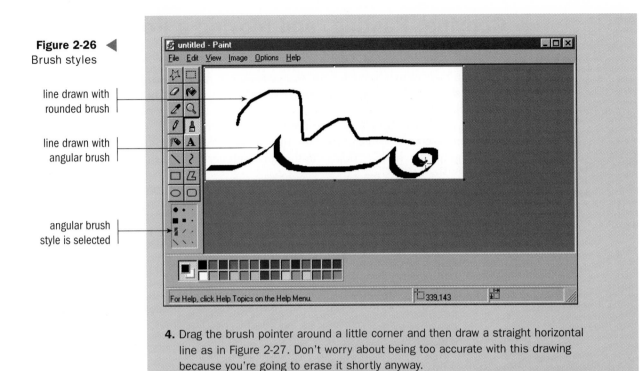

4. Drag the brush pointer around a little corner and then draw a straight horizontal line as in Figure 2-27. Don't worry about being too accurate with this drawing because you're going to erase it shortly anyway.

Figure 2-27 ◄
Drawing a ski
using the
angular brush

start here, then drag
pointer around a corner

angular brush helps
you draw a ski

Now that you have an idea of how the brush tools work, you can clear the screen and try drawing the real ski. This time, rather than using the New command, you'll use the Image menu's **Clear Image** command, which erases the entire image all at once and lets you start over with an empty canvas.

To clear the graphic and then draw the ski:

1. Click **Image** then click **Clear Image**. Your drawings disappear as the canvas is cleared.

2. Now try drawing the ski. This time try to make it look like the ski in Figure 2-27. Click Undo if you aren't satisfied and try again.

   TROUBLE? If you have a difficult time holding the mouse steady to draw the straight line, you could try controlling the pointer with the arrow keys rather than the mouse. Use the MouseKeys option available through the Accessibility Options dialog box. You could also try drawing just one section of the ski at a time.

Copying, Pasting, and Moving a Portion of a Graphic

Once you have drawn a satisfactory ski, you want to draw a second ski that has the same size and shape as the first ski. To ensure a consistent look, you can make a copy of the first ski and then paste it on the graphic as the second ski. To copy a portion of a graphic, you select it, and then you choose the **Copy** command on the Edit menu. Your selection is copied into memory. You can then use the Edit menu's **Paste** command to paste the copy into the graphic, where it "floats" in the upper-left corner of the canvas.

REFERENCE window

COPYING, CUTTING, AND PASTING GRAPHICS

- Click the Select or Free-Form Select tool.
- Drag a selection box around the area you want to copy or cut.
- Click Edit, then click Copy.
- Click Paste. The selection appears in the upper-left corner of the canvas.
- Drag the selection to the new location, then click outside the selection box to anchor the selection into place.

You are ready to copy the first ski, paste it, then move it just above the existing ski. So that your drawing will match the one shown in the figures, you'll open a copy of the drawing of the ski, which is stored on your Student Disk in the Brush file. You'll then save this file with the name Kiana.

To copy and paste the first ski and then position it:

1. Click **File**, click **Open**, then locate and open the **Brush** file on your Student Disk. Click **No** if you are prompted to save changes to the untitled graphic you were just working with.

2. Click **File** then click **Save As**. Make sure the Save in box displays the drive containing your Student Disk. Type **Kiana** in the File name box, then click the **Save** button.

3. Click the **Select** tool 🔲 .

4. Draw a selection box around the first ski.

5. Click **Edit** then click **Copy**. The ski is copied into memory.

6. Click **Edit** then click **Paste**. The ski appears in the upper-left corner of the Paint window.

7. Place the pointer over the pasted ski. Make sure the pointer looks like ✛ .

8. Drag the ski down and slightly to the right. See Figure 2-28.

   TROUBLE? If you want to reposition the second ski after you release the mouse button, repeat Steps 7 and 8.

   TROUBLE? If the ski does not move when you drag it but the selection box changes size, you might have pointed at a sizing handle. Click Edit, then click Undo. Make sure the pointer looks like ✛ before you start to drag. Then repeat Steps 7 and 8.

Figure 2-28 ◀
Moving the
pasted ski

make sure pointer
looks like this
as you drag

selection box

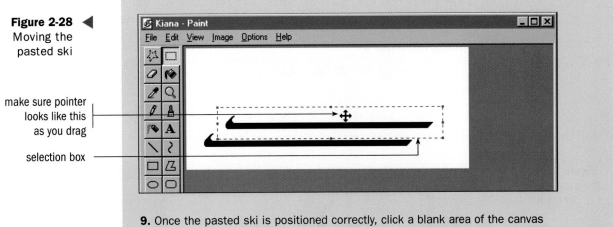

9. Once the pasted ski is positioned correctly, click a blank area of the canvas outside the selection box. The ski is anchored into place.

Flipping a Graphic

When you and Joe look at the skis, you decide you want them to point in the other direction. You can flip a graphic using the **Flip/Rotate** option on the Image menu. This option lets you reverse a graphic or rotate it by a specified number of degrees.

To flip the skis so they point in the other direction:

1. Click **Image** then click **Flip/Rotate**. The Flip and Rotate dialog box opens. See Figure 2-29.

Figure 2-29 ◀
Flip and Rotate
dialog box

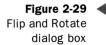

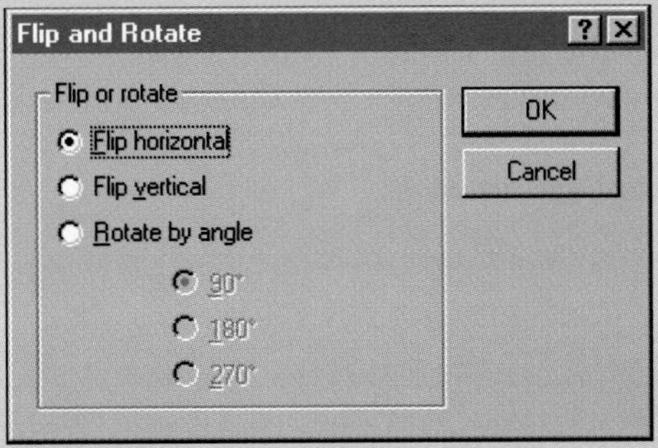

2. Click the **Flip horizontal** radio button, if it isn't already selected. This tells Paint to flip the graphic horizontally.

3. Click the **OK** button. The skis now point in the other direction. See Figure 2-30.

Figure 2-30 ◀
Skis now point
in opposite
direction

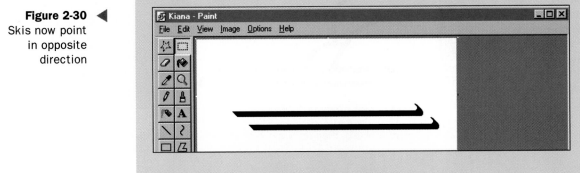

4. Click **File** then click **Save** to save the graphic.

Now you're ready to create the letter "K." You think you can create the look you want by using the rounded brush style, which is in the first row of brush styles.

To create the letter K:

1. Click the **Brush** tool [icon], then click the **largest circle** in the top row of brush styles.

2. Draw the letter K so it looks like a skier. Follow the steps shown in Figure 2-31.

   TROUBLE? If you make a mistake, use the Undo command.

Figure 2-31 ◄
Drawing the letter K

use these three brush motions to draw

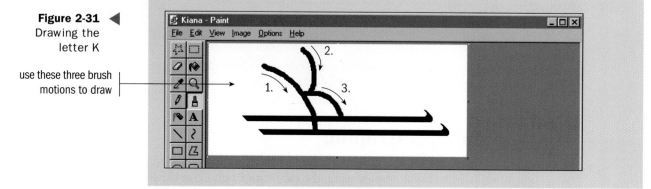

Drawing a Straight Line

Now you want to make the K look like it's moving. The **Line** command lets you draw straight lines, which you can place in your graphic to give the illusion of movement. You can create a horizontal, vertical, or diagonal line by pressing Shift while you drag the Line pointer in one of those directions. You can, of course, draw a line using the Pencil tool, but it's difficult to keep the line straight. You are going to draw a single line behind the K, and then you'll copy it and paste it a few times to add several "movement" lines.

To add straight lines to your drawing:

1. Click the **Line** tool [icon]. Notice that you can draw lines in several different line widths. You want the narrowest line (the default).

2. Press **Shift** and hold it down while you draw a horizontal line behind the K, as shown in Figure 2-32. Release **Shift**. The line is perfectly straight. You can copy and paste this line several times to create several speed lines that are all the same size.

Figure 2-32 ◄
Drawing a straight line with the Line tool

line you drew

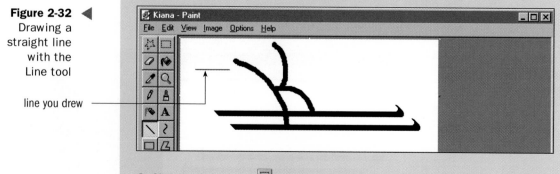

3. Click the **Select** tool [icon], then draw a selection box around the line you just drew.

4. Click **Edit**, click **Copy**, click **Edit**, then click **Paste**. Move the line you just pasted so that it is below and slightly to the right of the original line.

5. Click **Edit**, then click **Paste** twice more to add two more straight lines, moving both pasted lines until they match the position of those shown in Figure 2-33.

6. Click a blank area of the canvas to anchor the last line into place.

Stretching a Graphic

As a final touch, you decide to stretch the graphic to see if that effect enhances the illusion of movement. You can stretch a graphic either horizontally or vertically using the **Stretch/Skew** option on the Image menu. You specify a percentage, and Paint expands or contracts the graphic by that percentage in the direction (horizontal or vertical) that you specify.

To stretch the Skis graphic:

1. Click **Image** then click **Stretch/Skew**.

2. Click the **Horizontal** percentage box.

3. Replace the default value of 100% with **140%**.

4. Click the **OK** button. The graphic is stretched in the horizontal direction. Your graphic now looks like Figure 2-33.

Figure 2-33 ◀
Stretched
Kiana graphic
with action
lines

pasted lines ⎯

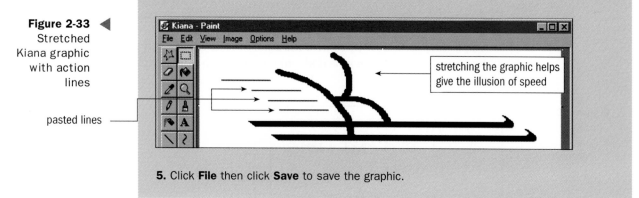

5. Click **File** then click **Save** to save the graphic.

You'll add the text to the Kiana graphic in the Tutorial Assigments at the end of this tutorial.

Creating Shapes

Joe suggests you next create a scenic image, such as a few mountains on a sunny day. You tell him that's a job for one or more of the shape tools—Line, Curve, Rectangle, Polygon, Ellipse, and Rounded Rectangle. These tools let you draw predetermined shapes. When you click one of the shape tools, a collection of options appears below the tool box. You can choose the shape as an outline, a filled shape without a border, or a filled shape with a border. See Figure 2-34.

Figure 2-34 ◀
Fills and borders

examples of each fill and border style

fill and border styles

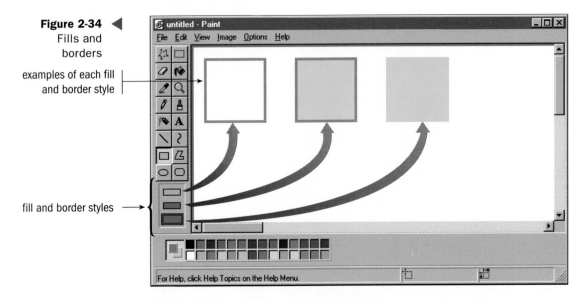

You'll learn later how to control the colors of the border and the fill for these shapes. Joe quickly sketches what he'd like to see, as shown in Figure 2-35, and asks if you can draw it.

Figure 2-35 ◀
Idea for a scenic graphic

It's Ski Time!

3.1 NOTE

The shape tools are the same for Paintbrush and Paint. However, in the Windows 3.1 Paintbrush accessory, there were separate tools for a filled shape and an outline. The Windows 95 Paint accessory combines them into a single button and then displays the fill and border options below the tool box.

To create the mountains, you can use the Line tool, which you've already used, and to create the sun you can use the Ellipse tool. Once you have drawn the shapes, you will color them and add text in Session 2.3.

You want to start by giving Joe a quick overview of the shapes you can draw.

To draw with a variety of the Paint shapes:

1. Click **File** then click **New** to open a new canvas.

2. Click the **Rectangle** tool, then drag a rectangle.

3. Click the **Ellipse** tool, then drag an ellipse.

4. Click the **Rounded Rectangle**, then drag a rounded rectangle. Compare your screen to Figure 2-36.

TROUBLE? If your screen doesn't look like Figure 2-36, don't worry. These shapes are just for experimenting.

Figure 2-36 ◄
Shape tools

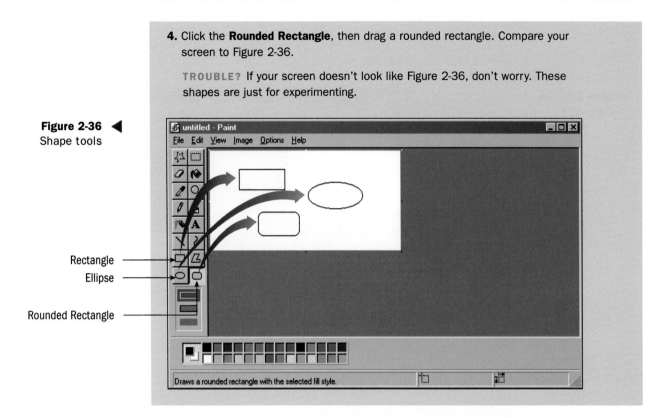

Rectangle

Ellipse

Rounded Rectangle

Now you're ready to create the new graphic. To save you time in this session, the mountains have already been drawn for you. They are stored in a file named Mountain. All you need to do is add the sun. In the same way the Shift key helped you draw a straight horizontal line, it also helps you draw a perfect circle when the Ellipse tool is selected. Likewise, if you use Shift with the Rectangle tool, you can draw a perfect square. When you draw a shape, you can use the **sizing coordinates**, immediately to the right of the pixel coordinates, to control the size of the shape you are dragging. For example, when you draw a circle, you might start at pixel coordinates 15,15 and drag with sizing coordinates of 30×30—so your circle has a 30-pixel diameter.

To open the Mountain file and add the sun:

1. Click **File**, click **Open**, then locate and open the **Mountain** file on your Student Disk. Click the **No** button if you are prompted to save changes.

2. Click **File**, click **Save As**, then change the name to **Mountain and Sun** so your changes won't affect the original file. Click the **Save** button.

3. Click the **Ellipse** tool.

4. Press **Shift**, then drag a circle starting at pixel coordinates **15,15**. Drag to sizing coordinates of **30×30**. See Figure 2-37.

Figure 2-37 ◄
Drawing a
circle

pointer

Ellipse tool

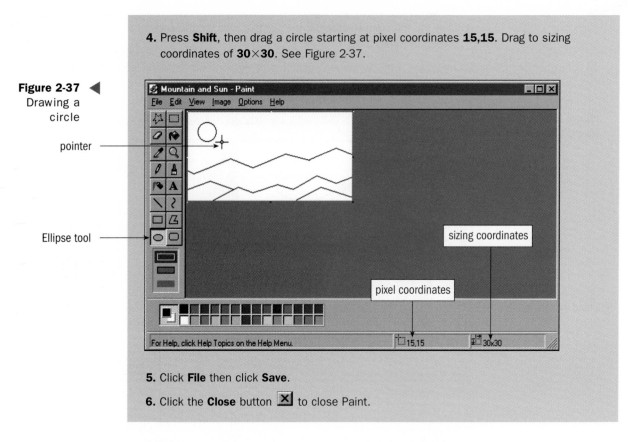

5. Click **File** then click **Save**.

6. Click the **Close** button ⊠ to close Paint.

Joe now has three graphics to choose from: the Skis graphic, the Kiana graphic, and the Mountain and Sun graphic. You remind him that you still plan to add text and color to two of these graphics. You'll work with text and color in Session 2.3.

Quick Check

1. How wide a line can you draw with the Pencil tool?

2. When you view the grid, what does each box represent?

3. What option can you use to view the magnified portion of your graphic in Normal view while retaining the magnification on the canvas?

4. Name three ways to clear a canvas.

5. How do you draw a perfect circle?

6. What is the diameter of a circle drawn to 50×50 sizing coordinates?

SESSION 2.3

In this session you work with color and text. You'll begin by filling enclosed areas with color using the Fill With Color tool, and then you'll paint with the Airbrush and work with background and foreground colors. Finally, you'll add text with the Text tool and format it using the Fonts toolbar.

Filling an Area with Color

Joe isn't sure when he'll be able to afford full-color printing, but he is interested to see what effect color has on his graphics. You can add color to a graphic in one of two ways: choosing colors as you draw, or coloring in shapes after you have finished drawing them. You decide to color the Mountain and Sun graphic, whose shapes are already in place. You'll learn to choose colors as you draw later in this session.

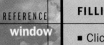

FILLING AN AREA WITH COLOR

- Click the Fill With Color tool.
- Click the color box color you want.
- Click inside the border of the area you want to color. Make sure the tip of the paint pouring out of the bucket is within the border.

In the Mountain and Sun graphic, the shapes you want to color are already in place. You click a color in the color box, then click an enclosed area in the graphic with the Fill With Color pointer ✍. The area within the borders of the enclosure fills with color. When you use the Fill With Color tool, make sure the area you click is a fully enclosed space. If there are any openings, color "spills out" of the boundaries you are trying to color.

You want to color each mountain range a different color to give the impression of distance and shadow. You decide to use a mix of blues and purples.

3.1 NOTE

The Fill With Color tool replaces the Windows 3.1 Paintbrush Paint Roller tool.

To fill the Mountain and Sun graphic with color:

1. Start Paint, and make sure your Student Disk is in drive A.

2. Click **File**, click **Open**, then locate and open the **Mountain and Sun** file on your Student Disk.

3. Click the **Fill With Color** tool ✍. The pointer changes to ✍. You'll color each layer of mountains a different color.

4. Click the **dark blue** color in the top row, 7th from the left.

5. Click inside the border of the **top mountain range** with the Fill With Color pointer ✍. The mountain range turns blue. See Figure 2-38.

   TROUBLE? If the sky turns blue instead of the mountain range, click Edit, then click Undo. You clicked the sky instead of the mountain range. You must click the area to be colored with the active part of the Fill With Color pointer, which is the tip of the paint pouring out of the can. Click Edit, click Undo, then repeat Step 5, and make sure the tip of the paint is within the border of the mountain range.

Figure 2-38 ◄
Filling first
mountain range
with color

Fill With Color tool ———

active part of pointer
is tip of paint drop

dark blue color for
first mountain range

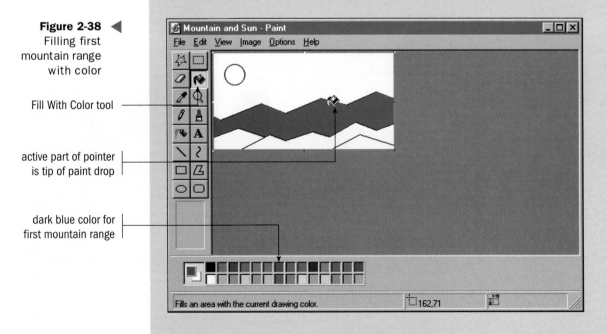

6. Click the **purple color** in the top row, 8th from the left, then click the front-left mountain range to color it purple.

7. Click the **bright blue** color in the bottom row, 7th from the left, then click the middle mountain range.

8. Click the **periwinkle** color in the bottom row, 3rd from the right, then click the right mountain range.

9. Finally, click the **yellow** color in the bottom row, fourth from the left, then click the sun. See Figure 2-39.

Figure 2-39 ◀
Adding colors

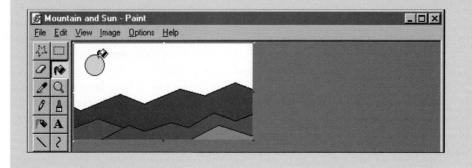

Coloring with the Airbrush

You have one more idea to enhance the Mountain graphic. You can sprinkle snow on the top range of mountains using the **Airbrush**, a tool that scatters color a few pixels at a time over the area you "brush." The Airbrush comes in three different sizes. The small size scatters color most thickly, whereas the largest size sprinkles it more sparingly. You'll use the largest size to sprinkle the top mountain range with snow.

To use the Airbrush:

1. Click the **white** color in the beginning of the second row.

2. Click the **Airbrush** tool 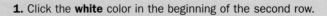.

3. Click the **largest Airbrush style** (on the bottom).

4. In one motion, drag the **Airbrush** pointer 🖌 over the top range of mountains. See Figure 2-40.

Figure 2-40 ◀
Using the
Airbrush

Airbrush tool ——————

largest Airbrush style ——————

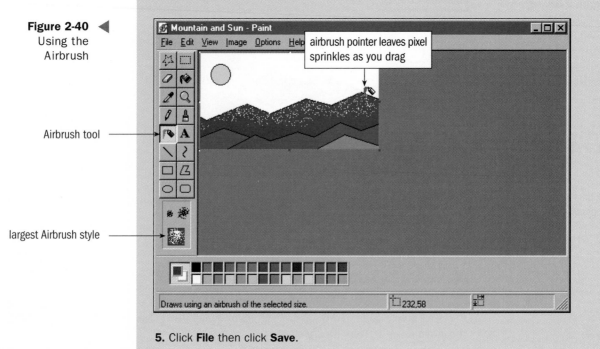

5. Click **File** then click **Save**.

Using Foreground and Background Colors

In looking over the graphic, you decide you don't like the stark contrast between the sun's black border and yellow color. You think a different border and fill will look more aesthetically pleasing. You've already seen how to color as you draw when you sprinkled the mountains with white snow using the airbrush. When you draw a shape, Paint can use two colors, not one. The **foreground color** determines the border of an object as you draw and the **background color** determines the fill. To set the foreground color, you click a color with the *left* mouse button. The foreground color box changes to that color. To set the background color, you click a color with the *right* mouse button. The background color box changes to that color. You can draw your shape using one of the three options located below the tool box: only the foreground color, both the foreground and the background colors, or only the background color. Figure 2-41 shows examples of each of these options.

Figure 2-41
Example of foreground and background colors

border only

border and fill

fill only

foreground color determines border color

background color determines fill color

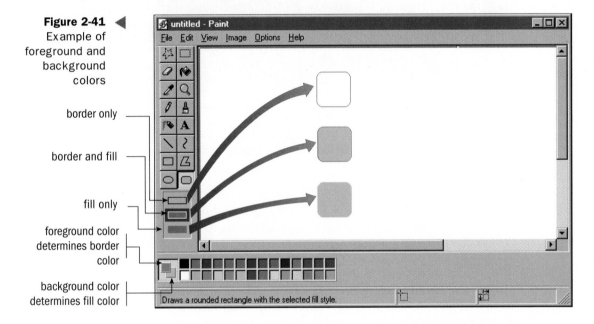

You decide to draw the sun with a foreground color of brown and a background color of orange. First, you'll need to erase the sun you've already drawn and colored. You could use the Eraser tool, but when the area you want to erase is off by itself where no other parts of the drawing interfere, it can be quicker to select the area and then cut it using the Edit menu's Cut command.

To draw a sun with different foreground and background colors:

1. Click the **Select** tool, then drag a selection box around the sun.

2. Click **Edit** then click **Cut**. Now change the foreground and background colors in the color box.

3. Click the **brown** color in the top row, farthest to the right, with the *left* mouse button. Notice that the foreground box turns brown. See Figure 2-42.

Figure 2-42 ◀
Selecting a
foreground
color

brown color ——

foreground color turns
brown when you
click brown with
left mouse button

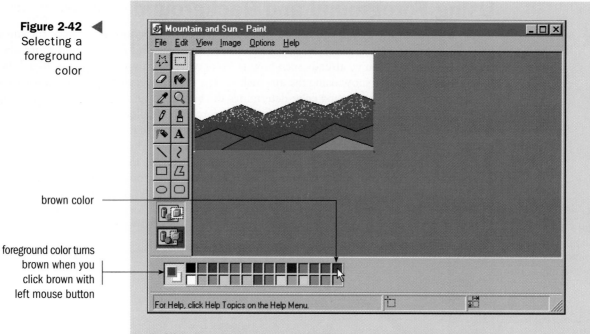

4. Click the **orange** color in the bottom row, farthest to the right, with the *right* mouse button. The background color changes to orange.

5. Click the **Ellipse** tool.

6. Click the **fill and border** option below the tool box (the middle option).

7. Press **Shift**, then drag a circle from pixel coordinates 15,15 and sizing coordinates 30×30. The new sun has a brown border and an orange fill. However, the orange looks too dark; you decide the original yellow color looked better.

As you've already seen, you can color an enclosed area using the Fill With Color tool. When you filled in the mountain ranges earlier with this tool, you clicked an area with the *left* mouse button, and Paint then applied the foreground color to the area. You can apply the background color by clicking the area with the *right* mouse button. Notice that this is different from when you draw a shape from scratch—there the foreground color determines the border and the background color determines the fill. When you use the Fill With Color tool on *an already existing shape*, you are working only with the fill, and you can switch between foreground and background colors using the left or right mouse button. You decide to change the fill color back to yellow.

To select a new background color and use it to fill a shape:

1. *Right*-click the **yellow** color in the bottom row, fourth from the left, to set the background color to yellow.

2. Click the **Fill With Color** tool, then *right*-click the **sun**. The fill color of the sun changes to yellow, the background color you just set. This sun, yellow with a brown border, looks good. See Figure 2-43.

Figure 2-43 ◀
Recolored sun

New users are sometimes confused by the way foreground and background colors take on different roles depending on whether they're drawing an object from scratch using a shape tool or coloring in an object using the Fill With Color tool. Just remember that for drawing an object from scratch, the foreground color is the border and the background color is the fill. When you are coloring an object with the Fill With Color tool, Paint uses the foreground color if you left-click and the background color if you right-click.

You and Joe are satisfied with the coloring of the Mountain graphic. Now you're ready to add the text.

Using the Text Tool

Joe had written the phrase "It's Ski Time!" on his sketch. To add these words to the graphic you will use the **Text tool**. To add text to a graphic, you first create a selection box using the Text tool, and then you type your text in this box. If your text exceeds the length and width of the selection box, you can drag the sizing handles to enlarge the selection box.

REFERENCE window	ADDING TEXT TO A GRAPHIC
	■ Click the Text tool, then drag a selection box on the canvas.
	■ Click View, then click Text Toolbar if the Fonts toolbar does not appear.
	■ Use the Fonts toolbar to select a font, font size, or attributes (bold, italic, or underline).
	■ Type the text in the selection box, resizing the selection box if necessary using the sizing handles.
	■ Adjust the font, font size, or attributes (bold, italic, or underline) and resize the selection box as necessary.
	■ Click outside the selection box.

You decide to type "It's Ski Time" just to the right of the sun in the Mountain graphic, and you decide the text should appear in the same shade of dark blue you used in the drawing set against a white background.

To select the text color and create the selection box:

1. Click the **dark blue** color in the top row, 7th from the left, with the *left* mouse button.

2. Click the **white** color in the bottom row, farthest to the left, with the *right* mouse button.

3. Click the **Text** tool `A`.

4. Create a selection box by dragging from pixel coordinates 54,15 to a size of 185×30. After you've created the selection box, the Fonts toolbar appears.

   TROUBLE? Recall that the pixel coordinates are on the status bar, and the sizing coordinates are to their right.

   TROUBLE? If the Fonts toolbar does not appear, click View. Notice that the Fonts toolbar appears as "Text Toolbar" on the View menu. Click Text Toolbar.

Any letters you type into the selection box will appear with the **font**—or typeface—style, size, and attributes shown in the Fonts toolbar. The font size of the letters are measured in **points**, where a single point is 1/72". **Attributes** are characteristics of the font, including bold, italic, and underline. You can change the font, font size, and the font attributes using the Fonts toolbar before you type, after you type, or as you edit the text. Once you are satisfied with the text and its appearance, you click outside the selection box. The selection box disappears and the text is "anchored" into place, becoming a part of the bitmapped graphic. Once text is anchored in a graphic, you can change the font or its attributes only by deleting the text and starting over with the Text tool.

You decide to use an Arial 12-point font. **Arial** is the name of a common font that comes with Windows 95.

To choose the Arial 12-point font and insert the text:

1. Click the **Font** list arrow ⬇. The list of fonts available on your computer opens. See Figure 2-44. Your list will probably be different.

Figure 2-44 ◀
Font list

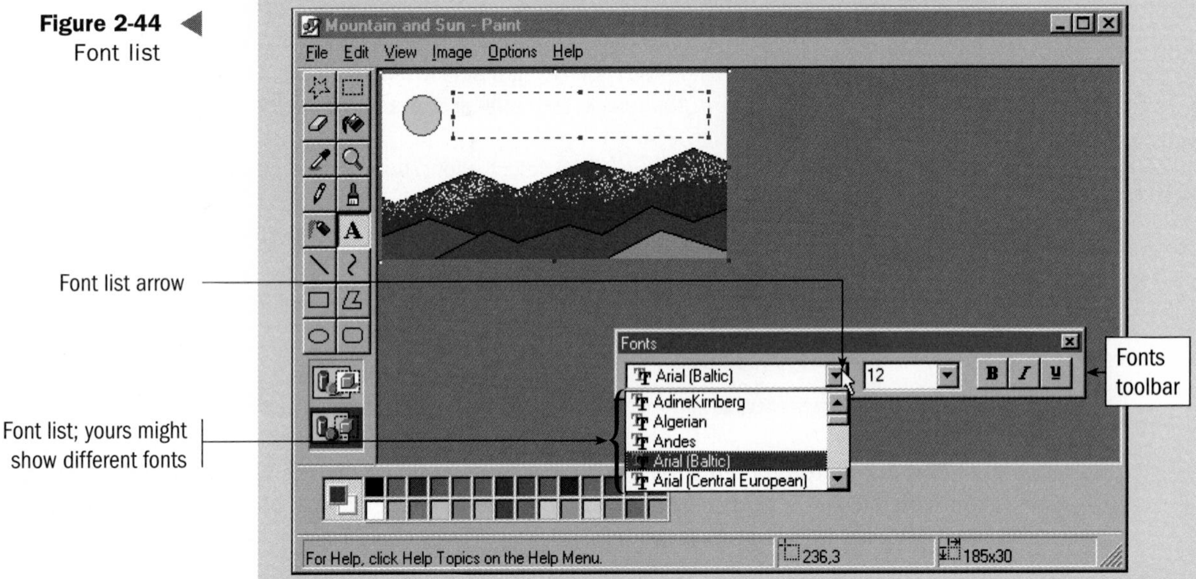

Font list arrow ——

Font list; yours might
show different fonts

2. Scroll the Font list until you locate Arial, then click **Arial**.

   TROUBLE? If your Arial font appears multiple times with a number of different styles, click any one of the Arial fonts, such as Arial (Baltic).

3. Click the **Font Size** list arrow ⬇, then click **12**. Make sure the Bold and Italic buttons are not selected; if they are, click them to deselect them.

4. Click inside the selection box.

5. Type **It's Ski Time!** Your text appears in the selection box in the Arial 12-point font. See Figure 2-45.

   TROUBLE? If nothing appears when you type, it's possible that you clicked the color white with the left mouse button instead of the right mouse button in the previous set of steps. White text will not appear against a white background. Make sure the foreground color is dark blue and the background color is white.

Figure 2-45 ◄
Adding text
using the Text
tool

text appears in
selection box

font is Arial

point size is 12

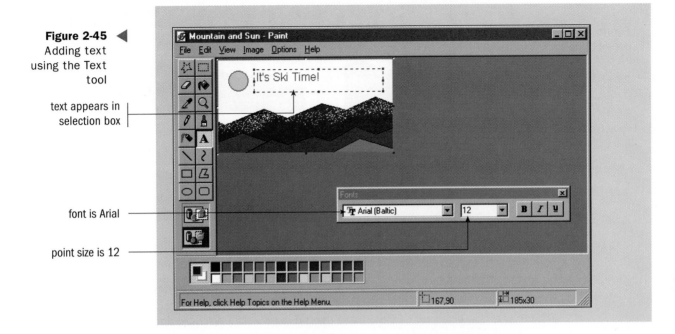

Joe would like to use a more interesting font. You decide to experiment with several fonts, sizes, and attributes to find the look you want. Windows 95 comes with a standard set of fonts, including Arial and Times New Roman, but most users add fonts so they can format text in a variety of styles. The fonts that appear on your computer will most likely differ from those shown in the figures.

To experiment with the font:

1. Click the **Font** list arrow ▼.

2. Scroll the Font list until you locate Times New Roman, then click **Times New Roman**.

   TROUBLE? If your Times New Roman font appears multiple times with a number of different styles, click any one of the Times New Roman fonts, such as Times New Roman (Baltic).

3. Click the **Bold** button **B** to see how the text looks bolded.

4. Click the **Italic** button **I**. You like the look of both bold and italic, though you'd like to keep looking at other font styles.

5. Continue to select different fonts and attributes, as shown in Figure 2-46.

   TROUBLE? If you can't find the fonts shown in Figure 2-46, experiment with fonts available on your computer. Although Windows 95 comes with a few fonts, your computer lab manager might have added more fonts to your computer.

Figure 2-46 ◀
Experimenting
with different
fonts

Braggadocio

Lucida Blackletter

FoxScript

CarawayBold

6. Joe likes bold and italic CarawayBold best. Click **CarawayBold** if you have it, using both the Bold and Italic attributes. Otherwise click one of your favorites. (You can also leave it as Times New Roman, which is a font that is installed with Windows 95 so every computer should have it.)

7. Now enlarge the font to make the text more visible. Click the **Font Size** list arrow ▾, then click **18**.

TROUBLE? If you are using a font that is especially large, 18 points might cause some of the letters to disappear. Repeat Step 7, but this time pick a smaller point size.

8. Click a blank area of the canvas outside the selection box to accept this style of text. The selection box and Fonts toolbar disappear, and the text is anchored into place. See Figure 2-47.

Figure 2-47 ◀
Completed
graphic with
text

9. Click **File**, then click **Save** to save the Mountain and Sun graphic.

10. Click the Paint **Close** button ☒.

Quick Check

1. To change a shape's fill color, you use the _____ tool.

2. What does it mean to say a font is "10 points?"

3. What font attributes can you work with in Paint?

4. If you can't see the Fonts toolbar, what option should you click on the View menu?

5. You just opened a graphic containing text, and you'd like to change the font of the text. Describe your options.

6 When you draw an object from scratch, the foreground color controls an object's
_____ whereas the background color controls
its _____.

7 If you select the Fill With Color tool and then right-click an enclosed area, which color
is applied, the foreground or the background?

End Note

Joe has enjoyed watching you work with the Paint program. Although he recognizes that
these graphics do not match the quality of those you could create with a full-featured
graphics program such as CorelDraw, he is, nevertheless, impressed with Paint's versa-
tility and ease of use. Now that he has a few usable graphics, he looks forward to creating
more attractive announcements and promotional materials for the Birkebeiner ski race.

Tutorial Assignments

1. Cropping a Graphic You are the coordinator for a university students' bowling league,
and you want to add a graphic to an informational promotion you are preparing.

    a. Open the Sports graphic in Paint.
    b. Use the Select tool to crop to the bowling ball hitting the bowling pins in
       the lower-right corner of the Sports graphic.
    c. Save the cropped graphic to your Student Disk as a monochrome graphic
       with the name Bowling Ball.
    d. Open the Bowling Ball graphic and, if necessary, erase any portions of it
       that aren't part of the graphic.
    e. Save and print the graphic.

2. Cropping a Graphic with the Free-Form Select Tool You work at Portage Electric—one
of the sponsors of the Portage Community Tennis League. You're helping design league
jackets. You want to crop the tennis rackets in the lower-left corner of the Sports graphic.
In Session 2.1 you used the Select tool to crop part of a graphic, but the selection box
included portions of other images that you then had to erase. You can avoid this extra
step using the Free-Form Select tool. With the Free-Form Select tool, you can draw a line
of any shape around the area you want to crop.

    a. Open the Sports graphic.
    b. Use the Free-Form Select tool to draw around the tennis rackets in the
       lower-left corner of the Sports graphic.
    c. Save the cropped graphic to your Student Disk as a monochrome graphic
       with the name Tennis Rackets.
    d. Open the Tennis Rackets graphic and ensure that you didn't include any
       unwanted portions of the Sports graphic.
    e. Save and print the Tennis Rackets graphic.

3. Drawing with the Brush Tool You work for Jensen Telecommunications. Jensen is host-
ing an engineering conference to share ideas on making high-speed fiber-optic data lines
available to homes. You're helping host the conference banquet, and you'd like to create a
classy design to imprint on the cocktail napkins and coasters. Use the Brush tool to draw
the graphic as shown in a through f, then save it as a Monochrome Bitmap graphic.

a. Create a vertical line as shown using the largest angular brush style in the third row.

b. Copy the vertical line and paste it as shown.

c. Draw the horizontal line to hook up with the vertical line.

d. Copy the horizontal line and paste it on top.

e. Copy a short section of the horizontal line and paste it in the middle.

f. Save the image as Letter J on your Student Disk. Print the image.

4. Drawing in Color Your company is one of the sponsors of the Olympics. Create a graphic of the Olympic rings so you can use the Olympic logo in your advertisements. The top three rings are blue, black, and red. The bottom two rings are yellow and green. Save the file on your Student Disk as a 256 Color Bitmap graphic with the name Rings. Print the file. Here are some tricks you can use to make this assignment easier:

- Use Shift to draw perfect circles.
- Use the sizing coordinates to ensure each circle is the same size (such as 30×30).
- Draw each new circle in a blank area of the canvas, then use the Select tool to select the circle and drag it into place.
- Use the pixel coordinates to ensure that you place all rings in each row on the same level.

5. Adding Text to the Kiana Graphic You and Joe decide to finish the Kiana graphic. You need to add the rest of the word "Kiana." First open the Kiana file that you created earlier in this tutorial and saved on your Student Disk.

a. Use the Text tool to insert a selection box, then type the letters "iana" and select a font and font size. Joe likes FoxScript—choose that font if you have it; otherwise, choose any font that you like.

b. Use the Fill With Color tool to fill each letter with a different color. Joe chooses brick, olive, moss, and midnight blue, respectively.

c. You can make the graphic take up less room on your disk by selecting the entire drawing and dragging it up to the corner of the canvas. Then resize the canvas to fit the drawing.

e. Give the graphic a background color that complements the letter colors. Joe likes a light mustard color. Compare your figure to Figure 2-48.

f. Print your graphic and save it as Kiana Color. Give the disk and hard copy to your instructor. If you don't have a color printer, your graphic will print in black and white.

Figure 2-48 ◀

6. Copying and Pasting to Create a Graphic at Stanton Junior High You coordinate the chess classes at Stanton Junior High. You want to create a simple graphic for a tournament brochure. Use the Rectangle tool and your copy and pasting skills to create the chessboard in a through f.

a. Use the Rectangle tool in combination with the Shift key to create a perfect square with dragging coordinates of 35×35. Don't forget to use the Shift key.

b. Copy the square, then paste it and drag it so the edges overlap. Do this three times to create the first four squares.

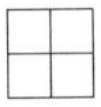

c. Copy the four squares, then paste that image and drag it to the right of the first four squares.

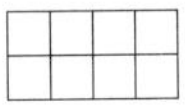

d. Copy those eight squares, then paste that image and drag it to the right of the existing eight squares.

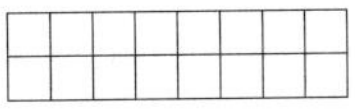

e. Copy those sixteen squares, and paste and drag them three times to create the rest of the chessboard.

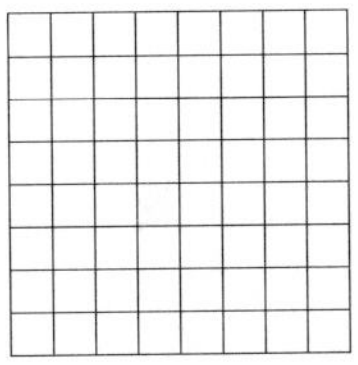

f. Save the images as Chess on your Student Disk, then print the image.

7. Adding Text and Color to the Stanton Junior High Brochure You just completed the Chess graphic in Tutorial Assignment 6. You now want to add text and color.

a. Color in every other square using the Fill With Color tool to create a chessboard.

b. Add the words "Stanton Chess Club" to the top of the chessboard. Choose a font style and size that complements the colors and board you drew.

c. Add the word "Tournament" below the chessboard.

d. Now use the Select tool to select just the word "Tournament." Then rotate the word and drag it to the right side of the chessboard, as shown in Figure 2-49. Using the Flip/Rotate command on the Image menu, click Rotate by angle, then click 270. Depending on your font, your graphic should look like Figure 2-49.

Figure 2-49 ◄

e. Print the graphic, then save it on your Student Disk as Chess with Text.

8. Designing a Font Style You work for a commercial graphics design company, Ace Design Group (ADG). ADG has just landed a contract to create a new font style for the posters and materials of the American Statistical Association's annual conference. Your boss has asked you to start drafting possible designs for the new font style. You decide to use Paint to create a few sample letters, specifically, a capital and lowercase "a" and "f." You'll probably want to use a combination of drawing tools for this assignment. You'll almost certainly need to zoom in and edit using the grid to ensure consistency from letter to letter. Tutorial Assignment 3 shows how you go about drawing a letter. When you are finished drafting a few ideas for a new letter design, save your file as Fonts and print it.

Object Linking and Embedding

OBJECTIVES

In this tutorial you will:

■ Create a WordPad document into which you will insert data from other documents

■ Use the Cut, Copy, and Paste commands to transfer data

■ Use the Calculator accessory

■ View the contents of the Clipboard with Clipboard Viewer

■ Use Object Linking and Embedding (OLE) to insert a graphic and a video clip into a WordPad document

■ Examine numerous methods of using OLE: Paste, Paste Special, Insert Object, and Link

■ Edit and update OLE objects

■ Work with the Windows 95 Media Player

CASE

Preparing for the Jugglers Guild Convention

The Tenth Annual Jugglers Guild Convention is scheduled for this summer in New Orleans. Maria Arruda, secretary of the Jugglers Guild, is chairing the convention, aided by a committee of which you are a member. Maria has assigned tasks to each committee member—yours is to work on gathering materials that will promote the event. Maria would like you to hire a designer to design a graphics file that can serve as a logo for informational flyers, posters, and convention T-shirts. Maria asks you also to look for an eye-catching video clip that will run on the computer screens used at the convention. A **video clip** is a file that contains a very short movie, either real-life or animated.

You get right to work. You hire a graphic designer to design the logo. You also hire a computer animation company to create an animated video clip. Once you receive the disks containing the graphics file and video clip, you give them to Maria so she can evaluate them. The next day she returns the disks and says she likes the logo and the animation, but she'd like feedback from the rest of the committee. She asks you to create a single WordPad document that will contain the graphics file and the video clip, and into which the committee members can add their comments. A document that includes a variety of media—such as text, graphics, and video—is called a **multimedia document**.

Windows 95 provides three ways to combine data from a variety of sources into a single multimedia document: pasting, embedding, and linking. You'll learn about pasting in Session 3.1, embedding in Session 3.2, and linking in Session 3.3. How do you decide which method to use in a given situation? It depends on what you need to do with the information after you've inserted it into the multimedia document—whether you need to use the tools in the program that originally created the data and whether you are likely to change the data once you've inserted it. As you proceed through these three sessions, notice how the pasting, embedding, and linking techniques offer you different options to meet these needs.

SESSION

3.1

In this session you will learn how the Windows 95 Clipboard makes data from one document or program available to another document or program using the Cut, Copy, and Paste commands. You will create a WordPad document that draws material from different sources—first from the Calculator accessory and then from another WordPad document. You'll then check to see whether the Clipboard Viewer is installed on your computer. If it is, you'll learn to examine the contents of the Clipboard.

Creating a WordPad Document

You start by creating the WordPad document that will contain the data you want other members of the committee to view. You'll format the document as a memo, beginning with a standard memo heading that includes To, Date, and Subject headings.

To start a new WordPad document:

1. Place your Student Disk in drive A. See the "Read This Before You Begin" page to make sure you are using the correct disk for this tutorial.

   TROUBLE? If your 3½-inch disk drive is B, place your Student Disk in that drive instead, and for the rest of this tutorial substitute drive B wherever you see drive A.

2. Click the **Start** button, point to **Programs**, point to **Accessories**, then click **WordPad**.

3. Type the following memo heading into the WordPad document. Press the **Enter** key twice after each line, and **Tab** after each colon.

   TROUBLE? You might need to press Tab twice to align the information, depending on how your tabs are set in WordPad.

   MEMO

   TO: Jugglers Guild Convention Committee

   DATE: 3/18/97

   SUBJECT: Tenth Annual Jugglers Guild Convention

4. Click **File** then click **Save As** to save the work you've done so far.

5. Click the **Save in** list arrow, then click the drive containing your Student Disk.

6. Click the **File name** box, delete the contents of this box if necessary, type **Feedback**, then click the **Save** button. See Figure 3-1.

Figure 3-1 ◀
Feedback
document

memo heading

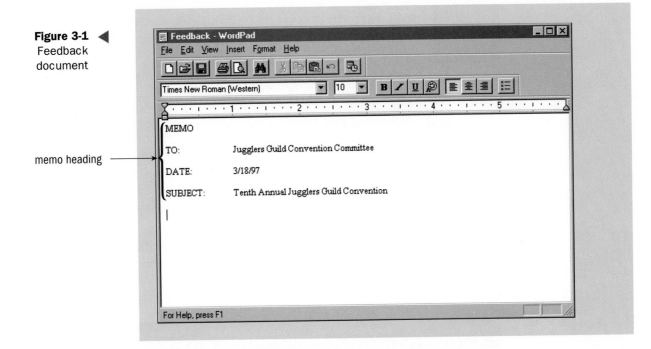

The Clipboard

Maria stops by your office and hands you a disk. She's decided that she wants the committee members to give their feedback on the graphics and video files in a specific way. She drafted a document that outlines the feedback procedure and includes her own feedback. She suggests you insert her document into your Feedback document.

Windows 95 offers several ways to transfer data from one document to another; the most basic technique is **Paste**, where you cut or copy data from one document and then paste it into another. This procedure uses the **Clipboard**, an area in your computer's active memory that temporarily stores the data you cut or copy. For example, suppose you had an e-mail message that contained information you wanted to paste into a WordPad document. Figure 3-2 illustrates how you copy the message to the Clipboard and then paste it into your document.

Figure 3-2 ◀
Using the
Clipboard

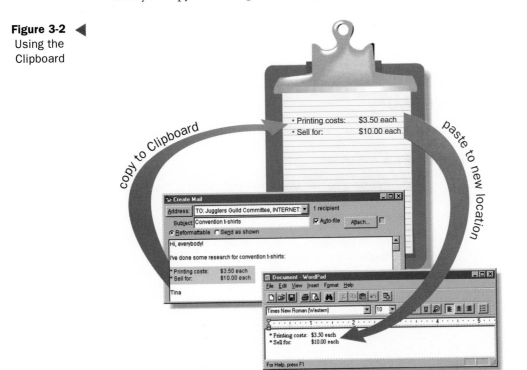

USING PASTE TO TRANSFER DATA FROM ONE DOCUMENT TO ANOTHER

- Select the data you want to transfer.
- Click Edit.
- Click Cut to remove the data from the document to the Clipboard or click Copy to place a replica of the data on the Clipboard while leaving the document intact.
- Switch to the second document.
- Click the second document where you want to paste the data.
- Click Edit, then click Paste.

The Clipboard is part of the operating system and is available in many (but not all) Windows programs through standard Cut, Copy, and Paste commands. Figure 3-3 shows the equivalent methods you can use to cut, copy, and paste data within a document or from one document to another.

Figure 3-3 ◀
Cut and Paste
options

Operation	Menu Command	Toolbar Button	Keyboard Shortcut
Cut	Edit, then Cut	✂	Ctrl+X
Copy	Edit, then Copy	📋	Ctrl+C
Paste	Edit, then Paste	📋	Ctrl+V

When you paste data from the Clipboard into a document, you do not remove the data from the Clipboard; you can continue to paste the data as many times as you want, into as many documents as you want. The Clipboard stores the data until you cut or copy new data.

If the Clipboard contains a large amount of data when you close a program, Windows 95 might prompt you to clear the Clipboard contents to free your system's memory. You can clear the Clipboard manually using the Clipboard Viewer, as you'll see at the end of this session. The Clipboard's contents are also cleared when you shut down your computer.

Copying and Pasting from the Calculator Accessory

You decide to open Maria's document from the disk she's given you to see what it contains.

To open Maria's document:

1. Open the document named **Maria** from your Student Disk in WordPad. Because you can open only one document at a time in WordPad, the Feedback document closes. See Figure 3-4.

   TROUBLE? Use the Open command on the File menu, and make sure the Look in list box displays the drive containing your Student Disk.

Figure 3-4 ◀
Maria's document

price estimate
information goes here

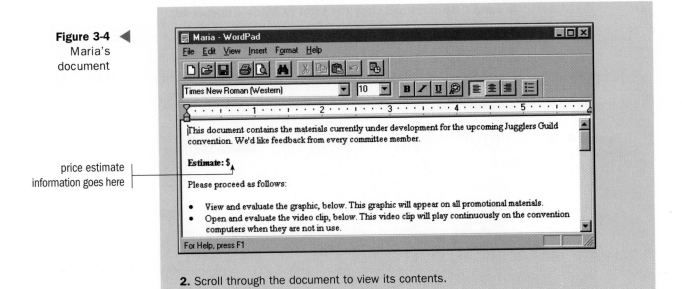

2. Scroll through the document to view its contents.

You see that Maria has left room to insert both the graphic and the video clip. Then you notice she left room for a price estimate at the top. You've received quotes from the two vendors: $235 for the graphic and $390 for the video clip. The graphic design vendor is also offering a 12% discount if you print your convention materials there. You want to inform the committee members of these quotes, so you decide to use the Windows 95 Calculator to calculate the total. The **Calculator** is a Windows 95 accessory that looks and functions just like a handheld calculator. It can appear in two views: **Standard** view, which provides basic arithmetic operations; or **Scientific** view, which includes a variety of algebraic, trigonometric, and statistical functions.

You are less likely to make a mistake entering the total into your document if you use the Clipboard to copy the data from Calculator to your document instead of typing it. Calculator includes a Copy command that copies the current entry to the Clipboard. You can transfer the answer to any program that offers Clipboard access.

To calculate the total you multiply $235 by .88 to calculate the 12% discount, then add 390. The equation would read .88 * 235 + 390 =.

To open Calculator and copy the total to Maria's document:

1. Click **Start**, point to **Programs**, point to **Accessories**, then click **Calculator**. See Figure 3-5.

   TROUBLE? If your Calculator window appears half this size, your Calculator opened in Standard view. You could click View, then click Scientific to match Figure 3-5.

Figure 3-5 ◄
Calculator
accessory

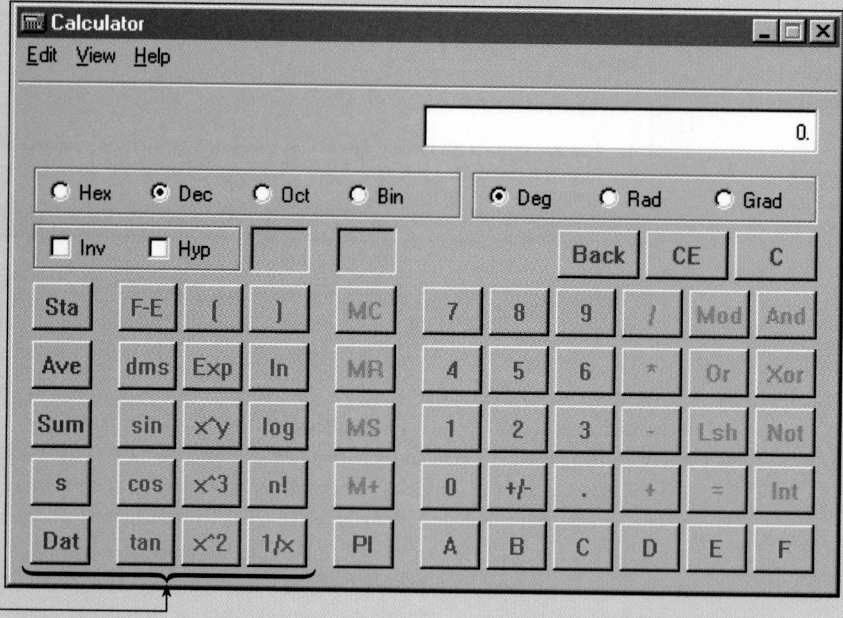

this part of Calculator
does not appear
if opened in
Standard view

2. Click the buttons [.], [8], [8], [*], [2], [3], [5], [+], [3], [9], [0], [=] to calculate the total of 596.8.

3. Click **Edit**, then click **Copy**. With Calculator, you don't have to highlight the data you want to copy. Calculator automatically copies the entry in the results box. Notice that when you copy, the information is not removed from the program. You have just made a copy of it on the Clipboard.

4. Click the **Close** button [X] to close Calculator.

The Clipboard now contains the value 596.8. You need to paste this value into Maria's document.

To paste the total into Maria's document:

1. Scroll to the top of Maria's document.

2. Click to the right of the $ next to the bolded **Estimate:** heading.

   TROUBLE? If the insertion point doesn't appear, repeat Step 2. WordPad might not have been activated, so you might need to click once to activate it and click again to place the insertion point.

3. Click the **Paste** button [📋]. See Figure 3-6.

   TROUBLE? If the Paste button doesn't appear, click View, then click Toolbar.

Figure 3-6 ◀
Pasting the
calculated
estimate

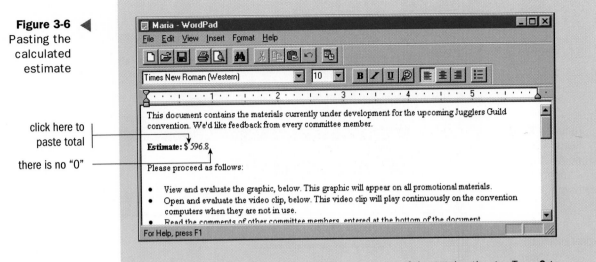

click here to
paste total

there is no "0"

4. Notice that there is no "0" in the cents column of the total estimate. Type **0** to complete the currency format.

Cutting and Pasting Between Two WordPad Documents

The next step in your project is to move the information from Maria's document to your document. This time, rather than copying the information over, you decide to cut it from Maria's document and paste it into yours. When you copied, the information remained in the program, as you saw with the Calculator accessory. However, when you cut, you permanently removed the information from the original program. Unlike with copying, with cutting you no longer have two copies of the same information and so you are using your disk space more efficiently.

To cut the contents from Maria's document to the Clipboard:

1. Click **Edit** then click **Select All**. The entire document is selected.

2. Click the **Cut** button [✂]. Windows 95 removes the selected material from Maria's document and places it on the Clipboard.

The Clipboard now contains the data from Maria's document. It will stay there until you copy or cut something else, until you manually clear the Clipboard, or until you shut down your computer. You can now open your Feedback document and insert the contents of the Clipboard.

To insert the contents of the Clipboard into your Feedback document:

1. Click **File**, then click **A:\Feedback**, which appears near the bottom of the File menu.

   TROUBLE? If A:\Feedback does not appear and you left the computer between the time you were working with the Feedback document in the WordPad window, other files opened more recently might appear at the bottom of the File menu. If this is the case, open the Feedback file using the Open dialog box.

2. Click **No** when WordPad prompts you to save changes to Maria's document. Under normal circumstances you would save changes, but because you might want to use Maria's file to go through this tutorial again, you don't need to save changes.

3. Click at the end of your Feedback document. The insertion point | appears where you click. Any text you type or paste will appear at the insertion point.

4. Click the **Paste** button 🖺 to paste the information from Maria's document into your Feedback document.

5. Scroll back to the top of the document. See Figure 3-7.

Figure 3-7 ◄
Feedback
document with
pasted
information

original information
you typed ⎤

information you
pasted from Maria's
document ⎤

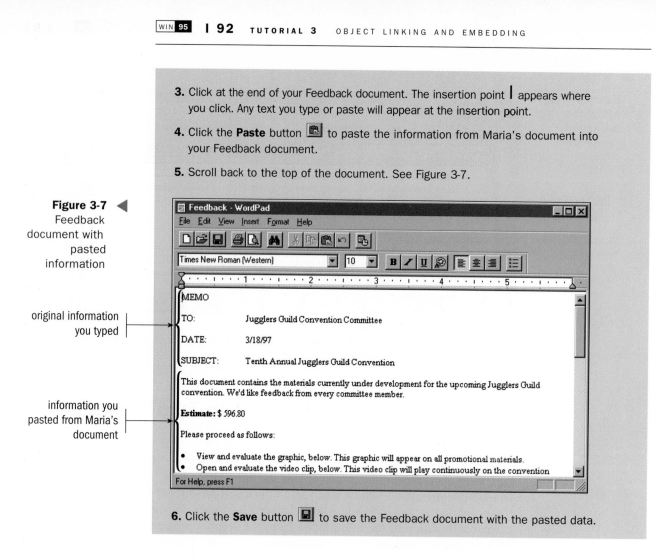

6. Click the **Save** button 🖫 to save the Feedback document with the pasted data.

Viewing Clipboard Contents

The Clipboard still contains the text of Maria's document. Remember that when you choose Paste, you are simply pasting a copy of the Clipboard contents into your document. The contents remain on the Clipboard in your computer's memory. If you need to free up memory, you can clear the contents of the Clipboard using a Windows 95 accessory called Clipboard Viewer. **Clipboard Viewer** lets you examine, save, and delete the contents of the Clipboard.

You decide to open Clipboard Viewer and delete its contents to free up memory. In reality, the amount of text you cut from Maria's document does not take up that much memory, but in practice you might find that cutting or copying graphics or large quantities of data could cause memory problems if memory is scant on your computer.

To view and clear the contents of the Clipboard:

1. Click the **Start** button, point to **Programs**, point to **Accessories**. Look at the Accessories menu to see whether Clipboard Viewer is installed.

TROUBLE? If Clipboard Viewer appears as an option on the menu, then Clipboard Viewer is installed on your computer and you can proceed. If Clipboard Viewer does not appear, then you cannot complete this session until Clipboard Viewer is installed. Check with your instructor or technical support person for assistance. If you are using your own computer and you have the installation disks, online Help can help you install Clipboard Viewer. Search for "installing" in the Index, then click "Windows components." The topic that opens is called "To install a Windows component after Windows has been installed." If you still can't install Clipboard Viewer, read to the end of this section without doing the steps.

2. Click **Clipboard Viewer**. The Clipboard Viewer window opens. The text you cut from Maria's document appears. See Figure 3-8.

Figure 3-8
Clipboard
Viewer

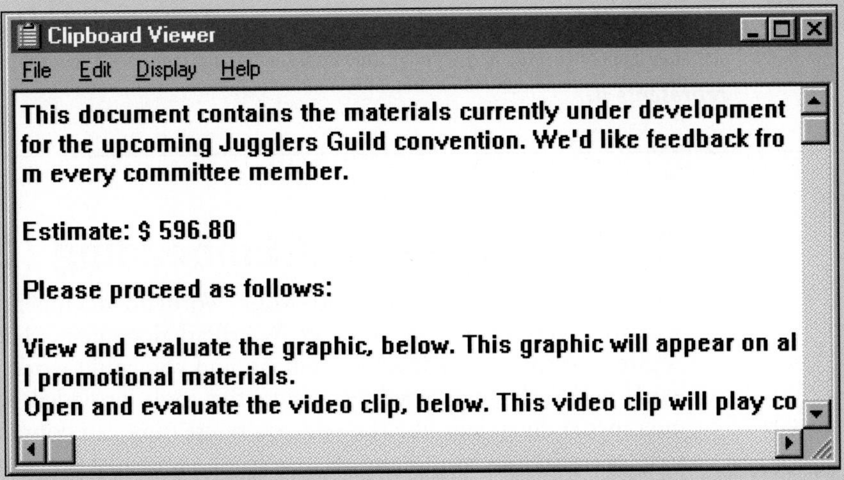

```
┌─────────────────────────────────────────────────────────┐
│ 📋 Clipboard Viewer                              _ □ ✕    │
├─────────────────────────────────────────────────────────┤
│ File  Edit  Display  Help                                │
├─────────────────────────────────────────────────────────┤
│ This document contains the materials currently under development ▲ │
│ for the upcoming Jugglers Guild convention. We'd like feedback fro │
│ m every committee member.                                │
│                                                          │
│ Estimate: $ 596.80                                       │
│                                                          │
│ Please proceed as follows:                               │
│                                                          │
│ View and evaluate the graphic, below. This graphic will appear on al │
│ l promotional materials.                                 │
│ Open and evaluate the video clip, below. This video clip will play co ▼ │
│ ◄                                                      ►  │
└─────────────────────────────────────────────────────────┘
```

3. Click **Edit**.

4. Click **Delete**.

5. Click **Yes**.

6. Click the **Close** button ✕ to close Clipboard Viewer.

7. Click the **Close** button ✕ to close WordPad.

Quick Check

1. What is the Clipboard?

2. What happens to the selected text in the original document when you cut it? When you copy it?

3. What keyboard shortcuts can you use to cut, copy, and paste?

4. True or false: Once you paste the contents of the Clipboard into a document, it is no longer available to be pasted into other documents.

5. How do you clear the contents of the Clipboard? Why would you want to do this?

6. Why would you use the Copy and Paste commands to transfer answers from the Calculator into other documents?

SESSION

3.2

In this session you'll learn how object linking and embedding (OLE) extends your ability to transfer data between files. You'll focus on embedding: you'll learn to embed a graphic object, and to change the size of and edit the embedded object. Then you'll display the embedded object as an icon, change its name, and change the icon that represents it.

Object Linking and Embedding (OLE)

So far you have pasted text into your WordPad document, first from the Calculator accessory and then from another WordPad document. The text you pasted actually became part of the Feedback document, and you could work with it in the same way you work with text you typed in—using the tools provided with WordPad. However, a multimedia document like the one you're creating can contain data from many different sources—graphics from Paint, charts from a spreadsheet, sounds from an audio file—as well as text.

3.1 NOTE

Windows 3.1 used OLE version 1.0, but Windows 95 uses version 2.0, which allows you to insert and edit objects from different programs without ever leaving your document.

How can you work with data in your multimedia document that comes from programs with different tools? For example, your WordPad document offers only text-editing tools. If you place a Paint graphic in this document, you can't use the WordPad tools to edit that graphic. Windows 95 provides the tools you need through a process called **Object Linking and Embedding**, or **OLE** (pronounced "oh lay"). OLE lets you insert an object into a document and access tools to manipulate the object. An **object** is a section of a text document, a graphic, a video, a sound, or any other unit of data. Figure 3-9 shows a WordPad document that contains an OLE object: a Paint graphic.

Figure 3-9 ◀
OLE object in
WordPad
document

text entered in
WordPad

OLE object from Paint

With OLE, you place objects into documents using either of two methods: you *embed* them or you *link* them. In this session, you'll learn how to embed objects, and in Session 3.3 you'll learn how to link objects.

To understand both embedding and linking, you need to know the terms listed in Figure 3-10.

Figure 3-10 ◀
OLE terms

Term	Definition
source program	The program that created the original object.
source file	The file that contains the original object.
destination program	The program that created the document into which you are inserting the OLE object.
destination file	The file into which you are inserting the OLE object.

Figure 3-11 applies the terms in Figure 3-10 to the document Maria wants you to create. Paint and Media Player are the source programs, and the Pins graphic and Video video clip are the source files. WordPad is the destination program, and Feedback is the destination file.

Figure 3-11 ◀
Multimedia document Maria wants you to create

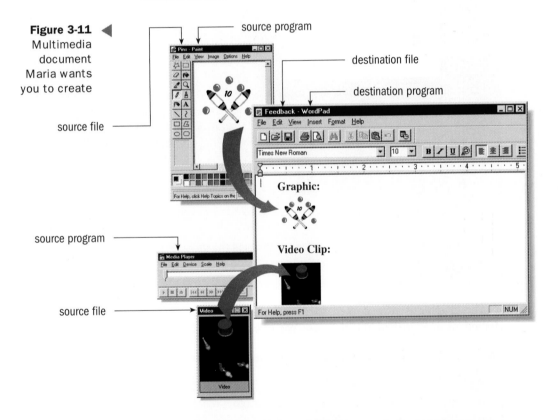

Embedding an Object Using Paste

You are ready to place the graphic into the Feedback document, but you want to retain the ability to work with the graphic with tools from the program that originally created it—in this case, Paint. When you want to be able to use the tools from the source program within the destination file, you should *embed* the object into the destination file. **Embedding** places a copy of an object into a document and "remembers" which program created the object, although it doesn't remember the name of the source file. There are several ways to embed an object. If both the source and destination programs feature OLE 2.0, you can simply paste the object from one to the other. Many of the programs designed for Windows 95 feature OLE.

The graphic provided by the graphic design company is called Pins. You want to embed a copy of this graphic into the Feedback document.

To copy the Pins graphic to the Clipboard:

1. Click the **Start** button, point to **Programs**, point to **Accessories**, then click **Paint**.

2. Open the **Pins** graphic from your Student Disk.

TROUBLE? If the Pins graphic did not open, click File, click Open, click the Look in list arrow, click the drive containing your Student Disk, click Pins, then click the Open button.

3. Click **Edit** then click **Select All**. A selection box appears around the graphic. See Figure 3-12.

Figure 3-12
Selecting the
Pins graphic in
Paint

selection box

4. Click **Edit** then click **Copy**. Windows 95 copies the graphic to the Clipboard.

5. Click the **Close** button ☒ to close Paint.

The graphic is now copied to the Clipboard. To embed it, you open the Feedback document in WordPad and then use WordPad's Paste command.

To embed the Pins graphic into the Feedback document:

1. Start WordPad and open the **Feedback** document from your Student Disk.

2. Scroll the **Feedback** document until you locate the boldface **Graphic:** heading.

3. Click the blank line two lines below the **Graphic:** heading.

4. Click the **Paste** button 📋. The Pins graphic is embedded in the Feedback document, and it appears in a selection box. See Figure 3-13.

Figure 3-13 ◄
Embedded
object

selection box

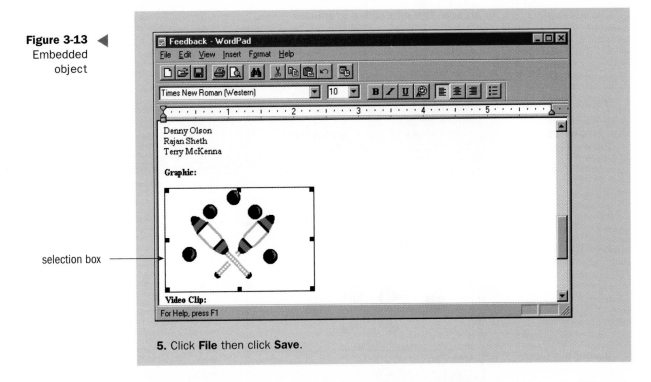

5. Click **File** then click **Save**.

New users are often confused by how the Paste command seems to function differently with different objects. In Session 3.1, Paste simply pasted text, but here Paste embeds an object. How can you tell what Paste is doing? There are no hard-and-fast rules for how each program takes advantage of the OLE 2.0 technology, although the following generalization often applies: when you use Paste to transfer the *same type of data* from one document to another, Paste inserts the data without embedding, as it did when you transferred text into WordPad. However, when you are transferring a *different type of data* from one document to another, and *both the source and destination programs use OLE 2.0*, Paste embeds the data. However, this is not always the case. As you'll see in the Tutorial Assignments, pasting WordPad text into Paint is not embedding, because Paint treats the pasted text as part of the bitmap—even though both Paste and WordPad are OLE 2.0 programs. When you copy and paste between Windows 95 programs, it's a good idea to examine what you've pasted so you can see how the program uses the Paste command. One clue is that if a selection box appears when you paste the data, it is embedded, and you can edit the data with the tools from the source program.

3.1 NOTE

In Windows 3.1, Paste inserts information without embedding it.

Changing the Size of an Embedded Object

As you examine the embedded graphic, you wonder if it might be easier to evaluate the image if it were a little bigger. You can easily resize an embedded object by dragging the selection box sizing handles. However, the object must first be selected, which you do simply by clicking it. The selection box and sizing handles appear. If you've just embedded the object, it is selected automatically.

To enlarge the embedded graphic:

1. Drag the lower-right sizing handle in a diagonal line, down and to the right. The pointer changes to ⬉ when you point at the sizing handle. The embedded object is enlarged. See Figure 3-14.

Figure 3-14 ◀
Enlarging the
embedded
Paint object

graphic is distorted
when enlarged

pointing at sizing
handle

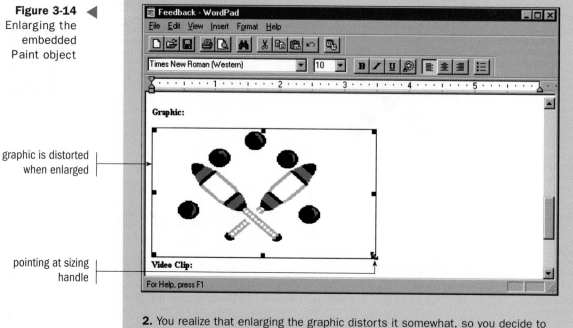

2. You realize that enlarging the graphic distorts it somewhat, so you decide to leave it in its original size. Click **Edit** then click **Undo**.

Editing an Embedded Object

The graphic is in place, but you decide that before the other committee members see it, you want to enhance it by adding color. You can edit an embedded object using the source program's editing tools. The ability to edit an object that has been embedded into a different program's document is called **in-place editing**—it gives you access to the source program's tools without making you leave the destination program. In-place editing is a valuable Windows 95 data-transfer feature, because it brings the tools you need to work with your document right to you, rather than making you fetch them.

When you use in-place editing, you sometimes might momentarily forget which program you are using. In that case, remember that the title bar identifies the program that contains your destination document, whereas the menus and toolbars identify what program you're using to edit the OLE object. See Figure 3-15.

Figure 3-15 ◀
In-place editing

title bar shows
destination document
and program

source program
menus and tools

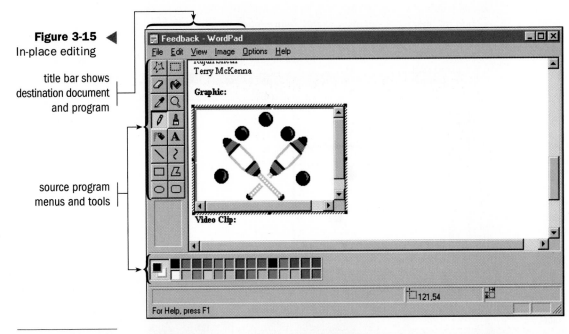

3.1 NOTE

*Although Windows 3.1
does not feature OLE
2.0, and so acces-
sories such as Write
and Paintbrush don't
feature in-place
editing, some
Windows 3.1
programs, such as
Microsoft Word and
Excel, do feature
OLE 2.0 and in-place
editing.*

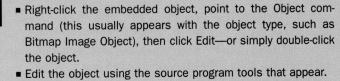

IN-PLACE EDITING

- Right-click the embedded object, point to the Object command (this usually appears with the object type, such as
  Bitmap Image Object), then click Edit—or simply double-click
  the object.
- Edit the object using the source program tools that appear.
- Click outside the selection box to return to the destination
  program.

To edit the Pins graphic within the WordPad document:

1. Right-click the **Pins** graphic to open its menu, then point to **Bitmap Image
Object**. See Figure 3-16

Figure 3-16 ◀
Opening an
embedded
object for
editing

right-click the
embedded object to
open menu

click to
edit
object

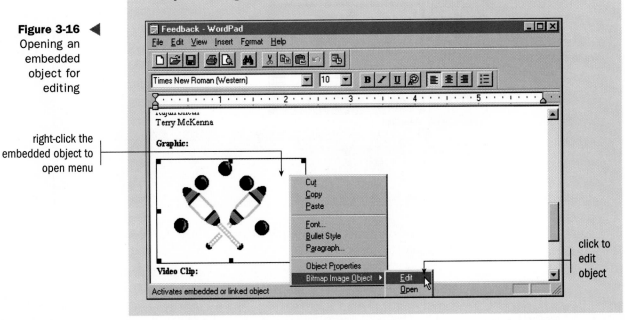

2. Click **Edit**. The graphic appears inside a selection box, the Paint tools appear, and the menu bar changes to the Paint menus, but the title bar identifies that you are still in WordPad. See Figure 3-17.

Figure 3-17 ◀
Using in-place
editing

Paint's Fill With
Color tool

selection box has
thicker borders to
indicate object is
ready for editing

red color

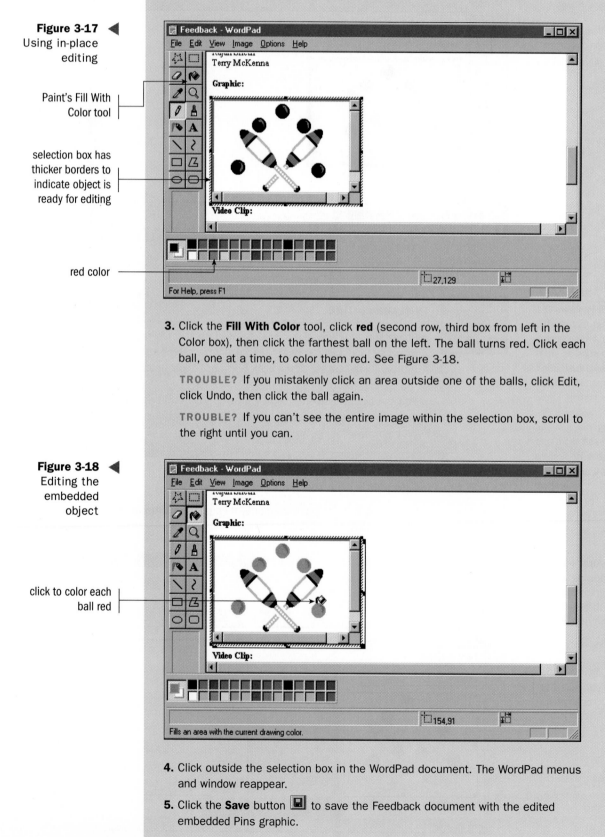

3. Click the **Fill With Color** tool, click **red** (second row, third box from left in the Color box), then click the farthest ball on the left. The ball turns red. Click each ball, one at a time, to color them red. See Figure 3-18.

TROUBLE? If you mistakenly click an area outside one of the balls, click Edit, click Undo, then click the ball again.

TROUBLE? If you can't see the entire image within the selection box, scroll to the right until you can.

Figure 3-18 ◀
Editing the
embedded
object

click to color each
ball red

4. Click outside the selection box in the WordPad document. The WordPad menus and window reappear.

5. Click the **Save** button 🖫 to save the Feedback document with the edited embedded Pins graphic.

As you'll see in Session 3.3, one of the important features that distinguishes embedding from linking is that *when you edit an embedded object, the source file is not affected.* You are accessing only the tools that created the object, not the original file. You can verify that the original graphic remains unchanged by opening the original Pins graphic in Paint.

To see that the original Pins graphic has not changed:

1. Click the **Start** button, point to **Programs**, point to **Accessories**, then click **Paint**.

2. Click **File** then click **A:\Pins** at the bottom of the File menu. Notice the original Pins graphic has not changed. See Figure 3-19.

Figure 3-19 ◄
Original graphic
in Paint

original graphic is
unchanged

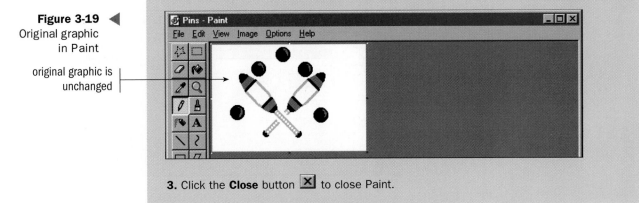

3. Click the **Close** button ⊠ to close Paint.

Embedding an Object using Insert Object

To paste an object into a different document, the object must be open and displayed on the screen so you can copy or cut it to the Clipboard. Most Windows programs that offer OLE technology also offer the **Insert Object** command, which lets you embed an object without having to open it and copy it to the Clipboard.

USING INSERT OBJECT

- Click the place in the destination file where you want to insert the object.
- Click Insert, then click Object. The dialog box that opens might look different depending on the program you are using. This is the dialog box that appears when you use Insert Object in WordPad.

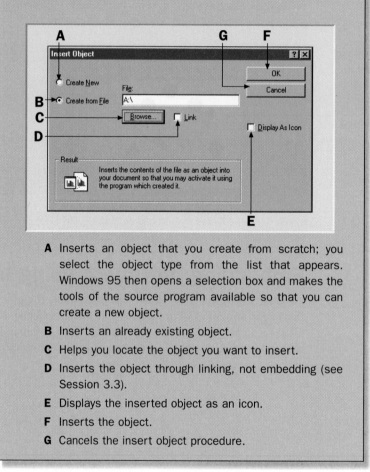

A Inserts an object that you create from scratch; you select the object type from the list that appears. Windows 95 then opens a selection box and makes the tools of the source program available so that you can create a new object.

B Inserts an already existing object.

C Helps you locate the object you want to insert.

D Inserts the object through linking, not embedding (see Session 3.3).

E Displays the inserted object as an icon.

F Inserts the object.

G Cancels the insert object procedure.

When you talked to the graphic designer on the phone the other day you mentioned that it might be nice to include the number "10" in the graphic, for 10th anniversary. The designer has just delivered a new disk with the revised file, called Pins10. You decide to embed Pins10 into the Feedback document using Insert Object.

To embed an object using the Insert Object command:

1. Scroll down the **Feedback** document until you see the boldface **Video Clip:** heading.

2. Click to the left of the **Video Clip:** heading. See Figure 3-20.

Figure 3-20 ◀
Location to
embed Pins10
graphic

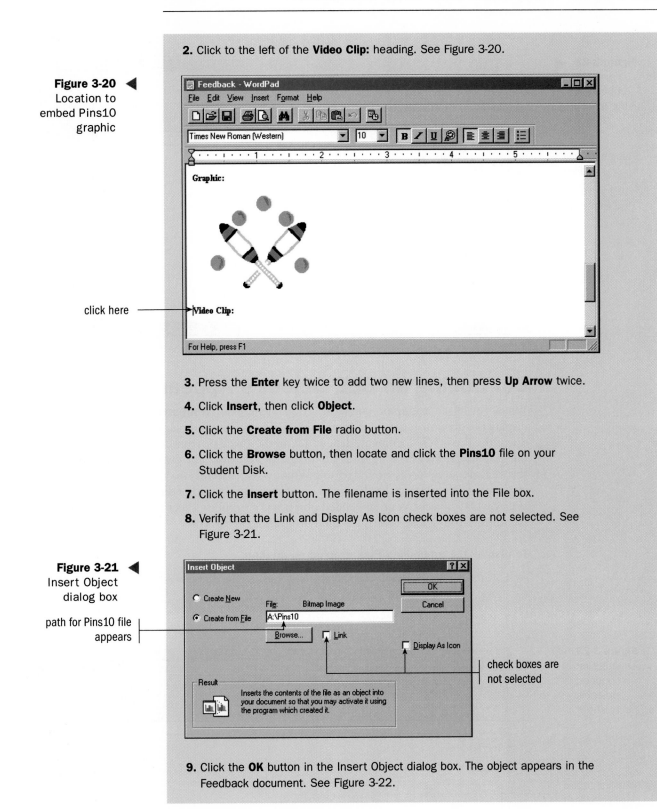

click here

3. Press the **Enter** key twice to add two new lines, then press **Up Arrow** twice.

4. Click **Insert**, then click **Object**.

5. Click the **Create from File** radio button.

6. Click the **Browse** button, then locate and click the **Pins10** file on your Student Disk.

7. Click the **Insert** button. The filename is inserted into the File box.

8. Verify that the Link and Display As Icon check boxes are not selected. See Figure 3-21.

Figure 3-21 ◀
Insert Object
dialog box

path for Pins10 file
appears

check boxes are
not selected

9. Click the **OK** button in the Insert Object dialog box. The object appears in the Feedback document. See Figure 3-22.

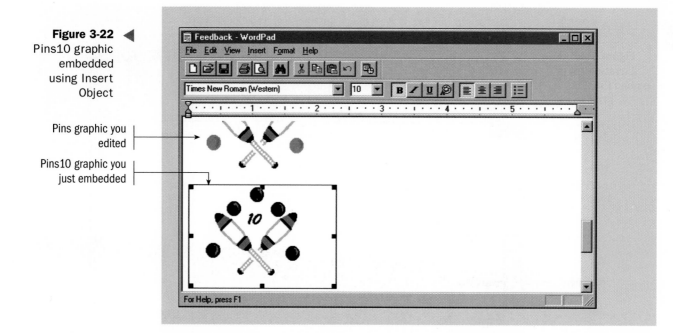

Figure 3-22 ◄
Pins10 graphic
embedded
using Insert
Object

Pins graphic you edited

Pins10 graphic you just embedded

Controlling an OLE Object's Appearance

When you place a graphic image in a document, your computer might take longer to display the document than if it contained only text. For example, when you scroll up and down the Feedback document, depending on the speed of your computer and the size of the graphics, it may take significantly longer to "redraw" the graphics as you scroll. For this reason, some users prefer to use Windows 95's ability to display OLE objects as icons, especially during the draft phases of creating a multimedia document. Like most Windows 95 objects, your embedded object has a property sheet that lets you work with the object. You decide to display the Pins graphic as an icon.

To display the embedded Pins graphic as an icon:

1. Scroll up the **Feedback** document so you can see the first graphic you embedded, the Pins graphic.

2. Right-click the **Pins** graphic. See Figure 3-23.

Figure 3-23 ◄
Opening an
embedded
object's
property sheet

right-click first graphic
you embedded

click to open property
sheet

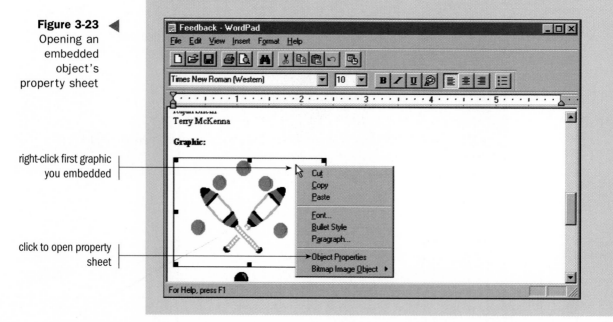

3. Click **Object Properties**.

4. Click the **View** tab.

5. Click the **Display as icon** radio button, then click the **OK** button. An icon appears that represents the graphic. See Figure 3-24.

Figure 3-24 ◀
Displaying an
object as
an icon

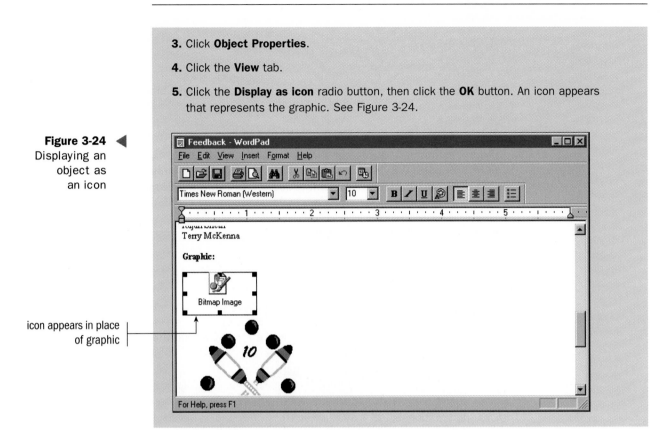

icon appears in place
of graphic

Changing the Display Icon

Because you changed the graphic to an icon and so can no longer identify the contents of the embedded object, you decide to change the label of the icon to make it more descriptive. You can change the icon label using the embedded object's property sheet.

To change the label of the icon:

1. Right-click the icon representing the embedded Pins graphic.

2. Click **Object Properties**.

3. Click the **View** tab.

4. Click the **Change Icon** button.

5. Delete the contents of the Label box, then type **Pins Graphic**. See Figure 3-25.

Figure 3-25 ◀
Change Icon
dialog box

type icon label here

6. Click the **OK** button.

7. Click the **Apply** button.

8. If necessary, drag the Properties dialog box out of the way in order to see the icon with the new label.

If your multimedia document includes icons in its final form, you might not like the look of the icons Windows 95 chooses to represent your embedded objects. You can change the icon representing the embedded object using the property sheet. Incidentally, you can use this method for any icon, including icons on the desktop.

REFERENCE
window

CHANGING AN ICON

- Open the icon's property sheet. You usually do this by right-clicking the existing icon to open its object menu, then clicking Properties, although for embedded objects the command appears as Object Properties.
- If necessary, click the tab in the Properties dialog box that contains the Change Icon button.
- Click the Change Icon button.
- Click one of the icons that appears in the Change Icon dialog box. You could also click Create From File, click the Browse button, and then locate and select the file containing the icon (switch the Files of type list to All Files if you are looking for a file with an extension other than ICO, the default type that appears).
- Click the OK button in the Change Icon dialog box and in the Properties dialog box.

You decide to change the icon representing the Pins graphic to a more descriptive icon. Your Student Disk contains a bitmap graphics file called **Icon** that you will use as the icon.

To change the appearance of the icon:

1. Click the **Change Icon** button.

2. Click the **From File** radio button, then click the **Browse** button.

3. Click the **Look in** list arrow, then click the drive containing your Student Disk.

4. Click the **Files of type** list arrow, then click **All Files**.

5. Click **Icon** then click the **Open** button.

6. Click the **OK** button, then click the **OK** button. The new icon appears. Click outside the selection box. See Figure 3-26.

TROUBLE? Windows 95 can be a little unpredictable when you change an icon in a document. If the new icon doesn't appear, wait a few seconds, then scroll up the document until the original icon is no longer visible on the screen. Then scroll back down. This forces Windows 95 to display the correct icon.

Figure 3-26 ◀
New icon for embedded object

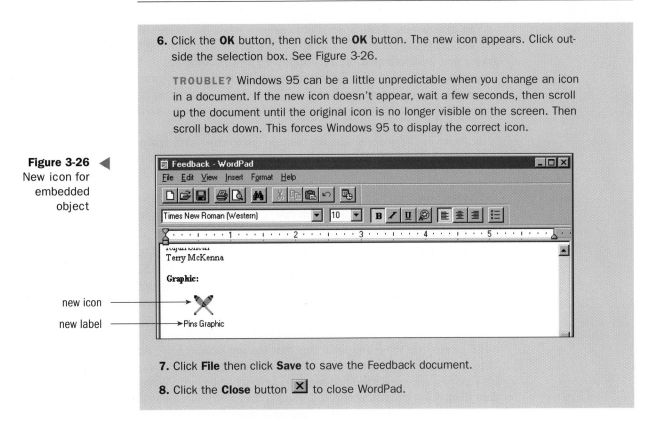

new icon

new label

7. Click **File** then click **Save** to save the Feedback document.

8. Click the **Close** button [X] to close WordPad.

Paste Special

In some cases you might not want to embed the data, because embedding often increases the size of the destination file more than linking does, which can be a problem if you're short on disk space. You might also be sharing the destination file with users who do not have the source program installed on their computer, in which case you might want to embed it with a different format. In these situations, you might want to use the **Paste Special** command on the Edit menu instead of Paste—it gives you more control over how you transfer the data into the destination file. For example, you might want to paste a Microsoft Excel chart into your WordPad document. If you use Paste, Windows 95 embeds it as an Excel chart, and you can use in-place editing to edit it, using tools from Microsoft Excel, in much the same way you did with the Pins graphic. However, if you don't need to edit the chart, you can use Paste Special to insert the chart simply as a bitmapped image, which requires much less space. Figure 3-27 shows the Paste Special dialog box as it appears when you paste an Excel chart as a bitmapped image into a WordPad document.

Figure 3-27 ◀
Paste Special dialog box

available formats

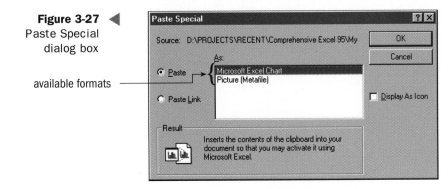

You can also use Paste Special in situations when the source file comes from a program that either doesn't feature OLE at all or uses an earlier version of OLE. The Microsoft programs that were released under Windows 95—including Paint, WordPad, and the Office programs—all feature OLE 2.0 technology; so when you are transferring data among these programs, you might not need to think about the complexities of Paste Special.

To summarize, there are three ways to embed an object into a document:

1. **Paste** If the source and destination programs both feature OLE 2.0, you can usually open the object in the source program, select the object, click Edit, then click Copy. Then open the destination program, click Edit, then click Paste.

2. **Insert Object** If you don't want to open the source program first, click Insert, click Object, then click Create from File. Locate the file you want to embed, then click the OK button.

3. **Paste Special** If you want more control over the data you're embedding, you can select the object in the source program, click Edit, then click Copy. Move to the destination program, click Edit, click Paste Special, complete the Paste Special dialog box, and then click the OK button. Using Paste Special lets you embed the object in specialized formats.

Be aware that there are programs that feature *neither* OLE *nor* Clipboard technology. You then must depend on the data transfer commands within those programs, commands which often appear on the File menu as Import or Export. When you attempt to transfer data from other programs and it doesn't seem to be working as you expect, the first thing you should suspect is that your program doesn't feature OLE 2.0.

Quick Check

1. What is OLE?

2. You just embedded text from a WordPad document into a PowerPoint presentation document. Identify the source program and the destination program.

3. When you use the Paste command, are you always embedding? Explain why or why not, and provide examples.

4. Name two ways to embed an object with OLE 2.0. Under what circumstances might you use these different methods?

5. What is in-place editing?

6. Under what circumstances might you use Paste Special rather than Paste?

7. True or false: You can use the Clipboard to transfer data between any two programs.

SESSION

3.3

In this session you will link a new version of the Pins graphic into your Feedback document. Then you'll work with the original file to see how linking lets you update the linked information in the source document. You'll learn how to delete OLE objects from your document. Then you'll link a video clip into the Feedback document and work with the Windows 95 Media Player.

Linking

The graphic designer you were working with has supplied you with another new version of the Pins graphic, called Pins2, that makes better use of color. You want the committee members to see this new version. But what if the graphic designer calls again with an even newer version? You don't want to have to re-embed the graphic every time you receive a new version. Therefore, you decide to link the Pins2 graphic into your Feedback document rather than embed it.

Linking is another way to insert information into a document, but with linking you insert a *representation* of the object. When you edit a linked object, you are editing the *original* object, the source file itself, whether you are in the source or destination file. For example, if you change the color of the balls with a linked object, you are changing the source file itself. Notice how this differs from embedding. With embedding you place a *copy* of the object into the destination file that does not connect to the source file, so any changes you make to the embedded object are not reflected in the source file. With linking, however, you maintain a connection between the source file and the destination file, and a change to one object, changes the other object. See Figure 3-28.

Figure 3-28 ◄
Linking vs.
Embedding

embedded
object is copy of
Paint graphic;
changing it does
not affect source
file

source file

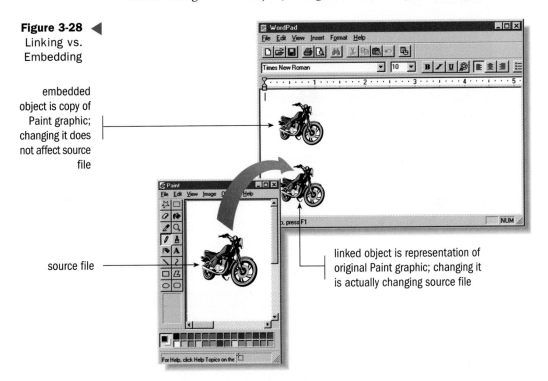

linked object is representation of
original Paint graphic; changing it
is actually changing source file

You link an object when you want only one copy of the object to exist. For example, you might want to use an object in several documents. When you update the object, all the documents use the updated version. There is one thing you should remember when you give a document to someone that contains links: Make sure to include the source files. When you embed objects, you don't need to include the source files, but when you link objects, you do.

Linking a Graphic File to a WordPad Document

You want only one version of the Pins graphic to be in use so you don't have to update it every time the file changes. You decide to link Pins2 to the Feedback document. There are two ways you can link an object: using the Insert Object command or, in some circumstances, using Paste Special.

REFERENCE window

LINKING AN OBJECT

- To use Insert Object, click the location in the destination file where you want to insert the object. Then click Insert, click Object, then click Create from File. Next click Browse, locate and select the file, and then click the OK button twice.
- To use Paste Special, first open the source file and highlight the information you want to insert. Click Edit, then click Copy. Next open the destination file and click the location where you want to insert the object. Click Edit, click Paste Special, click Paste Link, and then click the OK button. Note that Paste Special does not always allow you to paste with a link.

To insert the Pins2 graphic as a linked object:

1. Start WordPad, then open Feedback from your Student Disk.

2. Scroll down the **Feedback** document below the two embedded objects. Click to the left of the **Video Clip:** heading, press the **Enter** key twice to insert two new lines, and then press **Up Arrow** twice. See Figure 3-29.

Figure 3-29 ◀
Feedback document ready to accept revised graphic

insert linked object here

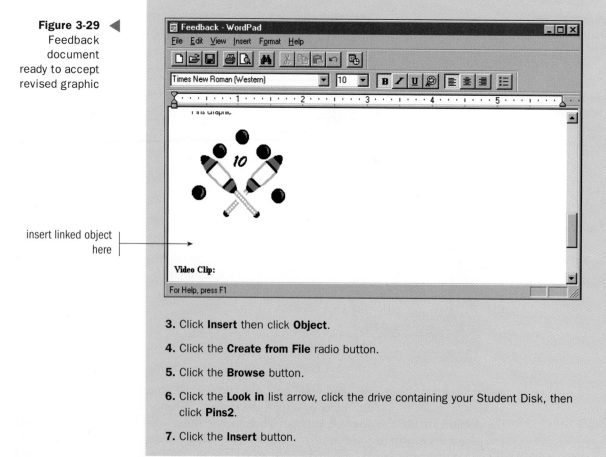

3. Click **Insert** then click **Object**.

4. Click the **Create from File** radio button.

5. Click the **Browse** button.

6. Click the **Look in** list arrow, click the drive containing your Student Disk, then click **Pins2**.

7. Click the **Insert** button.

8. Click the **Link** check box to place a check mark in it, then click the **OK** button. The Pins2 graphic appears in the Feedback document. See Figure 3-30.

Figure 3-30 ◄
Linked object

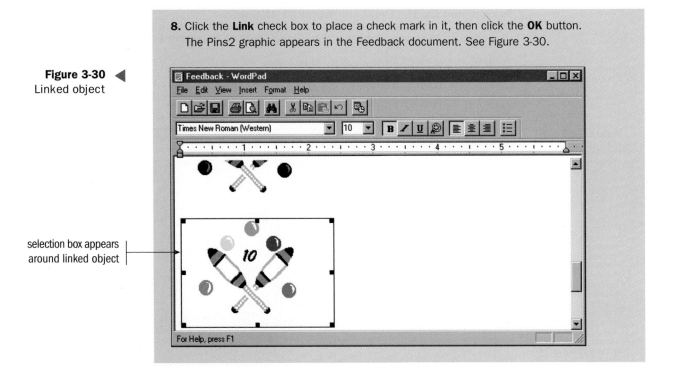

selection box appears
around linked object

Arranging Windows Using Tile and Cascade

You like the look of the color graphic, but you think it would look better if all the balls were one color. You decide to edit the source file, Pins2, in Paint. You can arrange the Paint and WordPad windows so both are open and visible at the same time. You could resize and drag the windows into place, or you could use the Tile or Cascade commands on the taskbar's menu. The **Tile** command arranges all open windows so they are all visible. You can tile vertically (side by side) or horizontally (one above the other). The **Cascade** command arranges all open windows so that they overlap each other and all their title bars are visible. Figure 3-31 shows these two arrangements.

Figure 3-31 ◄
Arranging
windows

tiled windows ➔

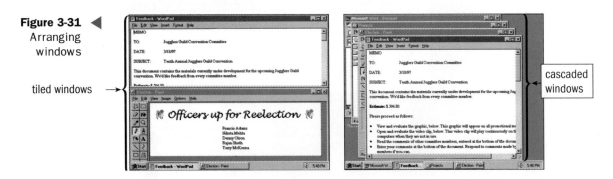

cascaded
windows

Tiling is useful when you have just a few open windows, whereas cascading is useful when you have many open windows. Arranging windows can be helpful when you work with data transfer, because you are often working with more than one open program, and you want to see what's happening in the open programs at the same time. You decide to vertically tile the WordPad and Paint windows.

To open and tile the Paint and WordPad windows:

1. Click the **Start** button, point to **Programs**, point to **Accessories**, then click **Paint**.

2. Open the **Pins2** file from your Student Disk in Paint. This is the file you just linked to the Feedback document.

3. Right-click a blank area of the taskbar to open the taskbar menu. See Figure 3-32.

Figure 3-32 ◄
Opening the
taskbar menu

click to tile open
windows vertically

taskbar
menu

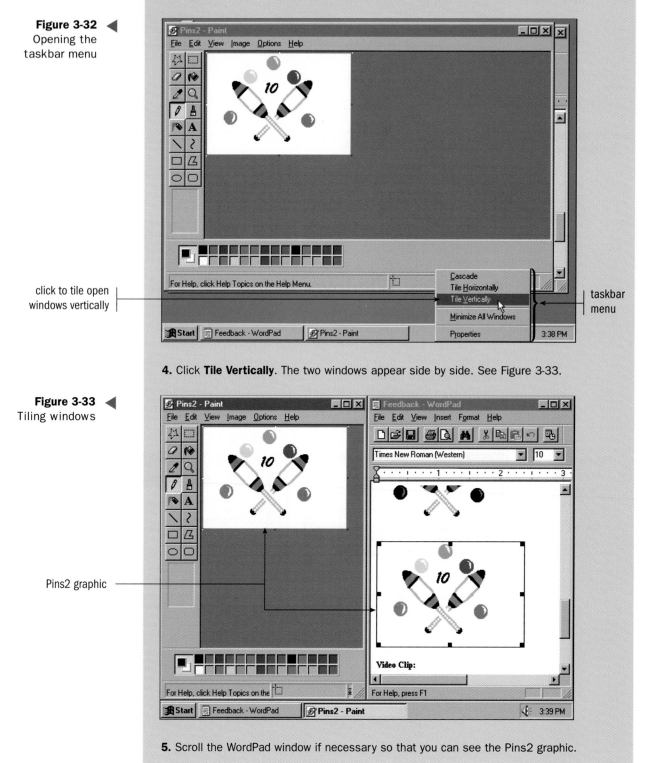

4. Click **Tile Vertically**. The two windows appear side by side. See Figure 3-33.

Figure 3-33 ◄
Tiling windows

Pins2 graphic

5. Scroll the WordPad window if necessary so that you can see the Pins2 graphic.

Editing a Linked Object in the Source Program

The object you just inserted is linked, so you can change it in either the source or destination file and your changes will be stored in the original file. You decide to color the balls red in the original file.

To edit the Pins2 graphic in Paint:

1. Click the **Fill With Color** tool 🎨 in Paint.

2. Click the **red** box (in second row, third box from left in Color box), then click each of the four balls that aren't already red. All five balls should be red when you finish. See Figure 3-34.

Figure 3-34 ◀
Editing linked object in source program

color balls red in source file

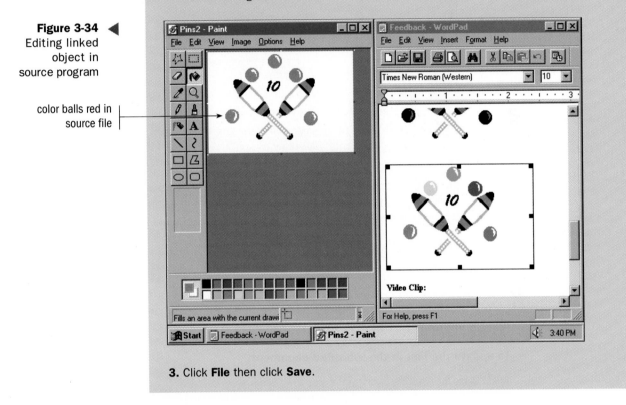

3. Click **File** then click **Save**.

Updating a Linked Object

If the destination file is closed when you change the source file, any linked objects will usually update automatically the *next* time you open the file. If the destination file is open when you change the source file, you have to update it manually using the Links command. This opens the Links dialog box, which gives you control over the links in your document.

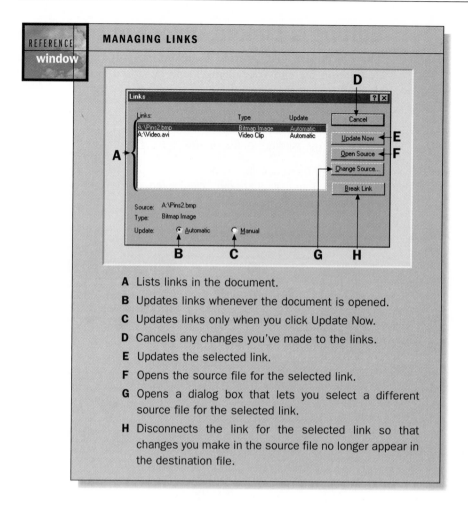

REFERENCE
window

MANAGING LINKS

A Lists links in the document.

B Updates links whenever the document is opened.

C Updates links only when you click Update Now.

D Cancels any changes you've made to the links.

E Updates the selected link.

F Opens the source file for the selected link.

G Opens a dialog box that lets you select a different source file for the selected link.

H Disconnects the link for the selected link so that changes you make in the source file no longer appear in the destination file.

You decide to update the link between the Pins2 source file and the Feedback destination file so you can verify that the changes take place.

To update the link in the WordPad document:

1. Click the **Pins2** graphic in the WordPad window.

2. Click **Edit** then click **Links**. Click the link that represents the connection between the linked object in the destination file and the source file. See Figure 3-35.

Figure 3-35 ◀
Links dialog
box

3. Click the **Update Now** button. The graphic is updated.

4. Click the **Close** button ⊠ to close the Links dialog box.

5. Click the **Close** button ⊠ to close Paint.

6. Maximize the WordPad window.

Deleting an OLE Object

As you look over your document, you notice that you have now inserted three graphic objects into the Feedback document. The first two are both older versions of the graphic. You decide you don't need to include them in the Feedback document, so you delete them. See Figure 3-36.

Figure 3-36 ◀
Three OLE
objects in
Feedback
document

delete two
embedded objects

you'll keep linked
object

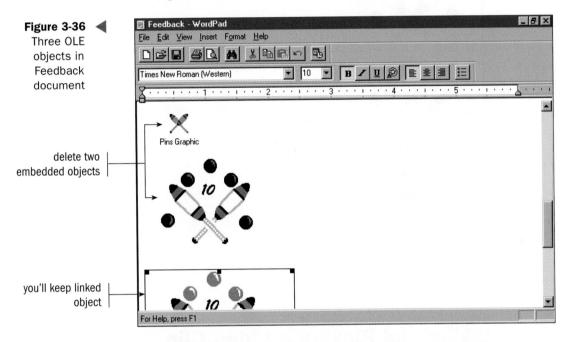

To delete the two old embedded graphics, Pins and Pins10:

1. Scroll up the **Feedback** document until you see the icon representing the first Pins graphic.

2. Click the icon labelled **Pins Graphic**. A selection box appears. See Figure 3-37.

Figure 3-37 ◀
Selecting the
first object to
be deleted

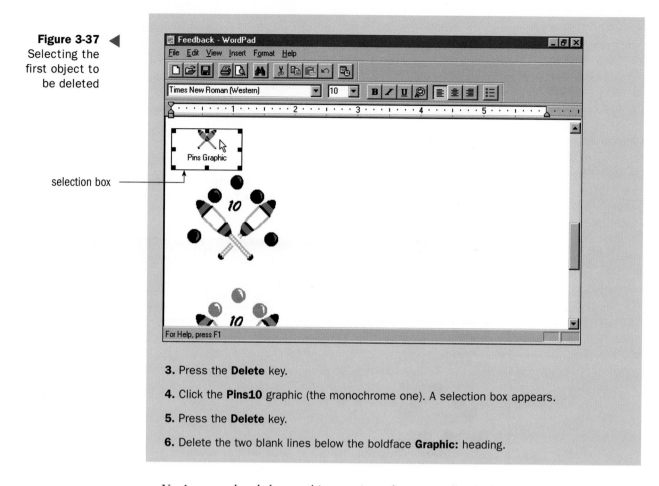

selection box

3. Press the **Delete** key.

4. Click the **Pins10** graphic (the monochrome one). A selection box appears.

5. Press the **Delete** key.

6. Delete the two blank lines below the boldface **Graphic:** heading.

You've completed the graphics portion of your Feedback document, and it's ready to be shown to the committee.

Linking and Playing a Video Clip

Now you turn your attention to the next object you want to show to the committee members: the video clip. You decide to link the video clip to your Feedback document so that if the computer animation vendor sends you an updated file, you don't have to reinsert the file. You can link a video clip in the same way you linked a graphic, using Insert Object.

To link a video clip to a document:

1. Scroll the **Feedback** document until you locate the boldface **Video Clip:** heading.

2. Click two blank lines below the boldface **Video Clip:** heading. See Figure 3-38.

Figure 3-38 ◀
Inserting a
video clip

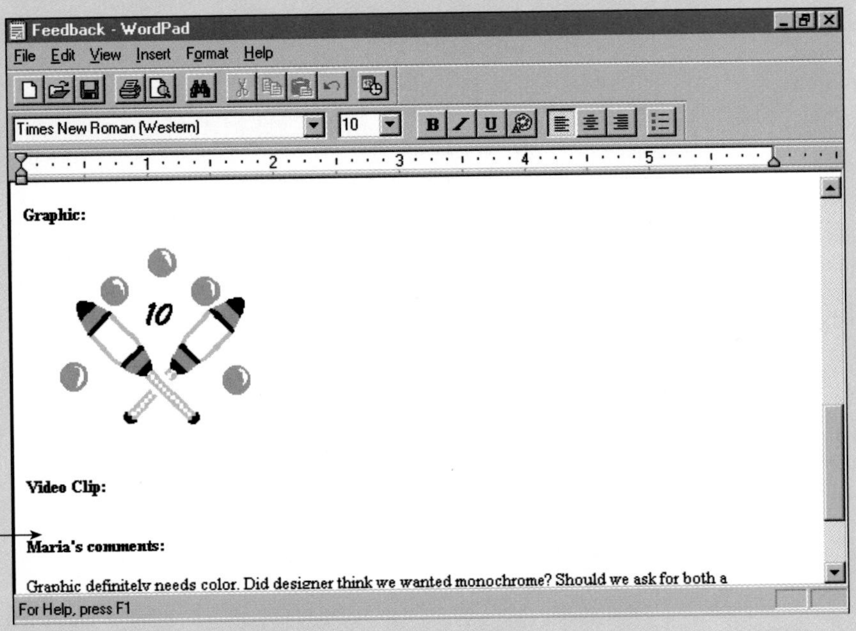

click here to insert
video clip

3. Click **Insert** then click **Object**.

4. Click the **Create from File** radio button.

5. Click the **Browse** button.

6. Click the **Look in** list arrow, then click the drive containing your Student Disk.

7. Click **Video** then click the **Insert** button.

8. Click the **Link** check box to place a check mark in it, then click the **OK** button.

The video clip looks like a graphic object, but of course it isn't. You can play the video clip by right-clicking it and using the Play Linked Video Clip Object command. Because it is a linked object using OLE technology, you don't have to leave WordPad or start a separate program to play it.

To play the video clip:

1. Right-click the video clip. The video clip's object menu opens.

2. Point to **Linked Video Clip Object**.

   TROUBLE? If this appears as "Linked Media Clip Object," click that instead.

   TROUBLE? If a message appears warning you that Windows 95 couldn't launch the server application, ask your instructor or lab manager to install the multimedia accessories.

3. Click **Play**. The video clip plays in a small window. See Figure 3-39. It might play once very quickly and then stop, perhaps even before it appears to reach the end, or it might play continuously. You'll learn momentarily how to control how the video clip plays.

   TROUBLE? If your clip plays very choppily your computer might not have sufficient memory to play it smoothly.

Figure 3-39 ◄
Playing a linked
video clip

video clip plays in its
own window because
it is linked, not
embedded

linked object is
representation of
source file

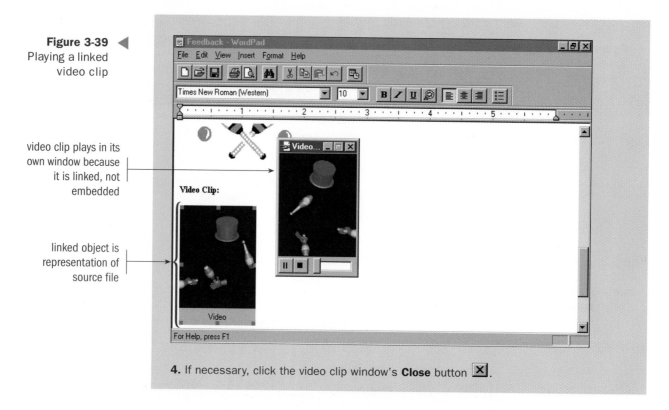

4. If necessary, click the video clip window's **Close** button ☒.

You've now inserted the video clip into the Feedback document. However, you'd like to refine how it plays.

Windows 95 Multimedia

The window that opened when you played the video clip was part of the Windows 95 **Media Player**, one of the accessories Windows 95 provides that handles multimedia files. The Windows 95 multimedia accessories, listed in Figure 3-40, let you create, edit, and play multimedia clips.

Figure 3-40 ◄
Multimedia
accessories

Accessory	Description
CD Player	Plays music CDs using your computer's sound card and speakers.
Media Player	Plays audio and video clips.
Sound Recorder	Records and plays audio files.
Volume Control	Adjusts your sound card's volume.
Sound Schemes	Lists sample sounds that you can attach to Windows 95 events (such as exiting a program or starting Windows 95).

Multimedia clips can use sound, video, or both. To play a clip that uses sound, you need a sound card and speakers. If your computer doesn't have these hardware devices, you can still hear sounds through your computer's internal speaker—such as the "beeps" you hear when the computer alerts you to something. The internal speaker, however, is inadequate for playing most sound files. Windows 95 works with two sound file formats: WAV and MIDI. The **Sound Recorder** accessory uses the **WAV** format, which is short for waveform-audio, to store and record sounds as realistically as possible. The Media Player accessory, on the other hand, uses the **MIDI** format, short for Musical Instrument Digital Interface. MIDI files use artificial, synthesized sounds to mimic a real sound and hence are usually much smaller than WAV files. Although you can't use MIDI files to store voices, you can use them very effectively to store the synthesized sounds of special MIDI instruments.

To play a video clip, you don't need a sound card or speakers, but the quality of the video will depend on your monitor's resolution, and the computer's video card capabilities and its speed and memory capacity. You use the Media Player accessory to play video clips in the **AVI** format, short for Audio-Video Interleaved. This format is sometimes called "Video for Windows." AVI files can contain both images and sound (of course, if you want to hear the sound you'll need a sound card and speakers). Media Player lets you scroll back and forth through a video clip, but you cannot use the Media Player to edit the clip itself.

Using Media Player

When you played the Juggler video clip, it might have played only once and then stopped, or it might have played continuously. You want to control how it plays. To do this, you need to start Media Player and edit the video's settings. Media Player plays a video one frame at a time, just like a filmstrip is shown. A slider appears that shows you which frame is appearing at any given moment, so you can move forward or backward through individual frames. Media Player also includes a set of buttons that resemble the buttons on a cassette tape player or a VCR, as described in Figure 3-41.

Figure 3-41 ◀
Media Player
buttons

Button	Name	Description
▶	Play	Plays the multimedia clip. Turns into the Pause button when multimedia clip is playing.
❚❚	Pause	Play button turns into Pause button when multimedia clip is playing; pauses clip.
■	Stop	Stops the clip at its current frame or track.
▲	Eject	Appears only when you are playing a clip off a CD-ROM; ejects the CD.
⏮	Previous Mark	Moves to the previous mark (like a track on a CD).
◀◀	Rewind	Moves backward in increments as you click.
▶▶	Fast Forward	Moves forward in increments as you click.
⏭	Next Mark	Moves to the next mark (like a track on a CD).
⤒	Start Selection	Starts the selection (if you select just a few frames to play).
⤓	End Selection	Ends the selection (if you select just a few frames to play).

You decide you want to make sure the video plays continuously. You can either start Media Player from the Start menu and then open the video clip, or you can start Media Player from within the Feedback document by opening the video clip for editing.

To make sure the video clip is set to repeat automatically:

1. Right-click the video clip, point to **Linked Video Clip Object**, then click **Edit**. Media Player opens. See Figure 3-42.

Figure 3-42 ◀
Media player

slider

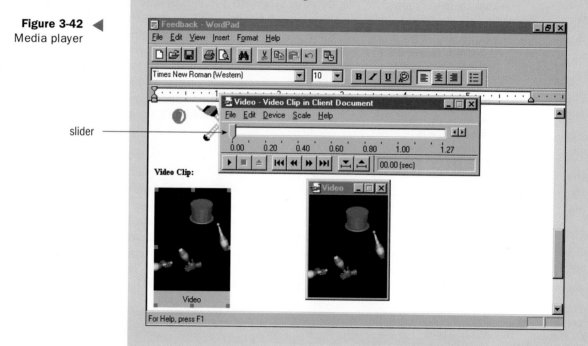

2. Click **Edit** then click **Options**. First see how the video plays when it is not set on Auto Repeat.

3. Click the **Auto Repeat** check box to deselect it, then click the **OK** button.

TROUBLE? If Auto Repeat is already deselected, skip Step 3. See Figure 3-43.

Figure 3-43 ◀
Media Player options

clip plays repeatedly
when check box is
selected

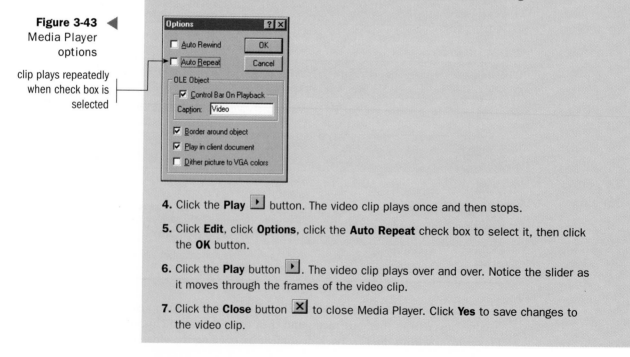

4. Click the **Play** ▶ button. The video clip plays once and then stops.

5. Click **Edit**, click **Options**, click the **Auto Repeat** check box to select it, then click the **OK** button.

6. Click the **Play** button ▶. The video clip plays over and over. Notice the slider as it moves through the frames of the video clip.

7. Click the **Close** button ✕ to close Media Player. Click **Yes** to save changes to the video clip.

The Feedback document now contains no embedded objects and two linked objects: the graphic and the video clip. You can send the document, along with the two source files, to the committee members for their feedback. They can easily view both objects and can then add their comments to the bottom of the document.

To save your work and close all open windows:

1. Click **File** then click **Save** to save your Feedback document.

2. Click the **Close** button ☒ to close WordPad.

Quick Check

1. What is the difference between linking and embedding?

2. If you change the source file for a linked object when the destination file is closed, what do you see when you next open the destination file?

3. If you want to share a document that contains embedded objects with another person, do you need to include the source files? Explain why or why not.

4. When you use the Insert Object method to insert an object into a document, do you first need to open the source file?

5. What's the difference between the appearance of tiling and cascading windows?

6. True or false: Media Player plays only video, not audio, clips.

7. Describe these three file types: WAV, MIDI, and AVI.

End Note

Your final version of the Feedback document used only linking, not embedding, because you decided that both objects were likely to undergo further revision and you wanted to be able to easily update the document without having to reinsert the objects. As you created the Feedback document, however, you used several different methods to exchange information between documents. New computer users will not be able to compare how these methods shift the historical focus of computing from programs to documents, but users of Windows 3.1 or DOS will appreciate how these techniques revolutionize the way we think about producing documents. As with other aspects of Windows 95, the focus is on the document, not the program that created it. You create a document by bringing in tools from other programs without even being aware that you are doing so. Many people see this focus on the document as the future of personal computing. Rather than a separate text-editing program or graphics program, there will be a document; and if the document contains text, text-editing tools will appear. If the document contains graphics, graphic-editing tools will appear. Windows 95 and OLE 2.0 take a significant step in the direction of the future.

Tutorial Assignments

1. Copying and Pasting Text A friend of yours owns a small tailor shop and wants to advertise his services in the *Yellow Pages*. He wants feedback from his employees and friends on his advertisement and wonders if you'd share your feedback process with him. You write him a note and then paste in the steps to your process.

    a. Start WordPad, then open Maria from your Student Disk.

    b. Highlight the bulleted list, then copy it to the Clipboard.

    c. Open Tailor from your Student Disk, and scroll to the boldface Follow this Procedure: heading. Add a few blank lines below the heading, then paste the copied information.

    d. Edit the information so it meets your friend's needs.

    e. Print and save Tailor.

2. Copying Text from Notepad to WordPad You work for the Internal Revenue Service and have been using Notepad to draft a brochure to inform taxpayers about on-line tax filing. Notepad, however, does not offer any text formatting options; and you'd like to format your document. You decide to move the text into a WordPad document.

    a. Start Notepad, then open IRS Text from your Student Disk.

    b. Start WordPad, then open New IRS from your Student Disk.

    c. In Notepad, select and then copy the entire document. Close Notepad.

    d. Switch to the WordPad window, click below the Online Tax Filing heading, then paste the text.

    e. Format the document using WordPad's formatting tools.

    f. Print and save the WordPad document.

EXPLORE

3. Pasting Text into Paint In this tutorial you pasted a Paint graphic into WordPad. Now you'll try pasting in the other direction. You are designing a banner that announces the names of incumbent officers up for reelection for the Jugglers Guild. You have created a Paint graphic called Election. You want to insert the names of the five officers into that graphic.

    a. Start Paint and open the Election graphic from your Student Disk.

    b. Start WordPad, open Maria, and copy the last five names (not including Maria Arruda) in the Distribution List to the Clipboard. These are the five officers up for reelection.

    c. Close WordPad, then return to the Election graphic. Paste the names into the Election graphic. Click Yes if Paint asks if you want to enlarge the bitmap.

    d. Drag the pasted names so they are centered below the heading.

    e. Print and save the Election graphic.

    f. On your printout, write a paragraph answering these questions: Is the text you just pasted inserted as an embedded object into the Paint graphic? How can you tell? How does the process you just completed differ from how you pasted a Paint graphic into a WordPad document in Session 3.2?

4. Linking and Editing a Graphic You are a clown named Chester, and you are attending the juggling convention. You want to distribute a flyer at the convention that advertises your clowning services. You have created the flyer in the WordPad document named Chester, and you want to link a graphic file into that document.

    a. Open the WordPad document named Clowning.

    b. Use Insert Object to insert the graphic named Chester into the bottom of the Clowning document. Make sure you insert the object with a link.

    c. After you've inserted the Chester graphic, open it for editing by right-clicking the object, clicking Linked Bitmap Image Object, then clicking Edit. Change Chester's hair color to brown. Close Paint, saving the changes to Chester, then return to the WordPad document.

    d. Update the link, if necessary, then print and save the Clowning document. On the printout, write a paragraph about how editing a linked object from the destination document differs from editing an embedded object.

5. Linking a Graphic and Displaying It As an Icon You are a member of the Tokunta Construction company. You are developing a training manual for new employees. You need to link a graphic that illustrates a construction principle, but you want to display it as an icon.

    a. Open the House document in WordPad.

    b. Use Insert Object to insert the House graphic at the end of the document. Make sure you link the graphic.

    c. Change the graphic display so that it displays an icon.

d. Change the caption of the icon to Cantilever.

e. Change the icon to the Tools icon on your Student Disk.

f. Print and save the House document.

6. Linking a Sound File to a Document Your Student Disk includes a sound file of J. F. Kennedy's "Ask not what your country..." speech. You'd like to link this sound file to a WordPad document that you are creating for a linguistics class in which you are studying American accents. Kennedy's sound clip exemplifies a Boston accent.

a. Create a new WordPad document and type "Linguistics, Bostonian accent" at the beginning. Save the document as Linguistics.

b. Use the Insert Object method to insert the Kennedy sound file into your document. Make sure you insert it with a link.

c. You'll be able to complete this task only if you have a sound card and speakers. Use the linked object's menu to first play the object and then open it for editing. When you open it for editing, what accessory does Windows 95 use? What other accessory could Windows 95 use to play this sound file?

Do not use your Student Disk for Tutorial Assignments 7-10. Instead, use a new, blank, formatted disk. Label this disk "OLE Disk." If you use your Student Disk, you might have disk space problems in later tutorials.

7. Creating a Multimedia Document You work at CarpetMaster, a company that specializes in residential and commercial carpet cleaning and restoration. A customer wants an estimate for repair costs for an Oriental rug that was damaged in a recent fire. You need to draw, a rectangle in Paint that approximates the carpet size and indicate the area that you'll be repairing. Then you need to embed that graphic into a WordPad document that gives the estimate.

a. Create a Paint graphic that shows the carpet and the damaged area. Save this graphic as Carpet. Close Paint.

b. Create a WordPad document that uses appropriate language for an estimate and a description of the necessary repairs. Save the document as CarpetMaster Estimate.

c. Open Calculator and calculate 6.5 hours at $47/hr. Paste this amount into the WordPad document.

d. Use Insert Object to embed the Paint graphic in the WordPad document.

e. Print and save the WordPad document.

8. Transferring Data Between Other Programs If you have access to other software programs, like a word processor, a spreadsheet program, or a database program, experiment with the data transfer operations available in those programs. Create new documents in these programs, add sample data, and then save the documents on your disk. Then try to copy and paste data between the programs. Next try embedding and linking. Write a short essay that answers the following questions:

a. In what situations were you able to copy and paste?

b. In what situations did Paste embed the data? In what situations did Paste simply transfer the data without embedding?

c. In what situations were you able to do inline editing?

d. Were there any situations where you were unable to link?

e. Based on your experiments, what conclusions can you draw about whether or not your programs feature OLE 2.0?

9. Using Sound Recorder If you have a microphone, a sound card, and speakers, you can create your own sound file using the Sound Recorder accessory that comes with Windows 95. You want to send a colleague an electronic "Happy Birthday" message, so you decide to sing the Happy Birthday song into the microphone and save it as a sound file and then embed it into a message.

a. Click the Start button, point to Programs, point to Accessories, point to Multimedia, then click Sound Recorder.

b. Click the Record button on the far right of Sound Recorder.

   c. Sing Happy Birthday into the microphone. Click the Stop button when you are finished singing.

   d. Click File, click Save As, then save the file as Happy Birthday to your OLE Disk.

   e. Play the Happy Birthday sound file.

   f. Compose a Happy Birthday message in WordPad, and embed the Happy Birthday sound file into this message. Print the message and save it as Birthday Message. Hand in the printout to your instructor. If you have access to e-mail and you know how to send a file, you could send the WordPad file to a friend who's celebrating a birthday.

10. Creating a New Embedded Object You own Circle K Ranch, a working ranch that welcomes families, summer campers, and groups for weekly stays so they can experience life on a ranch. You are working on a flyer that you will mail to former clients and travel agents.

   a. Create a WordPad document called Flyer. Write a brief description of the ranch. Mention that you are working on the summer schedule and that people should make their reservations as soon as possible.

   b. Use Calculator to calculate this year's weekly rate. You need to earn $15,000 this summer from your visitor income to make an acceptable profit. There are 12 weeks in the summer, and you have room for eight guests each week. To calculate a room change per person per week, you type 15000 / 12 / 8 =. Paste the Calculator results into your document.

   c. Use Insert Object to create a new bitmapped image in your advertisement. The Create New radio button should be selected, with an object type of Bitmap Image. Create a small Paint graphic that shows a letter K in an interesting font with a circle around it.

   d. Print and save the flyer.

Printers and Fonts

CASE

Chan & Associates

You are continuing to help plan the Tenth Annual Jugglers Guild Convention. You and other committee members have been designing materials ranging from convention schedules and announcements to souvenir T-shirt designs. You'd like to print some of these documents so you can send them to other members of the Guild. One of the other committee members, Wai Chan, owns a small desktop publishing company, Chan & Associates. He tells you that he recently ordered a color printer that should be arriving on Friday. He suggests that if you're free this weekend, you could help him install the color printer—and then you could use it to print some of your documents in color.

When you arrive at Wai's office on Saturday, he's already there, finishing up some paperwork. You ask if you could use his monochrome printer while you wait. You'd like to print the Pins graphic, which is black and white. He tells you to go ahead, and suggests that you spend a little time familiarizing yourself with Windows 95 printing techniques so that when the new color printer is installed you'll know how to select and use it.

SESSION

4.1

In this session you will print a document to an existing printer. You will then examine and work with the Windows 95 print queue to control print jobs. You also will learn how to pause and delete print jobs. However, you might not be able to perform all the procedures in this tutorial if you are working in a computer lab. Therefore, the steps in this tutorial include notes to alert you when that might be the case. When you can't perform a procedure, take special note of the information outside of the steps that will help you learn about the procedure.

Printing a Document

You have probably printed documents many times in Windows 95 without giving much thought to what goes on behind the scenes, even if you noticed signs that Windows 95 was processing your print request. You might have noticed a dialog box that tells you your document is printing, or you might have seen icons that look like printers appear and then disappear in the taskbar. You might even have heard your hard drive spinning for a second or two. Let's "look under the hood" and see what Windows 95 is doing with all that activity.

To print a document in Windows 95, you can drag a document icon onto a printer icon in Windows Explorer or on the desktop, or you can use a program's Print button. When you need more control over the printing process, however, you use the Print command on a program's File menu to open the Print dialog box, where you have more options. Regardless of which method you use to make the print request, Windows 95 processes your request the same way, as shown in Figure 4-1.

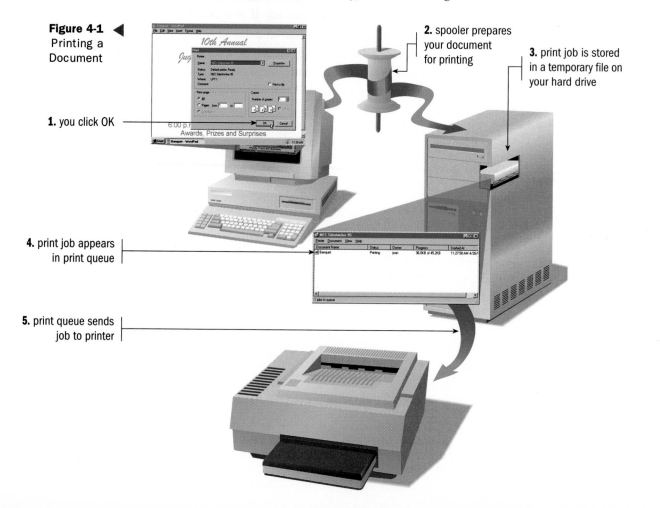

Figure 4-1
Printing a
Document

1. you click OK

2. spooler prepares
your document
for printing

3. print job is stored
in a temporary file on
your hard drive

4. print job appears
in print queue

5. print queue sends
job to printer

First, Windows 95 uses print spooling to quickly prepare your document for printing. **Print spooling** inserts the electronic codes that control your particular printer, such as the code to move down to the next line or to eject a page. As Windows 95 is spooling, it might display a dialog box such as the one shown in Figure 4-2.

Figure 4-2 ◀
Dialog box that appears during print spooling

3.1 NOTE

The Windows 95 print queue replaces the Windows 3.1 Print Manager. Unlike Windows 3.1, Windows 95 offers a separate print queue window for every printer available to your computer.

While the document is being spooled, you can click Cancel to cancel printing. Once print spooling is complete, the document, complete with the electronic codes inserted by the spooling process, is stored as a temporary file on your computer's hard disk. These temporary files are sometimes referred to as "print jobs." Once a print job is created, you can continue working on other documents—your document will print in the background while you do other computing tasks. By sending print jobs to your computer's hard disk rather than storing them in memory, spooling frees your computer's resources.

Print jobs are managed by a print queue. A **print queue** keeps track of the order in which print jobs were submitted and usually prints the jobs in this order. When the printer has finished with one job, the print queue sends the next job. You can control the print queue for a particular printer by opening its print queue window. Figure 4-3 shows the print queue for a printer that is used by several computers on a network. This is the situation you are likely to encounter in a school computer lab—many computers using the same printer. You'll learn more about network printers in the network tutorial.

Figure 4-3 ◀
Print queue window

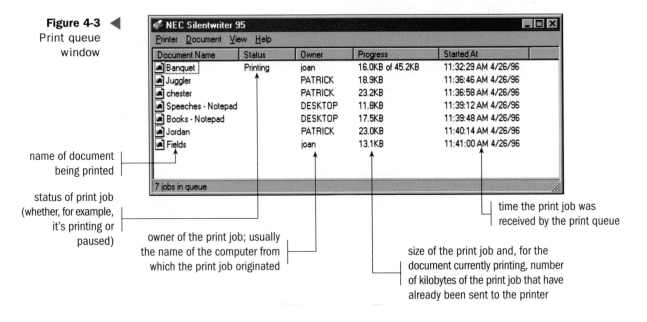

name of document being printed

status of print job (whether, for example, it's printing or paused)

owner of the print job; usually the name of the computer from which the print job originated

size of the print job and, for the document currently printing, number of kilobytes of the print job that have already been sent to the printer

time the print job was received by the print queue

The print job listed first in the print queue goes to the printer first. Once the entire job is transferred into the printer's temporary memory, it disappears from the print queue.

The print queue also gives you some control over print jobs waiting to be printed. For example, you can pause or cancel print jobs or change their order. You can do this for all jobs using the Printer menu or for just one print job using the Document menu. If you are on a network, you are likely to have limited control over print jobs. See the "Using the Print Queue" reference window for information on what options usually are available in the print queue window. Although you can open the print queue even when there aren't any print jobs in it, most of the time you'll need to open it only when you are printing something.

REFERENCE window

USING THE PRINT QUEUE

- Open the print queue as you print by right-clicking the printer icon that appears in the taskbar and then clicking the name of the printer (or simply double-click the icon). To use this method you must be quick if the print job is short—the printer icon appears only for an instant.

  or

- Open the print queue by clicking the Start button, pointing to Settings, then clicking Printers. Then click the printer you want and press the Enter key.

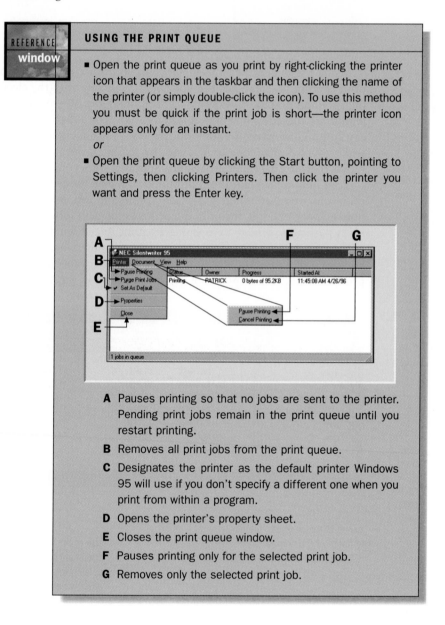

A Pauses printing so that no jobs are sent to the printer. Pending print jobs remain in the print queue until you restart printing.

B Removes all print jobs from the print queue.

C Designates the printer as the default printer Windows 95 will use if you don't specify a different one when you print from within a program.

D Opens the printer's property sheet.

E Closes the print queue window.

F Pauses printing only for the selected print job.

G Removes only the selected print job.

You decide to print your Pins graphic by opening it in Paint and printing it on Wai's printer, a monochrome NEC Silentwriter 95. If you are working in a computer lab where many computers use the same printer and where there are other students using this book, you might have a hard time telling which Pins print job is yours. For this reason, you should rename your Pins graphic before you print.

To open and rename the Pins graphic:

1. Place your Student Disk in drive A. See the "Read This Before You Begin" page to make sure you are using the correct disk for this tutorial.

TROUBLE? If your 3½-inch disk drive is B, place your Student Disk in that drive instead, and for the rest of this tutorial substitute drive B wherever you see drive A.

2. Start Paint, then open the **Pins** graphic on your Student Disk.

3. Click **File** then click **Save As**.

4. Click the **File name** box, then type your name after the word Pins so the name of the file becomes, for example, Pins Laura Smith.

5. Click the **Save** button.

Now you'll be able to identify your job in the print queue window. You are ready to open the print queue for your computer's active printer (the one currently handling your print jobs) so you can have more control over your print jobs.

To open the print queue for your computer's active printer:

1. Click **File** then click **Print**. The Print dialog box opens. In Figure 4-4, Wai's NEC Silentwriter 95 is the active printer. On your screen you will see the name of the printer Windows 95 will use to print your graphic.

Figure 4-4 ◀
Print dialog box

name of active printer
on Wai's computer

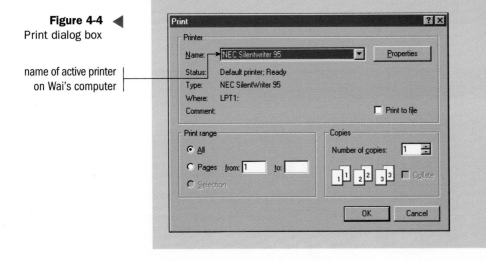

2. Now open the print queue for your computer's active printer. Click the **Start** button, point to **Settings**, then click **Printers**. Figure 4-5 shows the Printers window on Wai's computer.

Figure 4-5 ◀
Printers
window

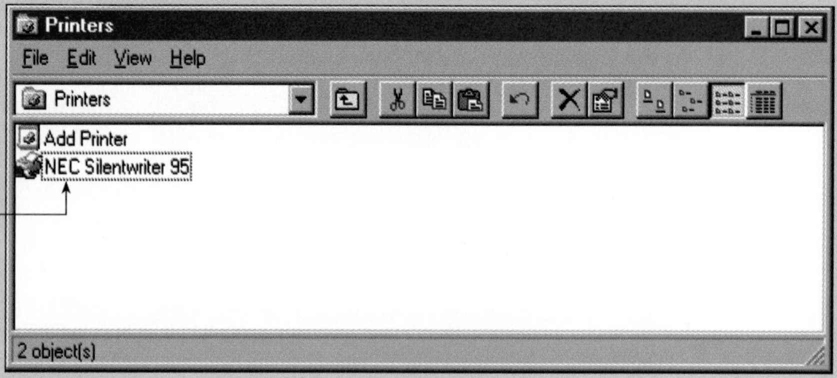

active printer on Wai's
computer

3. Locate your computer's active printer in the Printers window. This is the printer you saw in the Print dialog box in Step 1.

4. Click the name of the active printer.

5. Press the **Enter** key to display the print queue. Your print queue might be empty, or, if the printer is a network printer, it might show other documents being printed.

6. Switch to the Printers window, then close the Printers window.

7. Right-click the **taskbar** then click **Tile Horizontally** so you can see the Print dialog box and the print queue window. See Figure 4-6.

Figure 4-6 ◀
Tiling windows
to see Print
dialog box and
print queue

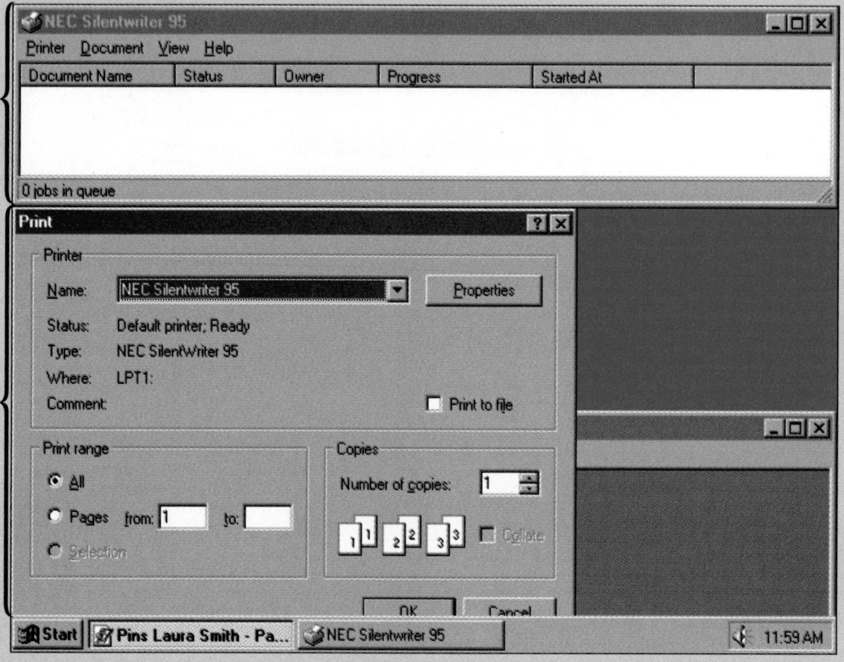

print queue window

Print dialog box

Now you are ready to print your document. Before you perform the next set of steps, read through them and study the figures so you will know what to watch for as you print.

To see what happens on the spooler and queue:

1. Click the **Print** dialog box to activate it.

2. Compare the printer name that appears in the Name box with the one in the title bar of the print queue window. They should be the same. See Figure 4-7.

Figure 4-7 ◀
Active printer

name in print queue
title bar matches
active printer in Name
box; yours might be
different

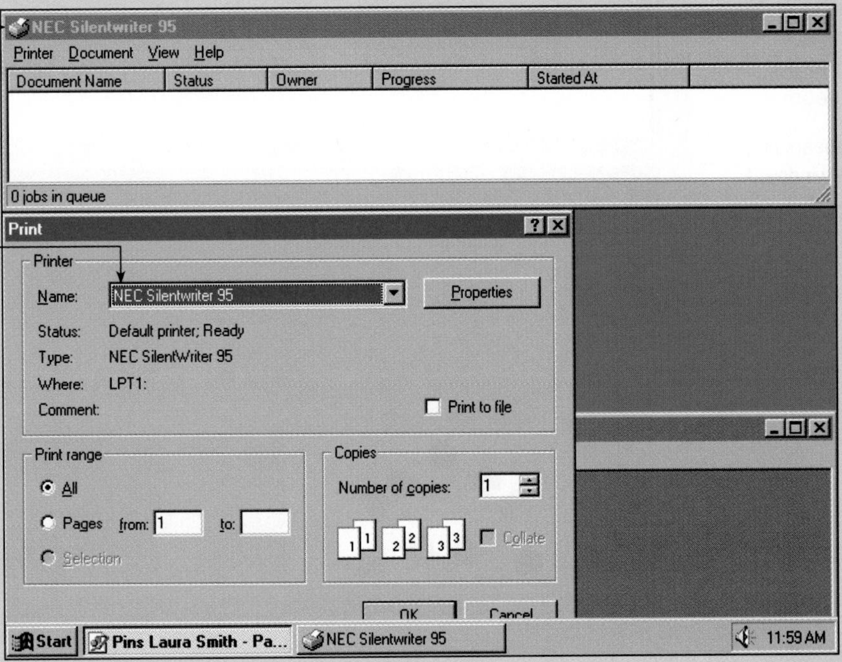

TROUBLE? If the printer in the Name box is not the same as the printer in the title bar of the print queue window, you might have opened the wrong print queue. Reopen the Printers window, and this time make sure you open the correct print queue window.

3. Click the **OK** button in the Print dialog box. As Windows 95 spools your print job, the dialog box shown in Figure 4-8 appears.

Figure 4-8 ◀
Spooling

> **Paint**
> Printing
> Pins Laura Smith
> on the
> NEC Silentwriter 95
> on LPT1:
>
> Cancel

TROUBLE? If you don't notice this dialog box as you print, don't worry. Your computer might process print jobs so quickly that you don't notice it. It's also possible that when you tiled windows, part of Paint was moved off the screen, and the dialog box might actually appear off-screen.

4. Locate the place on your screen—pointed out in Figure 4-9—where the printer icon appears once the document is spooled, and notice when the icon appears. The print job appears in the print queue window at the same time.

Figure 4-9 ◄
Print job
appears on
taskbar and
print queue

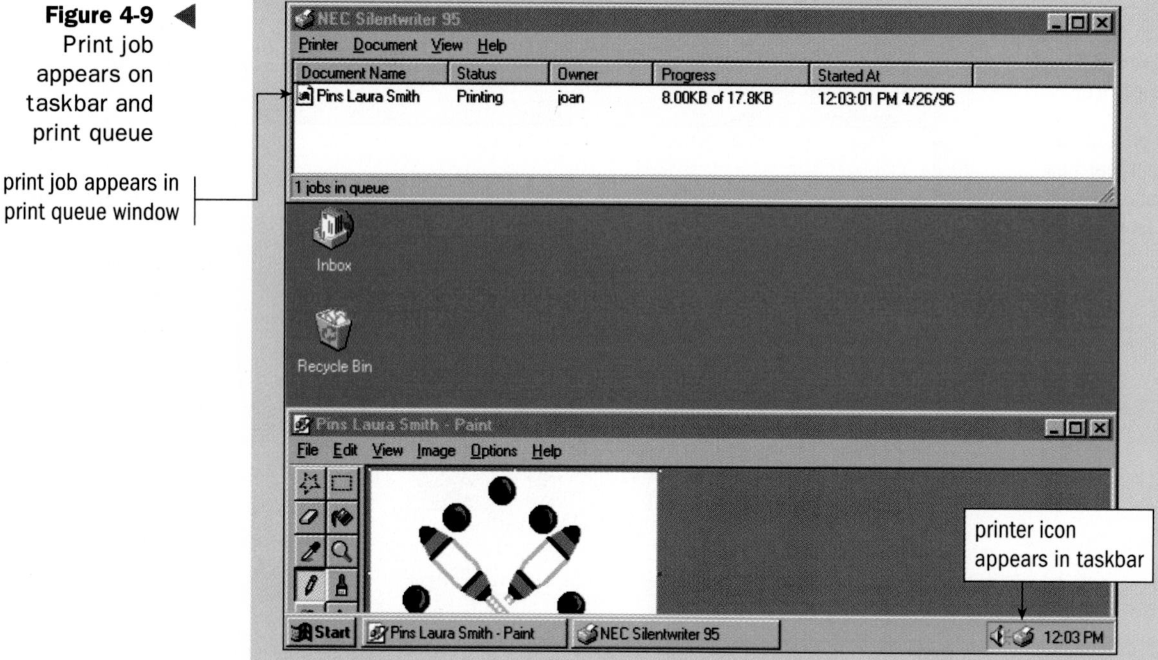

print job appears in
print queue window

TROUBLE? If you didn't notice the icon in the taskbar, don't worry. When you are printing a very small document such as the Pins graphic, the icon appears only momentarily and then disappears when Windows 95 has sent the document to your printer.

5. Watch as your print job disappears from the print queue window—this means it has been sent successfully to the printer.

Pausing One or All Print Jobs

On occasion you might want to delay your computer from sending jobs to the printer. For example, if you want to use a specific letterhead for a print job, you have to change the paper in the printer before you print a job. Windows 95 lets you pause all or one document in the print queue.

If you want to pause the entire queue, you would select the Pause Printing command from the Printer menu. This tells Windows 95 to stop sending jobs to the printer. Once you restart printing, the print queue starts sending all print jobs in the order shown in the queue. If you want to pause a specific print job, you would select the Pause Printing command from the Document menu. Pausing a single print job halts your job while allowing other print jobs in the queue to print. However, if you are printing to a network printer, you probably cannot pause printing at all.

Wai tells you he's almost ready to start installing the color printer. When you tell him you're experimenting with the print queue, he suggests you pause printing so you can learn how to manage print jobs in the print queue—a skill that comes in handy when you need more control over your print queue.

To pause printing:

1. Click **Printer** on the print queue window menu bar.

2. Click **Pause Printing**.

> **TROUBLE?** If you are on a network you might not be able to pause printing, because by pausing you might pause not only your jobs but also everyone else's. If that's the case, skip Step 2 and close the Printer menu.

Now that printing is paused, you can print your document and watch it move into the print queue and then pause.

To print the document with paused printing:

1. Click **File** on the Paint menu bar, then click **Print**.

2. Click the **OK** button. Watch the print queue window as your document appears. Notice that the printer icon appears in the taskbar. If printing is paused, the title bar shows "Paused," as in Figure 4-10, and the print job is not sent to the printer but remains in the print queue (stored temporarily on the hard disk).

   TROUBLE? If you were not able to pause printing, the print job appears only momentarily in the print queue and then moves directly to the printer.

Figure 4-10
Pausing printing

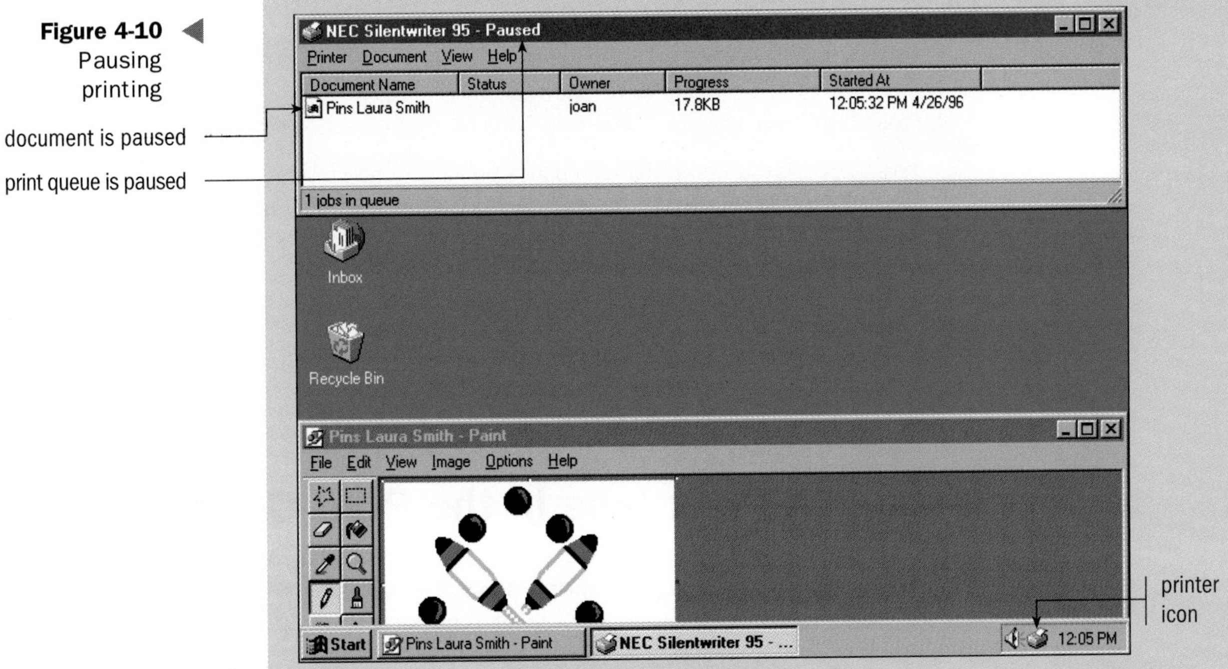

document is paused

print queue is paused

printer icon

Removing Print Jobs from the Print Queue

Suppose you mistakenly printed a document with the wrong printer selected. You might want to remove the job from the print queue to prevent it from printing. You can prevent Windows 95 from sending a print job to the printer by deleting the job from the print queue.

REFERENCE window	**REMOVING PRINT JOBS FROM THE PRINT QUEUE**
	■ To remove all jobs, click Printer then click Purge Print Jobs.
	■ To remove a single job, click the job in the print queue, then either press the Delete key or click Document then click Cancel Printing.

After you attempt to remove a job, you might discover that all or part of the document prints anyway. If this happens, Windows 95 has already sent part of the job—maybe even all of it—to the printer before you sent the cancel command. Your printer has memory too, and removing print jobs from the Windows 95 print queue does not affect the parts of a print job already in the printer's memory. You can clear your printer's memory by resetting your printer. How you do this depends on what type of printer you have. Some printers have a Reset button.

Because you have already printed the Pins graphic once, you decide to remove it from the print queue.

To remove a print job from the print queue:

1. Click the **Pins** print job in the print queue. This file appears as Pins with your name after it, as shown in Figure 4-11.

Figure 4-11 ◄
Removing a print job from the print queue

print job to remove is selected

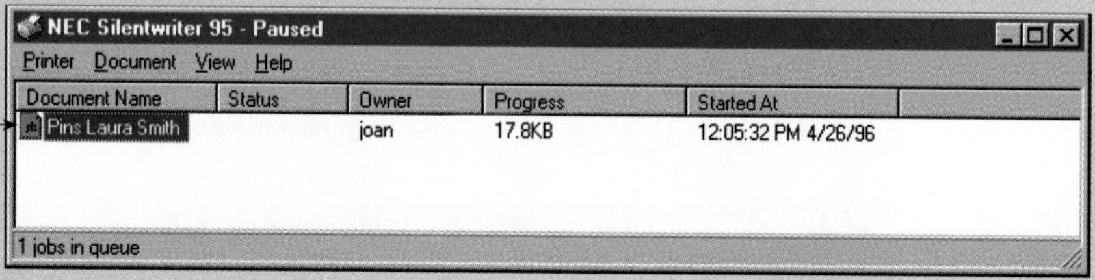

2. Press the **Delete** key.

TROUBLE? If you weren't able to pause printing in the previous section because you are printing to a network printer, the document might print so quickly that you don't have time to select and then delete it. Don't worry; just read through the steps and study the figures.

3. Click **Printer** then click **Pause Printing** to remove the check mark and return the print queue settings to their original state.

4. Click the **Close** button ☒ to close the print queue, then close Paint.

Managing Print Jobs in the Print Queue

Suppose you were working under a deadline and you needed to give your print job top priority over the jobs already in the print queue. You can rearrange the print queue order by dragging one or more print jobs to a different place in the print queue list, as shown in Figure 4-12.

Figure 4-12 ◄
Rearranging print jobs

drag print job to top of queue to print it first

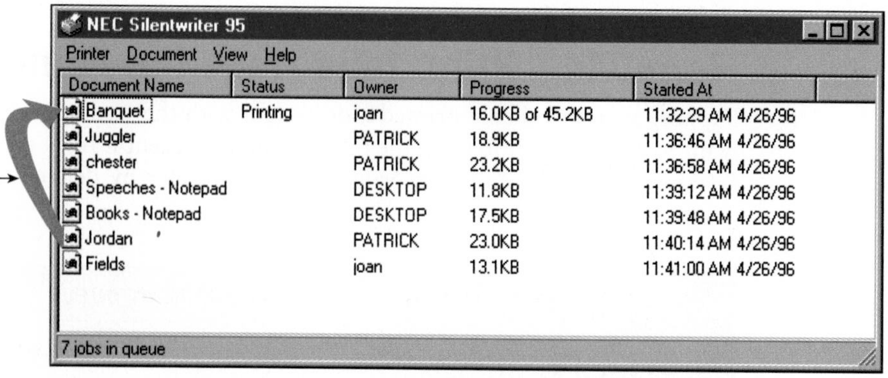

In Figure 4-12, a user on a computer named Patrick needs the hard copy of the Jordan document immediately, so he drags it to the top of the queue. To give his print job precedence over other print jobs in the queue, his computer had to be set so that he could override the jobs of other computers on the network. In many network situations, the only computer that can control the order of the print jobs is the network administrator's. You'll learn more about printing on a network printer in the next tutorial.

Quick Check

1. When you print a document, where does the printer icon appear?

2. How does Windows 95 prevent print jobs from using up your computer's memory?

3. You just started printing a 35-page term paper from your word processor. Suddenly you remember you forgot to add page numbers. You hate to waste paper, so you want to stop the job from printing. What should you do?

4. You've attempted to remove a job from the print queue, but part of it prints anyway. What happened?

5. How can you give your print job top priority among all the jobs in the print queue?

6. How does the process of print spooling differ from the process of queuing print jobs?

SESSION

4.2

In this session you will learn how to install a printer. You'll start by examining the property sheet for an existing printer so you can see what information you will need to provide when you install a new printer. Then you'll learn how to use the Add Printer Wizard to install a color printer. You'll learn how to print a document to a different printer and then how to troubleshoot problems that arise as you print. Even though you probably won't be able to install a new printer in a computer lab, you can read through the steps, even performing many of them, to learn how it's done.

Opening a Printer's Property Sheet

Wai is ready to install his new printer. He asks if you would help him by reviewing the properties of the printer already installed. This information will guide him in making changes to his system as he installs the second printer. A printer is a **hardware device**, a physical component of a computer system. As with objects on the desktop, hardware devices have property sheets that display the properties, or characteristics, of the device. You can use a device's property sheet to learn about the device and to change the device's settings.

To view the property sheet for your printer:

1. Click the **Start** button, point to **Settings**, then click **Printers**. The Printers window opens.

2. Right-click the icon for your printer, then click **Properties** from the menu.

   TROUBLE? Your computer might list several printers. Use the printer you used in Session 4.1.

3. Click the **Details** sheet tab to display the Details property sheet for your printer. See Figure 4-13.

Figure 4-13 ◀
Details
property sheet
for active
printer

port Wai's printer
is using

driver Wai's printer
is using

NEC Silentwriter 95 Properties   ? X

| Graphics | Fonts | Device Options | PostScript |
| General | Details | Sharing | Paper |

NEC Silentwriter 95

Print to the following port:

LPT1: (Printer Port)   ▼   Add Port...

Delete Port...

Print using the following driver:

NEC SilentWriter 95   ▼   New Driver...

Capture Printer Port...   End Capture...

Timeout settings

Not selected: 300   seconds

Transmission retry: 45   seconds

Spool Settings...   Port Settings...

OK   Cancel   Apply

The Details property sheet shows several important pieces of information about how Wai's existing printer is connected to his computer. Because a printer is located outside the computer's chassis, it is "external." To connect an external device to a computer, you plug a cable that comes out from the printer into a socket, called a **port**, on the computer. See Figure 4-14.

Figure 4-14 ◀
Connecting a
printer to a
computer

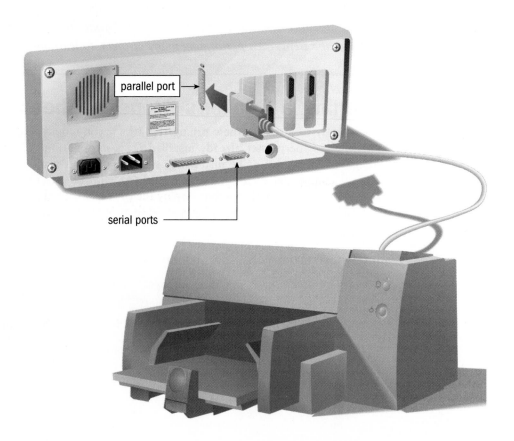

parallel port

serial ports

A computer usually has several different port types; a printer that you connect directly to a computer can use either a serial or parallel port. A **serial port** transfers data one bit at a time, whereas a **parallel port** transmits data eight bits at a time. A computer can contain up to four different serial ports, although most computers have only two. They are called COM1, COM2, COM3 or COM4 (COM stands for "communications"). A serial port is usually used for an external modem or mouse, although it can be used for some printers. Parallel ports are named LPT1, LPT2 or LPT3 (LPT stands for "line printer"). They are usually reserved for printers, and most computers have only one parallel port. In the property sheet shown in Figure 4-13, the printer is currently attached to the parallel port LPT1. Wai tells you that he'll add a second parallel port to his computer for the new printer.

The Details property sheet also gives you information on the driver that is installed for your printer. A **driver** is a file with program code that enables Windows 95 to communicate with, and control the operation of, a hardware device. When Windows 95 spools a document for printing, it is using information provided by the driver to insert the appropriate electronic codes. Wai's monochrome printer uses a NEC Silentwriter 95 driver.

Wai tells you that with this information from the property sheet, he is ready to install the new printer.

To close the Printer property sheet and Printers window:

1. Click the **Cancel** button to close the Printers property sheet without making any changes.

2. Click the **Close** button to close the Printers window.

Installing a Hardware Device

There are three steps to installing any hardware device, including a printer:

1. Check your existing configuration so you can see what ports are available and what information you will need to install the device—as you just did with checking Wai's existing printer's property sheet.

2. Connect the device to the computer. If the device is external, you usually plug in a cable. If the device is internal (like most disk drives, modems, or CD-ROM players), you shut down and unplug the computer first, then you remove the chassis and fit the device into your computer. Although installing internal devices is not difficult, it can be intimidating to new users, so you might want an experienced friend or a professional to help you.

3. Install the software (usually a driver) that enables your new device to communicate with your computer, then make any changes to your existing setup to accommodate the new device.

You have checked the settings of Wai's existing printer and connected the printer cable to the new parallel port. Now you need to install the driver.

Using the Add Printer Wizard

Wai installs a second parallel port on his computer and then connects the printer to that port. It doesn't take him long. Now that the new printer is attached to Wai's computer, he tells you to install the software that will allow his computer to communicate with the new printer. Windows 95 has greatly simplified this process by providing hardware installation Wizards. A **Wizard** is a series of dialog boxes that walk you through a complex task. Figure 4-15 shows a typical Wizard dialog box.

Figure 4-15 ◄
Typical Wizard
dialog box

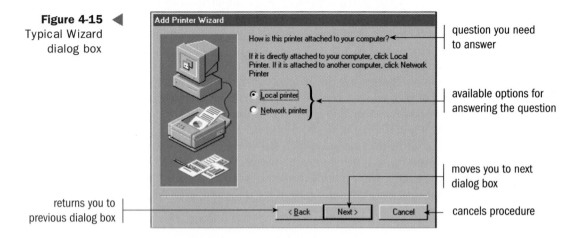

question you need
to answer

available options for
answering the question

moves you to next
dialog box

returns you to
previous dialog box

cancels procedure

The Wizard dialog boxes ask you questions, you provide the answers, and Windows 95 takes care of the rest. If you make any mistakes with the Add Printer Wizard, you can backtrack by clicking the Back button or cancel the installation altogether by clicking the Cancel button. The Add Printer Wizard helps you install your printer's driver software and configure your printer so that it doesn't conflict with the other devices in your computer.

3.1 NOTE

The hardware installation Wizards are new with Windows 95.

Although you aren't likely to be able to install a new printer in your computer's lab, you can still do many of the steps in this session. The steps tell you specifically when you should cancel the procedure. If you were really installing a new printer, you would need to have the Windows 95 installation disks or CD-ROM handy so Windows 95 could access installation data.

Now that the second printer is physically attached to Wai's computer, you decide to use Windows 95's Add Printer Wizard to complete the installation process.

To start the Windows 95 Add Printer Wizard:

1. Click the **Start** button, point to **Settings**, then click **Printers**.

TROUBLE? If you are worried that you haven't actually physically installed a new printer and should therefore not be going through these steps, don't worry. You can go through the steps in the Add Printer Wizard until Windows 95 prompts you for the installation disk. Then you'll need to cancel the procedure, as instructed in the steps.

2. Click the **Add Printer** icon, then press the **Enter** key. The Add Printer Wizard opens a dialog box that tells you about the installation process.

3. Click the **Next** button to open the Add Printer Wizard dialog box shown in Figure 4-16.

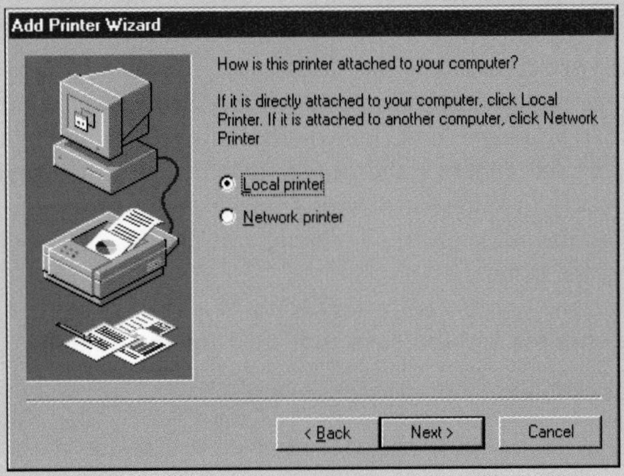

Figure 4-16
Add Printer
Wizard dialog
box ◀

Figure 4-16 ◀
Add Printer
Wizard dialog
box

The Add Printer Wizard now takes you step-by-step through the process of setting up Windows 95 to work with your new printer. The current dialog box asks whether your printer is a local or network printer. As you can see, you'll need to have the answers to some questions before you get too far into the Add Printer Wizard. You will enter the information needed to install an HP DeskJet 560C printer on your local computer's LPT2 parallel port—the port where Wai attached the new printer.

To continue installing the software for the new printer using the Add Printer Wizard:

1. Click the **Local printer** radio button, then click the **Next** button.

2. Now you must enter the make and model of your new printer. Drag the vertical scrollbar down the Manufacturers list, then click the **HP** manufacturer entry.

3. Drag the vertical scrollbar down the Printers list, then click the entry for the **HP DeskJet 560C Printer**. See Figure 4-17.

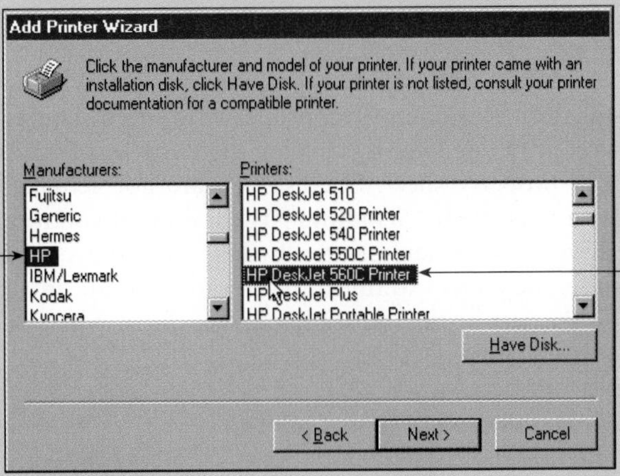

Figure 4-17 ◀
Selecting a
manufacturer
and printer

HP is manufacturer ——→

HP DeskJet 560C
is printer

4. Click the **Next** button.

5. Click **LPT2**, the port that Wai wants to use, then click the **Next** button.

> **TROUBLE?** If LPT2 doesn't appear, your computer might not have a second parallel port. Click LPT1, or one of the COM ports instead. You'll be cancelling the procedure at the end anyway, so it doesn't matter if these ports are already in use.

You have now given Windows 95 enough information to install the driver for the new printer. However, the Wizard still prompts you with additional questions. The next dialog box allows you to specify a name for the new printer. This is the name that will appear in the Printers window when you are finished with the installation. The name you enter could be the printer model (the default) or it could be a description of the printer's function (such as Marketing Printer). You decide to enter a name describing the printer's function. Next, you have to decide whether this printer will be the default printer on your system. The **default printer** is the printer that has been designated to handle all printing, unless you specify a different printer from within a program. Wai tells you he does not want to install the color printer as the default, because he won't use it as often as he uses his monochrome printer.

To name the printer and indicate that it is not the default:

1. Type **Color Printer** in the Printer name text box.

2. Verify that the **No** option button is selected so that this printer will not be the default printer on your system. See Figure 4-18.

Figure 4-18 ◄
Naming the printer

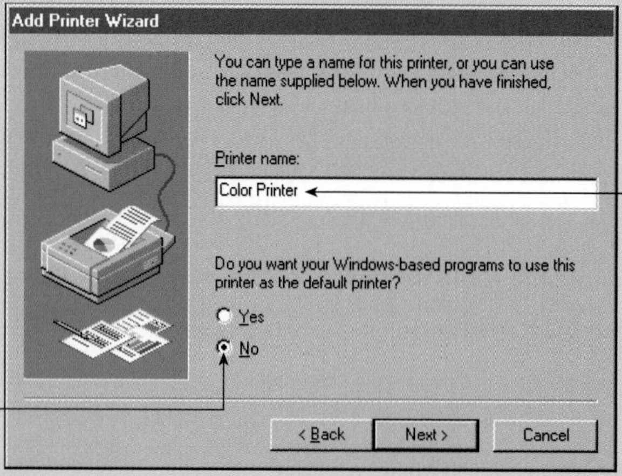

select so this will not be the default printer

name the printer here

3. Click the **Next** button.

Now the Add Printer Wizard asks you whether you want to print a test page to verify that the installation was completed properly. If you decide against printing a test page, you can always print one later by clicking the Print Test Page button on the General page of the printer's property sheet. Because you are not actually installing this printer, the steps direct you to click No. Windows 95 will prompt you to insert the disk that contains the printer driver for the new printer. If this were your computer and your printer, you would click the OK button to finish the installation, but in the steps you will cancel the procedure. In the rest of this tutorial, you will learn what would have happened if you had actually installed the DeskJet printer.

To cancel the installation of a new printer:

1. Click the **No** option button to prevent printing a test page.

2. Click the **Finish** button to finish the Add Printer Wizard.

3. Acknowledge any messages that appear to warn you that the installation process is incomplete, clicking the **Cancel** button when prompted for the installation disk.

4. Close the Printers window.

Installing New or Rare Printers

The last thing the Add Printer Wizard asked you to do was insert the installation disk so it could locate the driver for the printer you specified earlier in the Wizard steps. The drivers for some printers, however, are not on the Windows 95 installation disk and are not included in the list of printers provided by the Add Printer Wizard. This can occur when either your printer is so new that its drivers were not available when Windows 95 released its installation disks or if your printer is so rare that Microsoft didn't include it in the Wizard list. Most manufacturers include a disk along with the printer that contains the driver. If your printer does not appear in the Wizard's list of printers, you will need to install the driver from this disk. You can usually install the driver from within the Add Printer Wizard by clicking the Have Disk button when the Wizard asks for your printer model and by inserting the disk containing the driver when prompted. See Figure 4-19.

Figure 4-19 ◀
Using Have
Disk

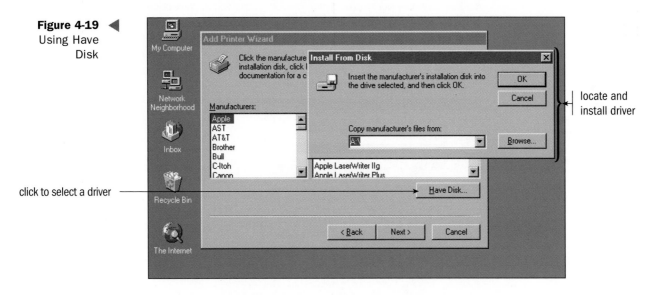

locate and
install driver

click to select a driver ──────

Manufacturers are constantly updating and improving their printer drivers. Some of these changes are made to remove bugs; others are made to increase printing speed. You can check with your manufacturer or with Microsoft to see whether a new version of your printer driver has been released. Although you might not be sure how to take advantage of this information now, you should know that many manufacturers make their new drivers available on their electronic bulletin boards or World Wide Web pages. Microsoft maintains a Web page with a list of drivers not included with the installation disk at *http://www.microsoft.com/windows/software/drivers/drivers.htm*. You can get more information about adding new drivers and additional software by the Microsoft Web page at *http://www.microsoft.com/support*.

Printing a Document to a Different Printer

Windows 95 will print your document to the default printer unless you specify a different printer from within a program. The printer you specified then becomes the active printer.

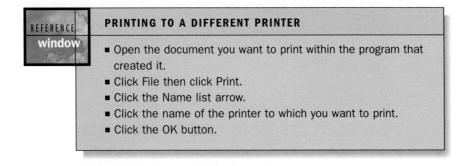

REFERENCE
window

PRINTING TO A DIFFERENT PRINTER

- Open the document you want to print within the program that created it.
- Click File then click Print.
- Click the Name list arrow.
- Click the name of the printer to which you want to print.
- Click the OK button.

Wai has more than one printer now. He still wants his monochrome printer as his default printer, but sometimes he'll want to print to the color printer. Wai is eager to see how that printer handles color print jobs. You tell him you were hoping to print Pins2, the full-color graphic, so he tells you to print it on his new printer.

To print a document on a different printer:

1. Open **Pins2** from your Student Disk in Paint.

2. Click **File** then click **Print**.

3. Click the **Name** list arrow.

4. Click the printer you want to use. Wai wants to use the one named "Color Printer." See Figure 4-20.

   TROUBLE? You won't see "Color Printer" in the Printer box because you didn't actually install that printer. If you don't see more than one printer on the list, there are no other printers available to your computer. Leave the default printer selected, then continue with Step 5. If there is more than one printer listed, ask your instructor or technical support person which printer you should use.

Figure 4-20
Printing to a different printer

available printers—yours will be different

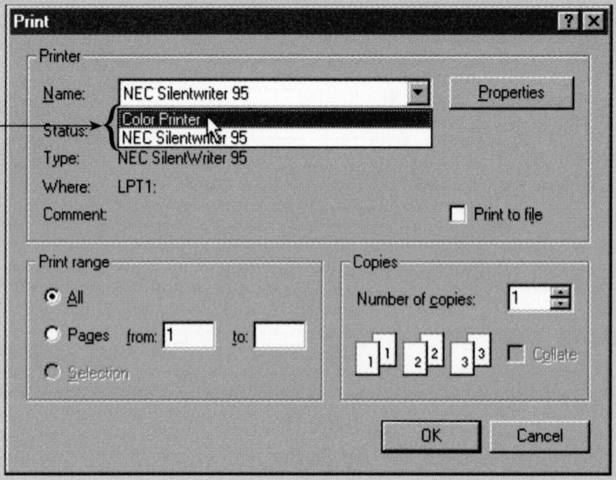

5. Click the **OK** button. The document prints on the selected computer.

6. Close Paint.

Changing the Default Printer

When you went through the installation procedure you had the opportunity to select the printer you were installing as the default printer. Windows 95 would print all documents to that printer. Just now, you saw how to print to a printer other than the default printer. Suppose, however, that Wai decides he wants his color printer to be the default printer. He can designate the color printer as the default printer by opening the print queue for that printer. He then would click Printer and Set As Default. See Figure 4-21.

Figure 4-21
Specifying a default printer

choose to set printer as default

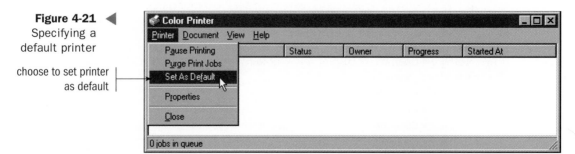

You won't change the default printer in this tutorial.

Using the Print Troubleshooter

Printers, like all devices, do not always work properly. On occasion you might have problems printing a document; or if the document does print, it might not print correctly. Windows 95 provides help in the form of a Print Troubleshooter that you can use to diagnose and correct printing problems. **Troubleshooters** are a part of the Windows 95 online Help system. They ask you questions about the problem, and you answer these questions by selecting one of the options that appear in the Troubleshooter dialog box. As you go through the Troubleshooter to test different solutions, Windows 95 gives you immediate access to the tools you need, such as a property sheet or an accessory. The Troubleshooter does not always successfully pinpoint the source of your problem, but it is an excellent place to start trying to find a solution.

You and Wai are finished installing the color printer on Wai's computer. The Pins2 printout looks great, and Wai asks you if you have any other documents to print in color. You tell him that Celia Koch, the committee member in charge of the convention banquet, sent you an announcement for the banquet. Because this is a festive occasion, Celia would like the announcement printed in color. She gave you a disk with the WordPad file, Banquet, and a black and white printout, as shown in Figure 4-22.

3.I NOTE

Troubleshooters are new with Windows 95.

Figure 4-22 ◀
Banquet
document

You decide to open the file and print it on Wai's color printer.

To open WordPad and view the Banquet document:

1. Click the **Start** button, point to **Programs**, point to **Accessories**, then click **WordPad**.

2. Open and then print the **Banquet** file from your Student Disk. As you look at the printout, you realize something has gone wrong. The printout in Figure 4-23 is different from the printout in Figure 4-22.

TROUBLE? If the file you opened looks identical to Figure 4-22, then your computer does not have the same problem as Wai's. You can follow the rest of the steps in this section, but keep in mind that in your case the problem you are solving doesn't actually exist.

Figure 4-23 ◀
Banquet
document
printed
incorrectly

font is different

The script font used to announce the banquet has been replaced by a different font. For some reason, your computer has substituted the incorrect font. You worry that something is wrong with Wai's printer, so you decide to use the Print Troubleshooter to see if you can figure out what happened.

To use the Print Troubleshooter:

1. Click the **Start** button then click **Help**.

2. Click the **Contents** sheet tab.

3. Click **Troubleshooting** then press the **Enter** key.

4. Click **If you have trouble printing**, then click the **Display** button.

5. Click the button to the left of the second option, "My document printed, but it doesn't look right, or it printed only partially." See Figure 4-24.

Figure 4-24 ◀
Using the Print
Troubleshooter

click button
corresponding to
current problem

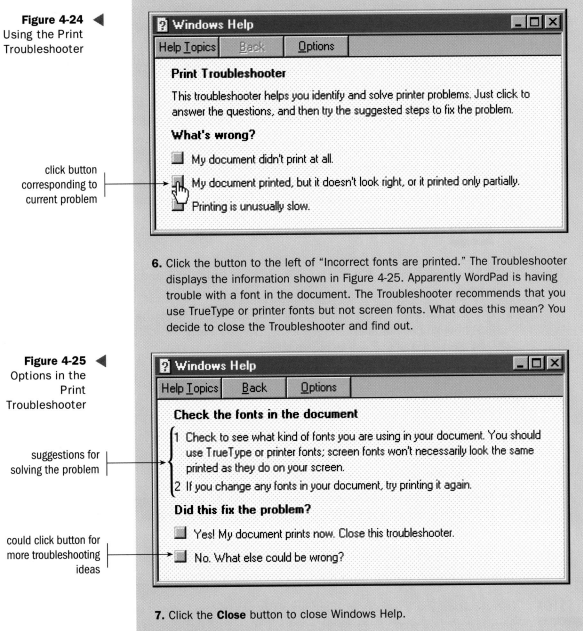

6. Click the button to the left of "Incorrect fonts are printed." The Troubleshooter displays the information shown in Figure 4-25. Apparently WordPad is having trouble with a font in the document. The Troubleshooter recommends that you use TrueType or printer fonts but not screen fonts. What does this mean? You decide to close the Troubleshooter and find out.

Figure 4-25 ◀
Options in the
Print
Troubleshooter

suggestions for
solving the problem

could click button for
more troubleshooting
ideas

7. Click the **Close** button to close Windows Help.

8. Click the **Close** button to close WordPad.

The information in the Troubleshooter suggests that you should examine the fonts used in your document. Notice from Figure 4-25 that you could continue to use the Troubleshooter to solve the problem if you wanted to. The Troubleshooter in many cases leads you all the way to a solution. For now, though, you're ready for a break. You'll work on a solution to the problem with the Banquet file in Session 4.3.

Plug and Play

The tools you've worked with in this session, including the installation Wizard and the Troubleshooters, are enhancements to previous versions of Windows that make it easier to manage your computer. One of the most significant ease-of-use features that Windows 95 includes is its Plug and Play technology. **Plug and Play**, or **PnP** for short, means that you can "plug" a device into your computer and immediately begin to "play" with it, avoiding the frustrations involved with setting up your system to work with the new device. In some cases, Plug and Play recognizes and configures a new device without your needing to do anything, whereas in other cases you can use one of the installation Wizards to install a new device on your system. In any case, the process of installing hardware and troubleshooting problems is much easier with Windows 95 than with previous versions of Windows.

When you plug a new hardware device into your computer, Windows 95 checks and corrects your computer's settings "behind the scenes" (including IRQs, I/O addresses, DMA channels, and memory addresses—the jargon alone is enough to frustrate a new user) to make sure your new printer doesn't cause any problems. To take advantage of Plug and Play, the device you are adding needs to meet a set of standards—not all devices do. For example, devices that you installed on your system many years ago, called **legacy devices**, came out before the Plug and Play standards were available. Thus, if your system has a modem you bought several years before Windows 95 was released, that modem is considered a legacy device. Windows 95 has added features to accommodate legacy devices, but to use the full power of Plug and Play, the device must be new enough to meet the new specifications. Most Plug and Play devices will advertise this fact.

Quick Check

1. Where should you look if you want to find out which port and device driver your printer uses?

2. Give an example of an external device, and then describe briefly (in three sentences or less) how you install one.

3. A file that enables a hardware device to communicate with your operating system is called a _____.

4. Once you have physically attached a new hardware device to your computer, what should you do next?

5. If Windows 95 doesn't seem to be able to locate the driver for a printer you just bought, what should you do?

6. How do you access the Windows 95 Troubleshooters?

7. True or false: Once you have installed Windows 95 on the computer you bought in 1993, you'll never have trouble with your old hardware devices again, because Plug and Play will handle them for you. Explain your answer.

SESSION 4.3

In this session you'll learn how Windows 95 manages fonts. You'll view a list of the fonts installed on your computer from within WordPad and then from within the Fonts window. Then you'll learn about the different font types available in the Fonts window. You'll open a font and learn how to install and delete fonts from the Fonts window.

Examining Fonts

At the end of Session 4.2 you saw that the fonts in the Banquet document did not appear as you expected them to. Perhaps the problem is that that section of the document was formatted with a font that isn't actually installed on your computer. You can find this out by first checking which font Windows 95 expects to find and then checking whether that font is actually installed on your computer. If it isn't, you might need to choose a different font for that section of the document.

In Figure 4-12, a user on a computer named Patrick needs the hard copy of the Jordan document immediately, so he drags it to the top of the queue. To give his print job precedence over other print jobs in the queue, his computer had to be set so that he could override the jobs of other computers on the network. In many network situations, the only computer that can control the order of the print jobs is the network administrator's. You'll learn more about printing on a network printer in the next tutorial.

Quick Check

1. When you print a document, where does the printer icon appear?

2. How does Windows 95 prevent print jobs from using up your computer's memory?

3. You just started printing a 35-page term paper from your word processor. Suddenly you remember you forgot to add page numbers. You hate to waste paper, so you want to stop the job from printing. What should you do?

4. You've attempted to remove a job from the print queue, but part of it prints anyway. What happened?

5. How can you give your print job top priority among all the jobs in the print queue?

6. How does the process of print spooling differ from the process of queuing print jobs?

SESSION 4.2

In this session you will learn how to install a printer. You'll start by examining the property sheet for an existing printer so you can see what information you will need to provide when you install a new printer. Then you'll learn how to use the Add Printer Wizard to install a color printer. You'll learn how to print a document to a different printer and then how to troubleshoot problems that arise as you print. Even though you probably won't be able to install a new printer in a computer lab, you can read through the steps, even performing many of them, to learn how it's done.

Opening a Printer's Property Sheet

Wai is ready to install his new printer. He asks if you would help him by reviewing the properties of the printer already installed. This information will guide him in making changes to his system as he installs the second printer. A printer is a **hardware device**, a physical component of a computer system. As with objects on the desktop, hardware devices have property sheets that display the properties, or characteristics, of the device. You can use a device's property sheet to learn about the device and to change the device's settings.

To view the property sheet for your printer:

1. Click the **Start** button, point to **Settings**, then click **Printers**. The Printers window opens.

2. Right-click the icon for your printer, then click **Properties** from the menu.

   TROUBLE? Your computer might list several printers. Use the printer you used in Session 4.1.

3. Click the **Details** sheet tab to display the Details property sheet for your printer. See Figure 4-13.

Figure 4-13 ◀
Details
property sheet
for active
printer

port Wai's printer
is using

driver Wai's printer
is using

| NEC Silentwriter 95 Properties | ? X |

| Graphics | Fonts | Device Options | PostScript |
| General | Details | Sharing | Paper |

NEC Silentwriter 95

Print to the following port:
LPT1: (Printer Port) ▼   [Add Port...]

[Delete Port...]

Print using the following driver:
NEC SilentWriter 95 ▼   [New Driver...]

[Capture Printer Port...]   [End Capture...]

Timeout settings
Not selected: 300   seconds

Transmission retry: 45   seconds

[Spool Settings...]   [Port Settings...]

[OK]   [Cancel]   [Apply]

The Details property sheet shows several important pieces of information about how Wai's existing printer is connected to his computer. Because a printer is located outside the computer's chassis, it is "external." To connect an external device to a computer, you plug a cable that comes out from the printer into a socket, called a **port**, on the computer. See Figure 4-14.

Figure 4-14 ◀
Connecting a
printer to a
computer

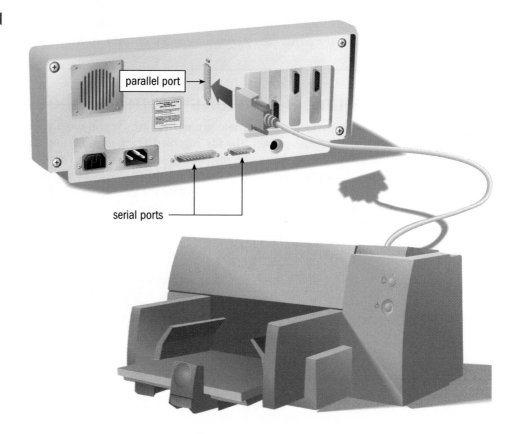

parallel port →

serial ports

In WordPad, you can assign a different font to any part of your document: to a section, a paragraph, a sentence, a word, or even a character. To see which font a particular section uses, you click anywhere within that section and then look at what font appears in the Font box in the WordPad toolbar.

To open the Banquet document in WordPad and open the Font list:

1. Start WordPad then open **Banquet** from your Student Disk.

2. Click anywhere in the title of the document (depending on the size of your WordPad window the title might take up two or three lines), which contains the text "10th Annual Jugglers Guild Banquet." The insertion point moves to the location you clicked.

3. Look at the Font box on the toolbar. The font name that appears is Kaufmann-Thin.

4. Click the **Font** list arrow ▾ to view all the available fonts.

   TROUBLE? If the Format bar doesn't appear, click View, then click Format Bar.

5. Scroll the Font list and notice that Kaufmann-Thin does not appear. See Figure 4-26.

Figure 4-26 ◀
Font list

font used for first line
appears in Font box
on Format bar

Kaufmann-Thin isn't
in Font list

Apparently this document uses a font named Kaufmann-Thin for the document's title. You've never heard of this font before. The fact that the font does not appear in the Font list suggests that there is a problem with this font or that it is not actually installed on your computer. You can find out which is the case by opening the Fonts window.

Using Control Panel to Display Fonts

From the Control Panel you can open the **Fonts window**, which manages the fonts installed on your computer. From the Fonts window, you can open fonts to look at their style and print a test to see how your printer produces the font. You can also install new fonts or delete unneeded ones.

The Control Panel Fonts window shows many more fonts than appear in a program's Font list because there are many fonts that Windows 95 needs but that are not available to programs.

To view the fonts installed on your computer:

1. Click the **Start** button, click **Settings**, then click **Control Panel**.

2. Click the **Fonts** icon then press the **Enter** key. Windows 95 opens the Fonts window displayed in Figure 4-27.

TROUBLE? If your fonts are listed differently, click View, then click Large Icons.

Figure 4-27 ◀
Fonts window

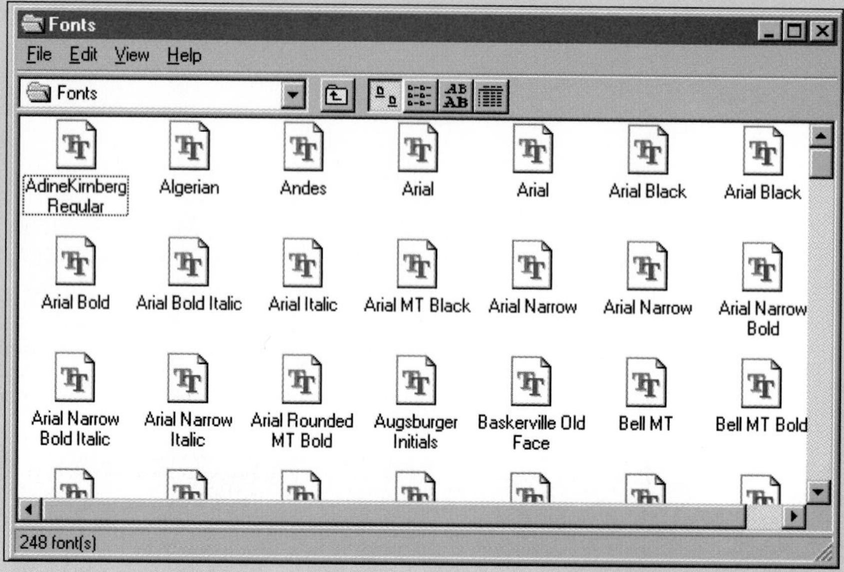

3. To display more details about your fonts, click **View**, then click **Details**.

4. Scroll down the list of fonts to see which fonts are installed on your computer. The Kaufmann-Thin font does not appear. See Figure 4-28.

TROUBLE? If Kaufmann-Thin does appear, it is already installed on your computer. Read through the rest of the session assuming that it is not installed on your computer.

Figure 4-28 ◀
Viewing font
details

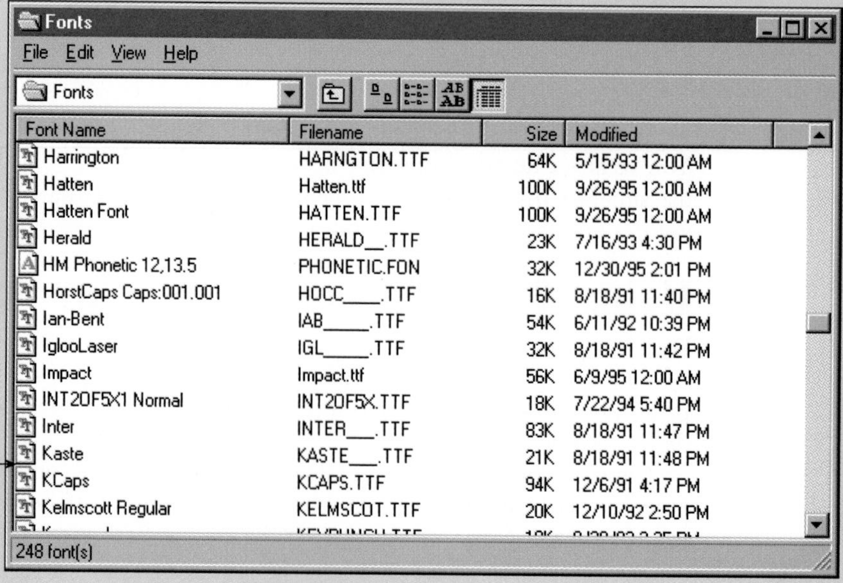

Kaufmann-Thin does
not appear

You believe you have pinpointed the problem: the reason your document didn't look right in WordPad is because the Banquet document used a font that was not installed on your computer. WordPad was able to display the name of the font in the Font box, but when Windows 95 tried to display the font, it didn't have the actual font file. In this case, it was forced to substitute a different font. You have two options: you can either try to locate and install Kaufmann-Thin, or you can review the fonts that are available and choose one to use in your document. The Fonts window can help you with either option.

Font Types

In Details view, the Control Panel Fonts window shows you both the name of the font and its filename. A **font file** contains the information Windows 95 needs to display the font on your monitor or print the font on your printer. The Control Panel Fonts window displays all the font files installed on your computer. A font file's name is not necessarily the same as the name of the font itself, as you can see from Figure 4-28. The Kelmscott Regular font, for example, is stored in a file named Kelmscot.ttf. To understand what fonts are available in the Fonts window and how you can use these fonts, you need to know a little bit about what font types you can use with Windows 95. Figure 4-29 describes the font types you are likely to encounter.

Figure 4-29 ◀
Font types

Font type	Description
Printer fonts	Fonts built into your printer. These are not stored in files on your computer and therefore do not appear in the Fonts window.
Screen fonts	Fonts used by your computer monitor to display the text that appears in dialog boxes, menus, buttons, icons, and other parts of the interface. Screen fonts are also used when you preview how your document will look when printed. When you create a document in a Windows 95 program, you choose a font and Windows 95 tries to match a screen font to it. However, screen fonts do not always perfectly match up with the fonts your printer uses. In some cases this causes your documents to print in ways slightly different from what you expect.
TrueType fonts	Fonts that are capable of both being displayed on your monitor and printed on your printer with minimal or no change in appearance. Windows 95 includes many of these fonts, and you will probably prefer to use them because there is no guesswork involved in how the printout will compare with what you see on the monitor. You can also **scale** a TrueType font—you can enlarge or shrink it without its losing its shape and appearance. You can also rotate a TrueType font, enabling you to print your text upside down or at different angles.
Postscript fonts	Fonts developed by a company called Adobe that are described by a special language called **Postscript** that produces fonts and graphics. You can scale and rotate Postscript fonts, but they require an extra software utility called the **Adobe Type Manager** to be converted into a form that can be displayed on a computer monitor (something Windows 95 can do automatically with TrueType fonts).

You probably noticed as you scrolled through the Fonts window that there are two different kinds of icons that represent fonts: 🆃 and 🅐. The first icon represents TrueType fonts, whereas the other icon represents screen fonts. The filenames for TrueType fonts end with the .ttf file extension, whereas screen font filenames end with .fon, as you can see if your computer's view options are set to display file extensions.

Some fonts use more than one file. For example, Times New Roman uses four files: Times.ttf, Timesbd.ttf, Timesbi.ttf, and Timesi.ttf—Times New Roman, Times New Roman Bold, Times New Roman Bold Italic, and Times News Roman Italic, respectively. See Figure 4-30.

Figure 4-30 ◀
Multiple files
for a single font

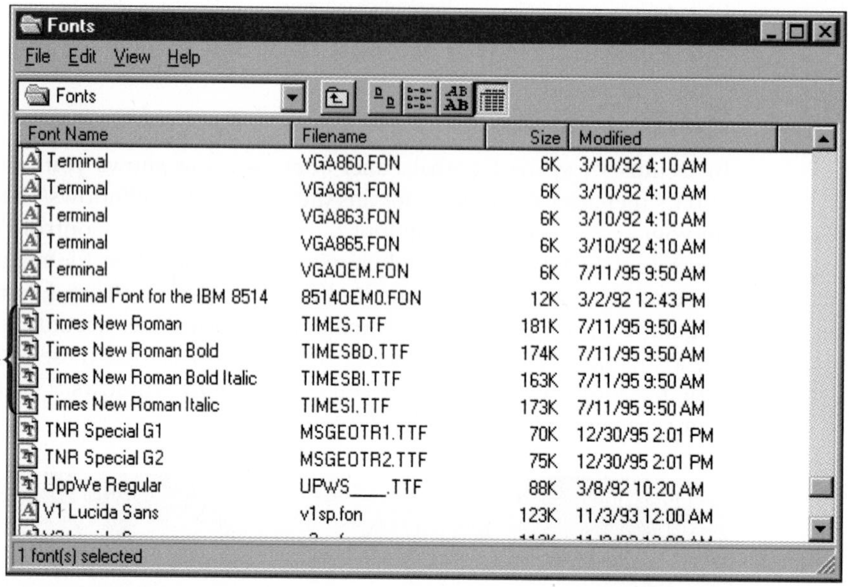

four files make up the
Times New Roman
font

When you choose an attribute such as bold or italic from within a program you are actually choosing an alternate file (though this is not the case with underlining). If you're interested in only viewing the font names and not these variations, you can use the Hide Variations command on the View menu. The Fonts window then hides the font variations, reducing the number of fonts you have to scroll through to find a font you want to use.

Font files are widely available. Windows 95 is shipped with 30 different TrueType fonts. Many programs, such as Microsoft Word, include fonts, and you can also find them on the Internet or in font collections you can buy on disk or CD-ROM.

Opening a Font

For the Banquet document you want to use only a TrueType font because those fonts give you the most flexibility, so you decide to search for a font that you might be able to use instead of Kaufmann-Thin. You can open a font in the Fonts window to see its characteristics and how it will look in a variety of sizes. One of the fonts that comes with Windows 95 is Braggadocio. Perhaps this font will look good on the Banquet announcement.

To open the Braggadocio font:

1. Locate then click the **Braggadocio** font icon.

   TROUBLE? If the Braggadocio font does not appear in your Fonts window, choose a different font to complete these steps.

2. Press the **Enter** key. Windows 95 opens a window that displays the font in different sizes, along with information about the font and its creator at the top of the window.

3. Maximize the Braggadocio window. See Figure 4-31. You don't think this font will work in the Banquet document.

Figure 4-31 ◀
Opening a font

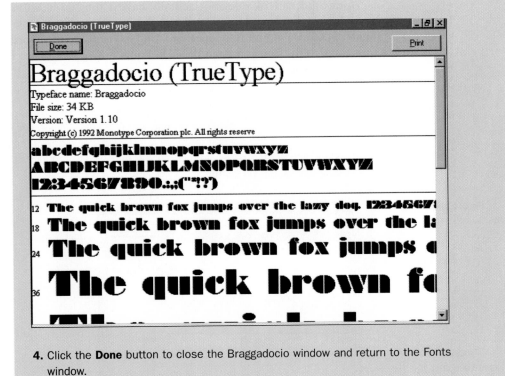

4. Click the **Done** button to close the Braggadocio window and return to the Fonts window.

Installing a Font

Rather than going through the other fonts on your computer to find a suitable replacement for the Kaufmann-Thin, it occurs to you that Celia, the creator of the Banquet document, might have realized you wouldn't have the font she chose. Perhaps she included the font on the disk. You decide to check, because then you'd simply be able to install the font and use it. When you examine the contents of the disk, you see a file called Kaufmann.ttf. You're in luck. You can install the font, and then the document should print correctly.

REFERENCE window	INSTALLING A NEW FONT
	■ Open the Fonts window from Control Panel.
	■ Click File, then click Install New Font.
	■ Select the drive and folder that contains the font you want to install.
	■ Click the font you want to install in the List of fonts list box.
	■ Verify that the Copy fonts to Font folder check box is selected.
	■ Click the OK button.

Your Student Disk does not actually have a font on it, so in this tutorial you won't actually install a font. However, if you did install the Kaufmann-Thin font on your computer, you would find that once the font is installed, the WordPad Banquet document prints correctly. You can open the Add Fonts dialog box to see how you would install a new font if you had one.

To open the Add Fonts dialog box:

1. Click **File** then click **Install New Font**. The Add Fonts dialog box opens. See Figure 4-32. If you needed to install a font, you would select the drive and folder containing the font. It would then appear in the List of fonts box. You would click it, then click the OK button.

Figure 4-32 ◄
Installing a font

lists fonts

locates folder
containing font you
want to install

installs selected
font or fonts

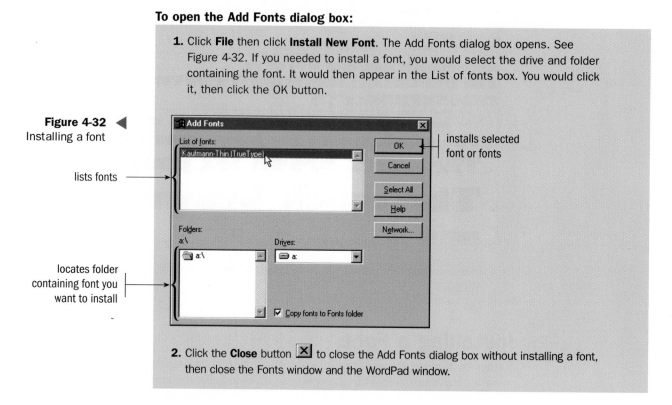

2. Click the **Close** button ⊠ to close the Add Fonts dialog box without installing a font, then close the Fonts window and the WordPad window.

When you install Kaufmann-Thin on Wai's computer, you find that the problem is solved. The Banquet document now prints correctly.

Deleting a Font

Many users collect fonts to give their documents variety. Once you start adding fonts, though, especially if you purchase them in batches, you might find that you have duplicates or many that you don't use very often. Fonts take up valuable disk space, so you should periodically review your fonts and delete those you don't need.

REFERENCE window	**DELETING A FONT**
	▪ Open the Control Panel Fonts window.
	▪ Click the font you want to delete.
	▪ Press the Delete key.

You need to be careful when you delete fonts, however. A document might use a font you deleted, and then, as you saw in this tutorial, that document would no longer print correctly. You also should not delete fonts with the 🅐 icon unless you are sure you understand what you are doing, because you might inadvertently delete a font that Windows 95 needs to display objects on the screen. If you are working in a computer lab, it is unlikely you will be able to delete fonts.

Quick Check

1. How can you tell which font a paragraph in a WordPad document is using?

2. True or false: If the name of a font used in an open WordPad document appears in the WordPad Font box, that means it is installed on your computer.

3. Is the name of a font necessarily the same as its filename?

4. Are printer fonts stored in the Fonts window? Explain your answer.

5. What are some of the advantages of using a TrueType font?

End Note

As you leave Wai's office, you reflect on how easy it was to install and work with his new printer—and how quickly you solved the font problem. From your previous experience with Windows 3.1 you realize that Microsoft has taken a step forward with Windows 95 in simplifying previously complicated procedures. Not only is the issue of printing and printers easier to handle, there is also a Wizard available for installing other types of hardware. One interesting thing to note about the font problem you encountered—if Celia had been using a word-processing program, such as Microsoft Word, she might not have needed to include the font file for the Kaufmann-Thin font. Many programs allow you to embed the fonts you are using into the document, so anyone with whom you share the document will be able to view and print the document without needing to install one or more font files.

Tutorial Assignments

1. Exploring Your Printer Open the Print dialog box (you can open it from WordPad or Paint), then answer the following questions on a piece of paper. When you are finished, close the Print dialog box.

    a. What is the name of your printer?

    b. What is your printer's type?

    c. Where is your printer? Do you see a port name or something else?

    d. Are there any other printers available from your computer? What are their names?

2. Exploring Your Printer's Properties Open the Printers window, then open your printer's property sheet. Answer the following questions on a sheet of paper.

    a. What port is your printer connected to?

    b. What driver does your printer use?

    c. Click the Paper tab, then describe how your printer processes paper when printing. For example, what paper size does it use? Where is the paper located? How many copies does it print?

3. Working with the Print Queue You work for Jacobson & Sons, a meat manufacturing company. You just started printing a big batch of bratwurst orders. Suddenly your boss knocks on the door and tells you he's on the phone with a local deli. He needs you to print a copy of the sales contract you have been negotiating with the deli. He asks you to slide it under his office door the second it's done printing. Write the steps you could take to print this document immediately. There are several ways to do this; just describe one way.

4. Installing a Printer You just purchased an Apple LaserWriter printer that you want to install as your default printer. You plan to install it locally on LPT1. You plan to name it Sales Printer. Go through the Add Printer Wizard and write down the options you chose for each dialog box.

5. Providing Printer Technical Support You are installing Windows 95 on several computers in your office. Afterwards, you receive a phone call from a fellow employee. He's having problems printing to his Postscript printer. His document printed, but it doesn't look right. Instead of the file he expected, he got pages and pages of Postscript text codes. He doesn't get a Postscript error message, he's just getting the wrong output. One possibility is that he is not using a Postscript driver for the printer. Because you're the one who installed his printer, you're sure that is not the problem. Using the Printer Troubleshooter, try to determine another explanation for his trouble. Write your answer on a piece of paper.

6. Previewing Fonts You work for a commercial graphics company. Your supervisor wants you to produce sheets of TrueType fonts styles so that users can refer to a book of styles when designing documents. You can open each font from the Fonts window as you did in this tutorial, and then click the Print button to print that font. Create sheets for the following fonts (substitute different ones if you can't find one or more of these):

    a. Arial

    b. Brush Script MT Italic

    c. Comic Sans MS

    d. Monotype Sorts

7. Previewing a Font's Appearance in WordPad You can preview the way a font will appear in WordPad without opening the Fonts window in Control Panel. Try picking a different font for the Kaufmann-Thin font used in the Banquet document. To preview different fonts from within WordPad:

a. Start WordPad and open the Banquet document from your Student Disk.

b. Select the title, "10th Annual Jugglers Guild Banquet."

c. Click Format then click Font. The Font dialog box opens. The Sample box shows a preview of the current font. See Figure 4-33.

Figure 4-33 ◀

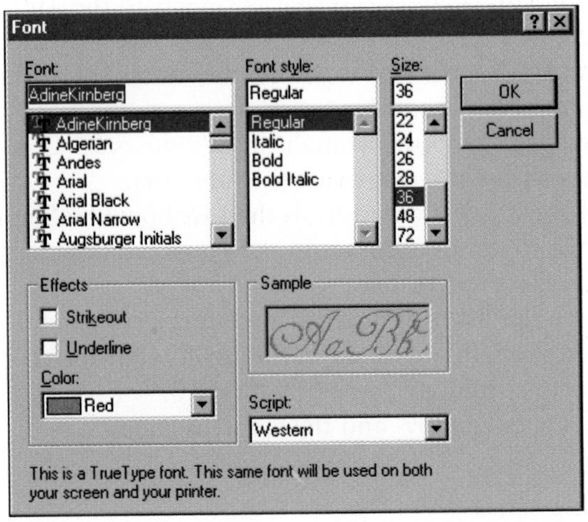

d. Select a different font from the Fonts list. Notice the Sample box.

e. Go through the list of fonts and pick out the font that you think looks appropriate for the announcement, then click the OK button.

f. Print a copy of the revised announcement to hand in to your instructor. Write the name of the font you chose on the printout. Close the Banquet document without saving your changes.

EXPLORE

8. Changing a Screen Font on your Desktop In this tutorial you saw that Windows 95 uses screen fonts to display the text in dialog boxes, title bars, and other elements on the screen. You can choose a different screen font for your desktop objects. You can use any screen font or TrueType font, allowing you a wide range of desktop appearances. Use the property sheet for the desktop display and change the font style for the icon titles.

a. Right-click a blank area of the desktop and click Properties from the menu.

b. Click the Appearance property sheet tab.

c. Choose Icon from the Item list.

d. Write down the font and size values entered in the Font and Size box for the Icon item.

e. Click the Font list arrow and choose the Comic Sans MS font (or a different font if that font is not available).

f. Change the Font size to 8.

g. Click the OK button.

    h. Press the PrintScreen key.

    i. Open a WordPad document and paste the image of the desktop into a blank document.

    j. Print the document to hand in to your instructor. Close WordPad without saving the document.

    k. Make sure to reopen the Appearance property sheet and restore the Icon font type and size to their original settings.

9. Judging Font Similarity You are creating a manuscript for a publishing house. You want to use a font in your manuscript that is similar to the Times New Roman font, but is not Times New Roman. Windows 95 allows you to list fonts by similarity. Use the View options in the Fonts window to list the fonts that are either very similar or fairly similar to Times New Roman.

    a. Open the Fonts window through the Windows 95 Control Panel.

    b. Click View then click List Fonts By Similarity.

    c. Choose Times New Roman from the List Fonts by Similarity to list.

    d. Remove the font variations from the Fonts window using the Hide Variations options on the View menu.

    e. Write down the list of fonts that are either very similar or fairly similar to Times New Roman and hand in the list to your instructor. If there are more than ten fonts listed, just write the first 10.

    f. Close the Fonts window and the Control Panel.

Network Neighborhood

QA Inc. Consumer Testing

CASE You are a new employee at QA Inc., a company that specializes in testing and then reporting the quality of consumer goods. QA occupies one large building and employs a workforce of 60, each of whom has a computer. Several years ago, QA connected all their computers together to form a network. A **network** is a collection of computers and other hardware devices linked together so that they can exchange data and share hardware and software resources.

Networks offer a company such as QA many advantages. Groups of computers on the network can use the same printer, so QA doesn't have to purchase a printer for each computer. Networks facilitate group projects, because one person can save a document in a folder that other users on other computers can access using the network. A network also improves communication in a company because coworkers can easily share news and information through the use of electronic mail.

Greg Bigelow, your supervisor, wants you to learn to use the QA network effectively, and he would like you to spend the next several hours exploring it. He decides to start you off by giving you an overview of the basic concepts of networking. Once you have been introduced to fundamentals, he says he will show you how to use Windows 95 to be productive on the company's network. You have not been assigned a computer yet, so you'll use Greg's. Although you won't be able to change anything on Greg's computer, you will at least get an introduction to the QA network.

SESSION

5.1

In this session you will explore the basic concepts of how a network operates. Then you will learn about some of the Windows 95 tools that help you understand and work with your network. Because every network is different, some of the topics in this tutorial will not apply to your network. You can discuss with your instructor any differences you notice between the network at QA Inc. and the network you are actually working on. You also might find that you are not able to do some of the tasks in this tutorial. If this is the case, you should still review those tasks to further your understanding of Windows 95's networking capabilities.

Network Concepts

Greg begins his overview by discussing the fundamentals of networks and network terminology. He believes that armed with these fundamentals, you will be better equipped to use the network effectively.

Each device on a network is called a **node**. Nodes are typically connected to each other using network cabling, although connections can also be established using phone lines, satellites, and infrared signals. If the network nodes are close together, as they would be in a computer lab or the testing lab at QA, the network is called a **local area network**, or **LAN**. Figure 5-1 shows a typical LAN.

Figure 5-1 ◀
A local area
network

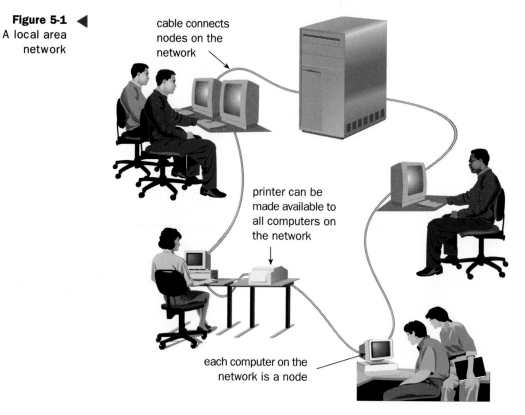

cable connects
nodes on the
network

printer can be
made available to
all computers on
the network

each computer on the
network is a node

If the nodes are spread out over a wider area, such as across a state or nation, the network is often called a **wide area network**, or **WAN**. For example, an insurance company with offices in many large cities might be on a WAN, so that an office in Detroit can access information on a client whose insurance history is located on a computer in the San Antonio branch of the company. A WAN might use satellite connections to exchange data among the nodes.

Individual networks can also be connected together to share information. A **domain** is the label given to a network so that it can be recognized by other networks. Just as information can be shared between nodes in a network, so too can information be shared between computers in different domains. The biggest and most famous example of this is the **Internet**, which is sometimes referred to as a "network of networks." With Internet access, a computer in one domain can communicate with a computer in a different domain if a path connects the two networks and these two networks communicate using the same standards and conventions that the Internet uses.

Because QA's computers are located in the same building, they are configured as a local area network. There are two models people follow to set up LANs: the hierarchical model and the peer-to-peer model. In the **hierarchical model**, often called the **client/server model**, computers called **servers** provide access to resources such as files, software, and hardware devices. A computer that uses these resources is called a **workstation** or **client**. Figure 5-2 illustrates the hierarchical model.

Figure 5-2 ◀
Hierarchical
network
model

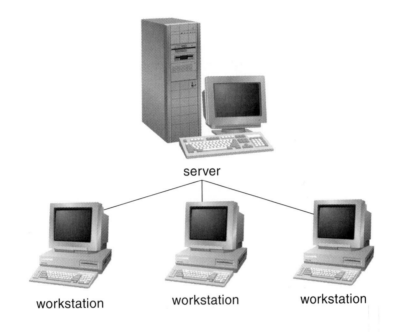

server

workstation   workstation   workstation

Servers offer many resources to the network. For example, a server might store a database, making it accessible to many workstations. In the QA testing lab, product test results are kept on a server so that all testers can refer to them as they write their reports. A server might also handle electronic mail, faxes, or printing for a network. If a network is large, it often has several servers, with each server dedicated to the needs of a separate group of users or to a specific task. QA, for example, has servers dedicated to each of its departments.

A hierarchical network requires special software on the server. This software, called a **network operating system**, manages the operations of the entire network. In addition, client software must be installed on each workstation so that it can communicate with the server. Although Windows 95 does not provide the network operating system software to allow your computer to act as a network server in the hierarchical model, it does provide the client software so your computer can work with a server using network operating systems such as Novell NetWare, Windows NT, IBM OS/2 LAN, and Banyan Vines. A network operating system is usually installed and maintained by an individual called the **network administrator**. He or she is ultimately responsible for how you interact with the network.

A second kind of network model is based on the peer-to-peer model. In the **peer-to-peer model**, a network does not require a server dedicated to managing network resources. Instead, nodes on a peer-to-peer network can act as both clients and servers, with each node sharing its resources with other nodes on the network. Figure 5-3 shows the layout of a peer-to-peer network.

3.I NOTE

Unlike Windows 3.1, which requires you to install special software on your computer for it to work as a client in a hierarchical network, no additional software is required for a Windows 95 workstation to act as a client.

Figure 5-3 ◀
Peer-to-peer
network
model

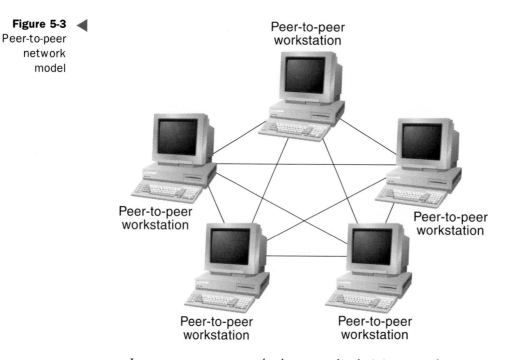

In a peer-to-peer network, the network administrator often organizes nodes into workgroups. A **workgroup** is a group of computers that performs common tasks or belongs to users who share common duties and interests. A network administrator for a business, for example, might organize computers used by the office staff into an Office workgroup and computers used by upper management into a Management workgroup. By organizing the network in this fashion, it's easier for the network administrator to manage the differing needs of each group.

An advantage of the peer-to-peer model for Windows 95 users is that the network can be set up without purchasing any additional software. Everything needed to create a peer-to-peer network is built into the Windows 95 operating system. One problem, however, with peer-to-peer networks is that performance of individual nodes can deteriorate as they manage tasks for other computers as well as performing their own duties. Moreover, a peer-to-peer network does not have the same extensive network management features offered by network operating systems under the hierarchical model. For these reasons, peer-to-peer networks are usually used for smaller networks with just a few nodes. The QA network, for example, is too large and complex to rely on only the peer-to-peer model.

Each network is different. The network administrator tries to create a network structure that best meets the needs of the users, sometimes including elements from both the hierarchical and peer-to-peer models. How a user interacts with the network can also vary from network to network. In some cases the network administrator will limit your ability to work on the network, whereas other administrators will give users great flexibility in sharing and accessing network resources. Greg wants you to understand that what you see on the QA network might not necessarily apply to other networks you encounter.

3.1 NOTE

Peer-to-peer networking was not provided with Windows 3.1. However, Windows 3.11, otherwise known as "Windows for Workgroups," included this feature.

Viewing Your Network

QA's hierarchical network includes several servers that are accessed by workstations running Windows 95. Greg explains that this model is very popular. For example, most university networks use a hierarchical model with students, faculty, and staff using workstations to access files and resources stored on servers across campus. Windows 95 workstations feature an icon on the desktop called Network Neighborhood 🖥️. **Network Neighborhood** is a window, similar to the My Computer window, that gives you access to the servers and workgroups on the network. It also helps you view your network's structure.

When you open Network Neighborhood, you see a list of computers in your network workgroup if your network administrator has set up your network to use workgroups. The first item on Network Neighborhood's list, however, is the Entire Network icon 👤, which you can open to view a list of servers not in your workgroup and to view other network domains. For example, suppose your company has two workgroups: Office and Marketing. You are in the Office workgroup. When you open Network Neighborhood on Bob's computer, you see the Entire Network icon and other computers in your workgroup. Figure 5-4 shows that there are three other computers in your workgroup named Bob, Terry, and Weber. When you open the Entire Network window, you see a list of the two workgroups on your network as well as other network servers.

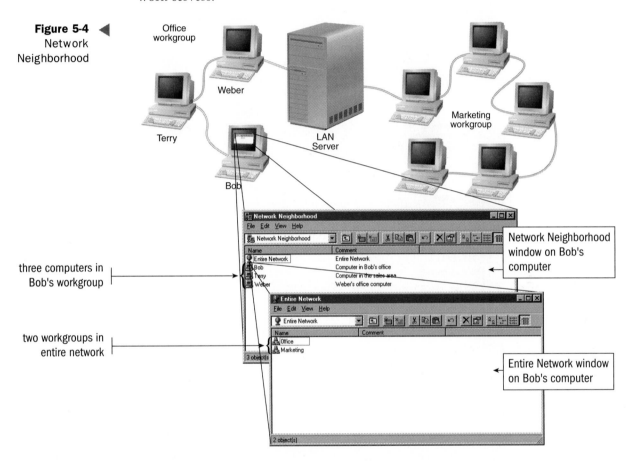

Figure 5-4 ◀
Network
Neighborhood

Network Neighborhood does not always give you the whole picture of your network, as it did for Bob's computer in Figure 5-4. If your workstation doesn't have access to other computers on the network, they might not appear in your Network Neighborhood window. Likewise, if you don't have access to other workgroups on the network, they might not appear in your Entire Network window. Much of what you see in the Network Neighborhood is determined by the network administrator.

Greg suggests that you open Network Neighborhood on his computer to get an overview of the computers on the QA network. To be able to perform these steps and other steps in this tutorial, your computer must have access to a network and Windows 95 must be configured to work with that network. Also, because networks use different network operating systems and they vary greatly depending on network resources, workgroups, and setups, the features and functions of your network might differ from those described in this tutorial.

To view the other nodes in your Network Neighborhood:

1. Click the **Network Neighborhood** icon 🖥 on your desktop, then press the **Enter** key. Examine the nodes listed in the Network Neighborhood window. Figure 5-5 shows the Network Neighborhood window at Greg's computer at QA Inc. His computer is named Bigelow.

   TROUBLE? If no objects appear in your Network Neighborhood window, ask your instructor or computer lab support person for help. You might not have access to the network from your computer or you might not be logged into the network. You'll learn more about logging on in Session 5.2.

Figure 5-5 ◄
Network Neighborhood as viewed from Greg's computer

Entire Network icon ——

other QA servers ——►

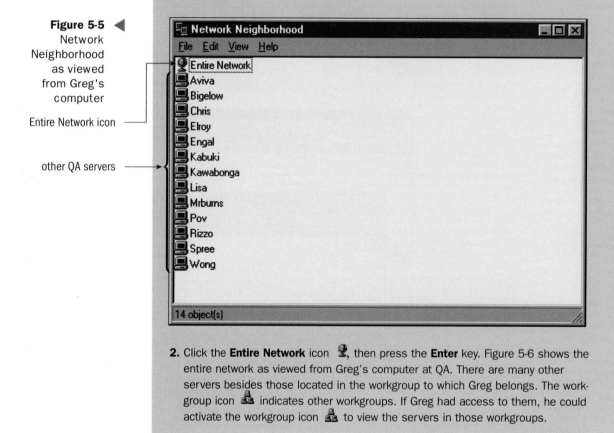

2. Click the **Entire Network** icon 🌐, then press the **Enter** key. Figure 5-6 shows the entire network as viewed from Greg's computer at QA. There are many other servers besides those located in the workgroup to which Greg belongs. The workgroup icon 🖧 indicates other workgroups. If Greg had access to them, he could activate the workgroup icon 🖧 to view the servers in those workgroups.

Figure 5-6 ◀
Entire Network
as viewed
from Greg's
computer

your list of servers
will be different

workgroups

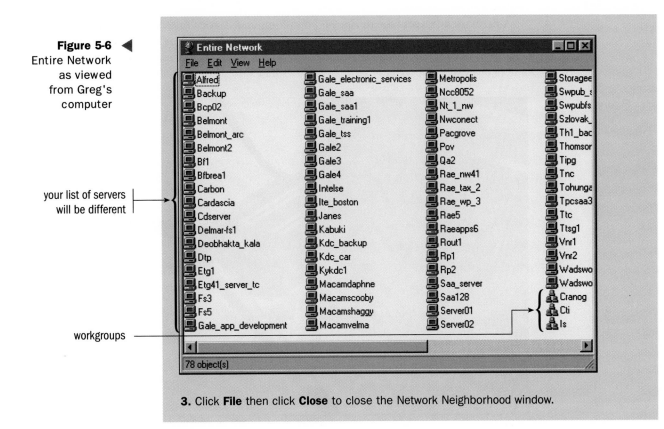

3. Click **File** then click **Close** to close the Network Neighborhood window.

The QA network is a large network. As you saw from the figures, it includes a number of computers and workgroups. Your network setup will likely be different.

Network Protocols and Standards

You tell Greg you've had some experience using networks because your college computer system was networked. Greg nods, but says that there are so many variations in how a network can be set up that you might find there are differences between what your college network could do and what the QA network does. He explains that to best understand how to use a network, it's useful to understand the different aspects of how a network operates. Windows 95 uses four components to provide network access: an adapter, a protocol, a client, and a service component.

A network **adapter** is the device on your computer that enables it to connect to the network. Adapters are usually cards, called **network interface cards**, or **NIC**s, inserted into a slot in the back of your computer (with the case taken off). The card includes a port into which a network cable is inserted. Figure 5-7 shows an example of such a network interface card.

Figure 5-7 ◀
Network
interface card

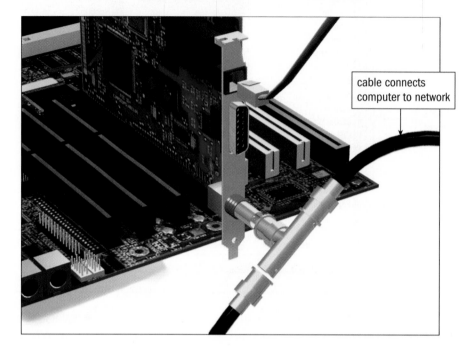

cable connects
computer to network

Your computer doesn't have to have an NIC and a network cable to connect to a network—you can connect, for example, using a modem. In these situations, Windows 95 uses the modem as a **dial-up adapter**, where the phone line acts as a network connection. A phone line does not transmit data nearly as fast as the combination of the NIC and network cable, but for many users phone lines are the only choice. For example, if you have a home PC and you have purchased access to the Internet using an Internet service provider, you most likely use your phone line to connect to the network.

Each NIC uses a **network standard**, which is the manner in which data is handled as it travels over the network cable. One of the earliest, least expensive, and most widely used network standards is the Ethernet standard. The **Ethernet** standard transfers data at 10 megabits per second—much faster than data is transferred over a phone line. Standards are often compared in terms of how fast they transfer data. The faster a standard can transfer data, the more efficiently the network can share resources among its pool of users. Another popular network standard is the Token Ring standard. Developed by IBM, the **Token Ring** standard is more expensive than the Ethernet, but it can transfer data at rates up to 16 megabits per second. As demands on networks increase, so too do demands for new standards that support faster transfer speeds. The newest standards, **Fiber Distributed Data Interchange** (**FDDI**) and **Asynchronous Transfer Mode** (**ATM**), can transfer data at 100 megabits per second and faster. A network that can transfer data this quickly can also handle more powerful tasks, such as video conferencing.

The communications protocol is the language computers use to communicate on the network. A **communications protocol** determines how computers recognize each other on the network and what rules they use to transfer data. Different network operating systems use different protocols. Computers that connect to the Internet use **TCP/IP** (Transmission Control Protocol/Internet Protocol) to facilitate communication. A NetWare network uses **IPX/SPX** for network communications. A Windows NT network uses the **NetBEUI** protocol. Windows 95 can handle most of the popular network protocols, but to use Windows 95 with these networks, you must have the appropriate protocol installed. Windows 95 also allows you to work with several different protocols at the same time.

The third component of your network setup is the **client** component, which gives your computer the ability to access shared resources on the network. Each network operating system requires a different client component. Windows 95 includes client components to support the Novell NetWare, Microsoft NT Server, and Banyan Vines networks.

The final component in your network setup is the **service** component, which enables your computer to share its resources with the network. It also enables a network administrator to remotely manage the software and hardware installed on your machine. The service component is used primarily in peer-to-peer networks, where each user controls how his or her computer shares its resources with the network. On many hierarchical networks, the network administrator will not make this component available to users.

Understanding which components have been installed on your computer helps you understand the capabilities and limitations of your computer on the network.

Viewing Network Properties

Now that you have an overview of the different aspects of network setup, you can examine Greg's computer to see which components are installed. The Windows 95 **Network property sheet** lists the network components installed on your computer. You can access the Network property sheet from Network Neighborhood or from the Control Panel. You decide to open it from Network Neighborhood.

To view network properties:

1. Right-click the **Network Neighborhood** icon 🖳 on the desktop.

2. Click **Properties**. The list of components installed on your workstation appears in the Configuration property sheet. See Figure 5-8. Your computer's components could look different.

   TROUBLE? On some networks, you might not have access to the Network property sheet. If this is the case, read the following steps without performing them on your computer.

Figure 5-8 ◄
Network properties of Greg's workstation

first part of components list

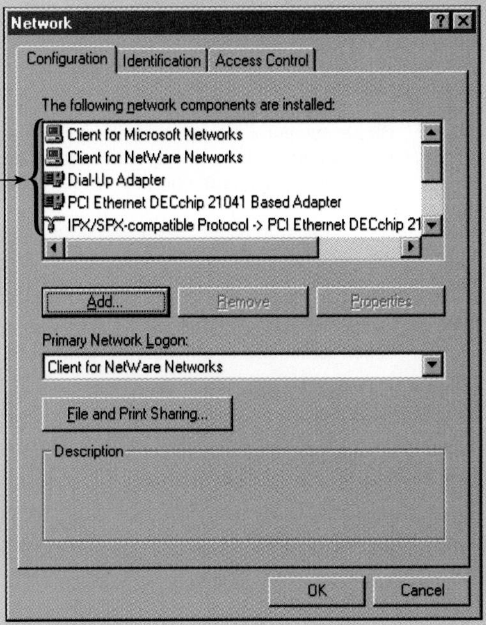

3. If necessary, scroll down to see other components installed on your computer. The rest of the components installed on this particular computer are shown in Figure 5-9.

Figure 5-9 ◄
More network
properties
of Greg's
workstation

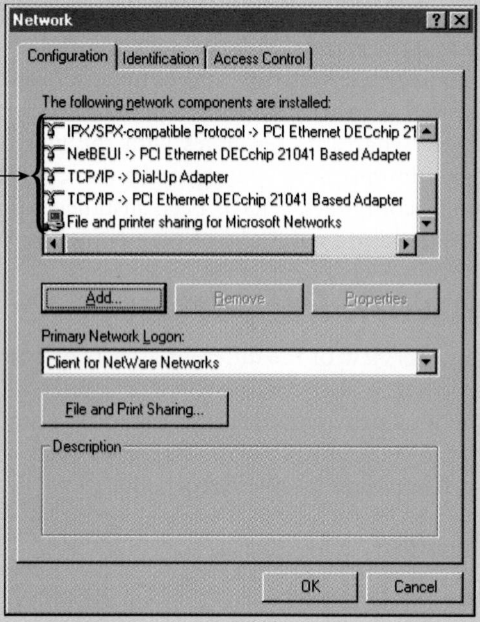

remainder of
components list

Greg's computer has several options for each of the network components. Figure 5-10 interprets the components available on Greg's computer.

Figure 5-10 ◄
Components
on Greg's
workstation

Component	Icon	Description on Greg's Computer
Adapter		Two adapters are listed: a PCI Ethernet adapter and a dial-up adapter. Greg's computer can connect to a network in two ways—through an NIC card and network cabling or over a phone line.
Client		Greg's computer can act as a client in both a Microsoft and a NetWare network. Note that Greg's computer is not limited to working with only one network operating system.
Protocol		Greg's computer uses the IPX/SPX protocol for NetWare networks, the TCP/IP protocol for Internet communications, and the NetBEUI protocol.
Service		Greg's computer can share both files and printers with other computers in a Microsoft network.

The other parts of the Network Properties dialog box shown in Figure 5-9 indicate the Primary Network Logon, which you'll learn about later, and options for file and print sharing. If you are allowed to share files and your printer, as you would in a peer-to-peer network, you would click the File and Print Sharing button to specify how you want your files and printers to be shared.

Identifying Your Computer on the Network

Recall that Greg's computer appeared with the name "Bigelow" in the Network Neighborhood window. You ask Greg how he knew which computer was his. He tells you that each network node has a name that identifies it to the other nodes on the network. Windows 95 limits this name to 15 characters and does not allow blank spaces. You can view your computer's name and description in the Identification sheet of the Network Property dialog box. This sheet also includes information about which workgroup your computer belongs to.

You decide to find out information about Greg's workstation. You are not likely to be able to change your workstation's name or description, but it is important that you know how to find this information to see how your workstation fits into the rest of the network.

To view network identification information:

1. Click the **Identification** sheet tab. This property sheet displays the name, workgroup, and description of your computer. See Figure 5-11. Yours will probably be different—and you might have no workgroup assignment.

Figure 5-11 ◀
Identifying
a computer
on a network

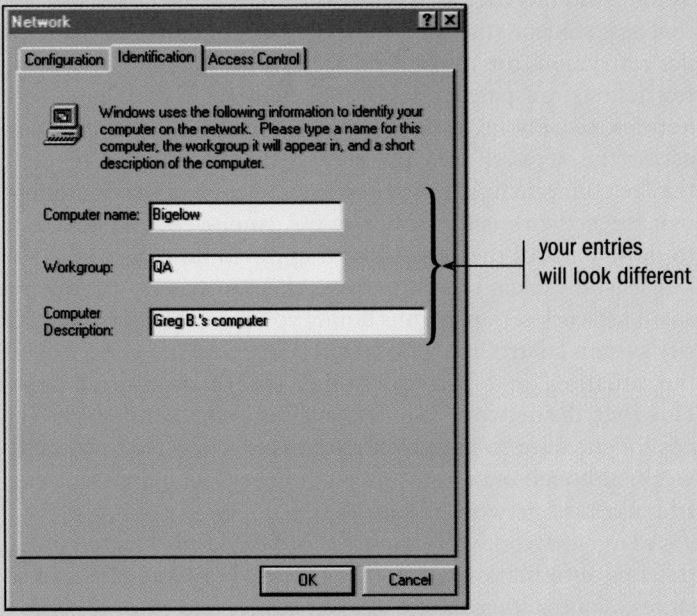

your entries
will look different

2. Click the **Cancel** button to close the Network property sheet without saving any changes you might have inadvertently made.

Quick Check

1. What is a network?

2. Define the following terms:
   node
   workgroup
   LAN
   WAN
   server
   client
   workstation

3. Name the two types of network models, then briefly describe each.

4. Name three tasks a network server might have to perform.

5. What are the four components needed to set up a Windows 95 machine to work on a network?

6. What is a communications protocol? Give an example of a communications protocol and describe what it is used for.

7. List four popular LAN standards.

8. List three popular network operating systems.

SESSION 5.2

In this session you will learn how to log on to your network and how Windows 95 manages access to different network resources with user accounts and access rights. You'll learn how passwords work and how to create a secure password.

Network Security and Access Rights

You mention to Greg that when you were at the university there were a number of things that as a student you were "blocked out" of doing on the network. Greg replies that similar restrictions are in place on the QA network for certain users. He explains that these restrictions are part of an overall plan for maintaining security on the QA network. **Network security** involves the control of two aspects of a network: the people who can access the network and the actions they're allowed to perform on the network once they're connected. At QA, Greg explains, the network administrator wants to make sure that the network is used only by QA employees and that each employee has access only to those parts of the network that apply to his or her job.

Measures taken to ensure network security vary for different networks. If you have a small network set up in your home, you probably don't need to have a sophisticated security system controlling who has access to the network. You are there to closely monitor the situation, and you have other means of controlling who gets into your home. However, the network requirements for a small business might be different. A small business might want to have security measures in place to control who gets access to the network; although once authorized employees who are connected might be given equal and free access to network resources.

A large network with hundreds of people working on different projects involving confidential information is another matter. For example, a university network server that stores, among other things, student grades and records needs tight security over who can access the system and what information they can view once they get access. Likewise, a network at a hospital must have severe restrictions in place on patient data to ensure the integrity of the doctor-patient relationship.

Network administrators don't just need to restrict access to data; they also need to restrict access to hardware. For example, the graphic arts department on campus might have purchased an expensive high-quality color laser printer, and they don't want students from other departments using it. The network administrator might therefore limit access to that printer to students and faculty in the graphic arts department.

Network administrators control who gets on the network—and what users are allowed to do once they are connected—through network accounts and access rights. A **network account** is the collection of information about you and the work you do on the network. Before you can use the network, the network administrator creates an account for you that identifies you as an authorized user of the network. In a network that has several different servers, you might have several network accounts. For example, a student who is getting an engineering degree but is taking a class in the art department might have two network accounts, one in each department.

Network administrators limit access to network data, software, and hardware through the use of user IDs and passwords. Your **user ID**, or **user name**, identifies you to other users on the network. A user ID might be your first name and last initial, separated by a punctuation mark, like Greg.B, or a number such as 445,228, or a word such as Tester. On some systems, user IDs are limited to eight characters and exclude spaces or special symbols.

Along with your user ID, you enter your password. Your **password** is a string of symbols, letters, and numbers, known only to you and the network administrator, that shows you are the legitimate user of the account. Passwords are a security device to prevent other people who might know your user ID from using your account. Once you have entered both the user ID and password, the server checks to see if these are valid before allowing you network access.

Once you're connected to the network, your ability to use network resources is controlled by a set of guidelines, set up by the network administrator. The ability to use a resource is called an **access right**. Access rights can be limited to **read-only access**, which allows you to view the contents of a file but not to edit or delete the file. This might occur if you were a physician who needs to be able to review patient records stored on a hospital network database. Your network administrator might grant you read-only access so that you could view the files without accidentally changing or deleting a record. In other situations you might need **read and write access**, which gives you the ability to view, edit, and delete a file. Read and write access is often granted on networks where your files are stored in folders located on a network server.

Network Logons

3.1 NOTE

Logon dialog boxes and user profiles are a new feature of Windows 95. Earlier versions of Windows were not easily configured to accommodate multiple users.

The process of accessing your account is called **logging on** or **logging in**. You are prompted for your user ID and password in a dialog box called a **logon dialog box**. The appearance of the logon dialog box differs slightly depending on the operating system used by your network. Figures 5-12, 5-13, and 5-14 show sample logon dialog boxes for Windows 95, a Microsoft network, and Novell NetWare.

If your workstation is part of a Windows 95 peer-to-peer network, you would see the dialog box shown in Figure 5-12. Completing this dialog box allows you to access the Windows 95 operating system after entering your user ID and password.

The Windows 95 logon dialog box also can be used in situations where a single workstation is shared by several people. Windows 95 allows each user to customize the desktop. Windows 95 stores the desktop each user designs in a file called a **user profile**. Logging onto Windows 95 accesses your user profile and loads the settings for your customized desktop. Not every network will have the Windows 95 user profiles feature installed.

Figure 5-12 ◀
Windows 95 logon dialog box

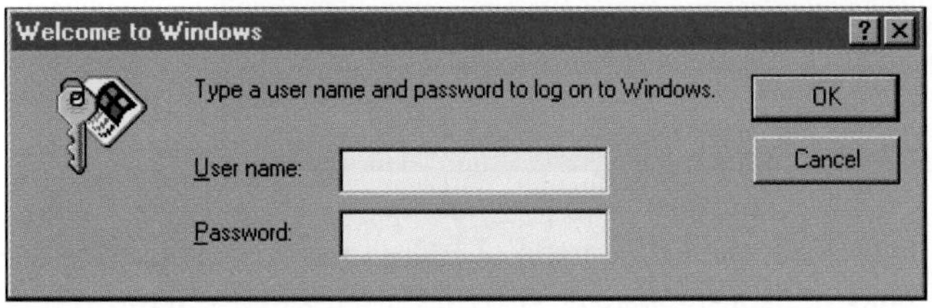

If your computer is set up to work on a Microsoft network such as one using the Windows NT server, you would see the dialog box shown in Figure 5-13. In addition to the user ID and password, you would have to specify the name of the domain that is managing your network account. Recall that a domain name is sometimes given to a network to identify it to other networks.

Figure 5-13 ◄
Microsoft
Network logon
dialog box

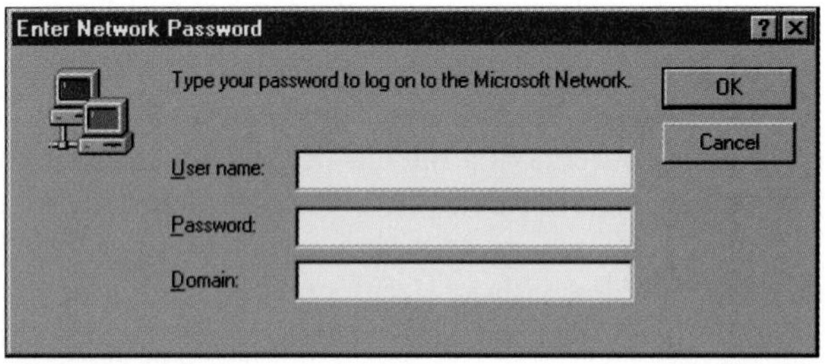

Greg tells you that the QA computers are connected to a NetWare network. He suggests that he take your place at the workstation for a minute in order to show you how he would log on to the network from his workstation. He tells you he doesn't want you to log on for him because company policy prohibits him from telling you his password. Greg shuts down his computer and then turns it back on. After the computer starts up, the logon dialog box appears. This dialog box requests Greg's user ID, password, and the name of the NetWare server that maintains the list of authorized users on the network. This server is called a **login server**, and like other workstations and servers on the network, it has a name. Greg tells you that the login server at QA is named Pov. Greg types Tester, his user ID, in the first box. He types a 12-character password in the Password box. As he types, asterisks appear, preventing you from learning his password. Finally, he types the name of his login server. Figure 5-14 shows Greg's logon dialog box after he has typed this information.

Figure 5-14 ◄
Novell NetWare
logon dialog
box

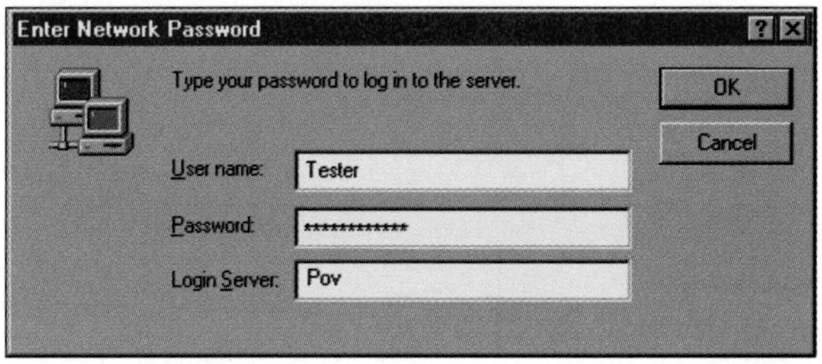

Greg then clicks the OK button. The login server checks his user ID and password and confirms that he is a legitimate network user. Greg's Windows 95 desktop appears, and Greg tells you he is logged on.

If you have accounts on more than one server, your network administrator might have set up your logon in one of two ways: You might be required to log on to each network using a separate dialog box. More convenient for you, however, would be a primary network logon. The **primary network logon** is the network that you are primarily using whenever you log into your computer. It could be a Windows NT network, a NetWare network, or Windows 95 itself. The advantage of designating one of your networks as your primary network logon is that if you use the same password for other accounts as you use for the primary network logon, Windows 95 automatically logs you on those networks. You see only one logon dialog box and have to remember only one password.

Attaching to a Server

Occasionally you will want to log on to other accounts on other network servers. Greg explains that this happens at QA when users want to access the database files located on the Kabuki server. The Kabuki server at QA is used only for special projects, so the network administrator has asked users to access that server only when they need to use those files. You are already logged on to the Pov server; now Greg wants to show you how to log on to Kabuki at the same time. Windows 95 allows you to log on to more than one server at a time using the Attach command in the Network Neighborhood window.

REFERENCE window

ATTACHING TO A SERVER

- Open Network Neighborhood.
- Right-click the server to which you want to attach.
- Click Attach As.
- Enter your user ID and password in the Enter Network Password dialog box, then click the OK button.

A Enter your user ID.

B Enter your password, which appears as a series of asterisks.

C Saves your password in a password list so that the next time you attach to this particular server, the password will be filled in automatically for you. On some networks, this feature might be disabled.

D Connects you as a guest, a temporary user with limited access to network resources. If you need to use a guest account, you should talk to your instructor or network administrator about the process of logging on as a guest.

E Attaches you to the server shown to the right of Resource:.

F Cancels the procedure.

Greg again tells you he'll attach to the Kabuki server because he wants to protect the security of his password. If your network allows you access to only one network server, read through the next set of steps without performing them.

To attach to a network server:

1. Open the Network Neighborhood window.

2. Move through your Network Neighborhood and locate the network server you want to access. Greg locates the Kabuki server.

TROUBLE? You might have other network servers displayed in your workgroup or you might have to click the Entire Network icon 🌐 to locate other servers. Ask your instructor or technical support person for the location of additional servers available to you.

3. Right-click the icon for the server to which you want to attach, then click **Attach As**. Greg chooses the Kabuki server from the list of servers in the Network Neighborhood window. Figure 5-15 shows the list of servers Greg sees.

Figure 5-15 ◀
Attaching to a network server

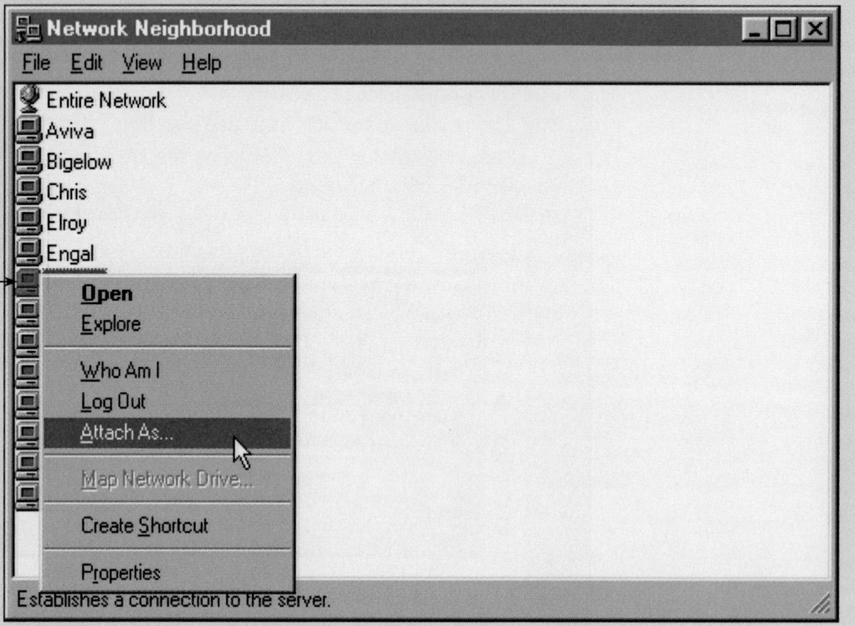

Greg right-clicks the
Kabuki server,
which is hidden
behind the menu

4. Enter your user name and password in the Enter Network Password dialog box. Greg's is shown in Figure 5-16.

TROUBLE? If you see the message, "You are logged in to this server. Do you want to log out first?" click the No button. You receive this query because you are trying to attach to a server that you're already logged in to. Try to find another server that you are not already attached to.

Figure 5-16 ◀
Logging on to a network server

5. Make sure the Save this password and Connect as guest check boxes are unselected.

6. Click the **OK** button. Windows 95 might notify you that you've been connected to the server.

7. If necessary click the **OK** button.

8. Click the **Close** button ❎ to close the Network Neighborhood window.

Password Protection

You have already seen how network administrators enforce network security through the use of User Ids and passwords—and that Greg is very careful not to share his password with anyone. Greg emphasizes that keeping your password secret helps maintain the security of a network and its resources. If you are allowed to create your own password for your account, you should keep the following principles in mind:

- Do not use fewer than seven characters in your password.

- Do not use your name, birth date, nickname, or any word that an unauthorized user might be able to guess.

- Try to include numbers or special symbols (!@#%&*) in your password, because they make it harder for other users to guess your password.

- Never write down your password where others can see it or share your password with other users.

You also should change your password every few months. On some networks this is a requirement, and the network administrator will set up an automatic prompt that appears when you are supposed to change your password. In the process of changing your password, you will be prompted to enter your old password and then to enter your new password twice. You enter the new password twice to reduce the possibility of a typing error.

REFERENCE window	CHANGING YOUR WINDOWS 95 PASSWORD
	■ Click the Start button, point to Settings, then click Control Panel.
	■ Click Passwords then press the Enter key.
	■ Click the Change Windows Password button.
	■ Type your current password in the Old Password box.
	■ Type your new password twice: once in the New Password box and once in the Confirm Password box.
	■ Click the OK button to save the new password.
	■ Close the Windows 95 Control Panel.

Greg tells you that password protection is one of QA's network security measures, and you will be required to change your password every two months. Greg suggests that you review the dialog box you would use to do this—but he doesn't want you to know or change his password.

If you are in a university computer lab, you might not be able to change your password. You should ask you instructor or network administrator about your network's policies for changing passwords. In the next set of steps, you will be directed to click the Cancel button to prevent making any changes to your current password.

To review the techniques for changing your Windows 95 password:

1. Click the **Start** button, point to **Settings**, then click **Control Panel**.

2. Click the **Passwords** icon 🔑 then press the **Enter** key. The Passwords Properties dialog box opens. See Figure 5-17.

Figure 5-17 ◀
Passwords
Properties
dialog box

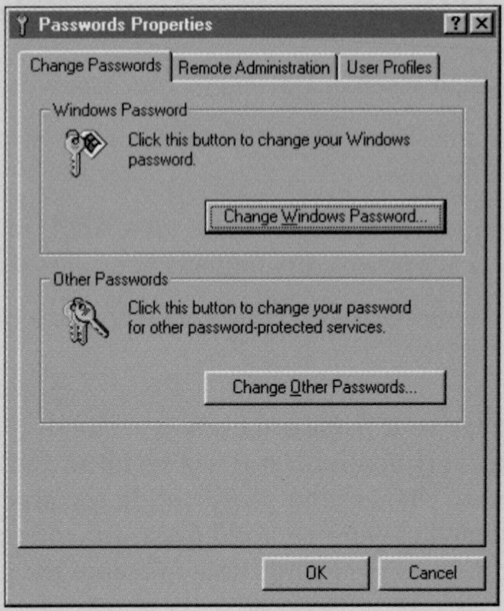

3. Click the **Change Windows Password** button. The Change Windows Password dialog box opens Figure 5-18.

Figure 5-18 ◀
Change
Windows
Password
dialog box

Type old password
here; asterisks
appear as you type

Type new password
twice to prevent
a typing error

4. Type your current Windows 95 password in the Old password box, then press **Tab**. Notice that asterisks appear as you type to prevent anyone watching you from discovering your password.

5. Type your new Windows 95 password in the New password box, then press **Tab**.

6. Retype your new password in the Confirm new password box, then press **Tab**. *Because this is just an example, you should exit the Change Windows Password dialog box without saving your changes.*

7. Click the **Cancel** button.

8. Click the **Close** button ⊠ to close the Passwords Properties dialog box, then close the Control Panel.

To change your password for a network account, you might be required to send a command to the appropriate network server. To change your password on a NetWare network, for example, you have to run the SETPASS command from the MS-DOS prompt. If you need to change your password on a NetWare network, you should talk with the network administrator or your instructor.

Viewing Your Current Accounts

If you've logged onto a network that has more than one server, you might not be sure which servers you are using. The QA network, for example, has many different servers, and you are currently logged on to both Pov and Kabuki. Greg tells you that you can use Windows 95 to view your user ID and the servers you are currently logged in to with the **Who Am I** command. He invites you to sit at the computer and obtain this information.

To view your user name and a list of servers to which your computer is connected:

1. Right-click the **Network Neighborhood** icon 🖳 on the desktop, then click **Who Am I**. Figure 5-19 shows the Kabuki server, where Greg is logged on with the user ID Greg.b; and the Pov server, where he is logged on with the user ID Tester. The Who Am I dialog box also shows the connection number for each server. Greg is the third user logged into the Kabuki server and the eighth user on the Pov server.

   TROUBLE? If you are running Windows 95 in a peer-to-peer network, the Who Am I command will not display any account information and might not even be available.

Figure 5-19 ◀
Who Am I
dialog box

server name

User ID

connection number

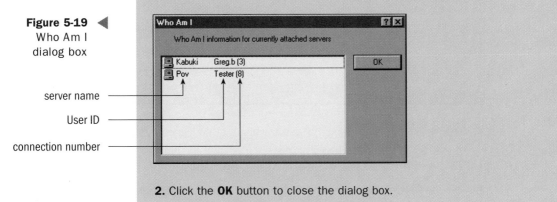

2. Click the **OK** button to close the dialog box.

Logging Out from a Network Server

As you have seen, at QA, Greg has access to several servers. Yet some, like the Kabuki server, should be used only temporarily. When you're done using a server, you should log out. **Logging out**, or **logging off**, is the process of exiting your account on the server. Greg explains that QA's network administrator has asked all employees to log out of servers as soon as they are finished working with them. Some of the QA servers allow only a limited number of users on at any given time, and the administrator wants to avoid tying up servers with non-active users. You can log out of a server at any time during your Windows 95 session without affecting your accounts on other servers. Greg tells you to log out of the Kabuki server so you don't tie it up from other users.

You should not actually log out from your account on the server. Instead, review the next set of steps so that you understand how to log out of a server if you need to do so in the future, but *do not perform these steps.*

To log out from a network server:

1. Open Network Neighborhood.

2. Locate the network server from which you want to log out.

3. Right-click the icon representing the server you are connected to, then click **Log Out**. See Figure 5-20.

> **TROUBLE?** If you are running Windows 95 in a peer-to-peer network, the Log Out command will not be available.

Figure 5-20 ◄
Logging out of
a network
server

the Kabuki server is
hidden behind the
menu

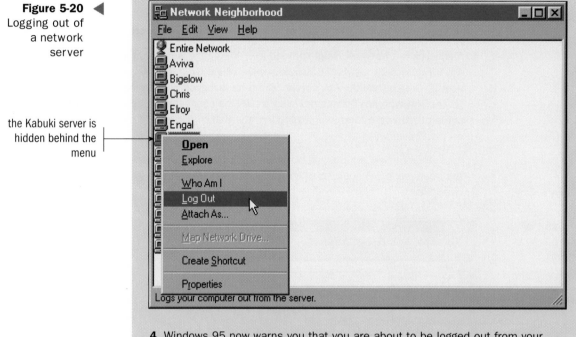

4. Windows 95 now warns you that you are about to be logged out from your account on the server. Although if you really wanted to log out, you would click Yes, *you should click the **No** button to stay logged on.*

5. Click the **Close** button ☒ to close the Network Neighborhood window.

Logging Out from Windows 95

In the previous section you logged out from an account on a server. However, your account on your workstation is still open. When you are finished working on your workstation, you should log out from not only all your network accounts but also from your workstation account. Depending on your network, your network administrator might want you to leave the computer on for those following you to use, so make sure you understand the procedures in your computer lab before you follow any of the instructions here.

There might be several options available to you when you are ready to stop working with Windows 95 on your workstation. You can:

■ *Shut down the workstation:* This option unloads the Windows 95 operating system. The next user will have to restart the workstation and reload the Windows 95 operating system. You should check with your instructor to see whether this option is allowed on your network. Many network administrators request users *not* to shut down individual workstations.

■ *Restart the workstation:* This option reloads the Windows 95 operating system. The next user will have to enter his or her user ID and password in the logon dialog box before using the computer.

■ *Close all programs and log on as a different user:* This option keeps the Windows 95 operating system loaded, but closes any active programs or network accounts, returning the user to the logon dialog box. Network administrators whose workstations are shared among several users often request that you use this option for shutting down your account.

You should talk to your instructor or network administrator to determine which of these options you should select when you're finished working with Windows 95. At QA, the network administrator prefers the third option: that you log out of your account but you keep the Windows 95 operating system loaded. Greg shows you how to log out from Windows 95 using this option.

To log out from your workstation, leaving Windows 95 still loaded:

1. Click the **Start** button then click **Shut Down**.

2. The Shut Down dialog box appears. See Figure 5-21.

Figure 5-21 ◀
Windows 95
logout dialog
box

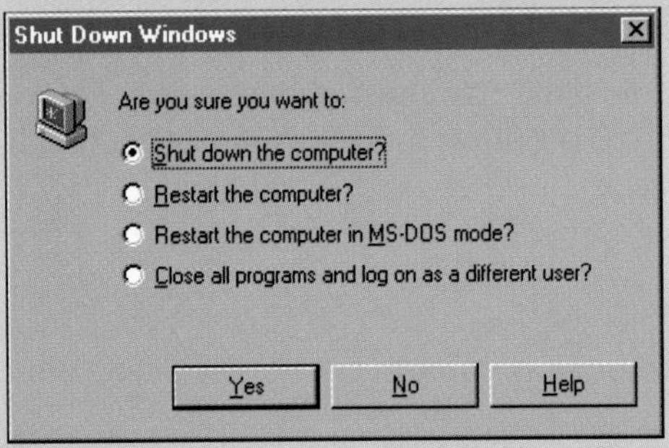

3. Click the **Close all programs and log on as a different user?** radio button.

4. Because this is an example, you should not actually log out from your workstation. If you really wanted to log out, you would click the Yes button, but for now you should click the **No** button to cancel the procedure.

Greg emphasizes that you should remember to log out of your account when you're done working. If you leave the workstation running, still connected to your network accounts, other users could access your work.

Quick Check

1 Give four guidelines you should follow in choosing a password.

2 What is a primary network logon?

3 What information do you need before logging on to an account on a NetWare network?

4 How would you discover your account name and the servers you're connected to?

5 How would you change your Windows 95 password?

6 Describe how you would log out first from a server on the network and then from your workstation account.

7 When you log out of your workstation account, which option or options leaves Windows 95 loaded for the next user?

SESSION

5.3

In this session you will learn how to access the resources on your network. You will access a folder on the network using Windows Explorer. Then you will explore different ways to represent the location of files on the network to your applications. You'll learn how to access a network printer. Finally, you'll learn about the Windows 95 Network troubleshooter, which can help you diagnose and fix a problem if the network is not working the way you expect.

Using Network Resources

Greg has logged back in to the Pov and Kabuki servers. He now wants to show you some of the available resources on those servers. You can view a list of the resources a server makes available through the Network Neighborhood window or through Windows Explorer. Greg decides to use Explorer because it gives a better view of the structure of the network.

To view available resources on a network server using Windows Explorer:

1. Click the **Start** button, point to **Programs**, then click **Windows Explorer**.

2. Scroll down the Folders list until you see the Network Neighborhood 🖳 icon.

3. If necessary, click the **plus box** ⊞ to the left of the Network Neighborhood icon to display the list of servers in your workgroup.

4. Click the **server** icon 🖳 representing one of the servers you're logged in to. Greg clicks the icon for the Kabuki server. The resources offered by that server appear in the Windows Explorer Contents list. Windows Explorer shows that three folders—sys, misery, and vol_a—are made available to the network by the Kabuki server. See Figure 5-22.

   TROUBLE? If you don't immediately see a network server that you have access to, you will have to look for servers elsewhere in the network. To do so, click the Entire Network icon 🌐 to display a list of additional servers and examine those. If you still cannot find a server you can use, talk to your instructor or network administrator.

   TROUBLE? You might have to enter a password before you can view the resources shared by a server. If you have trouble accessing the server, talk to your instructor or network administrator.

Figure 5-22 ◄
Kabuki server's
resources

server icon for Kabuki ⎯⎯⎯⎯⎯

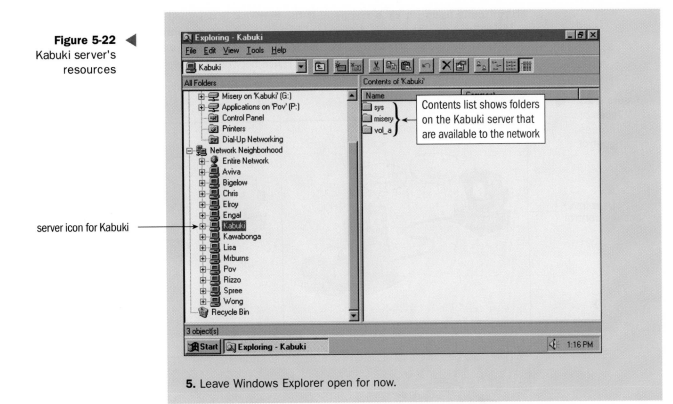

5. Leave Windows Explorer open for now.

Folders placed on servers and made available to the network are called **network folders**. Folders on your own computer are called **local folders**. You can work with the files in a network folder using the same techniques you apply to files in your local folders. For example, you could click one of the files and press Enter, and Windows 95 would open the file in the appropriate software program. However, remember that you might not have the same access rights for files on the network server as you do with your own files. You might not be able to move, modify, or delete files, or you might need to enter a password before you are allowed to manipulate network folders and files.

Windows 95 uses two methods to control access to network resources: share-level access control and user-level access control. With **share-level access control**, you need to enter a specific password for each network resource. Share-level access control is used primarily in peer-to-peer networks in which there is no dedicated server that maintains a list of legitimate users for each resource. If the network is designed around the hierarchical model, access to resources is determined by **user-level access control** in which only certain users have access to a resource. For added security, some networks employ both techniques. Figure 5-23 demonstrates the difference between the two methods.

Figure 5-23 ◀
Types of
access
control

User-level
access control

Share-level
access control

Drive-Mapping

For your software programs to access a file from a network folder, the program needs a way to locate the folder on the network. This location is called the file's **pathname**. Windows 95 pathnames follow the **universal naming convention**, or **UNC**, an accepted set of rules for expressing pathnames, including those for network folders. The general form is \\server\drive\folder\. The path name begins with a double backslash, followed by the name of the server, and then by the drive name and folder names, each separated by a single slash. For example, a pathname of \\Sirius\D\Documentation\ refers to the Documentation folder on drive D of the network server Sirius. If you wanted to access a file named Readme.doc located on this network folder, you would use the complete path, \\Sirius\D\Documentation\Readme.doc. Figure 5-24 shows this file's location on the Sirius server.

Figure 5-24 ◀
Chart of the
path to
\\Sirus\D\
Documentation
\Readme.doc

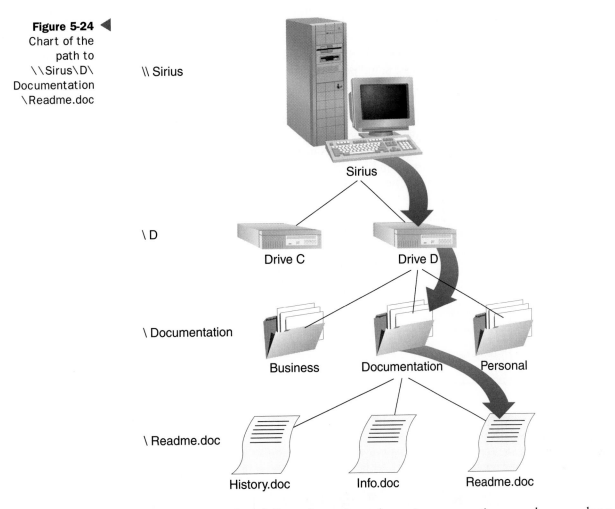

\\ Sirius

\ D

\ Documentation

\ Readme.doc

Pathnames that follow the universal naming convention can be very long and complicated for new users. They have the added disadvantage that Windows 3.1 programs cannot interpret them. To make a file available to a Windows 3.1 program, you must use drive-mapping to refer to the location of files on the network. **Drive-mapping** takes the UNC pathname and represents it with a single drive letter. This makes it appear as if you had an extra hard drive on your computer. For example, if you map the network folder located at \\Sirius\D\Documentation\ to the drive letter F, the pathname becomes simply F:\. The path for the Readme.doc file in that network folder is F:\Readme.doc.

You can usually tell whether a program needs to use drive-mapping by examining your program's Open dialog box. Figure 5-25 shows sample Windows 3.1 and Windows 95 Open dialog boxes. Some programs use different dialog boxes to open files, but they follow the same general structure as those shown. In a Windows 3.1 Open dialog box, you open the Drives list to view folders containing the files you want to access. If the network folder you need to open does not appear, you must use drive-mapping to assign a drive letter to that drive. Only then will the folder appear on the list, and only then will you be able to open a file it contains. On the other hand, the Windows 95 Open dialog box shows all the drives and folders available to your computer, including network drives and folders. To open a network folder with a Windows 95 program, you simply locate it on the network.

Figure 5-25 ◀
Accessing
network folders
in Windows 3.1
and Windows
95 programs

Windows 3.1
Open dialog box

mapped drives

mapped drive letter

UNC path

Windows 95
Open dialog box

drive c on Michela
appears through
Network
Neighborhood
without requiring
drive-mapping

drive C on Michela
server appears as drive
d on your workstation

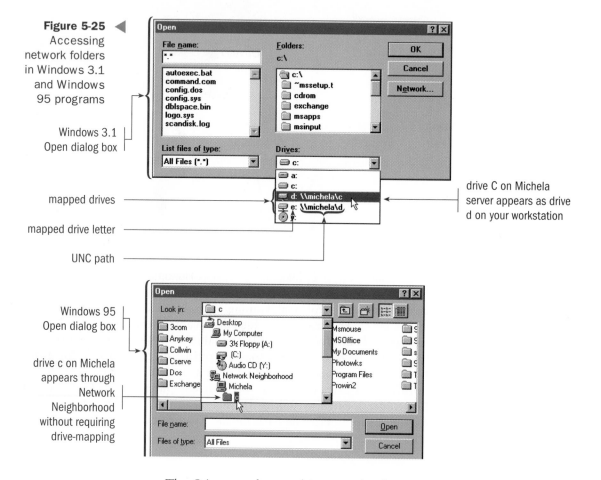

The QA network uses drive-mapping because it runs some Windows 3.1 programs along with their Windows 95 software. Greg decides to show you how to map the vol_a folder located on the Kabuki server to the E drive letter on his computer.

To map a network folder to the drive letter:

1. If Windows Explorer is not open, start Windows Explorer and access the list of folders on a network server. On Greg's workstation, you can still see the vol_a folder in the Folders list.

2. Right-click the icon representing the network folder you want to map to a drive letter. Greg right-clicks the vol_a folder.

3. Click **Map Network Drive** from the menu.

   TROUBLE? Your network administrator might not have given you the ability to do drive-mapping on your computer. If that is the case, review the steps listed here, but do not actually complete them.

4. Click the **Drive** list arrow ▼, then click the drive letter you want to use for the network folder. Greg chooses drive E. In Figure 5-26, the pathname \\Kabuki\vol_a is mapped to the drive letter E.

Figure 5-26 ◀
Mapping a network folder to a drive

network folder you want to map

drive letter you are going to use

UNC path

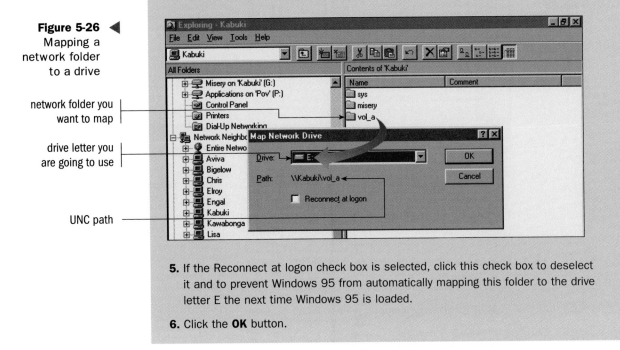

5. If the Reconnect at logon check box is selected, click this check box to deselect it and to prevent Windows 95 from automatically mapping this folder to the drive letter E the next time Windows 95 is loaded.

6. Click the **OK** button.

After a few seconds the Windows Explorer Folders list is updated to reflect the addition of the new drive letter to your system. The new drive letter appears in the list of drives, making it appear as if you had an extra hard drive. Figure 5-27 shows the updated Windows Explorer, displaying the new drive letter, E. Now you can reference files in that folder using either the UNC pathname or the mapped drive letter.

Figure 5-27 ◄
Mapped
network folder
appears under
My Computer

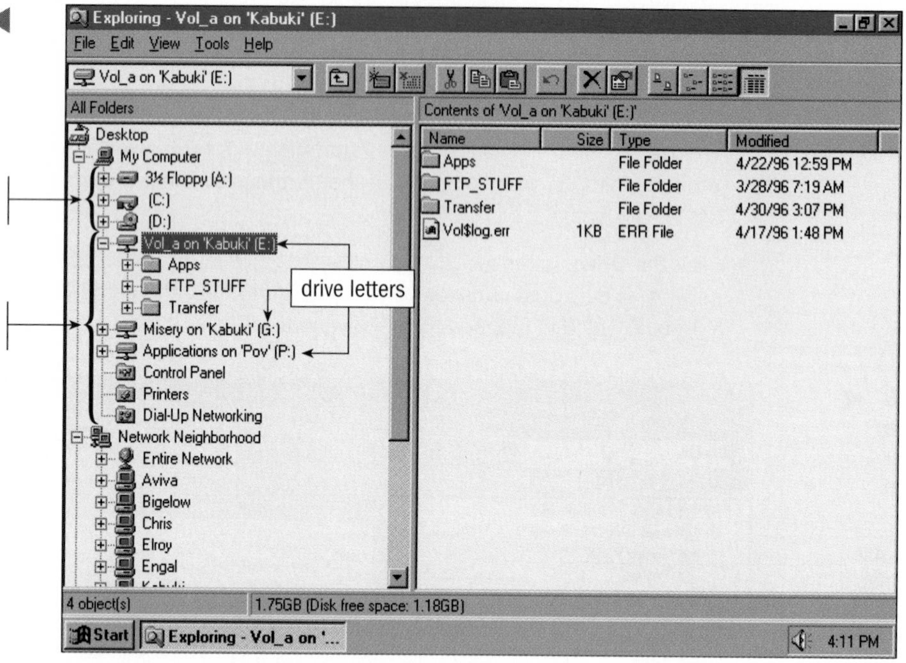

local drives on
My Computer

network folders
mapped as drives
on My Computer

Next Greg wants to show you how to discontinue mapping a network folder. Windows 95 refers to removing drive-mapping as **disconnecting** from the network folder. Disconnecting from the network folder does not remove your access to that folder. You can still access the folder using the UNC pathname through the Network Neighborhood.

To remove drive-mapping from a network folder:

1. Return to Windows Explorer.

2. Right-click the **mapped drive** icon ▣ in the list of drives found under My Computer.

3. Click **Disconnect** from the menu. The mapped drive is removed from the My Computer window.

4. Click the **Close** button ☒ to close Windows Explorer.

Network Printing

Greg would like to show you one other important resource on the network: the network printer. A **network printer** is a printer that handles printing jobs for network users. By contrast, a **local printer** is one that is connected directly to your computer and is not shared with the network. The operation of the network printer is managed by a server called a **print server**. As shown in Figure 5-28, when a user wants to print a document, Windows 95 sends the information needed to print the document to the network print queue located on the print server. A **network print queue** keeps track of the order in which print jobs are received and sends them, in order, to the network printer.

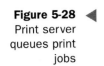

Figure 5-28 ◀
Print server
queues print
jobs

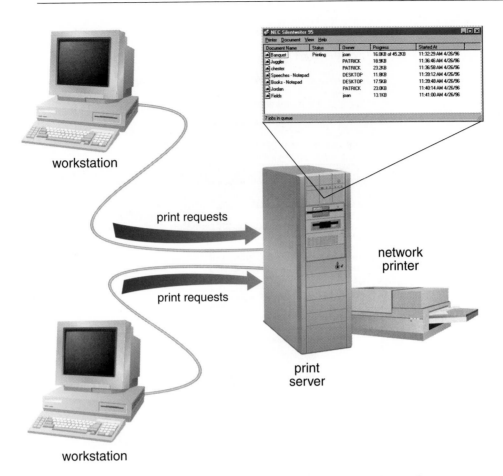

One of the printers available on the QA network is a color printer. It is usually reserved for final reports and special projects. Greg tells you that you can access this printer using the same techniques you use to access a local printer. Windows 95 lists all available printers, both local and network, in the same Print dialog box. To send a print job to a network printer, you simply select the printer name from the Name list, as shown in Figure 5-29.

Figure 5-29 ◀
Selecting a
network printer

Setting up your workstation to access the printer is a job usually reserved for your network administrator. However, you will need to know where on the network the printer server is located, if for no other reason than to know where to go to pick up your print jobs. Knowing this information is also helpful if you run into problems with a print job and need to track down the print server handling the request. Greg shows you how to determine the location of the color printer on the network.

To learn the location of a network printer:

1. Click the **Start** button, point to **Settings**, then click **Printers**.

2. Right-click the **network printer** then click **Properties**.

   TROUBLE? If you aren't sure which printer is a network printer, ask your instructor or network administrator.

3. Greg opens the property sheet for a printer named Color Printer. See Figure 5-30.

Figure 5-30 ◀
Accessing
printer
properties

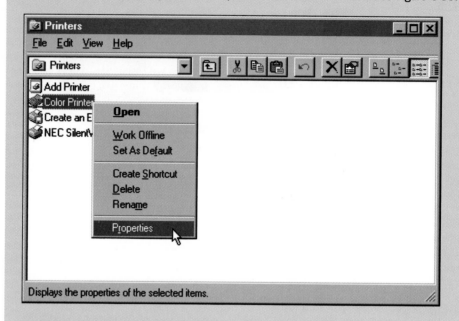

4. Click the **Details** sheet tab. The Port list box in the Details dialog sheet shown in Figure 5-31 displays the path to the network server. The location of the color printer on the QA network is \\Pov\deskjet.

Figure 5-31 ◀
Viewing the
location of a
network printer

port is path to ┐
network server ┘

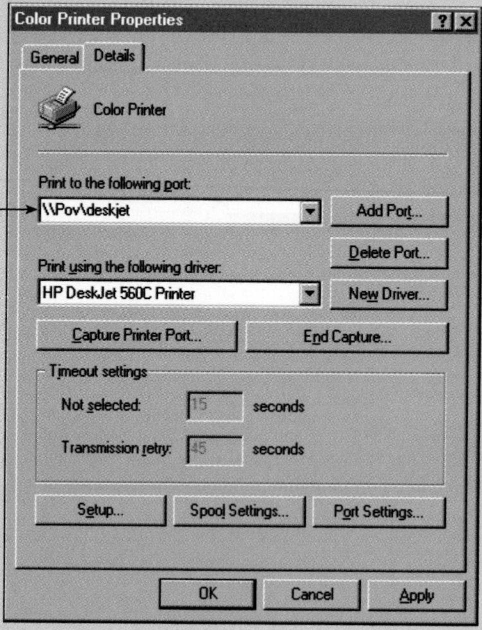

5. Click the **Cancel** button to close the Printer Properties dialog box without saving any changes you may have inadvertently made.

6. Click the **Close** button ☒ to close the Printers window.

Note that the path information is included in the Port list box on the printer's property sheet. Recall that a port connects you to an external device such as a modem or a printer. In this case, the port is the connection over the network to the network printer. The path to the network printer follows the same form as pathnames for network folders. The general format is \\server\printer. The pathname \\Pov\deskjet means that the printer is connected to the Pov server with the name deskjet. With this information, you know where to start if you're having problems printing to the color printer.

Network Troubleshooting

Occasionally, Greg explains, you will have problems working with the network. While you might be tempted to hunt down QA's network administrator to handle your problem, you should first try to solve the problem yourself. Windows 95 includes a Help tool called the Network Troubleshooter to help you diagnose the problem and, if possible, correct it. The Network Troubleshooter works in much the same way as the Print Troubleshooter you worked with earlier.

As a test, Greg asks what you would do if you were having problems connecting to a network server. You can see the list of resources offered by the server, but are unable to open any of the folders. Greg suggests you use the Network Troubleshooter to find one possible answer.

To start the Network Troubleshooter:

1. Click the **Start** button then click **Help**.

2. Click the **Contents** sheet tab.

3. Click **Troubleshooting** then press the **Enter** key.

4. Click **If you have trouble using the network**, then click the **Display** button.

5. Click the button to the left of the third option, "I can't connect to a specific computer." See Figure 5-32.

Figure 5-32 ◀
Network
Troubleshooter

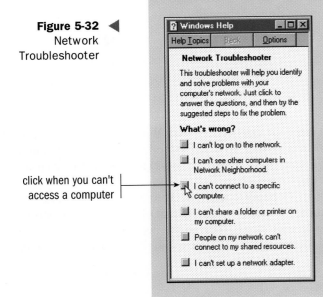

click when you can't access a computer

6. Click the button to the left of "I can view the shared resources but I can't connect to them." The Troubleshooter displays the information shown in Figure 5-33.

Figure 5-33
Possible
solution

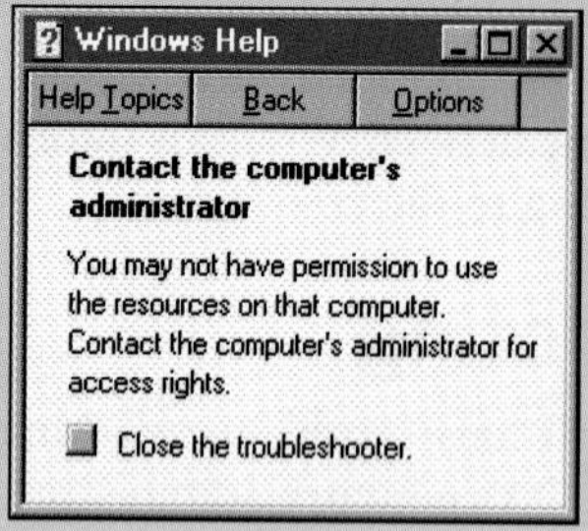

According to the Network Troubleshooter, one reason that you might not be able to use a network resource is because you don't have permission to do so. By using the Troubleshooter you have saved yourself a potentially embarrassing conversation with your very busy network administrator.

Quick Check

1. What is a local folder and what is a network folder?

2. What is share-level access control? In which network model would it usually be used?

3. What is user-level access control? In which network model would it most likely be used?

4. What is the pathname for a file named Intro.txt that is located in the Work folder on the C drive of the network server Sales?

5. Under what circumstances must you use drive-mapping?

6. What is the pathname for a printer named Work that is located on the QA network server?

End Note

As Greg concludes your training on using the QA network with Windows 95, the network administrator stops by. She has finished setting up a workstation for you and creating your network account. Because of a temporary hardware shortage, you will be sharing your workstation with a few other employees.

The administrator gives you a slip of paper containing your user information. She reminds you to keep your password confidential, explaining that QA has had some problems in the past with people getting unauthorized access to the network.

When she leaves, you thank Greg for taking the time to explain the QA network to you.

Tutorial Assignments

1. Diagramming Your Network One way to understand your network is to sketch a diagram of the network layout. Figure 5-34 shows a sample schematic drawing. Create a schematic drawing of the network you use. Identify the servers and the resources they share. If there is a large number of workstations on your network, show only a few of them, identifying them by their node names. Talk to your network administrator or instructor to get the information you need.

Figure 5-34 ◀

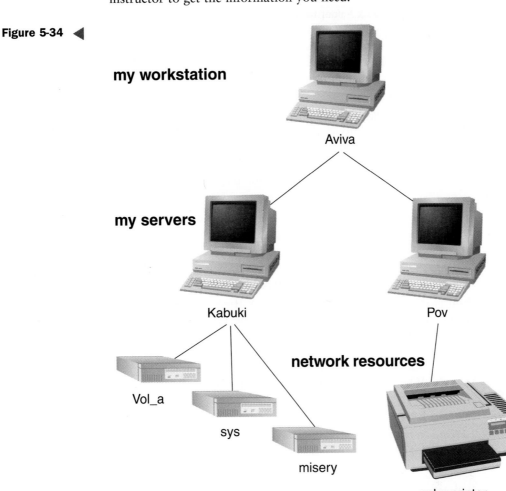

my workstation

Aviva

my servers

Kabuki

Pov

Vol_a

sys

misery

network resources

color printer

2. Reporting Your Network Configuration Write a description of your network. Include the following information in your report:
  a. The number of nodes on the network
  b. The network model (peer-to-peer, hierarchical, or mixed)
  c. The network operating system
  d. The network standard
  e. The communications protocol used

3. Password Protection Part of creating good passwords is understanding how password protection can be overcome by people trying to break into a system. Read books, magazines, or newspapers to learn the methods used to bypass password protection. Write a one-page report summarizing these techniques and include some suggestions for how you would protect yourself against them.

Note to Instructor: For your students to complete Tutorial Assignment 4, you must first place a file onto a network server for them to retrieve.

4. Transferring a File from the Network Folder Your instructor has placed a file on a network folder. With the filename and name of the folder given to you by your instructor, use Windows Explorer to copy the file to your Student Disk. Print a copy of the file's contents.

Note to Instructor: For your students to complete Tutorial Assignment 5, you must indicate to which network folder they should apply drive-mapping.

5. Mapping a Network Folder to a Drive Letter You can map network folders from within the Network Neighborhood window. Open the Network Neighborhood window and select a network folder indicated by your instructor. Map the folder to the driver letter U. Open the My Computer window on your desktop to verify that the network folder has been mapped to drive U. Print an image of the My Computer window. Remove the drive-mapping.

6. Learning About Mail Servers One of the uses of a network server is electronic mail. Servers that handle electronic mail are called "mail servers." Investigate the properties of your network to answer the following questions about your mail server:
   a. Which server handles your mail messages?
   b. In what network folder are mail messages stored?
   c. What client program do you use to retrieve your mail messages from the server?

Note to Instructor: If the network your students work on is not connected to the Internet, they will not be able to complete parts a and b of Tutorial Assignment 7.

7. Internet Connections Many university computers are now connected to the Internet. The Internet uses the TCP/IP communications protocol. Try to discover whether your computer is connected to the Internet by examining whether the TCP/IP protocol component is installed. Prove your findings by creating a printout of the Network Properties dialog box for your computer. If you decide your computer is connected to the Internet, examine the properties for the TCP/IP protocol component and answer the following questions:
   a. What is your computer's IP address? (This is the address that other Internet nodes use to uniquely identify your computer.)
   b. What is the domain for your node? (*Hint:* Look in the DNS Configuration property sheet in the TCP/IP Properties dialog box. The domain is the name for your network.)

Note to Instructor: To complete Tutorial Assignment 8, you must give your students the name of the server to find.

8. Finding a Computer on the Network You can use the Windows 95 Find command to find network servers as well as files. To access the Find Computer command, click the Start button, point to the Find command, then click Computer to open the Find Computer dialog box. Enter the name of the network server given to you by your instructor, and click the Find Now button. Print the Find Computer window.

9. Network Troubleshooting A friend is having trouble using the network. He is trying to locate the network server, but he can't find it when he looks through the Network Neighborhood window. Nor does it appear when he uses the Find Computer command. Use the Network Troubleshooter to explain one possible reason for this problem.

Disk Maintenance

OBJECTIVES

In this tutorial you will:

■ Scan a disk for errors using the ScanDisk accessory

■ Defragment a disk using the Disk Defragmenter accessory

■ Learn how to compress a disk using the DriveSpace accessory

■ Place a folder on your computer's hard drive and back it up using Backup

■ Restore a backed up file

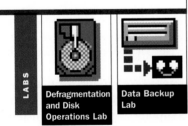

LABS
Defragmentation and Disk Operations Lab
Data Backup Lab

U.S. Patent and Trademark Office

CASE The United States Patent and Trademark Office (PTO) is a federal bureau under the Department of Commerce that examines and issues patents and trademarks for new inventions and discoveries. You are just starting a summer internship in the Office of Patent Quality Review. Your supervisor has organized an orientation program for you and the other interns, including a three-day seminar on learning to use Windows 95—the operating system on the computers at your office.

The third day of the seminar covers disk maintenance. Your instructor, Phil Adams, explains that **disk maintenance** involves checking your disks regularly for errors and ensuring that the data on the disks is efficiently stored and protected. Windows 95 provides several accessories that help you maintain the data on your disks. Phil says that today you will learn about scanning your disk for errors, defragmenting your disk to improve its efficiency, compressing your disk to make more space available, and backing up your data.

Phil explains that the Windows 95 disk maintenance accessories are most often used to maintain hard disks, which usually contain permanent data and are expensive to replace. Floppy disks, on the other hand, usually are used for temporary data storage, and if they are damaged they can be replaced easily and inexpensively. For the purposes of the seminar, however, Phil explains that you will practice disk maintenance techniques on floppy disks rather than hard disks, because access to the hard disks on the seminar lab computers is limited and disk maintenance procedures take much longer on a hard disk than on a floppy disk.

In this session you will learn how to improve the performance of your disks by scanning and defragmenting them. You'll also learn how you might compress a disk if you want more space. You might not be able to perform all the steps in this tutorial in your computer lab, so the steps include notes when that might be the case. Take special note of the information outside of the steps, because it will help you learn about procedures even when you can't perform them.

Windows 95 Disk Maintenance Accessories

Phil begins by talking about how disk maintenance is a critical part of owning a computer. Individuals and businesses are relying more and more on computers and the data they contain. If a computer's hard disk fails, it can be disastrous for some businesses. Backing up data is, of course, the primary way to prevent such a disaster, as you'll see in Session 6.2. But Windows 95 helps you prevent disk failure from occuring in the first place by providing some valuable disk maintenance accessories. In this tutorial, you'll learn about the four disk maintenance accessories shown in Figure 6-1.

Figure 6-1
Disk maintenance accessories

Accessory	Purpose
Backup	Creates a backup copy of your files
Disk Defragmenter	Restructures the files on your disk to maximize efficiency and to prevent future problems
DriveSpace	Compresses the data on your disk
ScanDisk	Checks a disk for errors and repairs some disk problems

Phil explains that if you have your own computer or are responsible for maintaining other people's computers, you should use these accessories as part of a scheduled comprehensive disk maintenance plan. You should begin a "cycle" of disk maintenance with a "spring cleaning," where you delete old or unneeded files. You then scan each disk on your computer to locate and repair errors. Then you defragment each disk so that it is organized most efficiently. Finally, you back up all the files on your computer. How often such a cycle occurs depends on how much you use your computer. If you are responsible for maintaining a computer that is used all day long, you might want to run these maintenance procedures monthly, weekly, or even daily. If, on the other hand, you use your computer more infrequently—if, for example, it is a home computer that you use only for correspondence, games, and maintaining your checkbook—you might not need to run disk maintenance procedures more than once every few months.

Scanning a Disk for Errors

Sections of the magnetic surface of a disk sometimes get damaged. Regularly scanning your disks for errors can be an effective way to head off potential problems that would make data inaccessible. The Windows 95 ScanDisk accessory not only locates errors on a disk but also attempts to repair them, or at least mark the defective portions of the disk so that the operating system won't attempt to store data there.

To understand what errors ScanDisk is looking for and how it repairs them, you need to learn a little bit about the structure of a disk. When you format a disk such as a floppy disk, a formatting program divides the disk into storage compartments. First it creates a series of rings, called **tracks**, around the circumference of the disk. Then it divides the tracks into equal parts, like pieces of pie, to form **sectors**, as shown in Figure 6-2.

Figure 6-2 ◀
A formatted disk

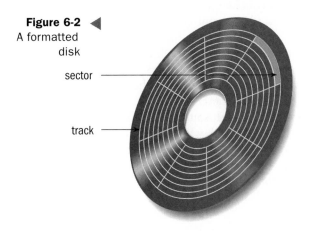

sector

track

The number of sectors and tracks depends on the size of the disk. A high-density disk, like your Student Disk, stores data on both sides of the disk. Each side has 80 tracks, and each track is divided into 18 sectors. Each sector can hold 512 bytes, for a total of 1,474,560 bytes or 1.44 MB (1,024 bytes make a megabyte).

Although the physical surface of a disk is made of tracks and sectors, a file is stored in clusters. A **cluster**, also called an **allocation unit**, is one or more sectors of storage space—it represents the minimum amount of space that an operating system reserves when saving the contents of a file to a disk. Most files are larger than 512 bytes. Therefore, a file might be stored in more than one cluster. Figure 6-3 shows a file that takes up four clusters on an otherwise empty disk.

Figure 6-3 ◀
File stored in clusters

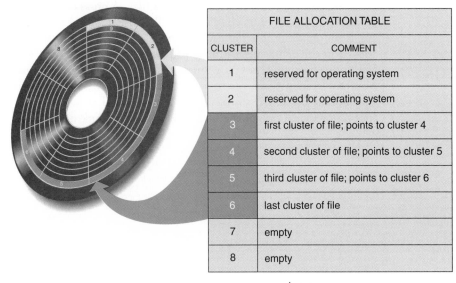

FILE ALLOCATION TABLE	
CLUSTER	COMMENT
1	reserved for operating system
2	reserved for operating system
3	first cluster of file; points to cluster 4
4	second cluster of file; points to cluster 5
5	third cluster of file; points to cluster 6
6	last cluster of file
7	empty
8	empty

...and so on

Each cluster is identified by a unique number; the first two clusters, shown in yellow, are reserved by the operating system. Windows 95 maintains a **file allocation table** (or **FAT**) on each disk that lists the clusters on the disk and records the status of each cluster: whether it is occupied (and by which file), available, or defective. Each cluster in a file "remembers" its order in the chain of clusters—and each cluster points to the next one until the last cluster, which marks the end of the file.

You can specify whether you want ScanDisk to check the physical surface of the disk, the files, or both the surface and the files. ScanDisk checks the disk surface by looking for damaged sectors. If it finds any, it marks those sectors and prevents data from being stored there. A damaged sector is called a **bad sector**.

ScanDisk checks the files on a disk by comparing the clusters on a disk to the FAT. It looks specifically for lost clusters and cross-linked files. A **lost cluster** is a cluster that contains data that the FAT can't match to a file. If your computer suffers a power surge, a power failure, or any problem that locks it up, the operating system might lose one or more clusters from a file that was open when the problem occured, and you might lose the data stored in those clusters. The presence of lost clusters on a disk is not damaging, but lost clusters do take up valuable space, and if there are too many of them, the confusion of clusters on your disk might lead to further errors. ScanDisk identifies lost clusters and either deletes them or saves them to a new file. Although sometimes you recover lost data from such a file, more often you won't be able to do much with the file and should simply delete it. Figure 6-4 shows how ScanDisk repairs lost cluster problems on a floppy disk.

Figure 6-4 ◀
Reparing lost clusters

You can set ScanDisk to delete or save these files; ScanDisk then marks these sectors as empty

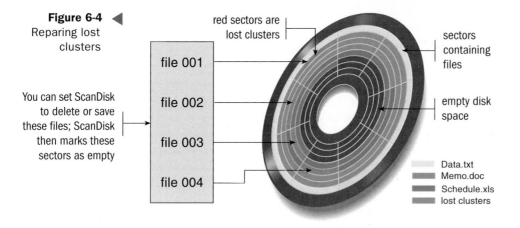

ScanDisk also checks for cross-linked files. A **cross-linked file** contains at least one cluster that belongs to more than one file. Because a cluster should be occupied by data coming from only one file, the FAT becomes confused about which clusters belong to which files. You can tell ScanDisk how you want it to handle such a file—by deleting it, copying it, or ignoring it. If you want to maintain the integrity of your files, it's best to allow ScanDisk to copy each file to a new location on the disk and remove the original files so they are no longer cross linked. This procedure often saves both files, although you might lose a portion of one of the files where the cross link occured.

REFERENCE window

USING SCANDISK

- Click the Start button, point to Programs, point to Accessories, point to System Tools, then click ScanDisk.
- Click the disk you want to scan.
- Click the Start button.

A Lists drives that can contain disks available for scanning—does not include CD-ROM drives or network drives.

B Checks only the file and folder structure for errors.

C Checks the file and folder structure and the disk's physical surface for errors; click Options to specify which parts of the disk's physical surface to scan.

D Automatically repairs errors it finds; click Advanced to specify how ScanDisk should fix the errors.

E Starts scanning the disk.

F Closes ScanDisk without initiating a scan.

G Lets you specify whether to display a scan summary or log file, how it should fix cross-linked files and lost clusters, and whether it should check invalid file names and dates.

H Lets you specify which parts of the disk's physical surface to scan—system and data, system only, data only—and lets you specify repair options.

Phil announces that the first thing he wants you to do is scan your disk for errors. He reminds you that although you'll be performing the scan on a floppy disk, this procedure is most useful for maintaining a hard disk.

To start ScanDisk:

1. Close all open programs—if a program is in use while a disk is being scanned, you could lose data.

2. Place your Student Disk in drive A. See the "Read This Before You Begin" page to make sure you are using the correct disk for this tutorial.

   TROUBLE? If your 3½-inch disk drive is B, place your Student Disk in that drive instead, and for the rest of this tutorial substitute drive B wherever you see drive A.

3. Click the **Start** button, point to **Programs**, point to **Accessories**, then point to **System Tools**.

4. Click **ScanDisk**. The ScanDisk dialog box opens. See Figure 6-5.

TROUBLE? If ScanDisk appears as an option on the menu, then ScanDisk is installed on your computer and you can proceed. If ScanDisk does not appear, then you cannot complete this session until ScanDisk is installed. Check with your instructor or technical support person for directions.

Figure 6-5 ◄
ScanDisk
dialog box

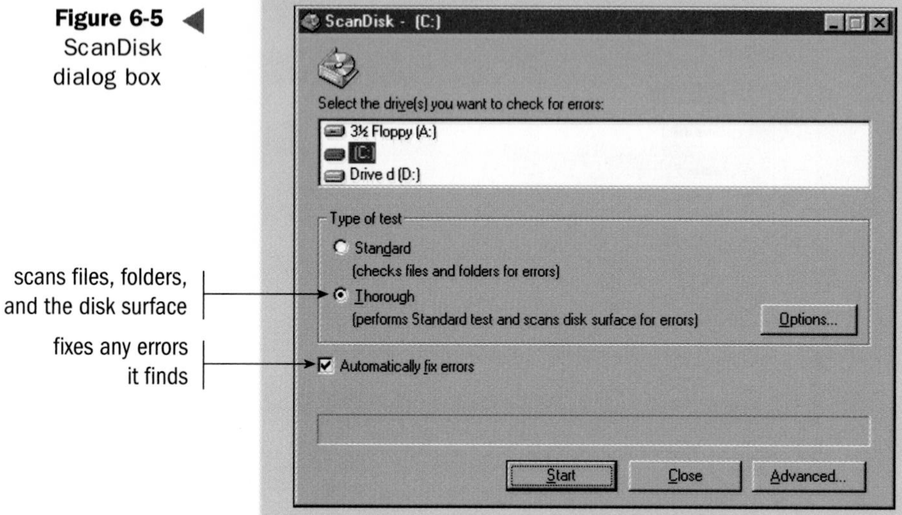

scans files, folders,
and the disk surface

fixes any errors
it finds

Two test-type options appear: Standard and Thorough. You look at the options, and decide to perform a Thorough test so ScanDisk will check both the files and the surface of the disk. Phil tells you that you should always try to use the Thorough scan unless you're in a hurry. A Standard scan is quicker—and useful when you want to make sure the file structure and filenames are okay but you aren't worried about the disk surface.

To scan your Student Disk for errors:

1. Click **3½ Floppy (A:)**.

2. If necessary, click the **Thorough** radio button.

3. If necessary, click the **Automatically fix errors** check box so it is selected.

4. Click the **Start** button. ScanDisk displays a status bar that tells you which particular cluster is currently being examined. See Figure 6-6. Your status bar might show different numbers.

Figure 6-6 ◀
Progress of
disk scan

area being scanned ─────

progress of scan ─────

cluster being
scanned

total clusters on disk
(your number might
be different)

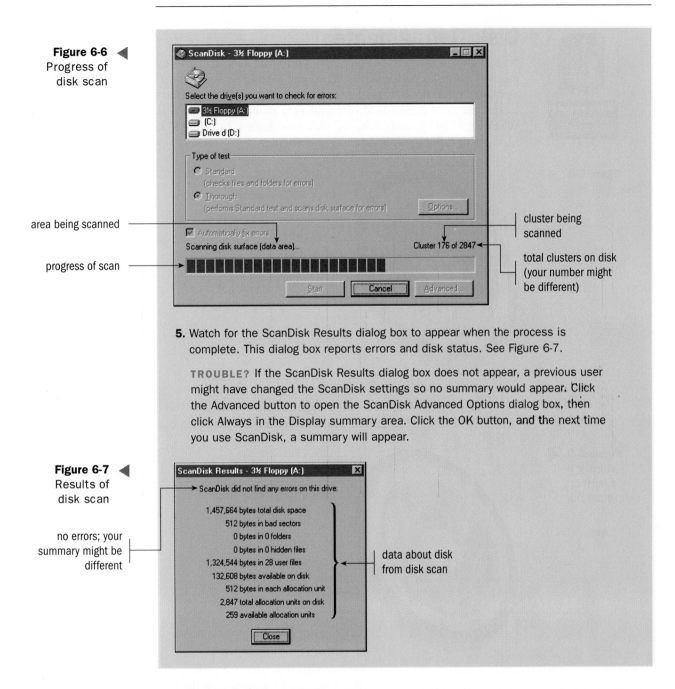

5. Watch for the ScanDisk Results dialog box to appear when the process is complete. This dialog box reports errors and disk status. See Figure 6-7.

TROUBLE? If the ScanDisk Results dialog box does not appear, a previous user might have changed the ScanDisk settings so no summary would appear. Click the Advanced button to open the ScanDisk Advanced Options dialog box, then click Always in the Display summary area. Click the OK button, and the next time you use ScanDisk, a summary will appear.

Figure 6-7 ◀
Results of
disk scan

no errors; your
summary might be
different

data about disk
from disk scan

Scanning a floppy disk takes a few minutes. However, scanning a hard disk could take an hour or more, depending on the disk size and whether you've chosen the Thorough scan option. When ScanDisk is finished, it opens the ScanDisk Results dialog box, which reports on the status of the disk. ScanDisk reports that for the disk in Figure 6-7, there were no errors. If there are errors on your disk, ScanDisk describes them.

To close ScanDisk:

1. Click the **Close** button to close the ScanDisk Results dialog box.

2. Click the **Close** button to close the ScanDisk dialog box.

Defragmentation and Disk Operations

Disk Defragmenter ✓

Now that you've corrected any errors on your disk, you can use Disk Defragmenter to improve the disk's performance. When you save a file, Windows 95 puts as much of the file as it can fit into the first available cluster. If the file won't fit into one cluster, Windows 95 locates the next available cluster and puts more of the file in it. The file is saved once Windows 95 has placed all the file data into clusters. In Figure 6-8, you have just saved two files to a new floppy disk: Address and Recipes.

Figure 6-8 ◀
Disk with two
files

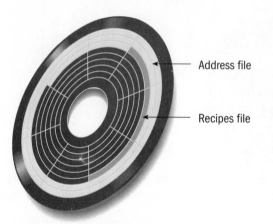

Address file

Recipes file

As you create and save new files, more clusters are used. If you delete a file or two, those clusters are freed. In Figure 6-9, you have saved a new file, Memo, and then deleted Recipes.

Figure 6-9 ◀
Adding a
file, then
deleting a file

Address file

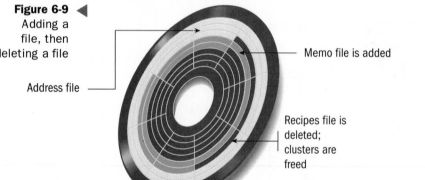

Memo file is added

Recipes file is
deleted;
clusters are
freed

The next time you save a file, Windows 95 searches for the first available cluster, which is now between two files. Figure 6-10 shows what happens when you save a fourth file, Schedule. It is saved to clusters that are not adjacent.

Figure 6-10 ◀
Adding a new
file in
fragmented
clusters

Address file

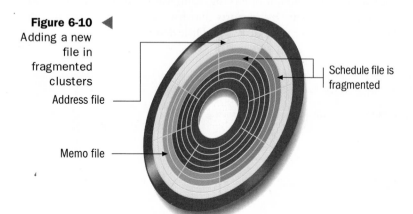

Schedule file is
fragmented

Memo file

The more files you save and delete, the more scattered the clusters for a file become. A disk that contains files whose clusters are not next to each other is said to be **fragmented**. The more fragmented the disk, the longer Windows 95 takes to retrieve the file, and the more likely you are to have problems with the file. Whenever a disk has been used for a long time, it's a good idea to defragment it. **Defragmenting** rearranges the files on the disk so they each occupy adjacent clusters. Figure 6-11 shows a fragmented disk. When a program tries to access a file on this disk, file retrieved takes longer than necessary because the program must locate clusters that aren't adjacent.

Figure 6-11 ◀
Fragmented files

next file to be saved will use these clusters

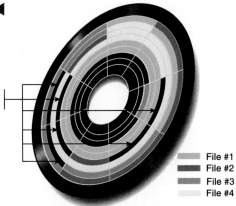

File #1
File #2
File #3
File #4

3.I NOTE

Disk Defragmenter replaces the DOS DEFRAG command available in Windows 3.1.

Before you begin defragmenting a disk, make sure your data is backed up. If your computer experiences a power loss while one of its disks is being defragmented, you could lose valuable data.

REFERENCE
window

DEFRAGMENTING A DISK

- Click the Start button, point to Programs, point to Accessories, point to System Tools, then click Disk Defragmenter.
- Click the drive list arrow, then click the drive you want to defragment.
- Click the OK button, then click the Start button.

Disk Defragmenter ? X

Drive C is 6 % fragmented.

You don't need to defragment this drive now. If you want to defragment it anyway, click Start.

| Start | Select Drive | Advanced... | Exit |

A   **B**   **C**   **D**

A Start defragmenting the disk.

B Select a different disk to defragment.

C Access advanced options that let you specify a defragmentation method, scan a disk before starting the defragmentation process, and save advanced settings.

D Exit without defragmenting the disk.

You're ready to defragment your disk. Phil tells you that he can't guarantee that your disk needs defragmenting. It's possible that you'll go through the defragment procedure but Windows 95 won't have to make any changes because your disk is not fragmented. If this is the case with your disk, you might not be able to perform all the steps in this section.

To start Disk Defragmenter:

1. Close all open programs to prevent losing data.

2. Click the **Start** button, point to **Programs**, point to **Accessories**, point to **System Tools**, then click **Disk Defragmenter**.

3. Click the drive list arrow, then click **3½-Floppy (A:)**.

4. Click the **OK** button. The Disk Defragmenter dialog box opens. See Figure 6-12.

   TROUBLE? If your disk is not seriously fragmented, the dialog box tells you that you don't have to defragment the disk. Normally you would cancel the procedure, but in this case you are learning how the Disk Defragmenter works, so continue with the next set of steps despite the message.

Figure 6-12 ◄
Defragmenting disk in drive A

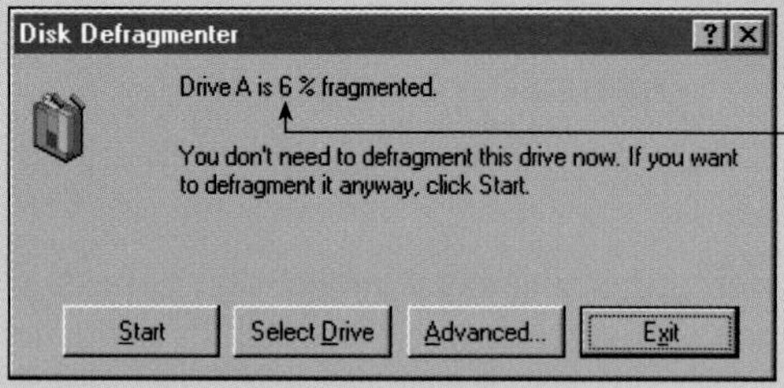

If your disk is 0% fragmented, continue with the procedure anyway

Before you click the Start button to defragment the disk, read through the rest of this section so you know what to expect. Once the defragmentation process begins, you are prompted to choose certain options. If you don't know what's happening ahead of time, you might miss the chance to view the defragmentation process.

To begin the defragmentation process:

1. Click the **Start** button in the Disk Defragmenter dialog box.

2. Click the **Show Details** button. The Disk Defragmenter shows the status of each cluster on your disk. See Figure 6-13.

   TROUBLE? If your disk is not fragmented, the process might go so quickly that you don't get an opportunity to view details. In that case, Windows 95 will ask if you want to quit Disk Defragmenter. Click the Yes button, then read through the rest of the steps.

Figure 6-13
Status of
clusters on disk

defragmented clusters

clusters being
rearranged

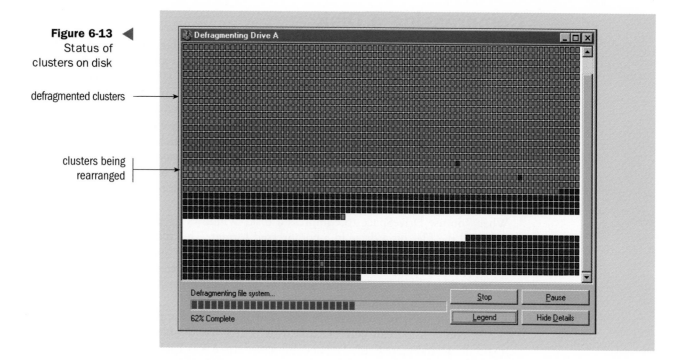

Figure 6-13 shows a map of the clusters on a disk that is being defragmented (each square represents a cluster). The blue clusters on the top have already been defragmented. Disk Defragmenter is currently rearranging the red clusters, and marking the other clusters for relocation to another part of the disk. You might see squares colored differently from those shown in Figure 6-13. Phil explains that you can interpret the squares by opening the defragment legend. You decide to do so.

To display the legend and end the defragmentation process:

1. Click the **Legend** button to display information on the meaning of each square's pattern or color. See Figure 6-14.

Figure 6-14
Interpreting the
defragmenta-
tion process

Defrag Legend ☒

☐ Optimized (defragmented) data
   Unoptimized data that:
   ☐ Belongs at beginning of drive
   ☐ Belongs in middle of drive
   ■ Belongs at end of drive

☐ Free space
☐ Data that will not be moved
☐ Bad (damaged) area of the disk
☐ Data that's currently being read
☐ Data that's currently being written

Each box represents one disk cluster.

[Close]

2. Watch the clusters as they are reordered, and compare the squares you see to those in the legend.

3. Click the **Close** button.

4. Wait until the defragmentation process is complete. This can take several minutes.

5. Click the **Yes** button when the defragmentation process finishes.

6. If necessary, click the **Close** button to close Disk Defragmenter.

Compressing a Disk

Phil tells you that the two accessories you've worked with so far are intended to correct and prevent disk problems. Now you're going to learn about an accessory that makes more space available on your disk. Most computer owners at one time or another run out of disk space. Sometimes the problem is easy to solve—you simply delete unneeded files. Other times, however, the disk space problem is more serious, and you are faced with the decision to either purchase a second hard disk or remove some programs and files. Windows 95 includes a solution: the DriveSpace accessory, which uses data compression to compact the files on a disk so they take less room. **Data compression** is the process by which a program like DriveSpace reduces the amount of space a file occupies on a storage medium. A 163 KB document, for example, could be compressed so that it requires only 54 KB on the disk.

When you use DriveSpace to compress a disk, Windows 95 creates a single file that contains all the files on a drive in a compressed format. This file is called a **compressed volume file**, or **CVF**. Windows 95 renames drive A as drive H and displays the CVF on drive H, called a **host drive**. Windows 95 then displays the *contents* of the CVF under the drive letter, A. This way, you can continue to work with drive A without ever realizing that you are really working with the CVF.

Because your files are now compressed, your floppy drive appears to be much larger. Typically, compression can make it appear as if disk has doubled in size. Consider the example shown in Figure 6-15. The uncompressed drive A is 1.44 MB in size. DriveSpace places the files in the compressed volume file. Drive A displays the contents of the CVF, and it appears to be a 2.88 MB drive.

Figure 6-15 ◀
File
compression

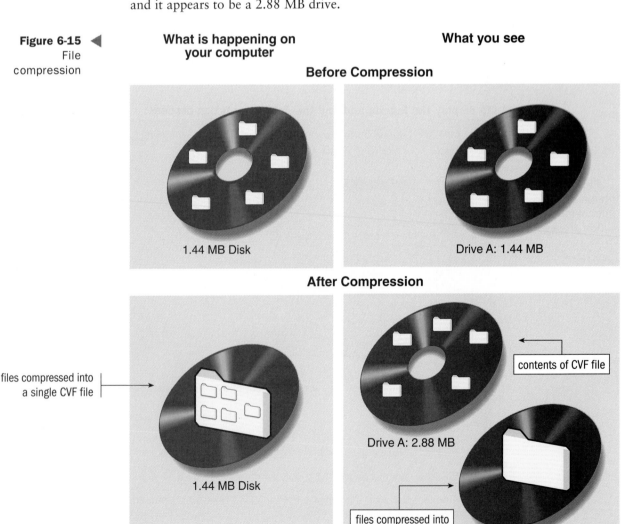

What is happening on your computer

What you see

Before Compression

1.44 MB Disk

Drive A: 1.44 MB

After Compression

files compressed into a single CVF file →

1.44 MB Disk

contents of CVF file

Drive A: 2.88 MB

files compressed into a single CVF file

Drive H: 1.44 MB

When you need to use a file, Windows 95 automatically retrieves and uncompresses the file from within the CVF without your even realizing it. Depending on your system, you might notice an increase in the time it takes to access your files as Windows 95 decompresses them. For this reason, computer users will sometimes shy away from using compressed disks unless they really need the extra space. When you save a file to a compressed disk, Windows 95 compresses the file and adds it to the CVF.

DriveSpace can compress drives up to 512 MB in size. If you want to compress a larger disk, you need a different file compression accessory. Microsoft offers a separate Windows 95 program called Microsoft Plus! that contains a fuller-featured DriveSpace disk compression accessory that can handle disks up to 2 G in size.

Phil explains that in lab settings, including the seminar lab, you might not have access rights to compress a disk, so you won't actually compress a disk in this seminar. However, it's a good skill to master, especially if you own your own computer.

REFERENCE window

COMPRESSING DATA ON A DISK

- Click the Start button, point to Programs, point to Accessories, point to System Tools, then click DriveSpace.
- Click the drive containing the disk you want to compress.
- Click Drive then click Compress.
- Click the Start button. Make sure you have several minutes to spare before you begin disk compression.
- Click Compress Now.
- Click the Close button twice when the process is complete.

When you start DriveSpace, it first checks your disk for errors and automatically defragments it. It then prepares the CVF. Even for a floppy disk, this takes time. When the process is complete, the Compress a Drive dialog box appears and shows you the free space you gained. See Figure 6-16.

Figure 6-16 ◀
Disk before and after compression

before compression ——→

→ after compression

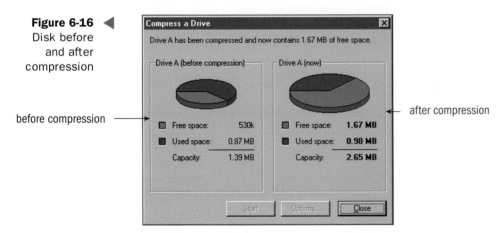

When you close the Compress a Drive dialog box, the DriveSpace window shows two drives, one for the CVF file (which appears to you as drive A) and one for the original drive A, renamed drive H. See Figure 6-17.

Figure 6-17 ◄
DriveSpace
window

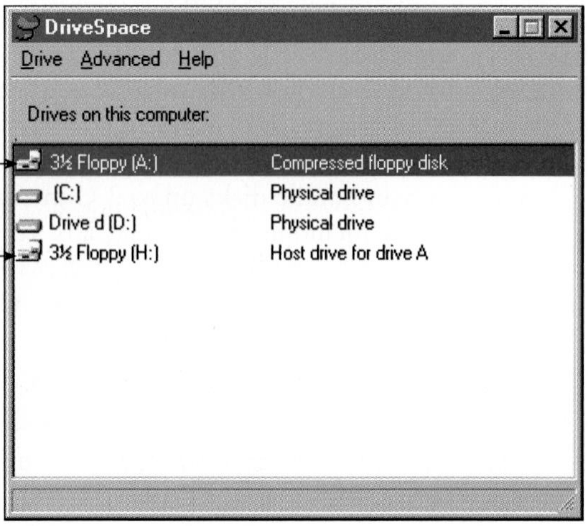

CVF appears
as drive A

drive A is renamed
drive H, the host drive

```
┌──────────────────────────────────────────────────────────┐
│ 🖳 DriveSpace                                    _ □ ✕     │
├──────────────────────────────────────────────────────────┤
│ Drive   Advanced   Help                                    │
│                                                            │
│ Drives on this computer:                                   │
│ ┌────────────────────────────────────────────────────┐    │
│ │ 💾 3½ Floppy (A:)        Compressed floppy disk     │    │
│ │ 💿 (C:)                  Physical drive             │    │
│ │ 💿 Drive d (D:)          Physical drive             │    │
│ │ 💾 3½ Floppy (H:)        Host drive for drive A      │    │
│ │                                                     │    │
│ └────────────────────────────────────────────────────┘    │
└──────────────────────────────────────────────────────────┘
```

Uncompressing a Disk

Phil tells you that because a compressed disk takes longer to access, many users choose to leave their disks compressed only when they really need the space. Uncompressing a disk reverses the compression process: it expands the files in the CVF back to their normal size, removes all traces of the CVF, and removes references to drive H from your computer.

REFERENCE window	**UNCOMPRESSING FILES ON A DISK**
	▪ Start DriveSpace, then click the drive containing the disk you want to uncompress. ▪ Click Drive, then click Uncompress. ▪ Click the Start button. ▪ Click the Uncompress Now button. When Windows 95 asks if you want to remove the compression driver, click No to leave the driver in place for other users. ▪ Click Close twice.

Quick Check

1. Why are the techniques you are learning in this tutorial especially important for hard disks?

2. Name two things you should do regularly to maintain peak disk performance.

3. What is a cluster?

4. What is the purpose of the file allocation table?

5. True or false: Windows 95 always stores a file in adjacent clusters.

6. How does a disk become fragmented?

7. If you were to compress a disk in drive A, a new drive would appear in My Computer: drive H. What is drive H?

8. If you want to open a file from a compressed disk in drive A, should you open drive A or drive H?

SESSION

6.2

In this session you'll learn how to use Backup to protect your data. You'll create and save a "file set" that specifies what files you want to back up. Next you'll create the "backup set" that stores a copy of the files you want to back up. Finally, you'll restore a file from a backup set.

Backup disks usually are created from data saved on a hard drive. Therefore, this session poses some unique problems for students working in a computer lab, because usually when you're working in a lab you must save all your data on a floppy disk. You can't use Backup to back up data from one floppy disk to another using the same drive. So in this tutorial you must first place some data on the hard disk, which you can then back up. You will save your backups on a blank disk, not your Student Disk, so bring a 3½-inch blank, formatted disk to the computer lab.

Read the conceptual material in this tutorial carefully so you understand how the backup process normally works when you are working from a hard disk rather than a floppy disk. If you are in a computer lab and are prevented from saving files on the hard disk or don't have permission to do so, you should either ask your instructor if you can back up the files in an existing folder on the hard disk, or you should read through this session and study the concepts without performing the steps.

Data Backup

Computer Backups

No one is safe from computer problems that result in data loss. A power surge, power loss, a failed section of a hard disk, a computer virus—these problems can strike at any time. Rather than risk disaster, you should make copies of your important files regularly. You probably have already learned how to copy data from one floppy disk to another and to copy a file from one disk to another. Making a copy of a disk or a file is one way to protect data. Copying a disk or a file is your only choice when you store your data on a floppy disk, as is usually the case in a computer lab, where you usually don't have access to a hard disk.

Phil points out that if you want to protect data on a hard drive, you will almost certainly want to use a backup program instead of a copy or disk-copy procedure. A **backup program** copies and then automatically compresses files and folders from a hard disk into a single file. The backup program stores this file on a **backup medium** such as a floppy disk or tape cartridge. Phil explains that such a software program, called **Backup**, comes with Windows 95.

Phil says that although in this seminar you will simulate backing up files to a floppy disk, in reality using floppy disks as your backup medium is impractical if you have more than just a few files to back up. A more practical solution, if you can afford it, is to add a **tape drive** to your computer that lets you back up your data to tape cartridges. Today's tape drives can store several gigabytes of data on a single tape, and you can find them for just a few hundred dollars.

When you back up a set of files with the Windows 95 Backup program, you go through the following steps.

1. You designate the folders and files you want to back up.

2. Backup creates a **file set**, a file that stores the list of the folders and files you designated for back up.

3. Backup copies the files and folders listed in the file set, compresses them, and stores them in a single file called a **backup set**.

4. Backup stores the backup set on the backup medium you specify.

Suppose you store all of your important files in three folders on drive C named Projects, Accounts, and Clients. Figure 6-18 shows how Backup backs up the files in these folders.

Figure 6-18 ◀
Backing up
data

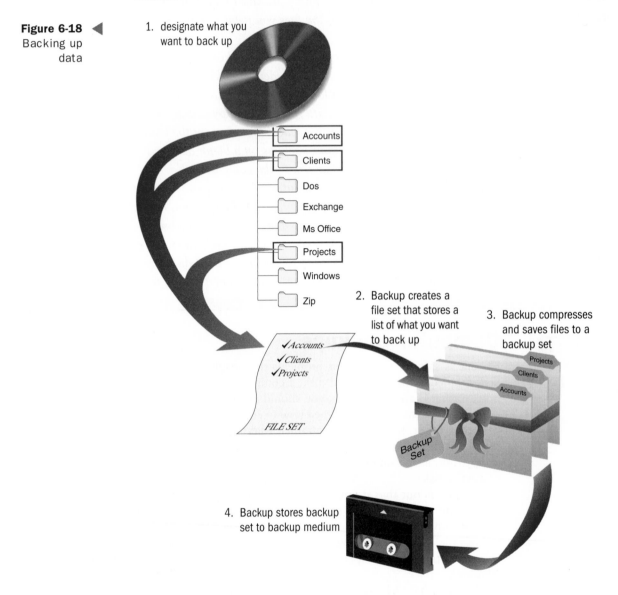

1. designate what you want to back up

Accounts
Clients
Dos
Exchange
Ms Office
Projects
Windows
Zip

2. Backup creates a file set that stores a list of what you want to back up

✓ Accounts
✓ Clients
✓ Projects

FILE SET

3. Backup compresses and saves files to a backup set

Projects
Clients
Accounts

Backup Set

4. Backup stores backup set to backup medium

New computer users sometimes have trouble understanding how the backup process differs from simply copying files. The biggest difference is that a backup copies files into a single, compressed file, whereas a copy simply duplicates the files. Figure 6-19 points out the differences between copying and backing up, showing why backing up files is a better data-protection method than simply copying files.

Figure 6-19 ◀
Copying vs.
backing up files

Copy	Backup
A copy of a file occupies the same amount of space as the original file. For this reason, making a copy of all the files on a hard disk is impractical.	Because it is compressed, a backup of a file is much smaller than the original file, depending on the file type.
It would take a lot of time and effort to copy all the files on a hard disk to floppy disks—not least because of the time it would take to swap disks in and out of the floppy drive. Copying 80 MB of data would require more than 56 floppy disks.	Backups are much quicker. If you have a tape drive, you can back up 80 MB of data to a single tape in a matter of minutes.
Because you can't split a large file over two floppy disks, you must manually break the file up into smaller parts and then copy them to separate floppy disks.	Backup is designed to split files across disks.
Every time you want to back up your data, you must either copy all the files on your disk again or you must painstakingly locate and then copy only those files that have changed.	Backup can automatically detect and back up only those files that have changed since your last backup.
If you do lose data because of a computer failure, there is no easy way to locate a file you need.	The Backup software keeps track of the files you have backed up, and it's very easy to find and recover a file.

Placing Files on the Hard Disk to Back Up

Phil emphasizes that you are *simulating* the backup procedure. The conditions under which you perform this backup are unusual because your data is on a floppy disk, not a hard drive. In normal circumstances, if you wanted to protect the data on your Student Disk, you would just make a copy of the disk from My Computer. Backup is designed to back up the contents of a hard drive (or several hard drives) onto a backup medium. To simulate using Backup, therefore, you need to place some of your data on your computer's hard disk, which you will do in this section.

You will create a new folder on your computer's hard disk named Projects. Then you'll copy the files onto your Student Disk into the Projects folder. You will then be ready to back up the files in the Projects folder. Figure 6-20 shows this process.

Figure 6-20 ◀
Placing files on
hard disk for
backup

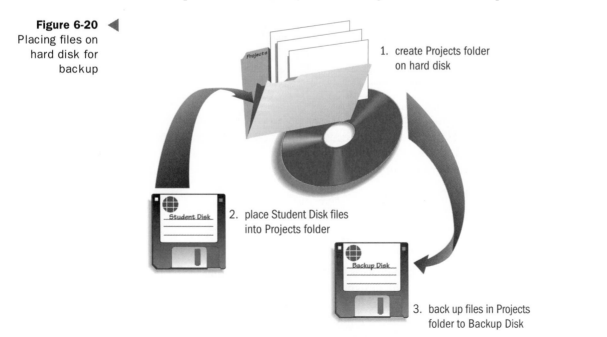

1. create Projects folder on hard disk

2. place Student Disk files into Projects folder

3. back up files in Projects folder to Backup Disk

You begin by placing the Projects folder on the hard disk.

To create a new folder on the hard disk and then copy files from the Student Disk into the new folder:

1. Click the **Start** button, point to **Programs**, then click **Windows Explorer**.

2. Scroll the Folders list until you see the (C:) icon ▭, then click the **(C:)** icon.

3. Click **File**, point to **New**, click **Folder**, type **Projects**, then press the **Enter** key.

   TROUBLE? IIf you are in a computer lab and are not permitted to save files to your computer's hard disk, close Windows Explorer, skip the rest of the steps in this section, and ask your instructor which folder on what drive you should use to back up.

   TROUBLE? If your hard disk already has a folder named Projects, give your folder a different name, such as your last name. Then substitute the name you gave your folder for the Projects folder throughout the rest of this tutorial.

4. Scroll the Folders list until you see the floppy drive icon ▭ for drive A, then click the **3½ Floppy (A:)** icon so its contents appear in the Contents list.

5. Scroll the Folders list until you see the (C:) icon ▭, then, if necessary, click its **plus box** ⊞ so its folders appear in the Folders list.

6. Scroll the Folders list until the Projects folder is visible.

7. Click **Edit**, then click **Select All** so all the files on drive A in the Contents list are highlighted.

8. Use the *right* mouse button to drag the files in the Contents list to the Projects folder. See Figure 6-21.

Figure 6-21 ◀
Copying files
from Student
Disk to
Projects folder
on hard drive

make sure Projects
folder is highlighted

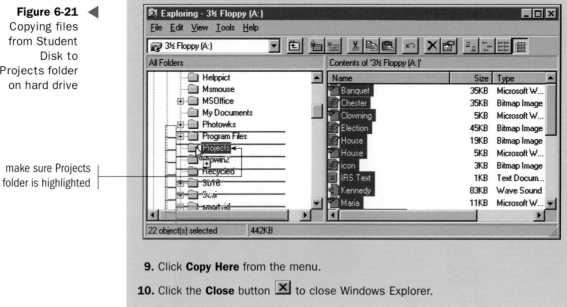

9. Click **Copy Here** from the menu.

10. Click the **Close** button ✕ to close Windows Explorer.

Backup Strategies

You start the backup process by designating which files and folders you want to back up. In this simulation, the designation is easy: you just tell your backup program to use the Projects folder. However, Phil explains that in reality, choosing which files you want to back up is a little more complicated because it is part of a larger backup strategy.

A **backup strategy** is a plan you develop to ensure you have a backup copy of all the files on your computer in their most current version. The backbone of a backup strategy is a backup of all the files on your computer, called a **full backup**. A full backup contains the Windows 95 program, all your system files, all your program files, and all the data files that existed on the day you performed the backup. Once you have a full backup, you can perform **partial backups** that back up only the files that have changed since the last time you backed up your data. There are two kinds of partial backups: differential and incremental. In a **differential backup**, the backup program searches for and backs up only those files that have changed since the last full backup. In an **incremental backup**, the back-up program searches for and backs up only those files that have changed since the last backup, regardless of whether it was a full or partial backup. Figure 6-22 helps you understand the difference.

Figure 6-22 ◄
Partial backup
types

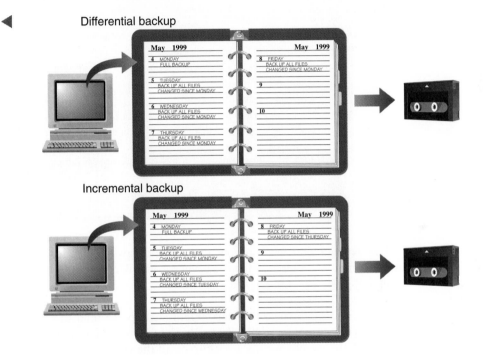

You might think that to be on the safe side, you should simply perform a full backup every time you back up your data. However, a full backup can take several hours, depending on how many hard disks you have and how big they are. For this reason, most users perform a full backup only once a week or once a month, depending on how substantially their files change from day to day. Many of your files don't change at all over the course of weeks or months. Your program files, for example, change only when you install a new version of software.

How often should you perform full and partial backups? It's best to develop a backup strategy based on a schedule. For the user in Figure 6-22, a backup strategy begins with a full backup at the beginning of the week. Then this user performs a partial backup on a daily basis. Perhaps the last thing he or she does before leaving the computer for the evening is run the backup software to back up any files changed during the day.

Some users might want to perform more frequent backups—especially those who can't afford to lose even a few hours' work. They might perform a partial backup more than once a day—at lunch time, after work, and then at midnight, for example. You don't want to overdo it, however. Even a partial backup can slow your productivity, because, even if the backup program is running in the background, it uses system resources. Only you can decide how many times to run a backup. If you can structure it so that your computer runs backups while you are busy doing something else, that's best. The important thing is that you back up your data often enough so that if your computer fails, your backup would contain enough of your data that it wouldn't take you too long to reconstruct the rest.

Creating the File Set

In this simulation, you are not going to perform a full backup—that would take too long, and you probably don't have access to a tape drive. Instead, you are going to perform a backup of only one folder: the Projects folder. There are circumstances where you might want to have Backup search only a few folders instead of all the folders on your computer. For example, suppose you habitually store all the files you work with on a daily basis in the Projects folder. You might want to backup just that folder. It will speed up the daily backup process considerably if Backup doesn't have to search your entire computer for changed files. Users who perform more than one backup a day especially might profit from searching just a few folders.

REFERENCE window

PERFORMING A BACKUP

- Click Start, point to Programs, point to Accessories, point to System Tools, then click Backup.
- Acknowledge any opening dialog boxes that appear.
- Select the folders or files you want to back up, then click the Next Step button.
- Click the drive where you want to store the backup set.
- Click Settings then click Options to check and correct options if necessary.
- Click File, click Save As, then save the file set on your backup medium.
- Click the Start Backup button.

Phil explains that the concepts and terminology you just learned are widely accepted in the computer industry. However, Microsoft's Backup accessory uses slightly different terminology that you might find confusing:

1. Microsoft uses the term "full system backup" to refer to a backup of all the files on your computer's hard drives. In the computer industry, the term "full system backup" usually means a backup of all the computers on a network.

2. Microsoft uses the term "full backup" to refer to a backup of all the files specified in the file set. In the computer industry, "full backup" usually means a backup of all the files on all the drives on a computer.

3. When you choose the backup type you want, your options are Full (which in Microsoft's terminology means just the files in a file set) and Incremental. If you choose Incremental, Backup searches the files in the file set and changes those that have changed since the last full or incremental backup (Phil wants you to know this because the description on the dialog box is slightly misleading). Microsoft's Backup accessory does not include the ability to perform a differential backup.

Computer owners who rely on their computers for important work usually require a backup program that gives them more options than Microsoft Backup, including the ability to perform differential backups and to schedule backups. Phil tells you, however, that the Microsoft Backup accessory is a great way to begin a backup strategy because it is free—it comes with the operating system. Now, he says, you're ready to start Backup.

To start Backup:

1. Click the **Start** button, point to **Programs**, point to **Accessories**, then point to **System Tools**.

TROUBLE? If Backup appears as an option on the menu, then Backup is installed on your computer and you can proceed. If Backup does not appear, then you cannot complete this session until Backup is installed. Check with your instructor or technical support person for directions. If you are using your own computer and you have the installation disks, online Help can help you install Backup. Search for "installing" in the Index, then click "Windows components." The topic that opens is called "To install a Windows component after Windows has been installed." If you still can't install Backup, read through this section without doing the steps.

2. Click **Backup**. The Welcome dialog box appears. See Figure 6-23.

TROUBLE? If this dialog box doesn't appear, don't worry. A previous user changed the settings to prevent this dialog box from appearing. Read Step 3, but don't perform it.

Figure 6-23 ◄
Welcome dialog
box

If selected, dialog box
won't appear again

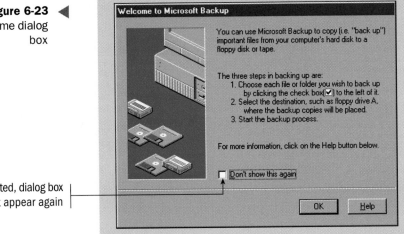

3. Click the **OK** button after reviewing the Welcome message. A dialog box appears indicating that the program has created a Full system backup set (a file that you can use to back up all the files on your computer). See Figure 6-24. Remember—in this simulation you don't want to back up all the files on your computer, just the files in the Projects folder.

TROUBLE? If this dialog box doesn't appear, don't worry. A previous user changed the settings to prevent this dialog box from appearing. Read Step 4, but don't perform it.

Figure 6-24 ◄
Notice about
Full System
Backup file set

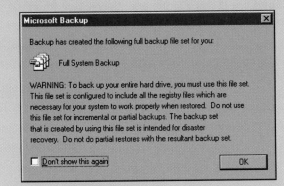

4. Click the **OK** button. You are now ready to back up the Projects folder.

TROUBLE? If a message appears warning you about a detected tape drive, click the OK button.

There are three tabs in the Backup window, as you can see in Figure 6-25. The **Backup** tab backs up your files. The **Restore** tab restores files from a backup set. The **Compare** tab compares backed up files with the original files to verify that the backup procedure functioned properly.

The Backup tab walks you through the steps to perform your backup. The first step is selecting the files or folders you want to back up. You navigate a window similar to Windows Explorer. To include a folder in the file set, you click the empty box ☐ next to the folder to place a check mark in it. For example, suppose you had a folder named Taxes that you wanted to back up. You display the folder in the Folders list and then click its box. See Figure 6-25.

Figure 6-25 ◀
Selecting Taxes
folder to
back up

indicates only some
folders and files will
be backed up

indicates all files will
be backed up

all files are selected

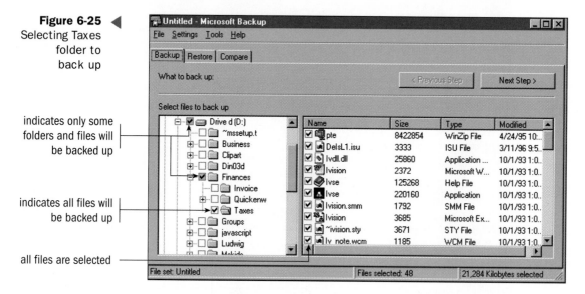

Notice that the box next to the Taxes folder is white whereas the boxes next to the Finances folder, which contains the Taxes folder, is gray. A checked white box ☑ indicates that the entire folder or file will be backed up. A gray checked box ☑ indicates that only part of the contents of that folder or drive will be backed up. If you want to include only one file in a folder, you click the folder's icon in the Folders list and then click the empty box just for that file in the Contents list.

You want to select the Projects folder on drive C to back up.

To select the Projects folder:

1. Click the **plus** box ⊞ next to the drive C icon 🖫 to display the folders on the C drive.

2. Click the empty box to the left of the Projects folder. A check mark appears in the box. The Contents list in the right window shows all the files in the Projects folder with their check boxes selected. See Figure 6-26.

Figure 6-26
Selecting the
Projects folder
for backing up

moves you to the
next step

all files will be
backed up

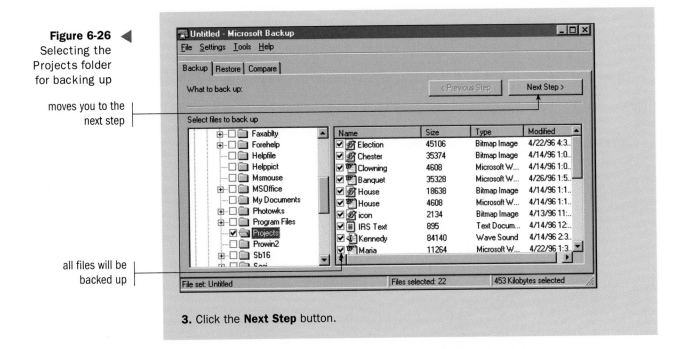

3. Click the **Next Step** button.

Backup displays the next step in the process: selecting the **backup device**, the drive that contains the backup medium. If your computer contains a tape drive, Backup automatically detects it. In this simulation, however, you will store your backup files on a blank disk. Do not use your Student Disk because there might not be enough space. You should also check your backup settings to make sure the backup will proceed according to your backup strategy. When you check the settings, you will see that you can choose either a Full or Incremental backup (see Figure 6-28). As you have seen, Windows 95 uses the term "Full backup" to refer not to a backup of all the files on your computer but rather to all the files you just selected—the files in your file set.

To select your floppy drive as the destination for the backup set and then check your backup settings:

1. Bring a blank, formatted disk to the computer lab, and write Backup Disk on the label.

2. Remove your Student Disk from drive A and place the Backup Disk in its place.

3. Click the **3½ Floppy (A:)** icon (not the plus box).

4. Confirm that the drive letter of the drive containing your Backup Disk appears, as shown in Figure 6-27.

Figure 6-27 ◀
Choosing the
backup device

make sure drive A
is specified

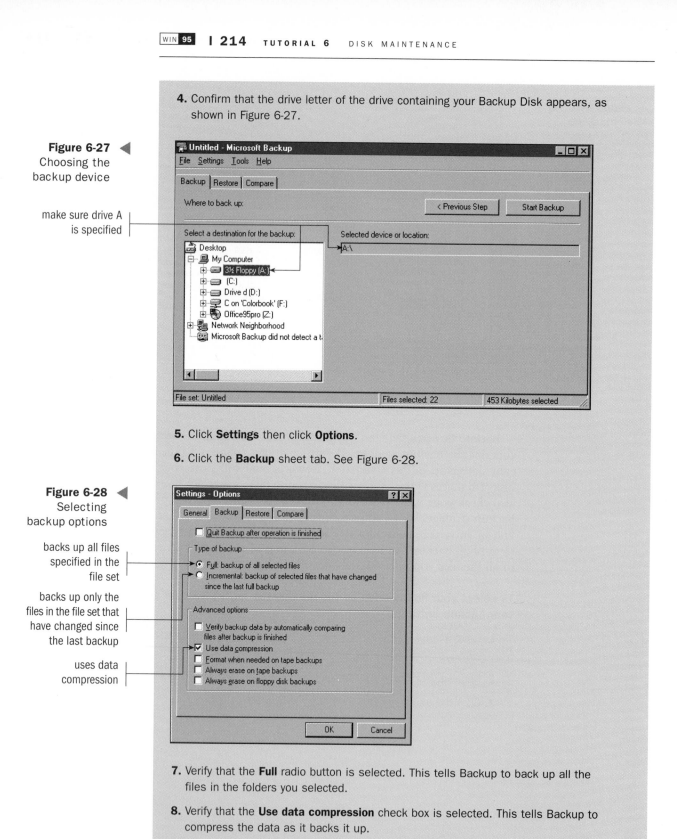

5. Click **Settings** then click **Options**.

6. Click the **Backup** sheet tab. See Figure 6-28.

Figure 6-28 ◀
Selecting
backup options

backs up all files
specified in the
file set

backs up only the
files in the file set that
have changed since
the last backup

uses data
compression

7. Verify that the **Full** radio button is selected. This tells Backup to back up all the files in the folders you selected.

8. Verify that the **Use data compression** check box is selected. This tells Backup to compress the data as it backs it up.

9. Verify that the other settings match those in Figure 6-28.

10. Click the **OK** button to close the Settings - Options dialog box.

Once you have selected the folders and files you want to back up, designated a backup medium, and have checked your backup settings, you can save those backup specifications in a file set. The file set not only remembers which files and folders you want to back up; it also stores the settings you've chosen. In the future if you want to back up the Projects folder again, you can simply open this file set in the first Backup window without having to go through the process of locating and selecting the Projects folder.

To save your choices to a file set:

1. Click **File** then click **Save As**.

2. Click the **Save in** list arrow, then click **3½ Floppy (A:)**.

3. Replace the default name with **Projects Folder File Set** in the File name box.

4. Click the **Save** button. Backup saves the file set on your Backup Disk.

Creating the Backup Set

You have now created the file set; all you need to do is start the backup. Backup will locate and copy the files you've selected and then compress the copies into a single compressed file—the backup set. You can store the backup set on the same Backup Disk you used to store the file set. When Backup is finished, it tells you how many files it backed up and how much space the backup set requires.

To back up your selected files:

1. Click the **Start Backup** button. Backup requests the label for your backup set.

2. Type **Projects Folder Backup** in the Backup set box, then click the **OK** button. The process of backing up might take a minute or two. Backup will notify you when the process is complete.

3. Click the **OK** button to acknowledge that the operation is complete. Backup displays a summary of the backup. See Figure 6-29.

Figure 6-29 ◀
Summary of the backup

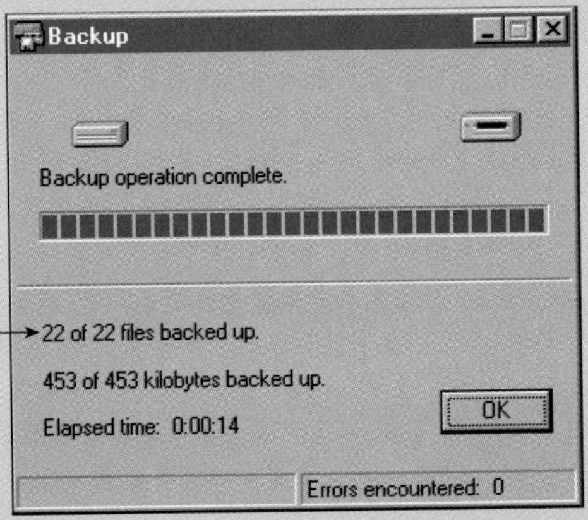

number of files backed up; your number might be different

> 22 of 22 files backed up.
453 of 453 kilobytes backed up.
Elapsed time: 0:00:14
Errors encountered: 0

4. Click the **OK** button to acknowledge the summary, then click the **Close** button ✕ to close Backup. Your disk now contains a backup of the files in the Projects folder. If you ever have computer problems, you can rest assured knowing that your data is safe.

Once you have the backup set, what should you do with it? Or more appropriately, what should you not do with it? You should not store it near your computer. A fire that destroys your computer would probably destroy your backup as well. If a thief wants your data, it's quicker to steal your backups than your computer. Many computer owners rent safe deposit boxes at banks and store their backups there. Business owners sometimes store their backups offsite at their own homes. Fire is not likely to strike in two locations at once.

Backup storage is part of your overall backup strategy. You need to decide how often you will put your backups into storage. Many users maintain two backup tapes: they store the backups for a single week on one tape, then at the end of the week they put the tape into storage. They use the other tape for the following week, and then at the end of the week they swap the tapes.

Restoring Files

Phil tells the class to imagine that disaster has just struck. Your hard disk fell victim to a lethal computer virus, and your computer maintenance person believes data recovery is hopeless—you're going to have to reformat your hard disk. "I hope," says your maintenance person, "you made a backup." If you did, then your problem is solved. You simply take the backup out of storage and run the Restore procedure on the backup set containing the files you lost.

REFERENCE window	**RESTORING A FILE FROM A BACKUP SET**
	▪ Start Backup then click the Restore tab.
	▪ Select the drive and folder containing the backup set in the Restore from list.
	▪ Click the backup set in the Backup Set list, then click the Next Step button.
	▪ Select the files or folders you want to restore.
	▪ Click the Start Restore button.
	▪ Click the OK button.

Phil says that to simulate a file restoration, you'll first delete the entire Projects folder from your computer's hard disk. In a real-life situation, these files might have been ruined in a power failure, by a disk defect, by a virus, or by some other misfortune.

To delete the Projects folder from the hard drive:

1. Click the **Start** button, point to **Programs**, then click **Windows Explorer**.

2. If necessary, click the **plus box** ⊞ next to drive C, then scroll down the Folders list until you see the Projects folder icon ▭.

3. Right-click the **Projects** folder icon ▭, then click **Delete**.

4. Click the **Yes** button if you are prompted to confirm that you want to delete the folder.

5. Click the **Close** button to close Windows Explorer.

Your hard disk now no longer contains the Projects folder or any of its files. You are ready to use Backup to restore the Projects folder to your hard disk. You must first identify the backup set that contains the Projects folder. In this simulation, there will be only one backup set on your disk: the Projects Folder Backup you created earlier.

In real life, how you restore data depends on what kind of loss you suffered. If you lost only a single file, you can choose the backup set that you made after you changed the file. If the file or folder you want to restore is not in that backup set, that means you didn't work with it since the last backup, in which case you'll have to check another backup set. If you have lost all the data on your disk, how you recover it depends on what kind of partial backups you use. If you use incremental backups, you would need to use all the backup sets you've created since your most recent full backup. You would start by restoring the full backup, and then restoring each backup set, one at a time, beginning with the oldest. If you use differential backups, you would restore the full backup and then the most recent differential backup.

You are ready to restore the Projects folder.

To select the backup set and check the restore settings:

1. Click the **Start** button, point to **Programs**, point to **Accessories**, point to **System Tools**, then click **Backup**.

2. Click the **OK** button as necessary to move through the Welcome dialog boxes.

3. Click the **Restore** tab. You now need to specify the location of your backup set, which is located on the Backup Disk in drive A.

4. Click the **3½ Floppy (A:)** icon [icon]. Your backup set appears in the Backup Set list on the right. See Figure 6-30.

Figure 6-30 ◄
Selecting a
backup set to
restore

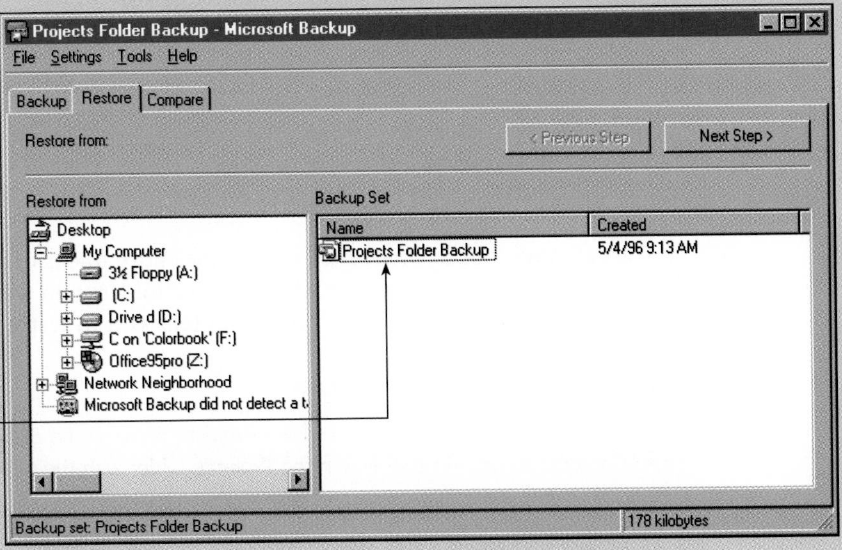

restore Projects folder
from this backup set

5. Click **Projects Folders Backup** in the Backup Set list.

6. Click the **Next Step** button.

7. Click **Settings** then click **Options**.

8. Click the **Restore** tab then click the **Original locations** radio button to restore the files to their original location on the hard disk. Compare the Settings - Options dialog box to Figure 6-31 and make sure the other settings are the same.

Figure 6-31 ◀
Checking
Restore
settings

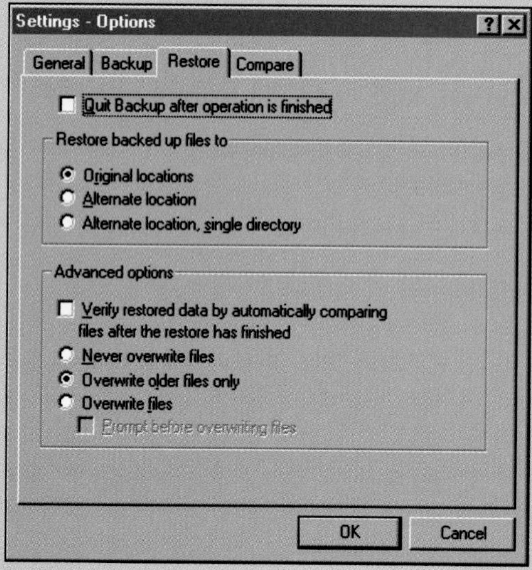

9. Click the **OK** button.

You can now choose whether to restore the entire folder or just one or two files. As you did on the Backup tab, you select which files or folders you want to restore by clicking the empty boxes next to each file or folder. Phil tells you to restore the entire Projects folder.

To restore the entire Projects folder:

1. Click the empty box to the left of the Projects folder in the Select Files list. The Contents list shows the files in the Projects folder with their check boxes selected.

2. Click the **Start Restore** button. Backup displays the status of the restoration procedure and informs you when the restoration is completed.

3. Click the **OK** button twice.

4. Click the **Close** button ☒ to exit Backup.

Now you should check whether the Projects folder was restored successfully to your hard drive.

To verify that the Projects folder has been restored:

1. Click the **Start** button, point to **Programs**, then click **Windows Explorer**.

2. Scroll down the Folders list until you see the Projects folder icon 📁.

3. Click the **Projects** folder icon 📁 and verify that the files in the folders have been restored along with the folder itself.

4. Delete the Projects folder to return the hard drive to its original state.

5. Close Windows Explorer.

Quick **Check**

1 How does copying a disk differ from backing up a disk?

2 Name two types of backup media. Which should you use when backing up a hard disk and why?

3 What is the difference between a file set and a backup set?

4 What is a full backup?

5 What is a partial backup? Identify and differentiate between two kinds of partial backups.

6 Why would you use a partial backup rather than just performing a full backup?

7 Which takes up more megabytes: all the files on your computer's hard drive or the full backup of your computer's hard drive? Why?

End Note

Phil ends the seminar by telling you that if you're lucky, you'll never have to use Restore to recover lost data. Then he tells you that Backup is probably one of the most important topics he's covered in the seminar. Practically everyone who has been around computers for very long has a data-loss story to tell. Many computer owners who now have tape drives learned the hard way how important it is to protect data. Many tape drives include specialized backup software programs that are even easier to use than Backup. A popular feature of many modern backup programs (although not the Windows 95 Backup program) is that you can schedule them to start automatically. As long as you leave a tape in your drive, the backup program will start your backup automatically. If you are a computer owner, put a backup strategy planning session at the top of your list, and then stick to your strategy scrupulously. You won't be sorry.

Tutorial Assignments

1. Scanning a Floppy Disk You are in charge of backing up the hard drives at Harrison's Tailor Shop. An employee tells you one of the backup disks is acting strangely, so you decide to scan the disk. Place the Backup Disk you used in Session 6.2 into drive A, then scan this disk. Make sure you perform a Thorough scan and that ScanDisk is set to fix errors automatically. When the scan is complete, print out the ScanDisk Results dialog box. Write a paragraph on the back of the printout that interprets the results reported in the ScanDisk Results dialog box.

2. Scanning a Hard Disk If you have your own computer or you have permission from your computer lab's staff to scan a hard drive, you can do this tutorial assignment. Otherwise, skip this assignment. Start ScanDisk, then click drive C. Make sure you perform a Thorough scan and that ScanDisk is set to fix errors automatically. Once you start the scan, be prepared to wait a few minutes. Print out the ScanDisk Results dialog box. Write a paragraph on the back of the printout that interprets the results reported in the ScanDisk Results dialog box.

3. Viewing the ScanDisk Log File When you scan a disk, you can have Windows 95 automatically maintain a log file that keeps track of the errors ScanDisk identifies and fixes. This log can be a useful way to keep a history of problems you've had with a disk. Windows 95 automatically saves the log file with the name Scandisk.log in the root directory of drive C.

   a. Place a floppy disk in drive A. Try to use a disk that has not been scanned recently and that has been used frequently. Use your Student Disk if you have no other disk, but recognize that you aren't likely to find any errors because you just scanned this disk in Session 6.1.
   b. Start ScanDisk, specify drive A, then click the Advanced button. Make sure the Append to log radio button is selected, then click the OK button.
   c. Click the Start button.
   d. When the scan is complete, start Notepad. Click File, then click Open. Select drive C, then select All files in the Files of type box. Click Scandisk, then click Open.
   e. If a number of scans have taken place on your computer, the log could be quite long. Scroll to the very end of the log file to find the report on your most recent scan.
   f. You should print the contents of this file to turn it in to your instructor, but if the log file is quite long, don't print all of it. If it's longer than a few pages, use your data transfer skills to copy just the results from the most recent scan (at the bottom of the log) into a new Notepad file, then print that file. You don't have to save the file.

4. Defragmenting a Disk When you defragmented your Student Disk in Session 6.1, it's possible your disk was not badly fragmented. This tutorial assignment gives you a chance to fragment a disk on purpose so that you can then watch Disk Defragmenter reorder the file clusters.

   a. Make a copy of your Student Disk and label this disk Fragmented Disk.
   b. Copy files from other disks onto your Fragmented Disk until you have filled the disk completely. Use any files you want—files from a hard disk, files from your Backup Disk, or files from other floppy disks. Once you get an error message that tells you the disk is full, delete a batch of files that were saved to the disk at different times. Then copy another batch of files to the disk until it is again full. Then delete another batch of files saved at different times. Fill the disk one last time.
   c. Run Disk Defragmenter on your Fragmented Disk, and click the Show Details button as soon as the defragmentation process begins. Continue on with the next step, part d., immediately—while the defragmentation process is going on.

d. Print an image of the details window that shows the reorganization of the clusters. If the defragmentation process goes so quickly that you can't get an image, just print what you see when the process is complete.

5. Backing up a Folder You work at Gemini Productions, a graphic design company. Create a folder on your hard drive called Gemini, then copy all the graphics files from your Student Disk into the Gemini folder. (If you can't copy files to the hard drive, then skip this tutorial assignment.) Then perform a backup of this folder. Name the file set Gemini File Set and save it on your Backup Disk. Name the backup set Gemini Backup and save it on your Backup Disk. When the backup is complete, open My Computer and then open drive A. Print an image of the drive A window so that it shows the file set and backup sets you have created so far.

6. Restoring a Changed File Continue with the previous tutorial assignment. Delete the Gemini folder from your hard drive (suppose a computer virus ruined it). Start Backup, then restore this folder from the Gemini Folder Backup backup set. Print an image of the summary dialog box that appears when the restoration procedure is complete.

7. Performing a Partial Backup You learned in this tutorial that you can perform partial backups as part of your backup strategy rather than always performing full backups to save time. Backup automatically detects which files have changed since your last backup and backs up only those files. Try changing one of the files in the Projects folder and then performing a partial backup.

    a. At the end of this tutorial you restored the Projects folder to the hard disk but then deleted it to restore the hard drive to its original state. Follow the steps in Session 6.2 to recreate the Projects folder and place your Student Disk files into this folder.

    b. Open Pins, and then color the balls in this graphic green. Save and close the Pins file.

    c. Start Backup, and place the Backup Disk you used in Session 6.2 into drive A. To perform a partial backup, you need to open the original file set.

    d. Click File, then click Open File Set. Locate and then open the Projects Folder File Set.

    e. Click Settings, then click Options. Click the Backup tab, then click the Incremental radio button.

    f. Click the OK button, then click the Next Step button.

    g. Click drive A as the destination, then click the Start Backup button. Type Projects Folder Incremental Backup as the backup set name, then click the OK button.

    h. The summary should tell you that only one file was backed up (because only one file changed, the Pins file). Print an image of the Backup summary dialog box before you close Backup.

    i. Now verify that the incremental backup worked by deleting the Pins graphic from the Projects folder on drive C and then restoring this file from the incremental backup. Click the Restore tab, then locate and select the Projects Folder Incremental Backup backup set. Click the Next Step button.

    j. Click the Projects folder, then click the empty box next to the Pins graphic. Print an image of the Restore window showing the file in your backup set, then hand this printout in to your instructor.

    k. Click the Start Restore button.

    l. Open Windows Explorer and verify that the Pins graphic has been restored.

8. Performing a Full Backup If you have your own computer and it has a tape drive, you can do this tutorial assignment. Otherwise, just read this assigment so you can see how you would back up an entire system. Backing up your full system is an important part of a comprehensive backup strategy, but it can take an hour or more, depending on the speed of your tape drive and the size of your hard disk or disks.

    a. Start Backup.

    b. From the Backup window, click File, then click Open File Set. Windows 95 has created a Full backup file set for you.

    c. Click Full backup, then click the Open button. It might take a few minutes for Backup to process the file set and select all the files it contains (all the files on your computer).

    d. Click the Next Step button, then click your tape drive as the destination.

    e. Name the backup Full backup 3/27/98. Substitute the current date for 3/27/98.

    f. Click the OK button. Backup starts the full backup. You can safely leave it alone; be prepared to wait an hour or more. When you come back, print an image of the Backup summary dialog box before you close Backup, then hand this printout in to your instructor.

9. Interviewing a Systems Manager Ask your instructor for the names of businesses whose systems managers might take a minute with you on the phone to be interviewed. You might ask the systems managers the following questions:

    a. What training did you receive to get this job?

    b. How many computers do you manage? Are they on a network?

    c. What backup media do you use?

    d. How often do you back up the entire system?

    e. How often do you perform partial backups?

    f. Do you perform incremental or differential backups? Explain why you chose to perform this type of partial backup.

    g. Are individual employees responsible for their own backups?

    h. If an employee has a problem with a computer, who is expected to fix the problem?

10. Restoring Lost Data You work at Hal's Food Warehouse in inventory management. You are responsible for backing up the computer system. You performed a full backup on Friday, and then on Monday you worked with a database file named Orders. You performed an incremental backup on Monday evening. On Tuesday you worked with the Orders file again, and Tuesday evening performed an incremental backup. When you attempt to open the Orders file Wednesday morning, you receive an error message that says the file cannot be found. How would you restore the file?

11. Devising a Backup Strategy If you have your own computer, do you use a backup strategy? If not, now's your chance to implement one. Ask yourself the following questions, and then write a backup strategy and schedule:

    a. How often do I install different software on my computer?

    b. How often do I work with important files and how much are they worth to me?

    c. What would I lose if the hard disk drive failed?

Lab Assignments

To start the Labs, click the **Start** button on the Windows 95 taskbar, point to **Programs**, point to **CTI Windows 95 Applications**, point to **Windows 95 New Perspectives Intermediate**, and click the name of the Lab you want to use.

Defragmentation and Disk Operations

Defragmentation and Disk Operations In this Lab you will format a simulated disk, save files, delete files, undelete files to see how the computer updates the FAT. You will also find out how the files on your disk become fragmented and what a defragmentation utility does to reorganize the clusters on your disk.

1. Click the Steps button to learn how the computer updates the FAT when you format a disk and save, delete, and undelete files. As you proceed through the Steps, answer all of the Quick Check questions that appear. After you complete the Steps, you will see a Quick Check Summary Report. Follow the instructions on the screen to print this report.

2. Click the Explore button. Click the Format button to format the simulated disk. Try to save files 1, 2, 3, 4, and 6. Do they all fit on the disk?

3. In Explore, format the simulated disk. Try to save all the files on the disk. What happens?

4. In Explore, format the simulated disk. Save FILE-3, FILE-4, and FILE-6. Next, delete FILE-6. Now, save FILE-5. Try to undelete FILE-6. What happens and why?

5. In Explore, format the simulated disk. Save and erase files until the files become fragmented. Draw a picture of the disk to show the fragmented files. Indicate which files are in each cluster by using color, crosshatching, or labels. List which files in your drawing are fragmented. Finally, defragment the disk and draw a new picture showing the unfragmented files.

Data Backup The Data Backup Lab gives you an opportunity to make tape backups on a simulated computer system. Periodically, the hard disk on the simulated computer will fail, which gives you a chance to assess the convenience and efficiency of different backup procedures.

1. Click the Steps button to learn how to use the simulation. As you work through the Steps, answer all of the Quick Check questions that appear. After you complete the Steps, you will see a Summary Report of your Quick Check answers. Follow the directions on the screen to print this report.

2. Click the Explore button. Create a full backup every Friday using only Tape 1. At some point in the simulation, an event will cause data loss on the simulated computer system. Use the simulation to restore as much data as you can. After you restore the data, print the Backup Audit Report.

3. In Explore, create a full backup every Friday on Tape 1 and a differential backup every Wednesday on Tape 2. At some point in the simulation, an event will cause data loss on the simulated computer system. Use the simulation to restore as much data as you can. Print the Backup Audit Report.

4. In Explore, create a full backup on Tape 1 every Monday. Make incremental backups on Tapes 2, 3, 4, and 5 each day for the rest of the week. Continue this cycle, reusing the same tapes each week. At some point in the simulation an event will cause data loss on the simulated computer system. Use the simulation to restore as much data as you can. Print the Backup Audit Report.

5. Photocopy a calendar for next month. On the calendar indicate your best plan for backing up data. In Explore, implement your plan. Print out the Backup Audit Report. Write a paragraph or two discussing the effectiveness of your plan.

Answers to **Quick Check** Questions

Introductory Tutorials

SESSION 1.1

1 a. icon b. Start button c. taskbar d. Date/Time control e. desktop f. pointer

2 Multitasking

3 Start menu

4 Lift up the mouse, move it to the right, then put it down, and slide it left until the pointer reaches the left edge of the screen.

5 Highlighting

6 If a program is running, its button is displayed on the taskbar.

7 Each program that is running uses system resources, so Windows 95 runs more efficiently when only the programs you are using are open.

8 Answer: If you do not perform the shut down procedure, you might lose data.

SESSION 1.2

1 a. title bar b. program title c. Minimize button d. Restore button e. Close button f. menu bar g. toolbar h. formatting bar i. status bar j. taskbar k. workspace l. pointer

2 a. Minimize button—hides the program so only its button is showing on the taskbar.
   b. Maximize button—enlarges the program to fill the entire screen.
   c. Restore button—sets the program to a pre-defined size.
   d. Close button—stops the program and removes its button from the taskbar.

3 a. Ellipses—indicate a dialog box will appear.
   b. Grayed out—the menu option is not currently available.
   c. Submenu—indicates a submenu will appear.
   d. Check mark—indicates a menu option is currently in effect.

4 Toolbar

5 a. scroll bar b. scroll box c. Cancel button d. down arrow button e. list box f. radio button g. check box

6 one, check boxes

7 On-line Help

SESSION 2.1

1 file

2 formatting

3 I-beam

4 insertion point

5 word wrap

6 You drag the I-beam pointer over the text to highlight it.

7 \ ? : * < > | "

8 extension

9 save the file again

10 paper

SESSION 2.2

1 My Computer

2 A (or A:)

3 Hard (or hard disk)

4 Filename, file type, file size, date, time

5 Root

6 Folders (or subdirectories)

7 It is deleted from the disk.

8 Yes

SESSION 3.1

1 Windows Explorer

2 Folders, Contents

3 F

4 F

5 subfolder

6 plus box

7 Drive A device icon

8 F

SESSION 3.2

1 T

2 device or folder icon

3 F

4 Details

5 Large Icons, Small Icons, List, Details

6 Shift, Ctrl

7 Modified

8 Windows 95 temporarily stores an image of the screen in memory. You can then paste the image into an accessory like WordPad and print it.

SESSION 3.3

1 When you use the left mouse button, the pop-up menu does not appear, so you might lose track of whether you are moving or copying files.

2 Refresh

3 T

4 T

5 F

SESSION 4.1

1 F

2 F

3 Here are three ways: 1) Click the document icon with the left mouse button then press Enter, 2) Right-click the document icon then click Open, and 3) Double-click the document icon.

4 You delete not only the icon but also the document.

5 You delete only the icon but not the document.

6 You place a copy of the document on the desktop rather than placing a shortcut to the original document.

SESSION 4.2

1 F

2 Right-click the object then click Properties.

3 Here are four: Background, Appearance, Screen Saver, or Settings. You could also mention the properties on each of these sheets, like the color palette, the resolution, and so on.

4 Activate a screen saver

5 There are 640 pixels across and 480 down.

6 640 × 480, because it displays the largest objects.

7 It requires extra video memory and runs more slowly.

8 Energy Star compliant

SESSION 4.3

1 MouseKeys, which lets you use the number keys on the keypad to take over the function of the mouse.

2 You select the icon.

3 Pointer trails and high contrast

4 5

5 Ctrl+Esc

6 Alt

Intermediate Tutorials

SESSION 1.1

1 T

2 You must choose drive A in the Look in box.

3 T

4 F

5 A wildcard is a symbol that stands in place of one or more characters. The asterisk wildcard stands in place of any number of consecutive characters in a filename, whereas the question mark wildcard stands in place of a single character.

6 All the files in the folder or drive specified in the Look in box.

7 The Current subfolder or file located in the Work folder on drive D.

8 Details.

SESSION 1.2

1 Enter nothing in the start date box; enter 12/31/96 in the end date box.

2 Advanced tab and Bitmap Image.

3 F

4 Date Modified tab: Find all files created or modified during the previous 1 day. Advanced tab: Of type WordPerfect, containing text "rap music."

5 Click the file in the Results list, then click the Enter key.

6 Click Edit, then click WordWrap.

7 Click At least then type 47.

8 On the desktop.

9 You might have forgotten to clear earlier criteria. For example, you might have specified a date range of a year ago, but this file was created last week, and thus wouldn't appear in the Results list.

SESSION 1.3

1 With Quick View

2 No. It uses a simple font with minimal formatting, and doesn't always display graphics or other objects.

3 You can use it to display a bitmap image, but not in a word processed document.

4 Increase Font Size.

5 Click the left page arrow repeatedly until it turns grey, or use the key combination Ctrl+End.

SESSION 2.1

1 Select the portion with the Select or Free-Form Select tool, click Edit, click Copy To, then give the file a different name and click Save.

2 Drag one of the canvas sizing handles.

3 T

4 pixels

5 More bits are required to define the colors.

6 No; Paint handles only BMP files. You must first convert it using a graphics converter.

SESSION 2.2

1 A single pixel

2 A single pixel

3 Thumbnail

4 Erase the screen using the Eraser tool, the Clear Image command on the Image menu, and the New command on the File menu.

5 Press Shift and use the Ellipse tool.

6 50 pixels

SESSION 2.3

1 Fill With Color

2 Its size is 10 x 1/72".

3 Bold, italic, and underline

4 Text toolbar

5 You must erase or cut the text, then click the Text tool and enter new text with the font you want.

6 border; fill

7 background

SESSION 3.1

1 An area in your computer's memory that stores data you cut or copy.

2 When you cut selected text, it is removed from the original document to the Clipboard. When you copy it, a replica of the data is moved to the Clipboard, but the original document remains intact.

3 Ctrl+X to cut, Ctrl+C to copy, and Ctrl+V to paste.

4 F

5 Open Clipboard Viewer, click Edit, then click Delete. Clearing Clipboard contents frees up memory.

6 It is more accurate than typing.

SESSION 3.2

1 Object linking and embedding—it is technology that allows you to transfer data from one program to another and retain the ability to access tools from the original program.

2 WordPad is the source program; PowerPoint is the destination program.

3 No. If you paste text from one WordPad document to another, you are simply pasting, not embedding. If you paste objects from Paint into WordPad, however, you are embedding. Paste's function depends on the type of data you are inserting.

4 Paste or Insert Object. Use Paste when the source file is open; use Insert Object when it is not.

5 Editing an embedded object using the source program tools without ever leaving the destination document.

6 When you want more control over how the data is inserted.

7 F

SESSION 3.3

1 Linking places a representation of the source file whereas embedding places a copy of the source file into the destination file.

2 The updated file (unless the file is set to update manually).

3 No. Embedded objects have been copied into the document.

4 No.

5 Tiling arranges open windows so they are all visible. Cascading overlaps open windows so their title bars are visible.

6 F

7 The WAV format records and stores sounds as realistically as possible. The MIDI format uses artificial sounds to mimic real sounds. The AVI format is the Windows video clip format.

SESSION 4.1

1 In the taskbar.

2 By storing them on the hard drive instead of in your computer's memory.

3 Open the print queue, select the print job, then click Cancel Printing from the Document menu.

4 That part of the print job had already been sent to the printer.

5 Drag it to the top of the print queue.

6 Print spooling inserts electronic codes that the printer uses to print the document. Print queuing simply orders the print jobs.

SESSION 4.2

1 Open the printer's property sheet, then click the Details tab.

2 A printer is an external device. You check your configuration and decide on a port to use, you connect the device, then you install the necessary software.

3 driver

4 Install the driver.

5 Use the disk that came with the printer.

6 From online Help.

7 F. A device created in 1993 will not meet the Plug and Play standards specified with Windows 95.

SESSION 4.3

1 Click the paragraph then look at the name that appears in the Font box.

2 F

3 No

4 No; they are stored on the printer.

5 It looks the same on the screen as it does when you print it and you can scale it without losing quality.

SESSION 5.1

1 A collection of computers and other hardware devices linked together so that they can exchange data and share hardware and software resources.

2 Node: Each device on a network.
Workgroup: A group of computers on a network that perform common tasks or belong to users who share common duties and interests.
LAN: A Local Area Network, a network in which the nodes are located close together.
WAN: A network in which the nodes are spread out over a wide area such as across a state or nation.
Server: A computer that provides access to its resources to other computers.
Client: A computer that uses the resources of a server.
Workstation: Another term for client.

3 The hierarchical model in which servers provide resources to the network and clients use those resources and the peer-to-peer model in which each computer can act as both client and server.

4 Store a database, handle electronic mail, manage printing.

5 Adapter, client, protocol, and service.

6 A communications protocol determines how computers recognize each other on the network and what rules they use to transfer data. TCP/IP is used on the Internet. IPX/SPX is used in Netware networks. NetBEUI is used in a Windows NT network.

7 Ethernet, Token Ring, FDDI, and ATM.

8 Novell Netware, Windows NT, IBM OS/2 LAN and Banyan Vines.

SESSION 5.2

1 Do not use fewer than seven characters in your password.
Do not use your name, birth date, nickname, or any word that someone might be able to guess.
Try to include numbers or special symbols.
Never write down your password or share it with others.

2 The network you are primarily using whenever you log into your computer.

3 Your username, password, and the name of your Login server.

4 Right-click the Network Neighborhood then click the Who Am I command.

5 Right-click the Passwords icon in the Control Panel, then click Open. Click the Change Windows Password button. Type your current password in the Old Password box and type your new password in the New Password box and in the Confirm Password box.

6 To log out from a server, right-click the server's icon from the Network Neighborhood window then click Log Out. To log out from your workstation, click the Start button on the taskbar then click Shut Down.

7 The Close all programs and log on as a different user option.

SESSION 5.3

1 A local folder is a folder on your computer, whereas a network folder is located on your computer on the network.

2 Share-level access control controls access to network resources through the use of a password. It is most often used on peer-to-peer networks.

3 User-level access control controls access to network resources through a list of approved users. It is most often used on hierarchical networks.

4 \\Sales\C\Work\Intro.txt

5 For working with Windows 3.1 and DOS programs.

6 \\QA\Work

SESSION 6.1

1 Hard disks contain more permanent data and are more expensive to replace.

2 Scan and defragment a disk.

3 The minimum amount of space an operating system reserves when saving the contents of a file to a disk.

4 Keep track of the status of each cluster on a disk.

5 F

6 File deletion can cause empty clusters between files. A file saved to a disk occupies the first available clusters, spilling over into clusters on other parts of a disk if necessary. A file that is not stored in adjacent clusters is thus fragmented.

7 The host drive—the original drive A, renamed to drive H.

8 A

SESSION 6.2

1 Copying a disk duplicates the disk contents, whereas backing up a disk compresses the files on the disk into a single, smaller file.

2 Floppy disks and tapes. Use a tape when backing up a hard disk because using floppy disks would be too time-consuming.

3 A file set contains the list of files and folders you are backing up. A backup set contains the compressed files that have been backed up.

4 A backup of all the files on your computer's local drives.

5 A partial backup is a backup of files that have changed since your last backup. An incremental backup backs up the files since the last backup, regardless of whether it was full or partial. A differential backup backs up the files since the last full backup.

6 It takes less time.

7 All the files on your computer's hard drive. Because they are not compressed.

Index

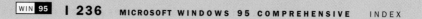

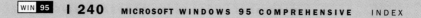

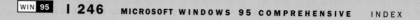

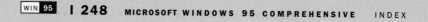

Microsoft Windows 95 **Task Reference**

TASK	PAGE #	RECOMMENDED METHOD	NOTES
Accessibility Options, open	130	Open Control Panel, open 🔧 (might need to install with Add/Remove programs)	
Backup, perform	I 210	Click **Start**, point to Programs, point to Accessories, point to System Tools, click Backup, select data to back up, click Next Step, click drive to store backup set, save file set, click Start Backup	See "Performing a Backup"
Backup, restore files from	I 216	Start Backup, click Restore tab, locate and select, backup set, click Next Step, click data to restore, click Start Restore, click the OK button	See "Restoring a File from a Backup Set"
Calculator, use	I 89	Click **Start**, point to Programs, point to Accessories, click Calculator	
Check box, de-select	21	Click the check box again	Tab to option, press Spacebar
Check box, select	21	Click the check box	Tab to option, press Spacebar
Clipboard contents, delete	I 93	Open Clipboard Viewer, click Edit, click Delete, click Yes	
Clipboard contents, view	I 92	Click **Start**, point to Programs, point to Accessories, click Clipboard Viewer	
Color palette, change	123	Right-click desktop, click Settings, click new color palette, click the OK button, then follow prompts to reboot computer	
Color, use in Paint	I 75	Click color in the color box with left mouse button to specify foreground color or right mouse button to specify background color	
Computer, view devices and folders	62	From Windows Explorer, scroll the Folders list	
Control Panel, open	125	Click **Start**, point to Settings, click Control Panel	See "Using the Control Panel to Customize Settings"
Data, cut or copy from one document into another	I 91	Select data you want to transfer, click ✂ to cut or 📋 to copy, click new document, click 📋	See "Using Paste to Transfer Data from One Document to Another"
Desktop document, creating	98	Right-click desktop, point to New, click document type	See "Creating a New Document on the Desktop"
Desktop, change background	112	Right-click desktop, click Properties, click Background, click pattern or wallpaper, click the OK button	
Desktop, change colors	116	Right-click desktop, click Properties, click Appearance, click item, click a color, click the OK button	
Disk, compress	I 203	Click **Start**, point to Programs, point to Accessories, point to System Tools, click Drive-Space, click drive, click Drive, click Compress Compress, click Start, click Compress Now	See "Compressing Data on a Disk"

Microsoft Windows 95 **Task Reference**

TASK	PAGE #	RECOMMENDED METHOD	NOTES
Disk, copy your	50	Place disk in drive A:, from My Computer click 🖥️, click File, Copy Disk, Start	See "Making a Backup of Your Floppy Disk."
Disk, defragment	I 199	Click **Start**, point to Programs, point to Accessories, point to System Tools, click Disk Defragmenter, click drive, click the OK button, click Start	See "Defragmenting a Disk"
Disk, format	30	Click 🖥️, click 🖥️, press the Enter key, click File click Format, click Start	
Disk, Quick format	58	From My Computer, click disk icon, click File, click Format, Click Quick (erase) button, click Start	
Disk, scan	I 195	Click **Start**, point to Programs, point to Accessories, point to System Tools, click ScanDisk, click disk, click Start	See "Using ScanDisk"
Disk, uncompress	I 204	Start DriveSpace, click drive, click Drive, click Uncompress, click Start, click Uncompress Now	See "Uncompressing Files on a Disk"
Document, open most recent	I 32	Click **Start**, point at Documents, click document you want to open	
Drop-down list, display	20	Click ▾	
Energy-saving features, use	124	Right-click desktop, click Screen Saver, click energy saving options, click the OK button	
File, copy		From My Computer, right-click the file, drag to the new location, press C	
File, copy in Windows Explorer	83	Drag file from Contents list to new location in Folders list using the right mouse button, then click Copy Here	Ctrl+drag the object, See "Copying One or More Files"
File, delete	49	From My Computer, click the file, press the Delete key, click Yes	See "Deleting a File."
File extensions, view or hide	I 14	Open My Computer, click View, click Options, click View tab, select Hide MS-DOS file extensions to hide	
File, locate by date	I 22	Click Find's Date Modified tab, click an option to specify range of dates	See "Locating Files by Date"
File, locate by type, contents, or size	I 24	Click Advanced tab, enter criteria you want	See "Using Advanced Search Criteria"
File, move	48	From My Computer, use the left mouse button to drag the file to the desired folder or drive	See "Moving a File"
File, move in Windows Explorer	81	Drag file from Contents list to new location in Folders list using the right mouse button, then click Move Here	Shift+drag the object, See "Moving One or More Files Between Folders"
File, open	37	Click 📄	

Microsoft Windows 95 **Task Reference**

TASK	PAGE #	RECOMMENDED METHOD	NOTES
File or folder, rename	67	Click file or folder, click label, type new name, then press the Enter key	F2, See "Renaming a Folder"
File, print	39	Click 🖨	
File, print preview	39	Click 🔍	
File, rename	49	From My Computer, click the file, click File, click Rename, type new name, press the Enter key	See "Renaming a File"
File, save	35	Click 💾	
File, search for by name and location	I 7	Start Find, type search string in Named box, click Look in list arrow, click drive to search, click Find Now	See "Searching for a File by Name"
File, search for in specific folder	I 15	Start Find, click Browse button, click ➕ on drive containing folder, click folder, click the OK button	See "Searching for Files in a Specific Folder"
File, view with Quick View	I 33	Right-click file to view, click Quick View	If Quick View is open, drag file into Quick View, See "Viewing Files Using Quick View"
Files, arrange	72	Click the Name, Size, Type, or Modified button	See "Arranging Files by Name. Size, Date, or Type"
Files, select all but one	77	Select the files you don't want selected, then click File, click Invert Selection	See "Selecting all Files Except Certain Ones"
Files, select in groups	75	Click Edit, click Select All for all, press Shift then click first and last for consecutive, or press Ctrl then click files one at a time for non-consecutive	Ctrl+A to select all, See "Selecting Files"
Files, view details	72	▦	
Files, view in Windows Explorer	71	Click 📁 in Folders list	
Find, start	I 5	Click 🏁Start, point to Find, click Files or Folders	
Folder, create	46	From My Computer, click File, New, Folder	See "Creating a New Folder."
Folder, create in Windows Explorer	66	From Windows Explorer, click File, click New, click Folder	See "Creating a Folder in Windows Explorer"
Folder or device, select	64	From Windows Explorer, click 📁 or device icon	See "Selecting a Device or Folder"
Folder or device, view or hide contents	63	From Windows Explorer, click ➕ to view; ➖ to hide	Right arrow to view, left arrow to hide, See "Expanding Devices or Folders in the Folders List"
Font size, change in Quick View	I 35	Click 🅰 to increase font size, 🅰 to decrease font size	
Font, change in Paint	I 78	Click Font list arrow, click font	

Microsoft Windows 95 **Task Reference**

TASK	PAGE #	RECOMMENDED METHOD	NOTES
Font, delete	I 152	Open Fonts window, click font, press the Delete key	See "Deleting a Font"
Font, install	I 151	Open Fonts window, click File, click Install New Font, locate and select font you want to install, click the OK button	See "Installing a New Font"
Font, open	I 150	Open Fonts window, click font, press the Enter key	
Fonts window, open	I 148	Open Control Panel, click Fonts, press the Enter key	
Graphic objects, cut, copy, and paste	I 66	Click ⬚ or ⬚, select area you want to cut or copy, click ⬚ to copy or ✂ to cut, then click ⬚ to paste, drag object to new location	See "Copying, Cutting, and Pasting Graphics"
Graphic, clear	I 65	Click Image, then click ClearImage	
Graphic, crop	I 50	Click ⬚ or ⬚, select the area you want to retain, click Edit, click Copy To, enter file name and location, click Save	See "Cropping a Graphic"
Graphic, erase portions	I 52	Click ⬚, drag area you want to erase	
Graphic, flip	I 67	Click Image, then click Flip/Rotate, click flip or rotate option you want, click the OK button	
Graphic, magnify	I 58	Click ⬚, click the canvas area you want to magnify	
Graphic, save in a different format	I 55	Click File, click Save As, click Save as Type list arrow, click file type you want, type file name, click Save	
Graphic, stretch	I 69	Click Image, click Stretch/Skew, enter a stretch or skew percentage, click the OK button	
Grid, show in magnified view of graphic	I 59	Click View, point to Zoom, click Show Grid	
Help topic, display	23	From the Help Contents window, click the topic, then click Open	
Help topic, open	23	From the Help Contents window, click the book, then click Display	
Help, start	21	Click ⬚Start, then click Help	F1, See "Starting Windows 95 Help"
High contrast, enable	136	Open Accessibility Options, click Display tab, click Use High Contrast, click the OK button	
Icon, change	I 105	Open icon's property sheet, click View tab, click Change Icon, click different icon or click Browse to select icon from file, click the OK button twice	See "Changing an Icon"
Icon, open	43	Click the icon, then press the Enter key or double-click the icon	See "Opening an Icon."
Icons, view large	45	From My Computer, click View, Large Icons	

Microsoft Windows 95 **Task Reference**

TASK	PAGE #	RECOMMENDED METHOD	NOTES
Insertion point, move	34	Click the desired location in the document Use arrow keys	
Keyboard shortcuts, perform with StickyKeys	134	Open Accessibility Options, click Keyboard tab, click Use StickyKeys, click the OK button	
Line, draw in Paint	I 68	Click ◣, then drag a line on the canvas	
Linked object, update	I 113	Click Edit, click Links, click link you want to update, then click Update Now	
List box, scroll	20	Click ▲ or ▼, or drag the scroll box	
Menu option, select	17	Click the menu option	
Menu, open		Click the menu option	Alt-underlined letter
Mouse pointer, control with keyboard	131	Open Accessibility Options, click Mouse tab, click Use MouseKeys, click the OK button	
Mouse, adjust double-click speed	128	Open Control Panel, open 🖰, click Buttons tab, drag Double-click speed slider to new location, click the OK button	
Mouse, adjust pointer speed	130	Open Control Panel, open 🖰, click Motion tab, drag Pointer speed slider to new location, click the OK button	
Mouse, configure for right or left hand	126	Open Control Panel, open 🖰, click Buttons tab, click Right-handed or Left-handed, click the OK button	
Mouse, turn on pointer trails	129	Open Control Panel, open 🖰, click Motion tab, click Show pointer trails, click the OK button	
Network account, view	I 175	Right-click 🖳, click Who Am I	
Network folder, map to drive letter	I 183	Right-click folder, click Map Network Drive, click Drive list arrow, click drive letter, click the OK button	
Network Neighborhood, open	I 162	Click 🖳, press the Enter key	
Network problems, troubleshoot	I 187	Click [Start], click Help, click Contents tab, click Troubleshooting, press the Enter key, click If you have trouble using the network, click Display	
Network properties, view	I 165	Right-click 🖳, click Properties	
Object, delete	I 115	Click object, then press the Delete key	
Object, embed using Insert Object	I 101	Click Insert, click Object, locate object, then click the OK button	See "Using Insert Object"
Object, embed using Paste	I 95	Select object, cut or copy it to Clipboard, click destination document, click 🗎	

Microsoft Windows 95 **Task Reference**

TASK	PAGE #	RECOMMENDED METHOD	NOTES
Object, insert using Paste Special	I 107	Cut or copy object to Clipboard, click Edit, click Paste Special, select paste options you want, then click the OK button	
Object, link	I 109	Click Insert, click Object, select file using Browse button, click Link check box, click the OK button	
Object menu, open	97	Right-click object	Shift+F10
Object, resizing	I 97	Drag sizing handle	
OLE object, display as icon	I 104	Right-click OLE object, click Object Properties, click View tab, click Display as icon, click the OK button	
OLE object, edit	I 98	Right-click OLE object, point to object command such as Bitmap Image Object, then click Edit, edit the object, then click outside the selection box	See "In-place Editing"
Paint tools, use	I 48	Click tool in tool box, click tool style if applicable, drag or click on the canvas to apply tool	See "Using the Tool Box Tools"
Paint view options, change	I 58	Click View, point to Zoom, then click View option you want to change	See "Using the View Options"
Paint, start	I 46	Click ⊞Start, point to Programs, point to Accessories, click Paint	
Password, change	I 173	Open Control Panel, click 🔑, press the Enter key, click Change Windows Password, type old password, press Tab, type new password twice, click the OK button	See "Changing Your Windows 95 Password"
Print problems, troubleshoot	I 144	Click ⊞Start, click Help, click Contents tab, click Troubleshooting, press the Enter key, click If you have trouble printing, click Display, follow Print Troubleshooter instructions	
Print queue, open	I 128	Click ⊞Start, point to Settings, click Printers, click printer, press the Enter key	See "Using the Print Queue"
Print queue, remove jobs from	I 133	Open print queue, click job, press the Delete key	See "Removing Print Jobs from the Print Queue"
Printer, change default	I 142	Open print queue, click Printer, click Set As Default	
Printer, install	I 138	Click ⊞Start, point to Settings, click Printers, click Add Printer, press the Enter key, follow Add Printer Wizard instructions	
Printer, locate on a network	I 186	Click ⊞Start, point to Settings, click Printers, right-click network printer, click Properties, click Details tab	
Printer, select different for printing	I 141	Click File, click Print, click Name list arrow, click printer, click the OK button	See "Printing to a Different Printer"

Microsoft Windows 95 **Task Reference**

TASK	PAGE #	RECOMMENDED METHOD	NOTES
Printing, pause	I 132	Open print queue, click Pause, click Pause Printing	
Program, quit	10	Click ☒	Alt-F4
Program, start	9	Click the Start button, point to Programs, to the program option, click the program	See "Starting a Program."
Properties, view	110	Right-click object, click Properties	Alt+Enter, See "Viewing and Changing Object Properties"
Quick View, start	I 33	Right-click file, then click Quick View	
Radio button, de-select	21	Click a different radio button	Tab to option, press Spacebar
Radio button, select	21	Click the radio button	Tab to option, press Spacebar
Resolution, change	120	Right-click desktop, click Settings, drag Desktop area slider to new resolution, click the OK button	
Results list, change column widths	I 18	Drag dividing bar between columns	
Results list, change view	I 17	Click View, then click view you want options	
Results list, sort	I 19	Click View, click Details, click column button to sort by that criteria	See "Sorting the Results List"
Screen saver, activate	118	Right-click desktop, click Screen Saver, click a screen saver, click the OK button	
Screen, print	78	Press Print Screen, start WordPad, click [icon], click [icon]	See "Printing the Exploring Window"
Search criteria, specify	I 7		See "Specifying Search Criteria."
Search, clear	I 31	From Find, click New Search button, click the OK button	
Search, save	I 30	Start Find, run search you want to save, click File, click Save Search	See "Saving a Search"
Server, attach to	I 171	Open Network Neighborhood, right-click Server, click Attach As, enter user ID and password, click the OK button	See "Attaching to a Server"
Server, log out from	I 175	Open Network Neighborhood, right-click server, click Log Out, click Yes	
Shape, draw	I 70	Click shape you want to draw: ▢, ▢, or ▢, then drag a shape on the canvas	
Shortcut, create on the desktop	102	Drag object's icon to desktop with the right mouse button, then click Create Shortcut(s) here	See "Creating a Shortcut"
Shortcut, delete	109	Click shortcut icon, press the Delete key, click Yes	
Start menu, display			Ctrl+Esc

Microsoft Windows 95 **Task Reference**

TASK	PAGE #	RECOMMENDED METHOD	NOTES
Student data disk, create	41	Click **Start**, click Programs, CTI Win95, Windows 95 Brief, Make Windows 95 Student Disk, press the Enter key	
Text, add to graphic	I 77	Click **A**, drag a selection box on canvas, type text	
Text, select	34	Drag the pointer over the text	
Thumbnail, view in graphic	I 60	Click View, point to Zoom, click Show Thumbnail	
Time-date stamp, insert on Notepad document	100	Type .LOG in uppercase letters at beginning of Notepad document	
Toolbar, view	69	Click View, click Toolbar	
Tooltip, display	19	Position pointer over the tool	
Video clip, play	I 116	Right-click video clip object or file, click Linked Video Clip Object if an OLE object, click Play, or just click Play	
Wildcards, use to find files by name	I 12	Start Find, type search string in Named box, using ? in place of single characters and * in place of multiple characters	
Windows, arrange	I 111	Right-click taskbar, then click Cascade or one of the Tile options	
Window, change size	17	Drag ▨	
Window, close	10	Click ✕	Ctrl+F4
Window, maximize	17	Click ▢	
Window, minimize	15	Click ▬	
Window, move	17	Drag the title bar	
Window, redisplay	16	Click the taskbar button	
Window, refresh view	88	Click View, click Refresh	F5
Window, restore	16	Click ▣	
Window, switch	12	Click the taskbar button of the program	Alt+Tab, See "Switching Between Programs."
Windows Explorer, adjust list width	68	Point at dividing bar between lists so pointer changes to ←|→, then drag dividing bar right or left	See "Adjusting the Width of the Folders List"
Windows Explorer, open	61	Click **Start**, click Programs, click Windows Explorer	
Windows 95, shut down	12	Click **Start**, click Shut Down, Click Yes	
Windows 95, start	5	Turn on the computer	